Changing Our Minds

Changing Our Minds

Negotiating English and Literacy

Miles Myers
Executive Director, NCTE

National Council of Teachers of English
1111 W. Kenyon Road, Urbana, Illinois 61801-1096

Grateful acknowledgment is made to those who provided the artifacts pictured on the cover: Gwynne M. Nicholaides, Elizabeth Nicholaides, the collection of Hugh W. and Jessie Owens Myers, Nancy and Ray Sanden, Karen Smith, Doug Bauling and the College of Agriculture of the University of Illinois at Urbana–Champaign, the Library of Congress, and the National Museum of American History at the Smithsonian Institution. NCTE also thanks the Early American Museum in Mahomet, Illinois, and its director, Cheryl Kennedy, for assistance in preparing the cover.

Manuscript Editor: Robert A. Heister/Humanities & Sciences Associates

Production Editors: Michelle Sanden Johlas, Michael G. Ryan

Interior Design: Tom Kovacs for TGK Design

Cover Design: Doug Burnett

NCTE Stock Number: 33045-3050

Library of Congress Cataloging-in-Publication Data

Myers, Miles.
    Changing our minds : negotiating English and literacy/Miles Myers.
      p.   cm.
    Includes bibliographical references (p.   ) and index.
    ISBN 0-8141-3304-5
    1. English language—Study and teaching—United States.
    2. English language—Study and teaching—Standards—United States.
    3. Literacy—United States.   I. Title.
    LB1576.M945   1996
    372.6'044—dc20   95-35855

Contents

List of Illustrations

Figures

Tables

Acknowledgments

My thanks to Jeanne Bohlen and John Kelley, who for the last year helped to keep this book afloat at the office; to the early, anonymous reviewers who gave very helpful advice; to the generous editors—Robert A. Heister, Michelle Sanden Johlas, and Michael G. Ryan—who salvaged matters many times; and, finally, to Celeste, who for the last ten years never seemed to waiver in her enthusiasm for the project, despite its elephantine presence around our home. I also want to thank NCTE's officers, who, when they hired me, made clear that they expected me to continue to do research while I was Executive Director of NCTE. Other acknowledgments to individuals and groups are referenced in the text.

Introduction

Standards debates have been going on in literate countries for years, Jonathan Swift's *Battle of the Books* (1704) being my first introduction to these matters in an English class at Berkeley almost forty years ago. The present debate about national curriculum content standards in the K–12 schools of the United States is the fourth or fifth major debate over literacy in this country, and, like the former ones, this current debate is likely to have far-reaching effects on the content and form of K–12 schooling, particularly on the content and form of English and English language arts.

"Standards" is, in some ways, a misleading word to describe the movement that is happening today in educational policy in the United States. We are not, for example, having an argument about whether to use American or British spelling conventions; that argument was a "standards" debate in another age. Instead, we are using the label "education standards" to refer to a broad range of changes in K–12 curriculum content, methods of student assessment, and requirements for teacher certification. All three of these variables are part of a larger movement to change the way minimum literacy is defined in this country. This larger movement involves efforts to change the way industrial production is organized and to improve the quality of public discourse on public issues, particularly issues of diversity. Changes in content standards and minimum literacy, of course, have far-reaching effects on how English is defined (and how other subjects are defined as well).

Why has this standards and literacy movement occurred? Some policy analysts and commentators believe that the present standards and literacy movement is necessary because the K–12 public schools, as a result of confusion about their goals, have failed their public mission. Therefore, we should either get clear about our goals for K–12 schooling and then reorganize K–12 schools or else abandon the whole idea of public schools and move to a system of vouchers and private schools. I believe that public schools in the U.S. have succeeded in attaining the goals of decoding/analytic literacy, which were adopted in 1916, but that today they are being asked to adopt a new standard of literacy, one not well understood by either the public or the profession. One purpose of this book is to outline some of the issues which the present standards and literacy movement must consider.

A second group of policy analysts and citizens supports the development of curriculum content standards in order to return the focus of K–12 English for all students to the cultural traditions of recitation literacy in the late nineteenth century and of decoding/analytic literacy in the early twentieth century. This group feels that a new standard of literacy is not needed—that, in fact, some of the trends of the new standard of literacy, particularly the focus on gender and ethnic differences and on problem-solving techniques, have undermined, not strengthened, our nation's cultural foundations. This group wishes to keep the traditional standards of decoding/analytic literacy and to maintain the world as it has been. One of the purposes of this book is to show that the proposals of this second group, which are intended to be mandates for all students, are not responsive to a number of essential social needs in the workplace, in civic forums, and in personal growth.

A third group opposes public schools, maybe all schools, and favors a broad choice in curriculum content, leaving the question of what English should be to families and students, not to schools. Some members of this group, for example, prefer the objectivity of decoding/analytic English because it focuses English on universal themes ("man versus nature") and tends to prevent schools from prying into a reader's attitude toward religious belief, gender, ethnicity, class, age, and so on. This third group believes that schools have become a public monopoly in which English teachers inquire into the feelings and beliefs of children; teach materials full of violence, skepticism, deceit, and the other values of pop culture; and hold up the traditional antischooling values of this third group for public criticism.

The concerns of this third group are very similar to the concerns of many radicals of the left in the 1950s. Those radicals, watching their values attacked as anti-American by a decade of pop culture McCarthyism, feared that the schools would inquire into their children's beliefs and feelings and then attack those values as "un-American and pro-communist." To deal fairly with this third group (and other groups like it), we, as the English teaching profession, need a multiliteracy awareness which has been missing from our professional rhetoric. We need to understand why this group and others like it resist particular forms of literacy and why we need to offer these students a broader range of alternative readings and assignments, giving them many more choices in schools and giving them privacy of opinion when they request it. One of the purposes of this book is to develop multiliteracy awareness by describing the different ways in which various groups have defined literacy and organized resistance to institutionalized literacy and English.

A fourth group, largely professionals, is pushing the standards and literacy movement as a way "to align" the curriculum content of K–12 English and English language arts with recent intellectual developments in literature, composition, language, and technology. This group points to various studies of the teaching of composition and literature as evidence that most English programs have not moved beyond the early assumptions of decoding/analytic literacy (A. Applebee 1981; Squire and R. Applebee 1968). This fourth group sees the new insights into literature, composition, language, and technology as promising a new standard of literacy which will democratize schooling by making school performances more public and offer new opportunities to many students by introducing alternative ways of knowing into K–12 English. One of the purposes of this book is to review the research which has contributed to this new definition of literacy.

A fifth group, largely nonprofessionals, is pushing the standards movement as a way to meet a set of social needs. This group believes a new standard of literacy will strengthen the economy and improve participation in citizenship activities. This group points to the failure of large numbers of citizens to vote and to the failure of basic U.S. industries to compete successfully worldwide, and it concludes that factories and public discourse must be reorganized to use new skills in problem solving and collaboration. Schools, of course, must teach these new skills. This fifth group, which is one of the major public influences on the standards movement, provides through foundations, commissions, and various committees of Congress a continuing stream of publications outlining why new social needs require a new standard of minimum literacy. One of the purposes of this book is to describe how a new standard of literacy could improve the quality of life in the workplace, in civic forums, and in places for personal growth.

Almost all of the groups who want a new standard of minimum literacy have agreed that this new standard is intended for *all* students. Over the last seventy-five years, decoding/analytic literacy has tended to track students, pushing many students away from academic work, for example, by denying the value of sign systems like actions and visuals, speech events like conversations, modes like narrative, and tools like groups for collaborative thinking. By expanding our views about how one can learn and know valuable knowledge, we are making it possible for many more students who desire to do so to enter academic domains or to enter any other area of life. We are also beginning to recognize that both academic workplaces and factory workplaces require higher-order thinking skills.

Many of the groups calling for a new standard of literacy agree on what some of the features of this new standard of higher-order skills might be. I am labeling these features "translation/critical literacy." There are those who argue that something like translation/critical literacy lost its chance in U.S. schools in the 1930s, when it was presented as "the experience curriculum" (Hatfield 1935) and was defeated by advocates of decoding/analytic literacy. Why was the "experience curriculum" defeated? Arthur Applebee points to one very important reason: "The ultimate difficulty was that the curriculum specified by the commission lacked a set of structuring principles" (Applebee 1974, 168). One purpose of this book is to suggest some of the "structuring principles" for a contemporary form of the "experience curriculum," a curriculum labeled here translation/critical literacy. These "structuring principles" are as follows.

Chapter 1: Different forms of literacy are the result of and the products of different kinds of English curricula, different kinds of factories, and different kinds of civic forums. Students bring to the classroom the history of various forms of literacy; thus, they bring to English classes various assumptions about English as an activity in school.

Chapters 2–4: The way a school is organized, the way a subject is taught and tested, the way we decide cut-off scores—each of these variables is shaped to a large extent by the way we define our standards of literacy. Two years ago, I heard the fascinating story about a federal testing "mistake." It seems that several years ago, the pass-fail cut-off score of a federal test for entry to training was mistakenly either ignored or lowered in the admission of recruits to various specialized schools. For a time, nothing happened. Then, teachers began to report that the recruits in the new classes seemed particularly challenging to teach.

The teachers responded by adding new incentives, like longer break times and various other rewards for success, and this helped some students. Then, some teachers changed their teaching methods—adding hands-on explorations of electrical systems in everyday tools, for instance—and this helped. Then, others added discussion groups to their courses so that the students got different perspectives on how to solve a problem or how to describe content. Finally, many teachers extended the time to learn, and many others split up their classes into smaller groups, with tutorials provided by the more successful students. This also helped. In time, most of the recruits graduated and went on to their assignments in critical positions—as radio or radar operators, and so forth. There remains a debate about whether these recruits failed at their jobs. The point I want to make is that a form of literacy is always a way of organizing the content and the form of learning and schooling and that our country has experienced four different forms of literacy prior to the present one.

Chapters 5–7: The new translation/critical literacy requires that we shift our primary focus as teachers from decontextualized parts to contextualized wholes, focusing the teaching and learning of English and English language arts, first, on language "experiences" and contextualized, communicative events and, second, on metacognition, analysis, and standing back from events.

Chapter 8: Each form of literacy acknowledges an implicit model of the self and of learners. Our new translation/critical literacy requires that learners be actively aware of their own efforts at metacognitive self-fashioning, particularly their efforts to fashion themselves as thinkers and learners.

Chapter 9: A form of literacy is shaped, in part, by the way we use particular forms of technology to solve problems. In translation/critical literacy, this technology includes the distribution of thinking to a complex array of people, information-processing machines, habits of talking to oneself, and various cognitive strategies.

Chapter 10: A form of literacy is shaped, in part, by particular forms of representation (or sign systems). Translation/critical literacy requires some flexibility in shifting sign systems and some experimentation with mixing sign systems—for example, adding charts where they formerly did not appear or adding videotapes to accompany printed documents.

Chapter 11: A form of literacy often privileges a way of speaking (a particular speech event). Translation/critical literacy requires that participants in literacy events be able to situate problems in different speech events and to experiment with mixing different speech events in some situations.

Chapter 12: A form of literacy often privileges particular modes. Translation/critical literacy gives a new status to narrative ways of knowing, requires some facility with mode shifting, and encourages some experiments with mode mixing in certain situations.

Chapter 13: Most forms of literacy attempt in some way to answer the question, "How do we distinguish between informational truth and imaginative fiction?" Translation/critical literacy distinguishes between literary and nonliterary readings or stances and encourages some facility with stance shifting on the same materials.

Chapter 14: The ideas of English and English language arts grow out of the domains of literature and public discourse (radio commercials, TV public debates and panels, cereal boxes, newspapers, posters, magazines) and are expressed in the concepts of love, hate, envy, and friendship. In translation/critical literacy, these concepts are examined from the points of view of ethnicity, gender, age, and the styles of common traditions.

This book grew out of five projects. The first was a study of speech events in which Wallace Chafe, Arthur Applebee, and Walter Loban were particularly helpful dissertation advisers. The second was a study of sign shifting in workshops I organized for Sophie Sa of the Panasonic Foundation and Benjamin Ladner of the National Humanities Faculty between 1982 and 1990. The third was a study of plant reorganization at New United Motor Manufacturing Incorporated (NUMMI) in Fremont, California, between 1985 and 1990. Various leaders of the California Labor Federation and Marty Morgenstern of the Department of Industrial Relations at the University of California–Berkeley were particularly helpful to me in this study.

The fourth project began with an article I wrote for the *English Journal* (M. Myers 1984), in which I made the claim that changes in curriculum and English education were *not* fads but instead were part of a society's efforts to meet its needs by changing its definition of minimum levels of literacy. This article led to a literacy conference sponsored by the Central California Council of Teachers of English and the California Federation of Teachers in 1988 at Asilomar, California. The thoughts of the primary speakers at that conference—Eliot Eisner, Shirley Brice Heath, Dennie Palmer Wolf, Joel Smith, Harold Berlack, and Michael Holtzman—were very important in helping me to think about where this book might be going. The discussions at that conference were focused primarily on secondary schools, and my experience has been, for the most part, secondary-level. Therefore, this book gives primary attention to secondary education; in fact, some of the structuring principles, while probably appropriate for secondary education, may not be appropriate for elementary education. The fifth project was an effort to describe a "new" form of literacy, beginning with an *English Journal* article in 1971 (M. Myers 1971).

Let me close this introduction with a story:

> It is a bright sunny April day as Si Mohamed drives the office car into the brand new Afriquia gas station in Berrechid, Morocco. When Allal, the gas station attendant, has filled the gas tank, Si Mohamed asks for a facture (receipt) for reimbursement. Allal rummages briefly through his leather money bag and carefully extracts a pad of blank *factures* and a blackened rubber stamp with the station's name and address. With a deep breath he exhales on the rubber stamp, moistening it slightly, and then presses it with deliberation into the *facture* paper. This small rubber stamp, like tens of thousands all over Morocco, serves as the guarantor of official literacy in Morocco. Allal, who cannot read or write, then hands the stamped paper to Si Mohamed, who fills in the date, amount of gas, and the price. (Wagner 1991, 17)

The point of the story is that because Allal, the gas station attendant, cannot write, his customer fills in the amount of gas and the price. This situation obviously puts Allal at risk. A form of literacy authorized by a culture always gives benefits to those who have it and losses to those who don't. It is our job as English teachers to help as many students as possible to cut their losses and increase their benefits.

1 Shifting Social Needs: From Clocks to Thermostats

> The way in which the historically established forms of human mental life correlate with reality has come to depend more and more on complex social practices. . . . New motives for action appear under extremely complex patterns of social practice. Thus are created new problems, new modes of behavior, new methods of taking in information, and new systems of reflecting reality. (Luria 1976, 9)

In September 1993, the National Assessment of Educational Progress (NAEP) announced that three-fourths of U.S. twelfth graders had reached the "basic level" where they "[developed] interpretations from a variety of texts . . . understood overall arguments, recognized explicit aspects of plot and characters . . . supported global generalizations . . . were able to respond personally to texts, and use[d] major document features to solve real-world problems" (Mullis, Campbell, and Farstrup 1993, 15). In other words, by 1993, three-fourths of the nation's twelfth graders had achieved the goals of decoding/analytic literacy outlined in the nation's standards projects of 1917–1918 in *Report on the Reorganization of English in Secondary Schools* (Hosic 1917) and in *The Cardinal Principles of Secondary Education* (Kingsley 1918).

Then why all the fuss in the public press about school failure and illiteracy? Because decoding/analytic literacy was no longer adequate. In the same September 1993 report that announced the achievement of decoding/analytic literacy, NAEP also announced that two-thirds of the nation's twelfth graders failed to achieve NAEP's new "proficient level" in reading where "they should be able to extend the ideas of the text by making inferences, drawing conclusions, . . . making connections to their own personal experiences and other readings, . . . [and analyzing] the author's use of literary devices" (Mullis, Campbell, and Farstrup 1993, 12–17). Thus, despite the gains in decoding/analytic literacy, our country, at the national, state, and local levels, was moving toward new definitions of what it means to be literate (National Commission on Excellence in Education 1983). This effort to define a new level of minimum literacy has taken the form of a national discussion about alternative methods of assessment (the New Standards Project,

1

the National Board for Professional Teaching Standards); about restructuring K–12 school sites (the Coalition of Essential Schools, the Alliance for School Reform); about factory restructuring (NUMMI and Saturn); about curriculum content (the Standards Project for English Language Arts, the College Board's Pacesetter Projects); and about new definitions of "proficiency" in reading and writing (the National Assessment of Education Progress). These projects—working within tensions between national and local cultures, between past and present social needs, and between our biological universals and our cultural particulars—are constructing a new definition of English and English language arts that is responsive to contemporary needs in the workplace, in civic life, and in "private" personal development.[1]

Reading these reports, it is possible to forget that changing the nation's standard of literacy will require changes in schools beyond just those in curriculum content. In secondary schools, students are attending fifty-minute classes with thirty to thirty-five students and with a teacher who has a daily load of five or six classes and from 150 to over 200 students. In addition, too many students attend schools without libraries, without computers for students, without paper towels in restrooms, without respect for the intellectual and social life of the students or the teachers, and often without safety in the halls of the school and in the streets nearby. Public leaders cannot simply point to students and teachers who go to school in these environments and say, "Here is our new standard of literacy and our new curriculum. Take it and learn it." Changing our standard of literacy and our curriculum will require many changes in many parts of the school system, not just changes in the curriculum guides or in the assessments. In my opinion, the whole idea of the publicly funded common school in the United States may now be at stake in these discussions.

Children do not invent their own forms of literacy outside the influence of the cultures in which they live, as you can see from the examples in Figure 1. If culture, local and/or national, does not encourage a particular form of literacy, then any predispositions toward that form of literacy will wither and die. Thus, children who live without verbal interaction cease to babble and to speak, even though they start life with the biological foundations necessary for the development of speech (Moskowitz 1978)[2]; children who are not encouraged to draw never have that artistic explosion for which they are biologically equipped.

Teaching English, then, is based on the universal capability of children and is not based on a universal model of intelligence or a universal model of literacy. English and other school subjects are shaped by a nation's national policy on minimum literacy. Thus,

A

B

C

D

E

Fig. 1. Children's drawings: A from Bali; B from Taiwan; C from Japan; D from Susan (first grade), U.S.A.; and E from Susan (third grade), U.S.A. (Source: illustrations #170, 171, 182, 183, 184 from *Artful Scribbles* by Howard Gardner. Copyright © 1980 by Howard Gardner. Reprinted by permission of BasicBooks, a division of HarperCollins Publishers, Inc.)

our models of mental functioning are, within universal biological constraints, socially constructed and socially contingent upon the specific literacy policies which we use to structure relationships between ourselves and our environment, between our voice and other voices within our own heads, all for the purpose of exploring, expressing, and shaping inner and outer worlds. Our biological constraints, the innate patterns of the mind, are always fundamental, and, thus, learning is not the opposite of innate structures. Learning is a result of a complex interaction between innate patterns and cultural patterns like literacy policies.

The present problems surrounding schooling and English classes are only the most recent of a long line of historical contingencies calling for changes in schooling and in the way English is taught—from Horace Mann's reports in the early 1800s (Mann 1842) to the Vassar Conference on English in 1893; the Reports of the Committee of Ten in 1894; Hosic's *Report on the Reorganization of English in Secondary Schools* in 1917 (Hosic 1917); The Ford Foundation's *Basic Issues in the Teaching of English* in the 1950s (see G. Stone 1964); NCTE's *A Report on the Status of the Profession* in the 1960s (Committee on the National Interest 1961); the College Board's *Freedom and Discipline in the Teaching of English* in the 1960s (Commission on English 1965); the Dartmouth Conference in 1965 (Dixon 1975); and the English Coalition Conference in the 1980s (Elbow 1990; Lloyd-Jones and Lunsford 1989). Each of these efforts was part of a movement to invent or reconceptualize a form of literacy, and new forms of literacy always have an impact on the way subjects like English get organized to meet a set of political and intellectual needs. It is important to remember that changes in English are almost always accompanied by changes in other subject areas. A literacy movement sits behind these changes.

The efforts above proposed quite different models of English teaching and, therefore, of course, different models of minimum literacy. For example, at the 1965 Dartmouth Conference, English teachers debated among themselves the validity of three models of mind and literacy—the *skills* or functional model based on a nation's needs for initial literacy in traditional factories and work; the *cultural heritage* model based on a nation's needs for socially unifying content and heritage; and the *personal-growth* model based on the needs of individuals to find significance in their lives (Dixon 1975). The cultural-critique model (Knoblauch 1990) was hardly mentioned. Earlier, the Basic Issues Conference of 1959 had recommended for all students a *cultural tradition* model organized around the triad of language, literature, and composition, and the early versions of Chapter 1 programs in the early 1960s had recommended a *skills* or functional model. The 1965 Dartmouth Conference, on the other hand, proposed the *personal-growth* model for teaching English.

Dartmouth's personal-growth model emphasized the importance of the "spectator" stance and the writing of stories, poems, and literary pieces; the use of expressive language to discover and to learn; and the centrality of the individual and the processes of psycholinguistics. A few schools adopted some of Dartmouth's approach, but most students throughout the 1960s and 1970s continued to attend schools dominated by a decoding/analytic model of literacy in which "low-track students" were given slot-filling exercises; the "college bound" were taught the forms of the triad—language, literature, and composition; and the "general students" got a mixture of both.

Many teachers of English and English language arts tend to treat recurrent social demands for change as meaningless "fads," as intrusions into a subject with universal form. This attitude disconnects the English classroom from culture and history, ignores the many forms of literacy long since abandoned by the dominant culture, and works against the possibility of historical and multiliteracy awareness in our teaching. Students actually bring to classrooms various forms of literacy from their histories and cultures, forms which, at one time, may have dominated in a nation's culture. Indifference in the classroom to these various forms of literacy is, I think, one of the major obstacles in contemporary schools to a good education for many students. The English teacher must become a kind of archeologist who recognizes the layers of past literacy practices in the classroom—what students call *The Way It Spozed To Be* (Herndon 1969)—and who recognizes that English and English language arts have been taught in our classrooms and in our society in many different ways. The present volume outlines the concept of historical and multiliteracy awareness, first by reviewing past literacy policies in the U.S. and then by describing a new literacy now being shaped by public and professional debate.

But the question remains: Why does a society decide to change its mind about its literacy practices? Societies do not develop something called intelligence or English teaching and then invent new standards of literacy from the possibilities of that intelligence or English teaching. Instead, a standard of literacy—what we call a skill—is the result of an interaction among such variables as urbanization (Lerner 1958), the political interactions of Protestantism and capitalism (Tyack 1974), the religious beliefs of Calvinism (Lockridge 1974), secularism (Clanchy 1979), technology like the printing press (Eisenstein 1979), mass media (Schramm and Ruggels 1967), fertility rates (Vinovskis 1981), and a failing and/or a growing economy (Reich 1992).

Although this book gives special importance to the needs of occupations and citizenship as shapers of literacy in the U.S., citizenship and occupations alone cannot create the cultural motives necessary for establishing a particular kind of literacy. Clanchy, a medievalist who takes a multivariate approach to the question of what shapes literacy in a given period, sees trends of secularization and the expansion of script literacy as shaping and triggering the cultural use of print in Europe (Clanchy 1979); but Eisenstein, who emphasizes the tool, sees the invention of the printing press as "a decisive turning point" (Eisenstein 1979). Harvey Graff gives special emphasis to religious influences on literacy, calling the Protestant Reformation the first Western literacy campaign that emphasized "individual literacy as a powerful social and moral force" (H. Graff 1987, 10); but Schramm and Ruggels (1967, 72), examining the correlation of literacy with growth in Gross National Product (GNP), urbanization, and mass media consumption in eighty-two countries in Latin America, the Middle East, and Asia, found from place to place no consistent correlation of literacy with the other three variables. For example, urbanization had a 0.04 correlation with literacy in Latin American nations and a 0.64 correlation with literacy in Asian countries.

This conflict over whether occupations (scribes), urbanization (industrialization), personal growth (the Reformation), tools (the printing press), markets (automobile sales), or some other variable is more important than anything else in the shaping of a nation's standard of literacy is repeated throughout the research on literacy and is a strong argument for a multivariate approach (Kaestle et al. 1991; Laqueur 1976). A multivariate approach, which will stretch the discussion from English classes to Xerox™ machines, will be used throughout this book. But the needs of occupations, citizenship, and personal growth are given a central position, nevertheless, because at this particular time education, in general, and English, in particular, appear to be essential for these three areas of need. The fourth area of need, the development of language knowledge as a cultural resource, is largely a professional concern.

Although literacy advocates today almost always claim that literacy produces humanitarian results, English teachers should understand that literacy has not always done so and will not always do so. Schooling and literacy have been used to label people as "intrinsically wicked and inferior" (Stuckey 1991); to exploit Southern blacks who were needed as cheap labor for Southern agriculture (Lemann 1991); to organize a Protestant-capitalist majority against an unorganized and desperate collection of dissenters, radicals, and religious minorities (Kaestle and Foner 1983); to control the working class through an agenda of classist and racist patterns of schooling (Katz 1968); and to solidify the control of "an interlocking directorate of urban elites" through professional and bureaucratic centralism (Tyack 1974, 7). Today, on many Navaho reservations, for example, literacy is regarded as an alien cultural artifact committed to the goals of American colonialism (Spolsky and Irvine 1980), and in many cities literacy is considered the creator of a basic alienation between home and school (Rodriguez 1983). The sad stories of children attempting to learn to read while at the same time attempting to avoid the self-contempt generated by literary lessons seem endless.[3]

However, school literacy appears to have produced, for many people, an enrichment of our cultural resources, an improvement in income, and for scholars like Goody and Watt, "the development of political democracy" (H. Graff 1987, 383). Despite the negative effects of many literacy campaigns and the inconsistencies in the data on the positive outcomes of literacy, education appears to have paid off better in the twentieth-century workplace because, in the twentieth century, there appears to be "a tighter fit between schooling and one's occupational fate" (Kaestle 1985, 35).[4]

This tighter fit has become particularly apparent in the income levels of college and high school graduates. College graduates show steady income increases, but high school graduates, for the first time, are showing income decreases as high school skills cease to be adequate for contemporary jobs (Murnane and Levy 1993). There also appears to be a tighter fit between schooling and one's ability to function as a citizen, a fit based on the increasing complexity of problems faced by citizens and the tendency of postmodern cultures to use literacy and schooling to define a society's coherence and to establish "the consensual basis of an existing political system" (Adamson 1980; qtd. in H. Graff 1987, 11). In order to recognize and respect the pluralism of our society, citizens need a clear understanding of society's democratic assumptions and the way those assumptions play out in public discourse.

The importance of literacy for the workplace, for enrichment of cultural resources, and for citizenship does not eliminate the need for literacy for personal growth. Increasingly, society has found that problems of drug abuse, teenage pregnancy, and gang violence are not only problems of personal growth, but also problems of civics and of the workplace. The questions of "What is difference," "What is love," "What is personal responsibility," "Who am I"—all crucial questions in the literature of English classes—are foundational issues for problems of personal growth, and at the same time, foundational problems for civics and the workplace.

The workplace relationship is probably the one of the three which is least understood by today's English teachers. For one thing, anyone who listens to some businesspersons and union leaders talk these days about a new education for a new workplace has to be struck by the fact that many of these businesspersons and union leaders have become energetic advocates for collaborative learning, for writing and reading whole pieces, for substantial interpretive work in schools, and for new forms of democracy in the workplace. There are those—and I am one of them—who think the close fit between workplace success and class-room success is often exaggerated. Glynda Hull (1993) has been particularly insightful on this point in her studies of the skills required in the workplace. But the exaggerations in the press of school-workplace relationships do not mean that there is not a significant fit. Bailey reports the effort of textile firms "to hire workers with some college education, even when they cost considerably more than high-school-educated workers" because in the new technology of textile plants, "literary skills are much more important in repairing looms today than in the past" (Bailey 1988; qtd. in Murnane and Levy 1993, 6). One result of this trend and others is that high-school-educated males "are the first generation of Americans in the post-World War II era who [are] earn[ing] less than their fathers" (Murnane and Levy 1993, 17). We, as English teachers, have to be concerned about such trends.

It is important to remember that the relationship between education and the workplace is an interactive one, not a delivery relationship from education to the workplace. Let me explain. In some recent United Automobile Workers (UAW) contracts, the union asked for training and education which go well beyond what is required in the workplace. Why do corporations provide them? Because corporations have found that this kind of education and training, although not immediately useful on the assembly line, helps to create company loyalty ("The company cares about me"), helps to create pride in one's work, and finally helps to change the way the company functions and defines its jobs as it makes use of available skills. Job descriptions are often the minimum requirements, and they do not necessarily represent typical or even potential practice. When an employee has skills, they are often used, and this use has the potential for changing the job description. The point is that the relationship between education and the workplace is interactive, not one-way.

Let's examine carefully the relationship between an English class and a reorganized workplace by comparing work at the old General Motors plant in Fremont, California, with work at the new, reorganized plant. The old GM plant—which in March 1982 laid off the last of its 3,000 workers after twenty years of auto and truck production—had many problems. For one thing, work was excessively routinized. One worker reported that working on the old GM assembly line was like "being paid to flunk high school for the rest of your life." For another thing, this plant produced poorly made cars. Why? One reason for the poorly made cars, almost everyone agrees, was the fact that the old factory was organized like a mechanical clock, with many parts or job categories, all of them fixed, prefabricated processes. Mechanical clocks, to borrow a metaphor from Kenneth Boulding (1956, 20–21), were reasonable organizing metaphors for the markets of the U.S. between World War I and 1970, but by 1982, many clock-like systems were no longer working well.

The GM plant which reopened as a joint venture between GM and Toyota in December 1984 replaced the old clock-factory with a thermostat-factory of just-in-time inventory, faster data processing (showing what was in stock, what was selling, what was not working), new roles for workers (the power to stop the line), and a new name—NUMMI (New United Motor Manufacturing Incorporated). All of these changes were necessary—not just one—because just-in-time inventory and the new data-processing equipment, for example, would not have worked any better than the traditional system if the culture of the workplace had not changed and if the workers were not given new equipment and new on-line responsibilities for identifying problems and proposing solutions.

The new NUMMI plant required three fundamental changes in production procedures—from numerous prefabricated job procedures defined in great detail to a few job categories with more on-line translations of appropriate procedures; from strictly individual work and individual definitions of intelligence to distributed work and distributed definitions of intelligence; and from generic problem solving to situated problem solving (SCANS 1991). It is important to remember that NUMMI did not look for new workers who had these new skills of negotiated, distributed, and situated intelligence and then build the new plant. Instead, NUMMI worked with the union (the UAW) to build the new plant and then taught these new habits of work and mind to the workers from the old plant.[5] And the workers easily learned these new habits of mind.

Why were these new skills needed? The need for these new skills grew out of, among other things, the new technology, which is both more costly and faster. Armano Ablaza told a group of us that the faster pace of the new plant makes waiting time too costly:

> I'm an electrician by trade, now working in the General Maintenance capacity at NUMMI. I'm also a member of the UAW Journeyman Card Committee, and the UAW-NUMMI Apprenticeship Committee. Traditionally, the lines of demarcation would mean that I would do only electrical work—specific jobs for specific classifications. For example, the job of installing a pump and motor would take 3 skills—a millwright, a pipe fitter and an electrician. There was too much waiting, one for the other, and the other. And here, a minute of downtime may cost thousands of dollars. (Ablaza 1989)

To reduce this wait time, GM and the union reduced the number of job categories in the contract with the United Automobile Workers (UAW) from over one hundred in the old GM plant to four in NUMMI, producing more flexible workers on-line and reducing the time spent waiting for "specialists." The dramatic reduction of job categories, according to George Nano, former bargaining chair of the UAW's local in Fremont, also gave workers a chance to escape the boredom of one lifetime job in the plant (Nano 1989).

The reduction in number of jobs also produced the need for workers who were better informed about the production process. In the old plant, where hiring and job training were a slot-filling process like the assembly line itself, Joel Smith, once the UAW International Representative at Fremont, told me, "We would hire people off the street, show them the spot to stand, hand them gloves, give them five minutes of review about the job, and tell them, 'Go!'" He added, "In the new job culture, they must be taught how to work in teams, how to problem solve, and how to do different jobs" (J. Smith 1988). In the new plant, the flexibility of job assignments requires workers who are knowledgeable about the whole system, and it requires managers who see themselves as part of the negotiations of solutions, not as the sole owners of information and the sole producers of answers, solutions, and directions:

> Flexible systems can adapt quickly only if information is widely shared and diffused within them. There is no hierarchy to problem solving: Solutions may come from anyone, anywhere. In flexible-system enterprises nearly everyone in the production process is responsible for recognizing problems and finding solutions. (Reich 1983, 135)

In the old plant, workers needed a tolerance for fixed, unchanging routines. In the new plant, workers need a tolerance for negotiated solutions to problems and an eagerness to think about new and better ways of doing the work. Some workers, of course, miss the simplicity of the fixed, delivered, prepackaged job. One complained to me, "This stuff looks like management's job to me." Another told me, "I wish we'd adopt a plan and not change it." Nevertheless, in the first ten months of 1988, two-thirds of the employees (1,600 out of 2,400) participated in NUMMI's voluntary suggestion program for restructuring and submitted an average of 3.9 suggestions per employee. NUMMI adopted more than 6,000 of these suggestions (Brown and Nano 1989, 2).

These changes in the workplace restructured the life not only of the workers, but also of the union leaders.[6] The primary job of union leaders in the past had been "work-to-the-letter" grievances in which the union leader argued that the worker was, in fact, doing every part of an assigned job description, neither more nor less, and/or that the worker should not be assigned to an unspecified task. Because there were over a hundred jobs in the old plant, each with a specific procedural description, the processing of grievances was a routine matter, and there were several thousand grievances filed each year. In fact, there were over 1,000 grievances still awaiting resolution when the old GM plant closed in 1982 (Stuller 1986).

In the new plant, union leaders still file grievances, but the issues require more on-line negotiations and appear to be more difficult to describe in checklists. In the first four years of NUMMI, only 257 grievances were filed (Brown and Nano 1989, 1), compared with the several thousand filed in the old plant during the same time period. The union leader in this situation, says Owen Beiber, must have new skills: "Instead of being a grievance handler, he/she [the union representative] becomes a more knowledgeable facilitator, adviser, and educator" (Beiber 1982). In summary, then, the reduction in the number of prespecified jobs created a need for both a worker and a union leader with a transformative habit of mind, a willingness to see the plant as a text to be negotiated, translated, and constructed, not as an immutable set of information and procedures.

This shift from delivered information to negotiated and translated information was accompanied by a second shift from individualized problem-solving assignments to distributed assignments and problem solving. In the old plant, the worker worked alone as an individual with individual responsibilities, and intelligence was defined as entirely an individual matter. In the new plant, each worker is assigned to a team and to a network with distributed responsibilities. Intelligence is now defined as, at least, partially distributed. This shift became necessary because in complex systems where information travels fast, where specialties of knowledge keep increasing, where technology assumes control of various tasks, and where change occurs frequently, problem solving and thinking must be a distributed, collaborative act.

In this new collaborative, distributed system at NUMMI, each team is led by a team leader who in many cases is also a union coordinator, and each member of the team is expected to learn how to do all of the jobs of the team. Thus, all jobs are systematically rotated within the team, and this rotation ensures the distribution of information and prevents situations in which all of the "unpopular" work is loaded onto one job or person. This teamwork creates the need for two new skills in the workplace. First, rotational teamwork places a new premium on teaching as a skill. Workers who can teach others how to do a new job or how to solve a new problem become critically important within this system of distributed intelligence. Second, rotational teamwork places a premium on interpersonal skills. NUMMI manuals, which describe

PT (the "personal touch") as part of everyone's job, require workers "to know and respect [the] individual team member's personal background." To support the development of PT, the company provides PT funds for teams to cover the costs of social events (Abbott 1989, 2).

In addition to a team of co-workers to which workers can distribute problems, workers need a larger collection of tools to which they can distribute intellectual problems. These tools include data-processing hardware—for example, electronic calendars and computers—and data-processing software—for example, Gantt charts, memorization tricks, and problem-solving steps. These new tools—Gantt charts and electronic calendars—process intellectual work, turning information into various sign systems, often on digital computers. The old tools of the industrial revolution processed physical labor—pliers to bend things, levers to lift things, drill presses to cut things, transport to move things. The new tools of the information revolution process intellectual labor and reduce the time we need to generate and store increasing amounts of information—leaving more time, I might add, for the interpretation of the information we have. In fact, interpretation has become an essential, basic skill, and our networks of people and machines have become foundational tools for this interpretive activity.

Finally, the new plant requires that problem solving be situated, not generic. In the old plant, information was slow and scarce, and, thus, production processes remained generally unchangeable because they were largely unaddressable. The workers were, said Tony DeJesus, former president of the NUMMI-UAW local, "so many cogs in a wheel" (DeJesus 1989). In the new environment, workers have much information available through computers and other tools. Thus, workers turn to information analysis and problems of translation—how to observe, how to use group discussions to solve problems, and how to translate data into different representations, from, say, lists to visual charts. Jim Jackson, who worked in the old GM plant for twenty-two years before being laid off and later rehired for the new plant, described how this process of situated problem solving works:

> Early last year, we formed an observation team with the goal of increasing our SPH, without increasing the pace of the machine—in other words, by reducing downtime. We were then averaging 310 SPH, and we wanted to meet a new production requirement of 380 SPH. The six members of our observation team included three production-line team members, a general maintenance worker, a die and tool worker, and an engineer assistant. The three production-line team members made all observations during the five months of the project (which continued from the first week in January to the last week in May); we were on temporary assignment then, and were not working our regular jobs. All six members of the observa-

tion team attended periodic joint meetings of the team. We started entering our observations on check sheets, on which we listed the check points for pieces of equipment like the crane saver (look for burrs, bent and wavy conditions, for example) or the sheet feeder (see if vacuum cups are making proper contact). . . .

Then we summarized our findings, as recorded on the check sheets, into a Process Observation Report (A-8) [see Figure 2]. This report totalled up the problems and the number of times they had occurred, and classified them into the categories of automation troubles (giving the number of loading and unloading misses, for example), and quality control troubles (giving the number of pimples, dimples, splits, and other defects, for example). (J. Jackson 1989)

Situated problem solving, with its emphasis on observation, charts, and analysis, requires that the new plant provide workers with an intensive training program on problem solving. Every year NUMMI provides its production workers with between 40 and 80 hours of training, much of it led by team members themselves and much of it focused on team building, motivation, leadership at all levels of work, and "Kaizen," a problem-solving sequence in which all workers are taught, among other things, the five "whys" and various ways of charting data such as histograms, scattergrams, fish-bone charts, and run diagrams (Abbott 1989; see Schonberger 1986; and Ishikawa 1972).

Richard Schonberger has observed that these data-analysis methods are particularly useful on the assembly line: "The tools are easy for staff people with a bit of math education to learn but hard for them to make use of. The tools, at least the more mathematical ones, are harder for the average shop employee to learn but easy to make use of" (Schonberger 1986, 126). The use of these data tools also contributes to a sense of expertise among assembly line workers about the patterns of their work. I heard several workers call one fellow employee "the glove lady" (she knew all about the flow of new and washed gloves in the plant, and she had the charts to prove it), and I heard other workers call another employee "the weather-stripping professor" (she knew all about weather-stripping patterns). The new patterns of literacy in this NUMMI plant—negotiated and translated meaning, distributed intelligence, and situated problem solving—are not restricted to industrial workplaces. Traces of these practices can also be found in academic workplaces.[7]

Similar literacy strategies are needed to deal with similar patterns of change in the civic life of the country, where change and diversity are dominant themes. During the 1970s, the Hispanic population increased by 61 percent and the Asian by 233 percent while the total U.S. population grew by only 11 percent (Gonzalez 1993). Every area of the country, especially the cities, has experienced some of this increase in population diversity (Crawford 1989, 14). In addition, the U.S. has been experiencing

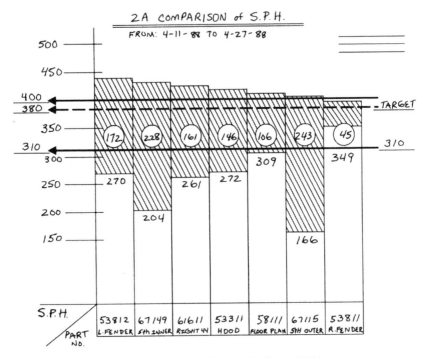

Fig. 2. Chart from Jim Jackson's team. (Source: Jackson 1989.)

increased information diversity in its civic life, as international networks of information bring to the U.S. diverse voices from around the world. We are, says Geertz, attempting to construct in our civic life a new world in which the old order, anchored in an educated class of the few and in U.S.-Soviet dominance of the world, has given way to multiple centers of influence throughout the country and the world:

> In particular, the hard dying hope that there can again be (assuming there ever was) an integrated high culture, anchored in the educated classes and setting a general intellectual norm for the society as a whole, has to be abandoned in favor of the much more modest sort of ambition that scholars, artists, scientists, professionals, and (dare we hope?) administrators who are radically different, not just in their opinions, or even in their passions, but in the very foundations of their experience, can begin to find something circumstantial to say to one another again. The famous answer that Harold Nicholson is supposed to have given to a lady on a London Street in 1915 as to why he was not, young man, off defending civilization—"Madam, I *am* civilization"—is no longer possible at even the highest of High Tables. (Geertz 1983, 160)

The key citizenship issue for the contemporary U.S. is
and our pluralism requires that we discover how to wea\
into a cohesive social pattern which maintains a respect fo\
tion of our differences. We need to construct a public disco\
knowledges the diversity of voices entering public discussions and
which also asserts that a common public policy can emerge from this diversity. Patricia Bizzell underlines the urgency of this social need: "Certainly the last [1988] Presidential campaign suggested that national
discourse is dead ... and that we have no way of sharing views and concerns on the challenges confronting us" (Bizzell 1990, 674). One of the
purposes of schooling, then, is to construct this public discourse in our
classrooms and to teach students how to participate and how they might
define themselves in the process. The key problem in the classroom is the
balance between participation and resistance, belief and disbelief.
Faigley has argued that conflicts and trends of thought within the larger
community end up as conflicts and trends of thought in composition
studies, and in both places, radical thoughts usually get domesticated
through demands for cohesion and audience satisfaction (Faigley 1992).

Throughout this book, I will be attempting to weave together our
cultural resources, the workplace, citizenship forums, our spaces for
personal growth, and our English classes into the larger patterns of literacy practice at a given time and place. I hope to avoid, if possible, the
tendency "to overestimate the degree of intellectual consensus in a
given society in the past" (Burke 1986, 443). But be forewarned: in the
chapters that follow, I will use categories of literacy to characterize and
to simplify very complex interactions from within the U.S. and from
other cultures. The only justification I have for these simplifications is
that these categories help me (and I hope they help you!) to imagine the
larger patterns of interactions which shape literacy practices in the U.S.
and in other cultures.

Four literacy shifts are outlined in the chapters which follow: (1) from
orality to signature literacy (from 1660 to 1776 in the U.S.); (2) from signature to recitation literacy (from 1776 to 1864 in the U.S.); (3) from recitation
literacy to decoding/analytic literacy (from 1864 to 1916 in the U.S.); and
(4) from decoding/analytic literacy to critical/translation literacy (from
1916 to 1983 in the U.S.), the latter being the shift now underway. Orality,
or *Oracy*[8] (the literacy of an oral society), served the needs of a stable agricultural society in which people lived in the same communities for years,
but *signature literacy* served a transient agricultural society in which people moved frequently. Oracy and signature literacy were also developed
as forms of literacy in other countries, and some of the similarities in different countries will be used to help us understand patterns in the U.S.

Recitation literacy served a society in which people were moving from farms to small factories and to cottage industries, but the literacy of *decoding/analytic comprehension* served a society where factories and industrial parks were large and centralized. Finally, in the 1980s, as international informational networks began to loom large in our lives and as the NUMMI story began to be repeated throughout the U.S. economy, a new standard of literacy began to emerge which some people call "higher-order thinking skills" or the new critical/translation literacy. Remember that the primary focus here is K–12 education and secondary education especially. But there is good evidence that some universities and colleges introduced similar forms of literacy at different times.

Let me emphasize, again, that it would be a mistake to take these periods too literally. These divisions into types of literacy suggest specific historical periods, but they disguise the erratic ups and downs of literacy efforts. What literacy periods give us is a sense of the mentality of a period.[9] There is no claim here that these forms of literacy dominated all parts of the country and all institutions. The forms were *generally*, not exclusively, dominant. A particular standard of literacy is often slow to develop, often overlapping with other standards of literacy, and sometimes declining (H. Graff 1979; Kaestle 1985, 31). Standards of literacy appear to undergo an initial period in which they are applied only to a few students and a subsequent period in which they become the minimum standard for the population at large.

The central problem in literacy theories is the problem of change—when, how, and why do people shift from one literacy to another. Forms of literacy always appear to be impervious to change during periods of dominance, despite various forms of citizen resistance. Furthermore, the explanation of change is almost always after-the-fact. Be forewarned: the chapters which follow assume that changes in standards of literacy are explained by (and associated with) occupational shifts, ideological shifts, national debate, and changes in the nation's form of schooling, models of mind, and literacy assessment.[10] My first purpose is to describe what the dominant patterns *might* be at any time, and my second purpose is to connect the teaching of English to those patterns. My third purpose is to describe public–professional tensions surrounding a form of literacy.

This book is founded on the hope that our present literacy campaign and its school reform movement have within them the possibility for a positive, democratic change, despite the negative effects of some literacy campaigns. This hope is based on the belief that our newer forms of literacy appear to acknowledge the different ways of being smart, as

well as the gains and losses in past literacy practices. But th[
new standard of literacy also depends, as Bolter has ob[
"dream" of continuous knowledge expansion fueling our
processing capabilities, the dream of "ever more powe[
energy" driving our factories, and the dream of the "economics o[
infinity" in which people continue to work, to interpret, and to read—
not just to consume more but to fulfill each person's need to use tools, to
symbolize, to create, and to build things (Bolter 1984). In this assumption of interpretive infinity, texts can continue to yield new interpretations (Tuman 1992) and, thus, can retain their status as the "repository
of secrets" (Kermode 1979, 144). Each of these assumptions (or dreams?)
underlies the hopes attached to literacy discussions in the U.S. today
(Bolter 1984; Tuman 1992, 7). Now, let's turn to the past literacy practices
(Chapters 2, 3, 4, and 5) which many of our students still bring to our
classrooms.

Notes

1. These projects have been joined by many others calling for new curriculum concepts, new teaching approaches, more teacher-training time, and more
class time for each curriculum area: *Building a History Curriculum* from the
Bradley Commission on History in Schools; *Changing a Course: Social Studies for
the 21st Century* from the National Commission on Social Studies in the
Schools; The Getty Art Project; Mathew Lipman's philosophy project; Rocke-
feller's *Chart Projects in the Humanities*; *Science for All Americans* from the American Association for the Advancement of Science; *Essential Changes in Secondary
Science: Scope, Sequence, and Coordination* published by the National Science
Teachers Association; *Reshaping School Mathematics* from the Mathematics Sciences Education Board of the National Research Council; *Everybody Counts: A
Report to the Nation on the Future of Mathematics Education* from the National
Academy of Science; *Curriculum and Evaluation Standards for School Mathematics*
from the National Council of Teachers of Mathematics.

2. "A boy with normal hearing but with deaf parents who communicated
with American Sign Language was exposed to television every day so that he
would learn English. Because the child was asthmatic and was confined to his
home, he interacted only with people at home where his family and all their vis-
itors communicated in sign language. By the age of three he was fluent in sign
language but neither understood nor spoke English" (Moskowitz 1978, 94–94b).

3. George Dennison reports: "When I used to sit beside Jose and watch him
struggling with printed words, I was always struck by the fact that he had such
difficulty in even seeing them. I knew from medical reports that his eyes were
all right. It was clear that his physical difficulties were the sign of a terrible conflict. On the one hand he did not want to see the words, did not want to focus his
eyes on them, bend his head to them, and hold his head in place. On the other
hand he wanted to learn to read . . . and so he forced himself to perform these ac-

tions. But the conflict was visible. It was as if a barrier of smoked glass had been interposed between himself and the words: he moved his head here and there, squinted, widened his eyes, passed his hand across his forehead. The barrier, of course, consisted of the chronic emotions I have already mentioned: resentment, shame, self-contempt, etc. But how does one remove such a barrier?" (Dennison 1969; Stuckey 1991, 68).

4. Although literacy is now usually associated with a nation's economic development, industrialization, and, sometimes, urbanization, this has not always been so. Seventeenth-century Sweden is an example of a broad expansion of literacy without any expansion of industrialization, urbanization, or economic development. In fact, the sole cause of the literacy effort in Sweden in the seventeenth century appears to have been a joint effort between the state and the Lutheran Church to use reading ability to establish national military preparedness (H. Graff 1987, 13). In addition, in his work on three Ontario cities in 1861, Graff concluded that literacy did not account for income or occupational status, but that ethnic heritage and family condition did (H. Graff 1979). However, the recent results of the National Adult Literacy Survey show a high correlation between employment and education among all types of workers and among all ethnic groups (Kirsch et al. 1993).

5. NUMMI mailed 5,000 employment applications to former workers in the old plant. About 3,000 of these applications were returned, and 2,200 of the old workers were eventually rehired (Nano 1989).

6. The problem-solving atmosphere of the plant soon found its way into the activities of the union. Most unions are run like their plants—stable, hierarchial, noncritical of the union itself. I speak here as an active union member throughout my teaching career. The UAW local which bargained contracts for workers at NUMMI was, throughout the period from 1984 to 1992, engaged in an open, extensive debate about whether the new organization of the plant was good for workers. Those supporting the new organization maintained leadership throughout the initial period from 1984 to 1992. By 1992, most of the critics had become supporters of the overall structure of the new plant and had begun to focus their critique on modifications, not revolution. Then, they began to be elected to union positions. The point is that the union saw a renewal of democracy in its operations, and the involved membership gave the critics most of the offices in the elections of 1992. I interviewed workers and managers, read union and company documents, observed developments at the plant from 1983 to 1990, and discussed these developments with the statewide union leaders. At that time, I lived in Oakland, California, and from 1985–1990 was president of the California Federation of Teachers, AFT, AFL-CIO.

7. I was serving on NCTE's David H. Russell Award Committee when the first collaborative award was given. There was an interesting discussion among the committee members about how collaborative awards are given in situations which traditionally have honored individuals.

8. The term "Oracy," meaning "oral literacy," comes from a personal communication with Andrew Wilkinson, at Asilomar, California, in the 1970s. He later served at the National Oracy Project (1987–1993) in the United Kingdom.

9. "In the last few years in fields as far apart as economic history and the history of science, a number of scholars have found it impossible to solve their problems without involving a concept like that of mentality..." (Burke 1986, 440).

10. This point is a critical assumption in the book. The assumption is that a form of literacy is part of what Gramsci calls the social or consensus hegemony, which gives a culture some coherence, some stability, and some ability to function in the care and feeding of citizens. Says Harvey Graff, "Antonio Gramsci's formulation of a concept of hegemony permits us to escape the crudities of social control theories, modernization and enlightenment notions . . ." (H. Graff 1987, 11).

2 From Oracy (or Face-to-Face Literacy) to Signature Literacy: 1660–1776

> Oral cultures can have schools, legal systems and political structures, and these institutions demand particular forms of language.
> (Barton 1994, 93)

The work of Anne McGill-Franzen and her research team at the Literature Center of the State University of New York at Albany suggests that school practices often define literacy in quite different ways. Their study of the literacy practices at five urban preschools found a startling contrast in the way those preschools defined literacy (McGill-Franzen 1993): one preschool teacher said, "I can't have an alphabet up in my room" (McGill-Franzen 1993, 183); another exhibited the alphabet and had the children copy and trace letters; another had children do exercises from a Zaner-Bloser workbook on handwriting readiness; and another, which also exhibited the alphabet, had the children learn the letters of their name and engaged the children in group work on the "letter of the week" (McGill-Franzen and Lanford 1993; McGill-Franzen 1992).

In one preschool, books were displayed, but there were almost no books available for the children to handle. In another, about thirty hardbound, unfrayed books were available for the children to handle, and in yet another, many books were always available for use by the children, both hardbound and softcover, frayed and unfrayed. In another preschool, writing and drawing materials were rarely available, and in still another, writing and drawing materials were almost always available. Says McGill-Franzen about the first center:

> Pencils with erasers were a novelty for the children, as was writing itself, and the children often pleaded with the observers to allow them to write. One youngster proudly showed a blue crayon stub that he had been carrying in his bookbag, and another puzzled over how the eraser part of the pencil worked.... (McGill-Franzen 1993, 12)

In an earlier study, Gordon Wells (1981) and Cliff Moon (Moon and Wells 1979) found similar differences in children's literacy experiences at home. For example, *looking at and talking about books, drawing and coloring, attempting to write,* and *listening to stories read aloud* were not equally distributed practices. In fact, *attempting to write* happened only twice in Wells's data. In addition, Wells found that for students who came to school with a good foundation for literacy, each of these activities was embedded within larger categories of cultural practice that shaped the child's conception of literacy. For example, Wells observed: "Thus, whilst part of the facilitating experience of the more successful children involved the shared activities of being read to, and looking at and talking about, equally important was the way everyday events were picked up in talk, and meanings developed and made more coherent through extended conversation" (Wells 1981, 263).

McGill-Franzen found that in some of the preschools, attitudes toward books were often like those in oral cultures. In these preschools, books were in the room as symbols of authority, not as objects to be opened and read. Students regarded books as objects that held a privileged position near the front of the room, like religious artifacts. They did not regard books as objects from which they might recite, decode, or secure pleasure throughout their daily lives. In these preschool cultures, books were to be honored, but not touched, just as a Bible might have a particular place in the front room at home and play the role of the authoritative place for family history, including birth certificates, family trees, and photographs of elders. Such a book was not to be touched by children.

Shirley Brice Heath (1983) has described how these vastly different attitudes toward literacy became woven into the work and home lives of the residents of Roadville, Trackton, and the townspeople in an area of South Carolina. In Trackton, young children were not viewed as conversational partners by adults, but in Roadville, young children were expected to be the adults' conversational partners. Trackton depended more on oral language, and Roadville brought more writing into everyday life. Similar contrasts are reported by Denny Taylor and Catherine Dorsey-Gaines (1988) in their study of literacy practices in an area of the Northeast.

How are we to understand this "startling" contrast in the way literacy is practiced in these various studies? I want to suggest that, in these studies, the researchers found traces of four different periods of past literacy practices. For example, the practice of not displaying the alphabet, not having books generally available for the children, using books as icons or shelf displays, and having no available writing materials—all of these features could be said to be characteristic of literacy practices during face-to-face or oral literacy. Wells's observation of routine "display questions" in some settings, on the other hand, is similar to the secular catechism of recitation and signature literacy, and the Zaner-Bloser workbook on handwriting readiness is reminiscent of decoding/analytic literacy.

I must at this point warn the reader that I am about to talk about *oracy, orality,* and *oral literacy* as if these terms represented a single thing. But all oral cultures do not have the same patterns of oral literacy (Bloch 1975). I am also going to talk about oracy as a form of literacy. Typically, literacy is reserved for paper marks, not oral language. Why, then, am I engaging in these distortions? I want to talk about oral patterns in the U.S. as one thing in order to show how these patterns can be found in other parts of the world, how these patterns represented a way of doing business in the U.S., and how these patterns come into conflict with the dominant culture's print literacy within the U.S. In other words, I am simplifying to make a point. I urge readers, however, to seek elsewhere the distinctions among different types of orality.

These distinctions are partly a result of the fact that the skills of a particular form of literacy are embedded in the everyday social practices of a community and are not isolated practices. Let me illustrate the "embeddedness" of literacy with the parable of how the skills of good manners originated among porcupines:

> One very cold night a group of porcupines were huddled together for warmth. However, their spines made proximity uncomfortable, so they moved apart again and got cold. After shuffling repeatedly in and out, they eventually found a distance at which they could still be comfortably warm without getting pricked. This distance they henceforth called decency and good manners. (qtd. in Wilson 1975, 257)

Good manners for these porcupines and, of course, for many humans require the "skills" of territorial distancing. A Mediterranean European will tolerate closer packing in restaurants than will a Northern European, and a German will go to almost any length to preserve his private space (E. Hall 1977). Among humans, social distance is regulated by literacy practices such as the skillful use of colloquialisms—for example, teaching children to avoid colloquialisms in formal situations and to use "ma'am" and "sir" with adults and strangers. Thus, a nation's conventional skills of pronoun use can be said to be a way of establishing social distancing and "good manners" in human relationships. So, too, a preschool's conventions of book use can be said to be a way of establishing social distancing rules for the relationships between human beings and print. Both pronoun use and attitudes toward books are part of the pattern of the nation's minimum standard of literacy.

Territorial practices and book customs are not the only matters embedded in literacy practices. Economic customs are another. Face-to-face or oral literacy interacted with the face-to-face economic relationships in the colonial U.S. of the 1600s and early 1700s, when one raised much of one's own food, exchanged goods with close neighbors, socialized the young at home, engaged in very limited travel to nearby village markets, and generally did not move much. New immigrants to the U.S. often brought with them the economic practices of English and European villages, where most people were accustomed to living in the same areas and engaging in face-to-face economic exchanges with the same families as their parents and grandparents. In these face-to-face economic relations, economic agreements were held together by "oral" memories of witnesses and by various memory techniques of oral literacy. Although in the U.S. of the late 1600s and early 1700s printed materials were fast becoming a dominant form of literacy among the educated, in the general population, face-to-face or oral literacy was the dominant form of everyday literacy practice.

The literacy event in an oral culture has always been a succession of vocal inflections, visuals, and physical movements passing between the ever-present "author" and "reader" (Goody and Watt 1968). The visuals were conventionalized in tokens, crosses, emblems, portraits, sculptures, tombstones, plaques, and family marks (including coats-of-arms), and movements were conventionalized in gestures, the nod, and the handshake, the latter of which is said to have originated in social situations where people had to assure one another "that they were not carrying weapons in their hands" (Ortega y Gasset 1963, 197). Over time, these various movements in face-to-face, oral literacy have become barely perceptible synchronizations between two people of finger, eyelid, and head movements (E. Hall 1977, 72).

In oral cultures, conventions developed for labeling, blessing, cursing, proclaiming, and entertaining, and these conventions began to cluster into specific practices embedded in particular communities. In African American neighborhoods in the U.S., for example, "playing-the-dozens," "sounding," "cappin'," and "signifying," including the subsets of "marking," "loud talking," "specifying," "testifying," and "rapping," became conventionalized oral exchanges ("Yo mama so skinny she can walk through the cracks in the door") (Lee 1993, 11, 98; Gates 1984, 286; Smitherman 1977).

One of the functions of the conventions of oral literacy was to preserve oral memory,[1] and, thus, the oral style used various linguistic devices for memory retention. These devices included, depending upon the culture, frequent redundancy (repeat expressions); frequent sequential and additive markers (*and, first, second*); infrequent subordinators which tax memory (*because, which, when, who*); frequent formulaic exchanges ("your mama," "Dear Sir: How are you? I am fine" and riddles); repetitions of epithets and formulaic phrases ("never judge a book by its cover," "clever Odysseus" in *The Odyssey*); adjective clusters ("sturdy oak," not "the oak"); an emphasis on meter and "rhythmic fluency" (football cheers, raps) (see Smitherman 1977, 121; Chafe 1982); and the development of devices of alliteration and various other "sound" patterns ("the Terror of the Terrible Twos"), including rhyme ("Rome," "home"). These characteristics of the oral style can be found in Homer (Parry 1971; Lord 1960), African American signifying (Smitherman 1977), oral conversational practices in the U.S. (Chafe 1982; Tannen 1985), Chinua Achebe's novels, *Beowulf*, and various practices of many oral cultures (Ong 1982).

It is important to remember that oral situations were also accompanied by a rich array of artifacts—seals, banners, tokens, crosses, and other religious figures, emblems of various kinds, tally sticks, good luck charms, and memory cords. One example of the memory cord is the *quipu* from Peru. A *quipu* is a collection of knotted cords of different lengths and colors which is worn as part of a headdress and used as a mnemonic system. Place and type of knot, color and length—each variation bears meaning representing dates, chronologies, and persons. The speaker uses the *quipu* to tell a story (Gaur 1987; Olson 1994, 99). I shall never forget a student teacher I had in Oakland, California, who triggered stories of family histories by having the students pass around a rope with forty knots, each student pausing, in turn, to hold one knot for fifteen minutes while reciting or telling one memory of family history.

These formulaic expressions of the oral style structured the way people began to think about the legal, religious, and epic facts of their lives (Yates 1966). To think in other patterns would have been a waste of time, says Ong:

> In an oral culture, to think through something in non-formulaic, non-patterned, non-mnemonic terms, even if it were possible, would be a waste of time, for such thought, once worked through, could never be recovered with any effectiveness, as it could be with the aid of writing. It would not be abiding knowledge but simply a passing thought, however complex. (Ong 1982, 35–36)

In the oral societies of the U.S. and England, where few people moved and where witnesses and their memories were used to authenticate ownership, kinship (births, marriages), agreements, wills, deaths, and oaths to carry out public business (Clanchy 1979), the courts opened their proceedings with an oral memory or the narrative of the case, not the formal features of the charges and counter charges typical in contemporary courtrooms based on a print literacy. Legal categories were "never … formalized" in the oral court as ways to organize oral memories (Epstein 1954, 29). As a result, "the nature of the case and the remedy sought often only emerged in the course of the hearing" as the oral narratives were told and oral interactions took place in the courtroom (Goody 1986, 153; see also the example in Epstein 1953, 26).

Fallers says that the transcripts of oral courts in oral societies "read like one non-sequitur after the other…interlaced with apparent contradictions" (Fallers 1969, 320–21). But he adds that "neither the non-sequiturs nor the contradictions really are such" (Fallers 1969, 314) because they are merely reflecting the conversational logic of an oral culture that bases evidence on narrative connections and proverbs, not legal principles. Says Ong, "The law itself in oral cultures is enshrined in formulaic sayings, proverbs" (Ong 1982, 35). These oral conventions, according to Goody, produced a legal system with processes of gradual adjustments to oral memories and, as a result, with "greater flexibility" than one might find in legal systems controlled by written records and precedent (Goody 1986, 136).

The following dialogue is an example of testimony by a Trobriand Islander who is using the conventions of orality or face-to-face literacy to testify in a Western court organized around print literacy.

(32.) Therefore, I came to reside in Teyava and saw my sister at a different veranda.

(33.) I had worked hard with them for our mother.

(34.) But because my sister had no one, I said to myself,

(35.) "O, this is not good. I will do a bit of Kaivatam of course."

(36.) People of Tukwaukwa I eat your excrement, compared to your gardens the one I made for her was so small.…
(Hutchins 1980, 68–69)

The Western judge called this a meaningless, rambling tirade, but Edwin Hutchins presents an analysis of the testimony showing that the logic of that testimony is based on the conventions of a face-to-face culture. He concludes:

Does Motabesi talk irrationally? No, he simply states a set of connected conditions in support of his case. This is quite reasonable, given the extreme complexity of the land tenure system which is unwritten and has no less than five different degrees of what we Westerners simply call "ownership." (Adapted from Hutchins 1980, 74; in Latour 1987, 189).

The Western judge's condemnation of the Trobriand Islander as illogical and rambling is reminiscent of Bereiter's early claims that expressions like "they mine" and "me got juice" are "a series of badly connected words" in the street talk of the cities (Bereiter et al. 1966, 114). Other researchers have argued that Bereiter's criticism confuses the notions of logic and explicitness (Labov 1972b; see also Latour 1987, 202–5). Logic in some black adult narratives, for example, is based on an episodic association which meanders "away from the 'point' [and] takes the listener on an episodic journey" (Smitherman 1977, 147–48).

Communities living entirely by the logic of a print-based legal system tend to dismiss these oral associations as illogical, as not sticking to the point, as lacking a governing thesis. But fragments in oral style may only be an effort to get one's partner into an oral exchange in order to share collaboratively in the construction of that exchange. In such a situation, talking too explicitly might look anti-social. In fact, starting every oral conversation with a clear thesis sentence may violate some of the social rules which prevail in some conversational settings. In summary, then, face-to-face oral literacy appears to encourage a conversational approach to discourse which violates the thesis and logic rules of *some* print-based institutions.

It is important to remember that this difference between oral- and print-based practices does not mean that speakers in oral literacy have no sense of their mental processes. They have a sense of mental processes and knowing as indicated in face-to-face interactions. Traugott has shown how numerous variations of the verb for "knowing" appeared in Old English, in Middle English, and even in Warlpiri, an aboriginal Australian oral language (Traugott 1987; on the Warlpiri, see Laughren 1992). Olson has argued that "[t]o make writing serve the same functions that speech has served, new verbs and concepts have to be invented, concepts such as 'literal' and 'metaphorical' as well as those expressed by the terms 'stated,' 'insisted,' or 'implied,' which when nominalized, could yield such entities as 'conjectures,' 'statements,' and 'implications'" (Olson 1994, 108). Verbs like *observe, state,* and *claim* became part of a modern consciousness which developed from writing (Olson 1994, 194). Hundert has suggested that in the seventeenth century there were "increasing lexical distinctions in many European languages between the verbs employed for knowing" (Hundert 1987, 194).

In addition to helping memory and shaping thought, "oral" language and its variations help establish group distinctiveness and group solidarity. Language in an oral culture often does not have "outside" textual references to which we can turn for an outside definition, and, thus, definitions in many "oral" usages are often inside the local group. As James Sledd, Geneva Smitherman, and others have shown us, in these dialects, embedded as they are in face-to-face encounters, usages like the following make perfect, convention-governed sense:

> It's against the rule; that's why don't so many people do it. (Labov 1972c, 812)
>
> I know a way that can't nobody start a fight.
> Won't nobody catch us. (Labov 1972c, 811)

It is increasingly necessary in English classes to recognize the rule-governed nature of these usages so that the translations to the English textbook in class make more sense to students. The remarkable and unnoticed fact of our English classrooms, in the cities especially, is that the students are an invaluable resource for explaining the oral literacy conventions of their neighborhoods and families and for helping others and themselves develop translations to textbook English. Understanding a student's awareness of his or her own structures is the first step toward helping students to translate the structures of print-based school texts.

Within the general conventions of face-to-face literacy, there are, of course, significant differences between one group and another and between men and women. Robin Lakoff points out that "Westerners see clarity and rapport as opposite strategies," but to the Japanese speaker, "the two are inseparably interrelated parts of every communication" (R. Lakoff 1990, 175). In addition, Deborah Tannen suggests that there are differences in the way men and women talk—for example, their tolerance toward overlapping talk:

> My father believes that only one person should speak at a time. As a result, he often has a hard time getting the floor in conversations involving my mother, my two sisters, and me, since we overlap and do not leave pauses between our comments. He also feels that once he begins to talk, he should be permitted to continue until he is satisfied that he has explained his point completely. My mother and sisters and I feel that in a casual conversation among friends or family, it is acceptable to chime in when you think you know what others are getting at….(Tannen 1990, 211)

In addition, Labov has suggested that in their oral narratives, middle-class whites and inner-city blacks tend to use different types of evaluations in their narratives. These evaluations are essential in narratives because they answer the question "So what?" ("Why are you bothering to tell me this story and to take up my time and attention?"). Middle-class whites in Labov's study tended to use external evaluations like "Hey, here's the point!" and "I had quite an experience." On the other hand, black teenagers in Labov's study tended to use internal evaluations embedded in the story:

> *J*: I just closed my eyes.
> *K*: I said, "O my God, here it is." (Labov 1972a, 372)[2]

In summary, then, oral cultures use a conversational logic in which things are connected through a large number of shared inferences, through memory devices like *and* or *then*, through gestures based on the spatial rules of face-to-face events, and through fragments and hesitations which help the speaker avoid looking unnecessarily authoritative and, thus, anti-social. It is easy to see these oral traditions at work in classrooms when students turn to personal stories to answer questions about larger generalities. In a class which was writing about "Should the U.S. have laws against smoking in the public places?" some students responded with the narrative logic of face-to-face literacy: "Maybe. I remember the time . . ." or "Well, I guess, but my friend told me the story about. . . ." Other students responded with the cause-effect relations of a print-based literacy: "The U.S. should ban smoking because . . ." or "One reason to ban smoking is. . . ."

English teachers should understand that the resistance to literacy in our English classrooms is not a simple matter of individual deviancy or irritability. Resistance to literacy has a long and honorable history. Writing, in fact, was not adopted even when it was available for use. The earliest written documents, even in Europe, became an artifactual support, not a replacement, for oral authority and oral ways of thinking. For example, the written ordinances issued by French emperors in the eighth and ninth centuries were not "usually" drafted in official, full texts by the royal chancery, but were notes or titles set down to recall the contents of royal commandments made orally. The messengers who "read" official letters announcing new laws or policies were often reciting aloud what they had memorized after hearing a scribe read the message back to the king or official. In this situation, the written document was used primarily as a visual symbol of the authenticity of the oral message (Street 1984, 119–20). Even the Magna Carta, which became a precedent for putting legislation in writing, was distributed primarily through oral readings (Clanchy 1979, 144), although a few people did read a little. Most documents posted in public places were typically addressed to those both "seeing and hearing these letters" (Clanchy 1988, 135).

Because the courts considered face-to-face evidence more trustworthy than written documents, written documents became a support for oral exchanges, not an independent, silent witness. As late as the thirteenth century, despite the widespread use of written documents, wills in London were probated through a detailed system of law based on oral testimony in which the witnesses "saw, were present, and heard" the testifier making his bequests "with his own mouth" (Clanchy 1988, 136). Written documents like the Bible served a symbolic role in the courts, representing the spirit of divine justice, but legal questions were answered not by consulting written documents, but by asking for "oral testimony" and oral guidance (H. Graff 1987, 66). In wills, sometimes courts made a distinction between those who "heard" and those who "saw" (Clanchy 1988, 137), giving priority to the "heard." This distinction was very important in those cases where, for example, a dying person had a communicable disease which prevented witnesses from being in the same room and actually "hearing" the will from the lips of the deceased.

Print in these situations still did not have the "trustworthiness" of face-to-face oral literacy. Even when written documents were eventually admitted to the courts as legal evidence—as new, silent witnesses, some thought—they still required validation by a notary system in which an eyewitness testified orally to the notary about the authenticity of a document. This validation of written documents was necessary because most people thought written documents were unreliable. After all, one could erase and modify alphabetic writing without necessarily getting the approval of the author. Nevertheless, the notary system was a way to let written documents enter the court as evidence. Because of the deep "distrust of written modes of proof," whether validated by notaries or not, an extensive notarial system did not develop in England on the Roman model until quite late (Clanchy 1988, 154). And as late as the Reformation in the 1600s, English businesses remained committed to the face-to-face literacy of watching, speaking, and listening, even though writing was used by many to conduct business (Street 1984; Clanchy 1979).

"Trustworthiness" was not the only reason to resist print. The protection of local authority was another reason because print tends to undermine local authority. Oral literacy's dependence on visuals, the mouth, and an individual's immediate memory always gives considerable authority to the local level and face-to-face relations, encouraging a highly decentralized system of governance; "a strong network of kinship and group solidarity" (Stock 1983, 16); a conservative, hostile attitude toward the outside world (Goody and Watt 1968, 30–31); and, according to some, a "regionalized, highly particularized" culture which is "more conscious of inherited status than of achievement through pragmatic social roles" (Stock 1983, 14). In England, emphasis on written texts produced an openness to change in worldviews not typical of oral communities and, in fact, resulted in outbreaks of heresy as early as A.D. 1050 in England (Stock 1983, 522–23).

In the colonies of North America in the 1600s, writing was conceptualized as an extension of speaking rather than as an artifact with qualities independent of speaking. In fact, the word *reading*, as late as the 1800s, sometimes meant not reading silently but hearing—as in "reading for a degree" by attending lectures and listening (Clanchy 1979, 217).[3] Thus, in the U.S. of the late seventeenth century, despite the rapid growth of printed materials and the increase in self-reported literacy rates, "the oral popularized, diffused, mediated, and endowed the society with much of its coherence and integration" (H. Graff 1987, 252).

Nevertheless, during this period of oral literacy in the U.S., there continued to be considerable tension between those pushing for print as a standard of literacy and those resisting written literacy. Revivalists in the U.S. during the eighteenth century's "Great Awakening" attacked the church's growing "habit of deference to the written word" and, according to Rhys Isaacs, rebelled against "the literacy culture of the gentry" (H. Graff 1987, 253). Earlier, leaders of the U.S. colonies had officially resisted English mandates for written reports to England's Lords of Trade and Plantations because they saw the emphasis on written records as an effort on the part of London to control U.S. colonial authorities and to deny the authority of local, U.S. cultures.

This tension between oral and written cultures is repeated in European and English history. Medieval France, in fact, became split between Southern France (*le Pays du Droit Écruit*), which acknowledged the written laws of Roman law, and Northern France (*le Pays du Droit Coutumier*), which acknowledged oral societies and local usage (Goody 1986, 130). A similar tension over print literacy developed between the Normans and the Anglo-Saxons when the Normans invaded England (1066–1307). The Normans wanted to eliminate the use of local, oral authentication of ownership of property in the England of the Middle Ages because those methods allowed the local, native Anglo-Saxons of England to control their own property through personal relations (oaths of witness) and other methods of local authentication. To get control away from these local agents, the Normans insisted upon detailed alphabetic and numerical records of the land they "owned" and demanded the hiring of a "literate mentality" in government positions—"a deliberate construction for political and economic purposes" to use print literacy "to centralize control and to remove power from local Anglo-Saxon communities" (Street 1984, 111–12; Clanchy 1979).

Print literacy has always been a way to colonize and to control other people (P. Cohen 1982, 33–34).[4] Henry VIII took control of the Pope's property in England by mandating the use of Arabic numerals in inventories of that property, thus removing control of legal records from local, oral counting systems which favored the Pope. The Greeks used paper, the Greek alphabet, and writing as "the first great sledgehammer blows of technology" to replace the clay tablets of oral cultures and to take power away from the decentralized local governments of oral cultures in Greek city-states, all for the purpose of organizing a more centralized Alexandrian Empire (Innis 1972, 10). English teachers who sense resistance to print culture in today's students should remember the resistance of the Greeks, the Anglo-Saxons, the French, and our colonial ancestors. We, as English teachers, like other print authorities, are always eroding some of the power of local, oral cultures when we teach print literacy, and we should expect from our students a resistance similar to that of our forebears.

I want to argue the unoriginal point that the shift of young people from oral to written literacy—from drawings to marks to alphabetic printing to invented spelling and to written messages—is largely a journey through different rule-governed conventions, not a pattern of decreasing error in one universal form of literacy. This journey is pushed in a given direction by one's culture. In the West, speed and economy have always pushed literacy in particular directions, and thus our schools tend to push children toward forms of literacy judged to be efficient transports and storage systems for information. Alphabetic writing in cursive, for example, appears to be privileged because it will transport information faster and cheaper.

But cursive was a slow development. Scribes, in order to save time and to make money, turned pictures of monetary tokens into a systematic, logographic writing (Schmandt-Besserat 1978, 50). But this logographic writing had its own inefficiencies. The scribes, for example, had difficulty writing proper names in the Sumerian script in which the names of trees, animals, and other concrete objects were expressed in a formulaic picture approximating the everyday appearance of things (Gelb 1952, 66–67; Sampson 1985, 54). Proper names did not necessarily correspond to the local appearance of concrete objects like "cow," "trees," or "rocks" and required a different sign: "If a proper name is a meaningless sound-sequence [which it often is], it can be written only phonographically [which means sound correspondence], unless one invents a special logographic sign just for the name…" (Sampson 1985, 55). In other words, a sound-based alphabet became a time-saving method for writing a large number of proper names. Later, to cut the labor costs of scribes even more, employers pushed for a shift from printing each separate letter, which was often like drawing a picture, to connecting each separate letter in a faster, cursive writing style (Clanchy 1979, 99; Street 1984, 113–49).

Today, many elementary schools teach cursive as if it were a prerequisite for intelligence when, in fact, history tells us that cursive was invented for reasons of efficiency—to cut costs and get more work out of the scribes. In other words, students should learn cursive because, in a society emphasizing speed and quantity of output, cursive enables students to write faster and, thus, to look smarter. True, the automaticity of cursive can possibly have cognitive consequences, but the motivations of cursive are a cultural matter, not a matter of progress toward universal, absolute intelligence.

It is important to remember that phonetic elements are present in all forms of writing—pictorial, logographic, and alphabetic. As any third grader's picture writing can tell us, when we translate 👁 into "I" or "eye," we are establishing phonetic relationships with the sign. In fact, as Coe has suggested: "All known writing systems are partly or wholly phonetic, and express the sounds of a particular language" (Coe 1992, 25). This point is important because the picture writing of young people is often dismissed as not "teaching" children anything about sound-symbol relationships. This is not the case. The drawings of children *are* connected to sounds, and the principles of this relationship *are* a key step in literacy development.

It is also important to note that our basic language relations of syntagmatic or horizontal relations and associative or vertical relations were established in the use of tokens, long before the alphabet (see Hawkes 1977, 26–27, for a discussion of these language relationships). Olson, referring to the work of others, has argued that "the decisive step from tokens to scripts occurs when symbols shift from token-iterative to emblem-slotting systems, or what I prefer to think of as acquiring syntax" (Olson 1994, 72–73). When ten tokens are collected as an associative class, one has one token for every cow one owns. When three tokens begin to have syntax, one has one token stand for *1*, another for *0*, and a third for *cows*. The latter, like syntax or sentences, is an emblem-slotting system.

Writing emerged as a standard of literacy in the U.S. as oral cultures began to disappear. Orality was a satisfactory standard of literacy in the U.S. as long as U.S. society had little geographic mobility and maintained stable, face-to-face relationships among people. During oral literacy in the U.S., dated here from 1600–1776, schooling for most children took place in or near the home or within religious institutions and focused on oral "readings" or recitations of the Bible, catechisms, psalm books, religious verse, and selections from books like Doddridge's *Rise and Progress of Religion in the Soul* (1748). But by 1776, an increasing amount of travel had helped to shift social practices from face-to-face interactions with acquaintances to interactions with strangers, and, as a result, the literacy standard of the colonies began to shift away from oral literacy to signature and recording literacy. Oral agreements are adequate when people do not move, but signatures and written records are necessary among strangers.

Signature and written records also became more important as printed materials entered people's lives. Throughout the early 1700s, an upsurge in the number of newspapers, almanacs, magazines, textbooks, manuals, sermons, legal codes, and pamphlets of every sort had helped to create a new attitude toward print literacy, an attitude first communicated by speeches and sermons to those who were unable to read:

> Non-literates had already begun to participate in literate culture, although indirectly. They were made aware that a text lay behind a sermon and they were given an indirect understanding of the principles of authentication, that is, of legal precedence and legitimization through writing. Although remaining unlettered, they could thereby comprehend how one set of moral principles could logically supersede another. (Stock 1983, 91–92)

In England, the widespread shift to a print literacy of multiple versions, either copying some letters and/or reading a little, was no doubt encouraged by the ideology of Luther's Reformation, which urged people to think of print as their sign system, not as the exclusive property of a religious elite (H. Graff 1987). Eisenstein says that well before Luther nailed his 95 theses on the church door, the new ideological issues posed by the printing press had begun to divide Western Christendom into churchgoers with Luther-like attitudes toward texts—that is, people who wanted to copy letters and read a little themselves—and churchgoers who insisted on assimilating the authoritative oral reading of text by someone else, usually a religious authority (Eisenstein 1979). Another way of saying the same thing is to say that without the printing press and without available books, society needed an elitist theory of textual authority to justify the individual's lack of access to reading materials. There are times when I think I hear the same rationalization to justify the shortage of books available to K–12 students. That is, school authorities claim they can tell children what is in books or show them at school.

Printing and Luther together certainly helped hasten the demise of oral literacy in England, although, says Stock, "Despite primary schools, cheap paper, spectacles, and the growing body of legal and administrative material, the masses of both town and countryside as late as the Reformation remained relatively indifferent to writing" (Stock 1983, 13; see also Davis 1975, 189–226; and Eisenstein 1979, 225–72). For one thing, printing and Luther helped undermine oral literacy's notion of a singular religious elite whose authority governed the singular Biblical text.

The Latin Bible had long been studied by monks and religious scholars as *the* literal, sacred text, but printing by everyman produced complete polyglot versions and numerous variations in the translations of the Bible from Latin to English. In addition, the translation of the Latin Bible into English vernacular made it possible for craftsmen, artisans, engineers, barbers, surgeons, painters, and others who had not mastered Latin to contribute to public productions of the sacred text.

As a result, scholars, Protestant and Catholic alike, became less certain about the literal sacredness of a given Bible (Eisenstein 1985, 21), and the text slowly ceased to be the exclusive property of one educated, elite class. Instead, in place of one authority, printing and Luther helped establish multiple religious authorities who interpreted texts for different groups. Luther's catechism, which became a model for the first textbooks used in U.S. schools, as Daniel and Lauren Resnick have pointed out, preserved the sense of an authority behind a text by inviting the reader not to interpret but to repeat back the text's predetermined, delivered meaning in response to a question (D. Resnick and Resnick 1977).

Printing and Luther also helped undermine oral literacy's definition of text as a sacred object or icon. Various institutions began producing not only multiple versions of the Bible, but also a "vernacular technical literature" (Eisenstein 1985, 29–30). This secular literature expanded the available data pools in astronomy, botany, geography, and many other fields, leading to the need for the development of cataloging, indexing, cross-referencing, and other aids to analysis. These aids became the new secular disciplines which began challenging religious authority by the time we reached the 1860s.

What is it that this history of oracy and face-to-face literacy can teach us as English teachers? The history of the shift from oral to signature literacy suggests several conclusions which, I think, should shape the attitudes of teachers toward the struggle of their students to attain literacy. First, teachers must recognize that a standard of literacy is socially and historically contingent and should not be regarded as a universal definition of intelligence. Thus, students who are good at a dominant form of literacy (print, oral, visual) are in many ways the accidental beneficiaries of society's policies for minimum literacy. Those students who are outstanding conversationalists but poor writers are the accidental losers of some social status in the shift from oral to signature literacy.

The second point is that, today in our classrooms, our children relive some parts of the history of literacy in their shift from logos and pictures to letters and words and finally to cursive. I am arguing that children feel some of the same resistance and that they sense that each change in literacy has its gains and losses. Children who are asked to move from drawing to writing probably end up discovering the old idea that the alphabet does not work as well as drawing for all purposes. The loss of drawing is the loss of a way of knowing and being. Teachers who understand this point about literacy's history should be better able to appreciate the tensions children face and should look for ways to value the past literacy practices that children bring to the classroom and often hang on to.

Third, teachers who find themselves facing learners who resist writing should remember the vigorous resistance to writing of many early colonists who regarded alphabetic and numerical literacy as a threat to oral culture, to local control, and to religious belief. Literacy is not a neutral activity. It does change self-identity, family relations, and politics. Resistance to literacy may be for many students an intuitive effort to preserve culture, self, and family and is *not* then a simple matter of anti-intellectual or remedial behavior. It may be, from one point of view, a heroic defense of another form of literacy valued by one's family and community.

One way to help many students enter contemporary literacy practices is to value the literacy of the cultures they bring to the classroom and to make apparent to all students the various forms of literacy used in the U.S. The history of literacy makes clear that people functioned effectively and imaginatively long before marking systems entered their lives. Imagine students who come from oral cultures and who enter a public school discussion where stories come from books, not the oral memories of people; where newspapers are the source of information, not the oral exchanges in the neighborhood; where one's writing is valued, not one's oral facility; and where one's dialect is ignored or disparaged, and another dialect called "standard English" is promoted for *all* social purposes. It is easy to see why many of our students join with our forebears, the founders of our democracy, in a rebellious effort to protect local dialects, local customs, and local group identity.

Remembering the history of the Norman imposition of print on an Anglo-Saxon oral culture, teachers might profitably approach the problem of alienation within large, centralized school bureaucracies by studying some of the ways past oral cultures retained a sense of local identity and control. First, one might experiment with translating every bureaucratic activity, if possible, into an oral activity. For example, at the end of the third, sixth, ninth, and twelfth grades, students might appear for review before school-site orals boards, very much like a town meeting or an "oral" court. Schools which have added the oral panel as a graduation requirement report a dramatic increase in the school's sense of community. Second, the process of hiring school personnel should include telephone and face-to-face interviews involving teachers, students, parents, administrators, and maintenance personnel—all members of the school-site community in a face-to-face setting. Third, new students should be required to go to an interview with other students and school personnel. The point here is to embed the importance of face-to-face relations of oral cultures in the network of social practices and values in our schools. We will return to this issue later.

Next, English classes should make more use of the oral forms of discourse still recognized within the communities which surround the schools, but which are often ignored in the schools themselves. For example, Heath has observed:

> The school has seemed unable to recognize and take up the potentially positive interactive and adaptive verbal and interpretive habits learned by Black American children (as well as other non-mainstream groups), rural and urban, within their families and on the streets. These uses of language—spoken and written—are wide ranging, and many represent skills that would benefit all youngsters. (Heath 1989, 370)

I am suggesting, for example, that we turn to the work of Marsha Delain (Delain, Pearson, and Anderson 1985), Carol Lee (1993), Geneva Smitherman (1977), Robin Lakoff (1982), Walter Ong (1982), and Deborah Tannen (1985) to see how we can make oral language an object of study in the English classroom and a means for enhancing both reading and writing.[5] When children see the structure in their oral language, they are not only learning that language has structure, but that *they* have structure, have reasons, have inherent sense. In these instances, students become researchers of the language around and in the school, making visible the literacy practices of their community and the structures their communities use. Then, new forms of literacy can be examined not only as structures, but as devices embedded in community goals.

All of our students are not embedded in the same literacy history. It is clear that in some communities, adults do not simplify their language to children, thereby encouraging children to label, to extend sentences, and to participate in language interactions (Schieffelin 1979; Heath 1986a), and they do not read to their children, thereby not encouraging them to engage with printed materials (Heath 1983). In addition, for some bilingual students, the development of their reading in the second language exceeds their oral fluency in that language, and some children begin their explorations of literacy with writing, not reading. In bilingual situations, we need to recognize that the movement between Language^1 and Language^2 is always accompanied by a movement between one form of literacy and another, from Literacy^1 to Literacy^2. One student moving from Language^1 to Language^2 may have come from a community organized around oral literacy, and another student may have come from a community organized around recitation literacy. The point is that some bilingual policymakers have treated bilingual education as a problem of shifting from one language or linguistic form to another while ignoring the problems of shifting from one form of literacy to another. In the classroom, English teachers must use *both* the resources of other forms of literacy and the resources of the first language to make the transition to a second language and to other forms of literacy. Now let's turn to the introduction of signature literacy into the U.S.

Notes

1. In 1928, Milman Parry argued convincingly that *The Iliad* and *The Odyssey* were creations of oral poets who passed the stories along in face-to-face relations. This upset the views of many that *The Iliad* and *The Odyssey* were written by a poet named Homer, who knew how to write (Parry 1971).

2. Keith Gilyard suggests that Labov may, at times, be telling us more about the Labov-African American interaction than about the internal practices of the African American community (Gilyard 1991).

3. This is a tradition which goes back to the early Greeks.

4. Similar resistance occurred in a number of literacy practices. A major impetus toward the widespread use of Arabic numbers was what Sir William Petty called "political arithmetic"—the use of numbers to centralize the administration of colonial properties, merged nations, and new markets (P. Cohen 1982, 32–34). Despite some of the great advantages of Arabic numbers, this system, like the alphabetic documents, did not find easy acceptance. Indeed, in 1299 the Italian city of Florence passed a law against the use of Arabic numerals because the citizens of Florence thought Arabic numbers were more easily falsified than Roman ones (P. Cohen 1982, 19). Florentine legislators argued that an Arabic zero could be easily mistaken for other numbers and that the addition of extra digits to the end of the Arabic number made falsification simply a matter of moving a dot, changing a 1.0 to a 10., for instance. The lawmakers of Florence felt that Roman numerals expressed numbers with unmistakable finality. A "XX" could not be taken for anything else except twenty. As a result, twelfth- and thirteenth-century Italian city-states conducted all of their trade, banking, and credit in Roman numerals, subtraction and division were carried out with an abacus or a counting board with lines representing an abacus, and coins or small stones were used as counting tokens (P. Cohen 1982, 18–19). Although Arabic numerals filtered into Europe in the tenth century through North Africa and Spain, they were hardly used throughout Europe before the

3 Signature and Recording Literacy: 1776–1864

By coding every sighting of any land in longitude and latitude ... and by sending this code back, the shape of the sighted lands may be redrawn by those who have not sighted them.... Instead of the mind of the scientists revolving around things, Kant explains, the things are made to revolve around the mind.... [M]any inventions have to be made to enhance mobility, stability and combinability of collected items. (Latour 1987, 224–25)

In the last chapter, we found that the development of the alphabet was not a fast, dramatic shift from oral language to pictures to alphabetic literacy, but rather a slow process based primarily on, among other things, the everyday functional need to save time and money in getting messages from one place to another (portability); in recording information so that it would be visible and not decay (stability); and in storing and producing information efficiently (storability) (Purves 1990). Syllable systems, for example, reduced the number of characters needed to write something in logographic systems, and alphabetic systems reduced the number of characters even more. For example, the Egyptians invented a logographic system with 2,500 characters; the Cherokee Indian leader, Sequoya, invented a Cherokee syllable system of 85 signs; and a long, historical process involving many countries produced the English alphabet of 26 characters (Coe 1992, 43).

The shift from oracy to print literacy was always a process of gains and losses. In these shifts from face-to-face literacy to print, some of the semantic and phonetic content is lost, and, as a result, literate readers and writers must re-create contexts of use, construct more and more inferences, and engage in acts of translation in which some meaning is always lost and some is always added. There are, as Ortega y Gasset has said, silences and exuberances in these translations. For one thing, different writing systems require learners to focus on different parts of language. Some stress syllables, others letters, others sound. "Syllable based systems such as Japanese," says Barton, "demand less detailed analysis of the spoken language" and "at the very beginning stages of learning to read, alphabetic systems such as English are overly complex"

(Barton 1994, 100). The point, once again, is that every language is a trade-off between silences and exuberances.

In our classrooms, students learn to translate from face-to-face literacy to drawing and then to the written alphabet, as shown in the seven instances of literacy development in Figure 3. These students, too, are contending with problems of lost context. In Figure 3, a child attempts to make a grocery list (A-1) which is *portable* and *visible* but is not *storable* because no one knows what it means after a few days. A-2 attempts to use some letter conventions, increasing the *storability* of the information. In B and C, the alphabetic efforts of the children merge with drawing and visual images. In B, the student writes her signature letter and then "reads" the letter as a picture, generating an accompanying oral drama of Flopsy, the talking rabbit. At the same time, the student attempts, as Ferrerio has noted in another case, "to find the frontier that differentiates drawing from writing" (Ferrerio 1984, 155). In C, we find the child inventing spelling to make visible and portable "mi bedroom," and in D we see a student experimenting with a visualization of the self in one's signature.[1]

Each of the events in Figure 3, which occur at school sites all the time, reflects in important ways various parts of the history of early signature literacy—from pictures to marks, from marks to the alphabet, from counting to art, and so forth. B, for example, reminds us of periods of signature literacy in which the alphabet itself was a branch of calligraphy or visual art, in addition to being a medium of alphabetic information (Tambiah 1968, 93–94). In fact, throughout the early days of signature literacy in England and the U.S., the alphabet did not have the same personal significance or moral force as a "picture" or other visual mark, and, as a result, many people placed the cross upon legal documents to invoke religious authority (Campbell and Quinn 1966, 752–53; Cressy 1980, 57). Still others used very personal marks to invoke ownership or family tradition (see Figure 4). These practices continue in classrooms today. Some teachers add smiles ☺ and exclamations (!) to their notes, and students practice over and over again the "art" of their own signature (as in Figure 3, item D). Many elementary students mix together pictures and the alphabet (as in Figure 3, item C), and still others draw pictures to tell stories (as in Figure 3, item B).

Robin Lakoff suggests that the use of some of these conventions could be viewed as efforts to sustain in print some of the conventions of oral language. She finds these practices in the differences between the comic strips that emphasize print conventions, like *Doonesbury*, and the older strips that approximate "a blend of oral and literate culture." She says that these older comic strips were among "the earliest

A-1   B-1   C-1

A-2   B-2   C-2

D

Fig. 3. Literacy development of children. (Sources: For A-1, A-2, C-1, and C-2: Harste, Burke, and Woodward 1984, 83–84. Reprinted by permission of Jerome Harste. For B-1 and B-2: Figures 11.2 and 11.3 from *Art, Mind, and Brain: A Cognitive Approach to Creativity* by Howard Gardner. Copyright © 1983 by Howard Gardner. Reprinted by permission of BasicBooks, a division of HarperCollins Publishers, Inc.)

forms of post-modern communication to attempt to convey essentially oral concepts in print" (R. Lakoff 1982, 252). In these older strips, sentences never ended with a period but with question marks or exclamation marks and attempted to reproduce nonstandard dialects and colloquialisms like "yuh," "Omigosh," "whuh," "wuz,"

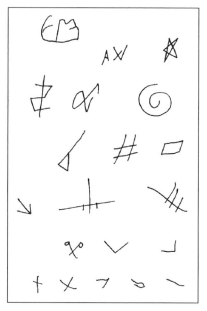

Fig. 4. Personal marks made on depositions in the diocese of Norwich 1580–1620. (Source: Cressy 1980, 60. Copyright © 1980 by Cambridge University Press. Reprinted with permission of Cambridge University Press.)

"ta," and "gotcha," always dropping the "g" in "ing" endings ("speakin'") (R. Lakoff 1982, 252). In the visual art of these strips, words were capitalized and darkened for emphasis (**WOW!**), repeated in different sizes for changing emphasis ("ssssssh"), written in invented spelling, and written at odd angles on the page to suggest action.

Of course, many of these conventions appear in the drawings and social notes of children where they interact with oral language, songs, actions, and gestures. Dyson's description of Jameel's singing fish (see Figure 5) illustrates how alphabetic print, letter sounds, physical gestures, acting out, and oral performance combine in one literacy event:

> Jameel, a first grader, combined his fledgling writing skills with his drawing and singing know-how to produce a text rich in the resources of popular culture, including pop songs, cartoons, and comics. He drew a singing fish, with "tunes" encased in air bubbles. . . . Moreover, he wrote that song to perform for his peers, to impress them and make them laugh....(Dyson 1993, 5)

Changes from art and gesture to writing, like other changes in literacy, always serve social needs. Signature and recording literacy became

Fig. 5. Jameel's singing fish. (Source: Dyson 1993, 4. Copyright © 1993 Teachers College, Columbia University. Reprinted by permission of Teachers College Press.)

necessary in the United States when more and more people moved and when they then needed new ways of making information portable, visible, and storable. During oral face-to-face literacy in the U.S., one lived and traded with people one knew in small, stable, familiar villages. But by the late 1700s, more and more people were moving as the Louisiana Purchase opened up the southern-central part of the country in 1803, the Erie Canal opened up upper New York in 1825, the Baltimore and Ohio railroad opened up the Midwest in 1830, and their railroad systems opened up the rest. In fact, U.S. railroad tracks increased from 23 total miles before 1830 to 52,922 miles by 1870 (Tyack 1974, 31).

As social and trade relations with strangers rapidly undermined the face-to-face relations of oral literacy (Braverman 1974, 53), people began to depend on written marks—a system of signature literacy—in order to carry out, to remember, and to record legally their economic and social dealings. In this new society of strangers and signature and recording literacy, the ability to record simple information and to sign one's name enabled one to borrow money, to post news for distant neighbors, to claim and settle land, to record an inventory of moving property, to file one's taxes, to record addresses, to certify marriages, wills, births, and deaths, to register to vote, to write messages to loved ones who had moved, and to sign petitions—to name only a few essential social functions of recording, remembering, certifying, and informing. The fundamental point is that the history of literacy is *not* an epiphenomenon of the history of the marketplace or the classroom (Laqueur 1976). Signature literacy, like other forms of literacy, grew out of many variables and helped shape those variables, creating the possibilities for trade with strangers as much as it resulted from that trade.

Changes in a form of literacy always have an impact on the way a culture defines contracts. The contract of face-to-face literacy "limited and sometimes denied contractual obligations by reference to the fairness of the underlying exchange" (Horowitz 1976, 923). Notice that this kind of agreement is based on a clear sense of community identity and values to dictate the meaning of "fairness" to all individuals. This assumption of a recognized group solidarity is typical of face-to-face literacy and its oral cultures. The modern conception of contracts, however, which emerged in the nineteenth century from signature literacy and from the social need to do business with strangers, says that "the extent of contract obligation depends upon the convergence of individual desires" (Horowitz 1976, 925). This "modern" notion of contract acknowledges that strangers are involved, that their sense of "fairness" cannot always be predicted, and that "fairness" is anchored in the convergence of individual desires, not in a local community's judgments about standards of "fairness."

In signature and recording literacy, as in other forms of literacy, practitioners of this literacy were divided into different levels of signature and recording performance. The lowest level of signature practice was represented by those who could not use pencils and pens to produce any kind of signature, and the middle was represented by those who could make a mark, possibly an X (Cressy 1980, 73). All of these and other marks (Figure 4) were considered a form of writing. There were many people who could only make an X, could not sign their names, and could not read at all or could read very little, but these people were still within the range of adequate literate behavior for everyday purposes: "He who is unable to write his name and make his mark is, not withstanding, a competent and legal witness to the execution of a will" (E. Stevens 1983, 63). In fact, Pennsylvania, which had a law in 1833 requiring signatures on wills, had to add a law in 1848 allowing marks like an X (Soltow and Stevens 1981, 225 [*n*1]).

At the highest level of signature and recording literacy were those who could sign their names and who could both read and write, at least a little:

> This is all we go to school for: to read common prayers at church and set down prices at markets; write a letter and make a bond; set down the day of our births; our marriage day, and make our wills when we are sick for the disposing of our goods when we are dead: These are the chief matters that we meddle with, and we find enough to trouble our heads withal. (Breton 1618; rpt. in Dunham and Pargellis 1938, 468)

Knowing how to sign one's name and knowing how to read generally went together, as Furet and Ozouf found in three sets of data—first, in an 1866 French census; second, in a reading test given to French military recruits; and third, in signatures by brides and grooms at French marriages (Furet and Ozouf 1982, 9–18). There were, of course, those like Richard Matthew of Kent, aged 38, who could sign his name in great Roman letters but could not read. At the other extreme were the few college-educated persons. The range of texts for most people was usually so limited that reading ability was often defined by the text that was read. And at one time, the levels of reading were suggested by the text, knowing one's letters being basic reading during signature literacy and reading the primer, the horn book, the "Testament," and the Bible being "higher" levels of reading (see Table 1).

In the middle range were those who could write using invented spelling. The following is a handbill showing this range of signature and recording literacy:

> This is to give Notis to badgers and fore Stallers of grain that there as Been sum in perticular a wocheing your Motions and ther whill Be in a wicks time some men Com ought of the Colepits by Nigt to Meak fire brans of all the abitations of the forestallers of grain. . . . (Thompson 1975, 279–80)[2]

During signature and recording literacy, central bulletin boards became the locations for posting handbills, like the one above, as well as posters, warnings, letters, and announcements—all of which often used invented spelling. The handbill above, in other words, is a conventionalized, written form which was "well understood by both parties in the market conflict, as one element within a regular and ritualized code of behavior" (Thompson 1975, 280). In these handbills

Table 1. Literacy rates. ("Literacy of boys entering Great Yarmouth Children's Hospital, 1698–1715.") (Source: Cressy 1980, 32. Copyright © 1980 by Cambridge University Press. Reprinted with the permission of the Cambridge University Press.)

Age	'knows not his letters'	'cannot read'	'in his horn book'	'in the primer'	'reads Testament'	'reads Bible'	Unknown	Total
6		3			2		1	6
7	2	10	2		5	1	1	21
8	1	10	4	6	2	1		24
9	2	6		6	2	1		17
10	4	13			9	5	2	33
11		5		1	1	1	1	9
12		3	1	2	2	4		12
13		3		2				5
14		1						1
Unknown	3	1						4
	12	55	7	17	23	13	5	132

and announcements, invented spelling was a way to preserve local dialects and, thus, some of the local character and group solidarity of local communities. The essential point here is that invented spelling was not just a stage of print acquisition. It was also a social practice which preserved some oral practices and which gave local authority to these handbills and announcements.

Reading in signature literacy usually meant intensive reading, which meant concentrated attention on small pieces of text, often involving the copying of pieces several times: "savoring the divine wisdom…taste the goodness of your redeemer…chew the honeycomb of his words…suck their flavor…" (Clanchy 1988, 147). In the typical form of intensive reading in colleges and universities, a book's singular meaning was derived by the careful analysis of "pronunciation, etymology, moods and tenses, and points of classical philology" (qtd. in G. Graff 1987, 29).

For the few college elite, English, which only slowly replaced Latin and Greek as the primary language studied in college, meant the recitation of a limited set of assigned lectures and books (Halloran 1990, 155–56). Debate, recitations, oral catechisms, orations—all of these were common in the "oratorical culture" of the colleges and universities of signature literacy (G. Graff 1987, 45), but the core, authoratative texts were limited. Thus, the text of signature literacy was an authoritative text which was always a delivered, fixed, sacrosanct object, not a variable text to be interpreted (Tambiah 1968, 94). In this view of reading, an "authentic" reading was the "original" reading or "an affinity with what came first," not a new or innovative reading (R. Williams 1976; Tuman 1987).

In colleges, intensive reading was said to have "a spiritual value" because concentration on such matters as tense and pronunciation was thought to focus the students on fixed human values; thus, the reading of selections from the Greek fused into the student's nature, according to Charles Frances Adams, "the imperceptible spirit of Greek literature, which will appear in the results of his [the student's] subsequent work, just as manure, spread upon a field, appears in the crop which that field bears" (G. Graff 1987, 30). At various times, intensive reading of a few books had to be defended. A Yale University report of 1828 argued that the intensive reading of a single textbook provided clarity and a common social life and that the extensive reading of a half dozen different books created "confusion in the student's mind" (G. Graff 1987, 27).

Throughout signature and recording literacy, weekly newspapers spread rapidly "in small towns and cities throughout the eastern states," and by 1828 more than five newspapers were produced each year for every person in the country (women and people of color were not necessarily counted) (Soltow and Stevens 1981, 76). These local papers were a source of primarily local information—obituaries, upcoming events, market prices—and secondarily a summary of local and national events.

Most people did not have books at home, but when books were present they were likely to be the Bible and an almanac—the latter, according to Benjamin Franklin, being "a proper vehicle for conveying information among the common people, who bought scarcely any other books." During signature and recording literacy, most people distributed information through lists, almanacs, newspaper announcements, ads, local bulletin boards, inventory systems, and, eventually, telegrams. A few people depended upon books and magazines. The telegram probably captures as well as anything the everyday practices of interstate reading and writing for everyman during signature and recording literacy. By the middle of the 1800s, the telegraph lines running alongside the national railroad system had become an essential part of a national system for recording, informing, remembering, and certifying among strangers.

For local communication, the pencil was the essential technology. In fact, signature literacy would not have worked very well if, in the U.S., it had depended entirely upon the technology of quill pens, ink, parchment, wax-covered tablets, and marking instruments like the stylus. But in 1847, a source of high-quality graphite was found at the top of Mount Batongal, and, within a few years, high-quality pencils with Chinese graphite became available throughout the U.S. (Petroski 1990, 56). In a very real sense, the cheap graphite pencil helped produce the practices of signature literacy. In fact, I would argue that the graphite pencil has been a critical influence on our postmodern conceptions of writing fluency. In other words, our notions of writing fluency are not just matters of cognition; they depend quite deeply on who gets the appropriate tools to engage in the practice. Quill pens are a lot of trouble for the average person who moves around. In fact, I want to suggest that the practice of "expressive writing" seems to depend upon the ease and comfort of postmodern tools like the pencil.

One of the important differences between "oral literacy" and signature literacy was the creation of schools to teach children signature literacy. In 1838, almost fifty years after Jefferson's initial proposal, Horace Mann became the secretary of the Massachusetts Board of Education and issued the first of his twelve annual reports describing the organization of and necessity for a common school curriculum. His reports, which were distributed across the country, became the nation's first national standards movement in curriculum content. He argued that the shift of economic activity out of the home and into a village market required the invention of a public school system to guarantee economic access for all citizens, to reduce crime, and to preserve our democratic society (Cremin 1961, 8–14). Mann won his arguments for public schools partly because the 1820s and 1830s were also a time when people were generally organizing children and youth into numerous institutions—"infant schools, Sunday and common schools, a special juvenile literature, and pediatrics as a medical specialty" (P. Cohen 1982, 137; Bremner 1970).[3]

Mann's notion of curriculum was a joining together of literacy drills and character development, suggesting that politeness was always inseparable from handwriting and spelling and that learning to write one's name was inseparable from morality and spiritual salvation. In Horace Mann's schools, one could teach someone to spell in the same way that one could teach someone to resist evil ways or to sit up straight at the dinner table: tell them and punish them. Signature literacy's mind-as-a-muscle or original-sin model of mind assumed that the "pain" and dreariness of drills exercised the muscle of the mind and soul and could lead both to morality—a cleansing of the spirit—and some facility with print. Of course, if facility with print did not develop, then there must have been a failure of character, which could only be corrected by more silent drill.

The primary texts of signature literacy in elementary schools were copying books with blank pages and widely spaced lines, which generally took "up a great part of your day" and generally ignored matters like meaning[4] (Robinson et al. 1990, 18) (see Figure 6). In the Oregon course of study in the 1800s, students copied their script from the bottom of the page up "in order to see the copy at the top of the page." The meaning was the same, no matter what direction one copied, it was said. The purpose of schools was to teach students to sign their names, to make lists, to record information, to copy word lists, to read a few essential words, to read a few things aloud from memory, to have some awareness of how devotional books were organized, to know some religious passages "by heart," to know how to write a few numbers, to be able to arrange numbers in inventory columns, and, possibly, to be able to do a few, simple arithmetic calculations.

Pedagogy, such as it was in the U.S., consisted of teachers reading aloud to their students and using various handwriting systems. One of the original U.S. "inventors" of a handwriting and copying system was John Jenkins, who, finding schoolmastering difficult because he had poor handwriting, decided to write *The Art of Writing* in the early

Fig. 6. Copying book, James French, 1840–1842. (Source: Nash 1969, 222.)

1800s, the "earliest native treatise on the subject" (Nash 1969, 4). This book "demonstrated that by the dissection of the round-hand letters and analysis of their interchangeable parts, practically the entire alphabet can be made up of a dozen principal strokes" (Nash 1969, 4). Jenkins, insisting that drill on these strokes could teach anyone to write in a neat and legible hand, organized handwriting into a subject to be studied, objectified, and taught through silent copying drills. Later, handwriting, as an objectified subject, became a folk indicator of intelligence and an expression of character and personality.

Jenkins's ideas were heretical to Boston writing masters who, following the British tradition, believed that students needed an elaborate apprenticeship with a master in penmanship. In his books, Spencer, for one, returned the teaching of handwriting to professionals in the "science" of handwriting by arguing that handwriting exercises were more complicated than Jenkins had suggested (see Figure 7). Throughout the early 1800s in the U.S., these handwriting "scientists" debated in numerous publications and programs whether handwriting should be taught as a product (an analysis of letters) or as a process (a series of hand and arm movements).

Typically, teachers taught students using both product and process, forming "letters in due proportion, of joining them aptly together; by practice of drawing the pen upon the figures of shadowed letters, then writing without shadowed letters, imitating copy, lastly of writing without a copy" (Kempe 1588; qtd. in Cressy 1980, 20). This alphabetic or spelling method, which "had already been in use in England for several centuries" (Robinson et al. 1990, 17), often had the following sequence of instruction:

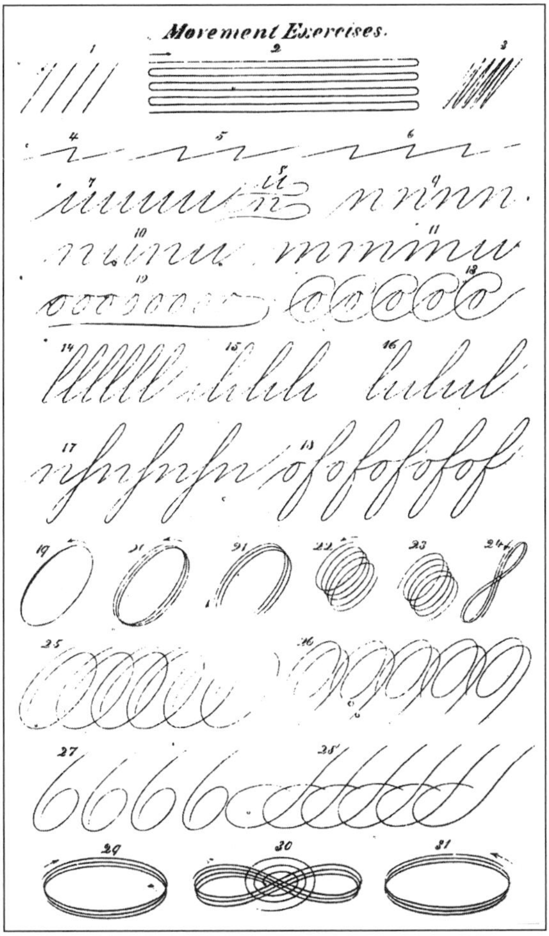

Fig. 7. Movement exercises. Platt Rogers Spencer: *Spencerian Key to Practical Penmanship*, 1866. (Source: Whalley 1980, 327.)

1. Learn the alphabet by rote, forward and backward [this could be a process or product approach].

2. Point out the individual letters . . . as they appear in words. (There appears to have been some use of squares of wood or ivory with pictures and letters on them.)

3. After mastering all the letters, proceed to the syllaborium (organized groups of consonant-vowel clusters) and learn them by rote: *ba, be, bi, bo, bu,* and so on.

4. Then, using the ability to name the letters, spell out lists of short words. . . . (Robinson 1977, 46)

In addition to the blank copying books, the most popular school texts of the period organized spelling and some reading around secular catechisms, often modeled after the world's first mass primer, Luther's *Little Catechism* (D. Resnick 1991b). Noah Webster's *Blue-Backed Speller,* which used a catechism focused primarily on words and parts of words, was first published in 1783, was reissued in 1787 as the *American Spelling Book,* and eventually sold approximately *three million* copies between 1787 and 1810 (Hodges 1977, 3). In this book, no sentence problems appeared until page 101. One of the primary purposes of these spellers, according to Webster, was to eliminate invented spelling and local dialects. Said Webster, "Small causes such as a nickname ... have actually created a dissocial spirit between the inhabitants of the different states.... Our political harmony is therefore concerned in a uniformity of language" (N. Webster [1789] 1967; Jacoby 1994, 61). One wonders whether Webster would feel that U.S. culture today had succeeded in becoming too homogenized.

The New England Primer, the first mention of which was in 1690 (Carpenter 1963, 24), also used the question-answer format with a set of 100 questions and answers. Cobb's *Spelling Book* (1844), featuring a twelve-page, ninety-item, question-answer format about the "Rudiments of the English Language," did the same. Cobb's book included the following exchange:

> *Q:* What are letters?
>
> *A:* Letters are marks of sounds, and the rudiments of written language which are presented to the eye. (Cobb 1844; qtd. in Robinson et al. 1990, 16)

Often, the question-answer format focused on general information and one's moral and ethical obligations.

In summary, then, in the signature classrooms of secular catechism, teachers asked students to memorize the alphabet, to answer short-answer questions aloud, to copy answers silently, and to spell words aloud. This was sometimes called the "spelling method" of teaching reading (Robinson 1977, 46). Teaching was ungraded, took place in a one-room schoolhouse or great hall, required the teachers or masters to walk up and down the aisles and to read aloud to students, and required the students to sit in a ranked position, to do silent drills, to speak when spoken to, to look at the various charts and wall bands of letters, to listen to the reading of questions, and sometimes to look at questions on a chalkboard.[5] In general, the copying of the alphabet and the spelling method of instruction, using oral, secular catechisms as the basic text, had remarkable success teaching students how to write their names and how to read a little. This mixture of reading aloud, dictation, and alphabetic copying apparently enabled so-called "illiterates" to participate in signature and recording literacy events (Clanchy 1988, 149), an accomplishment which some observers had considered impossible.

To measure attainment of signature literacy, literacy data was collected in both England and the United States. In the late 1600s, some local agencies in the U.S. began measuring the attainment of signature literacy by counting the signatures and marks appearing in wills, inventories, marriage oaths, and catechetical records (H. Graff 1987, 6–7). Of course, some parts of the country recorded higher levels of signature literacy than others. Of those making wills in 1660 in New England, 61 percent of the men and 31 percent of the women could write their names, and others made a mark (an X or some other mark) (Lockridge 1974, 38). By 1710, 69 percent of the men and 41 percent of the women could write their names on wills, and by 1760 these figures had increased to 84 percent of the men and 46 percent of the women (Cressy 1980, 183). These figures reflect the achievement only of those willing "to sign" wills and only of the population of New England, which was more highly educated than the population of the rest of the country.

Signature data from around the country began to be collected with a question in the U.S. census asking citizens whether they were literate. An illiterate, according to the 1870 census, was one who reported to the census taker that he or she was "not able both to read and to write a simple message either in English or any other language" (U.S. Bureau of the Census 1971, 5). These self-reports from the U.S. census suggest an increase in something approximating signature literacy—from 89.3 percent in 1850 to 93.8 percent in 1900 (Kaestle et al. 1991, 257; Folger and Nam 1967, 113–14).

These self-reports showing higher levels of signature literacy in the U.S. are confirmed by trends in the actual signatures recorded by the U.S. Army, starting in 1800, and recorded by the U.S. Merchant Marine, starting in 1798. Army enrollment records show a dramatic increase in signature literacy—from 58 percent of U.S. Army enlistees being able to sign their names in 1800, to 65 percent in the 1840s, to 75 percent in the 1850s, to 83 percent in the 1870s, and to 93 percent in the 1880s (Soltow and Stevens 1981, 52). The U.S. Merchant Marine data, which resulted from a 1798 federal law requiring American seamen to register by signing their names, shows that 58 percent of the seamen attained signature literacy by 1840 (Soltow and Stevens 1981, 50).[6]

Several states also mandated measurements of signature literacy by requiring reports on how many students could spell or write the alphabet. The 1847 legislature of New York State amended the "Statutes of the State of New York Relating to the Common Schools" to require school superintendents to file a comprehensive report with the county clerk showing "Number of pupils learning the alphabet, Number of pupils learning to spell without being able to read, Number of pupils learning to read, [Number of pupils learning] to define words." (Robinson et al. 1990, 18). Notice that this comprehensive report puts the basic emphasis on knowing the alphabet and spelling and puts a secondary emphasis on "learning to read," which often meant that someone had memorized some written material. It is interesting to note, I think, that states today do not ask for information on how many students know the alphabet. That part of literacy no longer has special importance.

Although the U.S. concept of signature literacy was borrowed directly from Europe, only a minority of the European population attained signature literacy by 1850, even in the most developed European nations (Schofield 1968). For example, in 1850, Europe showed a literacy rate of 50 percent, 40 percent if Russia is included (Cipolla 1980, 7). This is far below the 75 percent literacy rate of enlistees in the U.S. Army in the 1850s. In England, despite the push for signature literacy in the sixteenth and seventeenth centuries, signature literacy was not achieved by most English persons until the end of the nineteenth century, about the same time that this standard was achieved in the United States. In England of the 1600s, about 25–30 percent of the males could sign their names, and by the 1750s this figure had increased to 50–60 percent (L. Stone 1969, 119–32).

England's early start in literacy did not push that country ahead of the U.S. in universal signature literacy because, it appears, this goal did not have the backing of many influential leaders in England (Spedding 1868, 252–53; Cressy 1980, 187). Francis Bacon, for example, felt that to avoid disturbances of the social order, the government should restrict print literacy to a few people. Similar attitudes existed among some people in the United States. Soame Jenyns opposed print literacy for the mass population because he believed ignorance was "the only opiate capable" of making the poor accept the "miseries" and "drudgeries" of their lives (W. Joyce et al. 1983, 304; qtd. in Altick 1983, 31–32). But U.S. leaders largely favored some kind of minimal literacy for the masses, although U.S. educators, by and large, had few printed materials available, beyond the Bible, and continued to believe in the authoritative text with a singular meaning.

Some of the initial proposals for public education in the U.S. seemed to aim for something beyond signing one's name and copying texts. Thomas Jefferson, who initiated the first major educational reform debate in the United States in the 1780s, suggested that because democracy could not survive without education, the nation should establish public schools to teach every person to read the newspapers. But Jefferson intended that a republican gentry would deliver meaning to the masses, and by 1825, when a few people were beginning to claim some of their own authority as interpreters of meaning, Jefferson lamented the change (Wood 1992, 367–68).

Despite gains in signature literacy in the U.S., particular groups did not achieve levels of literacy equal to or similar to that of the general population. For example, in the 1900 census, only 55.5 percent of non-whites said they were literate, compared with the 93.8 percent making such a claim in the white population (Kaestle 1985, 31–32). In addition, women lagged behind men in all measures of signature literacy, although in New England about one-third of the women who died prior to 1670 had left wills with their signatures (H. Graff 1987, 164). The fact that these women could sign their names did not assure them of higher paying jobs or social class status (see H. Graff 1979). Most of the problems of equity in literacy policies remained generally unaddressed in the U.S. until the 1960s.

In summary, signature literacy had a national measure (the army and merchant marine requirements and later a U.S. census question); a technology (pencils, printing presses, and cursive writing procedures); ranges of achievement (from marks to signatures); a national reform report (Horace Mann's annual reports); a model of learning (mind-as-muscle); a set of texts (copying books, *American Spelling Book*); and a model of schooling (one-room schoolhouse, the Palmer method). Four sources of evidence—public records, U.S. census information, registrations of merchant seamen, and army enrollment lists—all suggest a dramatic increase from 1776 to 1864 in the number of people who could sign their names, possibly reaching nearly 80 percent by the 1870s in the adult male population of the U.S. By that time, the nation was in the middle of a debate about whether to change the national standard of literacy (see Table 2).

What does this history tell us about English teaching? The history of signature and recording literacy teaches us again that skill and intelligence are embedded in a culture, are not autonomous mental constructions, and can be developed by many people when cultural incentives are provided. Print literacy grew during signature literacy because people needed to record, remember, certify, and convey information in a world of strangers and in a nation communicating with telegrams and a struggling postal system. As noted earlier, many educated people during the signature literacy period doubted that the masses could learn to sign their names or to read a little, an

Table 2. Literacy periods.

Literacy for Masses	Education: religious Knowledge: transparent Consciousness of Literacy: inactive		Education: secular Knowledge: objectified Consciousness of Literacy: symbolic and textual		Education: diverse Knowledge: interactive Consciousness of Literacy: conceptual
Cultural Variables	1600 Oracy	1776 Signature	1864 Recitation	1916 Decoding	1983 Translation
Population	Local networks bonded people who knew each other and who generally did not move	Westward movement, increased mobility, regional networks of trains, canals, and roads, population became strangers	Male migration to factories, large immigration into country of diverse ethnic groups, people of color	National network of highways, trains and air travel, nationalization of government, centralization of institutions	Decentralization in government and private companies, international travel, diversity
Occupation	Family agriculture	Regional agricultural economy, tenant farmers	Declining family agriculture, growing industrialization, early fragmented urbanization, oratory for social memory, copying for memory	Government centralization, information storage/combinations, centralized newspapers, cities, mass production in large industrial complexes, publications, computers	Growth in technological services and information industries, translation of information becomes priority
Markets, travel, and work relationships	Stable, face-to-face, little travel, family to family	Stranger-to-stranger, village markets, some written relationships, a more mobile population, need for mobile records	Urbanized markets among fragmented population, new mobility, factories, written agreements. Need for stable records, categories	Increased automobile mobility, centralized corporations and markets, written contracts, corporate law. Need for combinable information centralized	Increased air travel, decentralization of institutions, new diversity of population, new diversity in world recognized

	At home: literacy as memory storage of stories, people and transactions	In halls: literacy as hand/eye coordination, print as art, memorization through copying	In classrooms: literacy as touchstones, as recitations of tradition, as memory of information, as copying texts	In school systems: literacy as decoding, extracting knowledge from unfamiliar works, analyzing parts.	Literacy as construction and reconstruction and translation of past and present
Literacy Education					
Purpose of Reading	Listening to oral exchanges, memorizing the Bible, understanding gestures, body knowledge	Intensive copying of a few texts, intensive hearing and reading of Biblical works.	Extensive copying, oral (rhetorical) learning, memory of many works, extensive "reading" of secular works, learn to copy	Silent analyzing, decoding of unfamiliar texts, efficient communication to others, learning to objectify texts, combining information	Interpretation of many texts, producing multiple translations of many different kinds of texts in many sign systems
Purpose of Literacy	Maintain oral traditions. Maintain oral records of social compact, develop conversational skills	Begin written records/contracts-inventories. Records were lists and visual designs. Handwriting was a visual art	Establish national cohesion among immigrants, new urban populations after Civil War, develop presentational skills, copying skills	Decode/analyze/produce new knowledge in scientific records, establish records through writing, process information for storage, academic skills	Develop multiple perspectives, translations of culture, negotiation of differences, flexibility among speech agents
Types of Student	Listener/Reactor face-to-face	Copier, listener	Reactor, copier, impression reader	Analyzer, decoder, analytic reader	Translator, interpreter
Mind	Mind as memory container	Mind as muscle	Mind as wax tablet	Mind-as-conditioned behavior	Mind as multiple frames of intelligence

assumption proven wrong by the literacy data of the 1890s. "They cannot do it" has up to now been proven false when the standard of literacy proposed has some evident value in the culture and some support in the nation's organization of schooling and teaching. Employment and jobs, for example, have a major impact on a nation's form of literacy (see Figure 8).

Teachers should remember that students bring to the classroom a collection of beliefs about literacy accumulated from literacy's history. One of the most "injurious consequence[s] of medieval literacy" was the "notion that literacy is identical with rationality," according to Stock (1983, 31). The folklore of print literacy as exclusively rational still prevails, denying the functions and values of oral narratives, the value of pictures and paintings as communicative arts. It should be obvious from the brief history in the last two chapters that rationality was not absent from oral cultures and, furthermore, was not the driving force behind the development of signature literacy. Signatures became necessary because people moved quite often and needed portable, visible, and storable forms of information and because the increased use of telegrams, quill pens, and primitive pencils made signature records possible.

In time, travel and many other cultural variables of signature literacy began to centralize information and to diminish the economic importance of face-to-face relations. Signature literacy, while undermining face-to-face relations, afforded increased status to a new way of putting one's personal stamp on the world. One's signature and handwriting became a visual representation of one's personality. Although signature literacy is no longer the nation's standard, the nation's folklore still celebrates the elegance of one's handwriting as an indicator of one's level of literacy—in fact, even as an indicator of one's intelligence. In the early days of the Bay Area Writing Project, I had dozens of language arts coordinators tell me their district was teaching writing in the elementary schools and then hand me a handwriting book to prove it. One of the most dramatic incidents occurred in the early 1980s, when almost a dozen people, after having flown halfway across the country, arrived at the offices of the Bay Area Writing Project (University of California–Berkeley) to learn "how the Bay Area Writing Project taught writing." Keith Caldwell stuck his head into my office and asked, "Do you know anything about the Palmer method? That's what they want." For them, writing meant handwriting and little else. The notion that writing in schools could be more than copying and refining one's handwriting is still a rather radical idea in some elementary schools, even in the 1990s.

Teachers need to remember that the literacy lessons of schools are simply various forms of social relations, economics, self-definition,

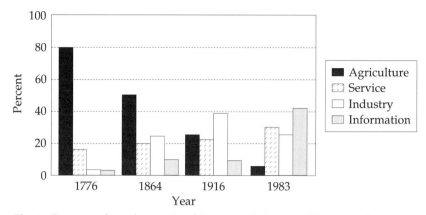

Fig. 8. Patterns of employment in literacy periods. Note: Because of inconsistencies in the data, these trends must be regarded as "gross" estimates. (Sources: Braverman 1974, 238–70; U.S. Bureau of the Census 1976, 167–81; and Straussman 1983, 115–21.)

labor issues, and politics of the contemporary world. For example, the shift from hand printing to cursive, which reduced labor costs in message production, has become for us today a third-grade event packaged as an intellectual shift of great social significance. We should recognize that third-grade cursive is a socially constructed value, not an intellectual absolute. The same can be said for the distinction between drawing and alphabet writing.

In our schools, efforts like those in C of Figure 3 are generally devalued. Nevertheless, art is still a way for many students to find their way into print because handwriting or one's "drawn" letters are still privileged as art among those students who carry the past of signature literacy into the classroom. A nation's definition of literacy must not blind a nation's teachers to the range of literacies in the classroom, even those literacies long since abandoned and devalued by culture. Notice that I use the word "literacies" here, not abilities, the usual word in schools. I am suggesting that one thing we often mean by "abilities" or "range of abilities" is literacies, the persistent histories of our past literacy practices.

The essential point is this: Most children older than three years can identify the McDonald's sign, according to Frank Smith, and it is not likely that this widespread ability is unrelated to hamburgers and French fries. I would add that knowing a sign is related to both getting hamburgers and knowing a particular set of literacy practices. By three years of age, many children have learned that print can be used to certify the contents of packages, that writing can be used for remembering and recording, and that reading can be used to enjoy stories and to tell others information aloud. On the other hand, many other children have also learned that print is an intrusion into one's local customs.

Every teacher who faces a classroom is facing many layers of historical assumptions about how literacy should be defined. Part of the art and science of teaching is learning how to help students get "through" these layers of folklore and history to an understanding of contemporary conceptions of literacy. A teacher, then, is not just teaching reading or writing—some absolute mental activity which everyone accepts as the goal of schools. Teachers are teaching contingent definitions and constructions of reading and writing. Invented spelling, for example, is not just a teaching device. Invented spelling was at one time a recognized, conventionalized form of writing, and as a part of public discourse, it had a respectable, functional role in society. For one thing, it preserved in print the sound of local oral dialects.

But invented spelling was defeated by the project of Webster and others to standardize in print the language of what was formerly an oral culture. This standardization obviously had some beneficial results for the country in the attempt to communicate from the East to the West. The printed standard became like etiquette and good manners in public, and it also helped make communication more efficient. But some things were lost—for instance, the sound of the local dialect. This mixture of "literacy" with etiquette is a "gain" or addition which has not disappeared. In *Eating on the Street*, David Schaafsma (1993) describes how some of these mixtures of etiquette and literacies persist in the arguments among teachers in the Dewey Center Community Writing Project in Detroit's inner city. These arguments, ranging from whether to allow the students to use Black English in class or to eat on the streets while on field trips, show how the tensions over definitions of literacy persist among teachers themselves.

Teachers and students bring with them different histories and different definitions of what it means to be literate—reading is copying, for instance, and writing is handwriting style, another instance. Teachers, it seems to me, need to inform students and each other about some of the history of literacy in the U.S.—not only to help students but also to help other teachers make the necessary translations across the gap or barrier between their historical assumptions and their students' contemporary needs. For example, many students go through a period when they practice writing their names in many different styles as part of what children and adolescents do to define their public face and to discover the power of language. They use signatures to draw a "picture" of themselves (see D in Figure 3 for one example).

Using this student inclination, many teachers have asked students to pick a pen name and a signature style as their public writing name for class assignments. One teacher whom I know brings to class examples of the signatures of famous people. George Plimpton (1990) has suggested that his career as a writer may have started when he spent much of his time in seventh grade writing his name over and over again in order to find the right signature and pen name for his career as a writer; his signature became for him an image, a kind of portrait of his future self as a writer. We must begin, then, to acknowledge the importance of signature to the young who are seeking their identity through the kinship of art and writing, and we need the help of scholars to understand this neglected practice. Yetta Goodman told me she was beginning a study of how children experiment with signatures as a way into writing and into self-definition.

And, finally, we need to remind ourselves that the histories of other literacies still persist in our classrooms. Signature literacy still lives. I will not soon forget the look on the face of one of my students at Oakland High in Oakland, California, who, after watching me write on the blackboard for a few minutes, commented, "Mr. Myers, with handwriting like that, you gotta be dumb!"

Notes

1. A-1, A-2, C-1, and C-2 come from Harste, Woodward, and Burke (1984, 83–84); B-1 and B-2 come from Howard Gardner (1982, 112).

2. "This is to give Notice to badgers and forestallers of grain that there has been some in particular [a worsening (of) your actions (motions)], and there will be in a week's time some men come out of the coal pits by night to make fire brands of all the inhabitations of the forestallers of grain."

3. Harvey Graff notes that in the eighteenth century "reading often was taught in the home from worn books, spellers, catechisms, primers, and Bibles. The young learned largely from imitation and only partly from explanation . . . no epochal shift from family to institutions took place in the eighteenth century" (H. Graff 1987, 254).

4. Signature literacy also included the copying of numbers, although it was common for arithmetic and numbers to be ignored in the elementary grades. Daniel Webster was first introduced to arithmetic when he entered Phillips Academy at Exeter in the 1790s, having learned only letters in his elementary school (D. Webster 1875). During signature literacy, students copied numbers and problems in their copybooks, which were widely used as a substitute for textbooks. A study of sixty of these surviving copybooks, written between 1739 and 1820, shows good penmanship, an emphasis on accuracy in copying, and a progression in copied problems from addition to subtraction, next to multiplication, then to division, and finally to the "Rule of Three." In this study, most of the schoolboys who copied the books were older than ten years, and all of the books appear to have been copied for later reference (P. Cohen 1982, 120). Of course, all of this copying did not mean that either the teacher or the students knew much about arithmetic.

4 Recitation and Report Literacy: 1864–1916

The workers themselves used to pay twenty-five to fifty cents a week and would hire a man to read to them during work. A cigar factory is one enormous open area, with tables at which people work. A platform would be erected, so that he'd look down at the cigar makers as he read to them some four hours a day. He would read from newspapers and magazines and a book would be read as a serial. The choice of the book was democratically decided. Some of the readers were marvelous natural actors. They wouldn't just read a book. They'd act out the scenes. Consequently, many cigar makers, who were illiterate, knew the novels of Zola and Dickens and Cervantes and Tolstoy. And the works of the anarchist, Kropotkin. Among the newspapers read were *The Daily Worker* and *The Socialist Call*.

The factory owners decided to put an end to this, though it didn't cost them a penny. Everyone went on strike when they arrived one morning and found the lecture platform torn down. The strike was lost. Every strike in my home town was always lost. The readers never came back. (Terkel 1970, 109–10)

Signature and recording literacy (1776–1864) served the needs of a society where population mobility was weakening the effectiveness of oral literacy in business and politics, but by 1864, signature literacy was failing to serve adequately a society shifting to an early industrial economy. During the signature and recording period, schools taught students the alphabet and "moral" behavior, but the basic introduction of young people to culture—to knowing about the world—was usually left to parents who, along with their children, were typically employed in or near the home and who taught their children discipline, the Bible, national culture, and some information about the world.

Then things changed. Occupations and production left the home.[1] From 1839 to 1869, the amount of nonhousehold manufacturing increased in value from $240,000,000 to $1,630,000,000 (Tyack 1974, 31) as more and more production became institutionalized in early factories. Males abandoned home employment, primarily agriculture, and went to work in these factories, leaving the daily teaching of children to mothers and others. In 1810, only 13 percent of adult males worked away from the home in industry or service, but by 1870 nearly half did, by 1900 nearly 60 percent, and by 1980 over 90 percent.[2] Thus, from 1870 onward, most males were employed away from the home, away from their children, and largely away from the all-day responsibility for the assimilation of their children into culture.

These shifts in adult occupations changed the responsibilities of schools. Because there was now only one parent at home during the day, the school was asked to assume more responsibility for teaching self-discipline and the habits of punctuality and attention (Harris and Dorty 1874). The home, however, still had the primary responsibility for providing cleanliness and tidy clothes: "Any scholar coming with untidy clothes, or with unwashed face or hands, or unbrushed hair, would be sent home at once" (Tyack 1974, 50).

Barbara Finkelstein, who examined almost one thousand descriptions of elementary classrooms from 1820 to 1880, concluded that schools had three ways of teaching recitation literacy: (1) the "Intellectual Overseer," who assigned material to memorize and assigned punishment for error; (2) the "Drillmaster," who led students in unison through their lessons; and (3) the "Interpreter of Culture," who clarified ideas and explained content. She found almost no examples of the latter. She found many examples of the drillmaster method in which the student was "expected simply to answer the questions which are put to him, but not to ask any of his instructor, or dispute his assertions" (Bagg 1871; qtd. in Russell 1991, 39). Thus, in schools "the acquisition of knowledge represented a triumph of the will as well as the intellect" (Finkelstein 1970, 134–35; qtd. in Tyack 1974, 55).

To achieve their goals in self-discipline, teachers used disciplinary devices in oral recitations, such as the bench, the toe-the-line, volume controls, and mouth-movement exercises. In the bench method, the child came to the front of the room, sat on the bench, faced the teacher, and recited. In the toe-the-line approach, elementary children were expected "to stand on the line, perfectly motionless, their bodies erect, their knees and feet together, the tips of their shoes touching the edge of a board in the floor" (Joseph Rice 1893; qtd. in Tyack 1974, 55). College preparatory students in secondary schools were expected to "read aloud twice a day; the several classes standing while they read and toeing a chalk line" (Corson [1896] 1908, 22; qtd. in G. Graff 1987, 43). One teacher asked, "How can you learn anything with your knees and toes out of order?" (Tyack 1974, 55–56).

These toe-the-line drills—"toe-the-line" has now become a formulaic expression in our culture—often included disciplinary exercises in attention and volume control:

> [The] teacher had a queer contrivance nailed to a post set up in the middle of the room. It was known as a "spelling board." When he pulled the string to which the board was fastened the school gave attention. If he let the board half way down the scholars could spell out words in moderate tones. . . . If he proceeded to pull the board up tight everybody spelled to themselves. When he . . . gave the cord a pull . . . down dropped the plank and the hubbub began. Everything went with a roar. Just as loud as you pleased, you could spell anything. People along the road were happy to know the children were getting their lessons. (Felton 1919)

Some teachers added a mouth-movement exercise to recitations:

> After entering the room containing the youngest pupils, the principal said to the teacher, "Begin with the mouth movements and go right straight through." . . . About fifty pupils now began in concert to give utterance to the sounds of a, (as in car) e, and oo, varying their order. . . . [T]hus [maneuvering] the jaws, the teacher remarked, "Your tongues are not loose." Fifty pupils now put out their tongues and wagged them in all directions. The principal complemented the children highly on the superiority of their wagging. (Rice 1893, 176–77)

These disciplinary devices were thought to help teach discipline to children with "working" fathers and to introduce new immigrants to the ways of their new country, the United States. The cities, especially, faced an enormous immigrant education challenge by the 1880s: "In a single year, 1847, Boston added more than 37,000 Irish immigrants to its population of 114,000" (Tyack 1974, 30). By 1908, 58 percent of the schoolchildren in thirty-seven cities had fathers who were born abroad, New York City leading with 72 percent, followed by Chicago with 67 percent (Tyack 1974, 230). At first, many U.S. schools valued the diversity of these immigrants, and many encouraged the teaching of subjects in the native language. For example, in 1853, the president of the Cincinnati school board argued that teaching German in the public schools was essential because immigrants felt that the native language was "that link without which all family and social ties are lost" (qtd. in Tyack 1974, 107). But this tolerance of a variety of languages began to disappear after the Civil War, when the country was concerned about the fragmentation created first by the Civil War and second by the increased immigration needed for new factories.[3]

The Civil War and immigration were not the only reasons the country was concerned about national cohesion. Urbanization was another. Urbanization from 1864 to 1900 did not mean, as it does today, a centralized network of government and services; it meant fragmentation and decentralization. By the late 1890s, nearly three-fourths of the population lived in or near fragmented, decentralized cities as "urbanization proceeded at a faster rate between 1820 and 1860 than in any other period of American history. . . . A muddy small town in 1830, Chicago, became a metropolis of over 109,000 by 1860" (Tyack 1974, 30).

The patterns of fragmentation in urban governance produced intense ethnic isolation and competition for resources. Although cities were often labeled as single school districts, the actual power was usually in the subdistrict school board and neighborhood political machinery (Tyack 1974, 79). In Pittsburgh, until 1911, each of the thirty-nine subdistricts had its own tax system designed by its own board (Tyack 1974, 89). In Philadelphia, each of the forty-two wards had a dozen board members, plus the ward bosses who "normally gave final approval" on the hiring of any teacher (Tyack 1974, 101) and who waged, said one observer, "a war of extermination against all teachers who are not their vassals" (Tyack 1974, 98). These diverse districts, which were often organized around specific ethnic communities, mandated that their own values be taught, thereby increasing the ethnic tensions among different groups and providing a continuing rationale for the drive to have schools socialize students into a "unified" national culture with a unified national language. This emphasis on national unification helped shape recitation literacy as a uniform way to report to others what one knows and to create the myth of the U.S. "melting pot."

In addition to helping solve problems of discipline, immigration, and national cohesion, schools had to assume more responsibility for teaching children the new knowledge and the new norms for success which followed the Civil War. Even parents who stayed home and who were not immigrants found that the nation's "ways for success were becoming increasingly uncertain" (Soltow and Stevens 1981, 60).[4] For one thing, information flowed into the lives of common people at what some considered an alarming rate. First of all, circulating libraries were established in all parts of the country—one library for every 600 free adults in 1850 (Soltow and Stevens 1981, 81)—the publication of cheap books increased, daily newspapers increased in number and got cheaper, mail-order systems like the Sears catalog began to grow, and U.S. post offices spread throughout the country.

One way to help people assimilate this new information and these new networks of communication was to have students in school memorize cultural information, especially what immigrants and new city dwellers "needed to know." This produced the need for new and larger almanacs and encyclopedias of essential information and authoritative lists. For example, Hugh Blair's *Lectures on Rhetoric and Belles Lettres* went through 130 editions between 1783 and 1911 and established

Blair, according to E. D. Hirsch, as "the first definer of cultural literacy for the English national language" (Hirsch 1987, 85).[5] John Bartlett's *Familiar Quotations*, first published in 1855, was another important indicator of the canon of printed materials used in recitations and taught in the schools. One-third of the book came from the Bible and Shakespeare, and the other two-thirds came chiefly from British selections (Milton, Pope, Wordsworth), with a small selection from Americans (Longfellow, Irving, Lowell). Memorizing, describing, and defining this cultural information and reporting for "directory" information—street signs, the population of a city, addresses of businesses, the distance to a railroad, "cures" for colds—became a necessary skill for all citizens. Students were expected to be able to read aloud this information and to write some.

In 1859, at the beginning of recitation literacy, only about half the population had books at home (Soltow and Stevens 1981, 69). During signature literacy, the shortage of schools produced public disputes about the location of the school—Tyack (1974) reports that one group of irate parents moved the school overnight—but during recitation literacy, it was book shortages which produced numerous public disputes.

> The recitation pedagogy of the nineteenth and early twentieth cen-
> tur[ies] was invariably tied to textbooks. If children could not
> bring a schoolbook to class, they often simply did not attend. As a
> result, there was considerable agitation for free textbook laws in all
> the states of the Middle West. (Theobald 1991, 2)

For one thing, recitation literacy, unlike signature literacy, emphasized "extensive exposure to many printed texts rather than repeated, intensive examination of the same ones" (Altick 1983, 302).[6] Recitation literacy's extensive reading required more books, and although there was a rapid growth of printed matter in the early nineteenth century (Schudson 1978, 31–34), there was still a shortage. Of course, recitation teaching, because it did not require everyone to have a book in hand, helped in many ways to solve the problem of a shortage of books in many classrooms (N. Smith 1965).

In recitation schooling, one's intelligence was determined by how many written materials one could recite. In colleges, these recitations often took the form of a catechism about cultural information:

> Date of birth and death? In whose reign did he flourish? Repeat
> Thomson's lives. What is said of his parentage? What does Gibbon
> say? How did he enter Cambridge? (Cleveland [1849] 1851, 765;
> qtd. in H. Graff 1987, 39)

Joseph Rice observed a similar approach in the 1,200 K–12 classrooms he visited in thirty-six cities during a six-month period in 1892:

> When the map had been found each pupil placed his forefinger upon "Cape Farewell," and when the teacher said "Start," the pupils said in concert, "Cape Farewell," and then ran their fingers down the map, calling out the name of each cape as it was touched. …After the pupils had named all the capes on the eastern coast of North America, beginning at the north and ending at the south, they were told to close their books. When the books had been closed, they ran their fingers down the cover and named from memory the capes in their order from north to south. (Rice 1893, 139–40; qtd. in Cuban 1984, 22)

In a school curriculum of this kind, English, as we know it today, was not a mainstream school subject (Applebee 1974, 21) but rather was a conglomeration of oral recitations based on rules of elocution (Porter 1838), rules of English grammar based on Latin models, a collection of literary devices, and later the use of modes as guides for writing (Bain 1866). By the end of the century, Matthew Arnold had made literature the core of the English class, arguing that English literature should be used to socialize the young through contact with the touchstones of "the best which has been thought and said in the world," thereby teaching the young to turn "a stream of fresh and free thought upon our stock notions and habits" (Super 1973, 5: 6). English literature could become, said Arnold, the moral guide for students, replacing the authority of religion, which, in Arnold's view, had been seriously undermined by science.

To ensure that only the best works served as canonical, moral guides for students, Arnold, a school inspector, sorted English literature into two classes of "cultural touchstones": Class I, including Shakespeare and other secular "saints," and Class II, including Chaucer, Burns, and other comedians, satirists, and middle-level writers. Below these two classes were the lower classes, which were not appropriate "touchstones" for cultural imprinting and recitation and, therefore, were not recommended for the English literature program of U.S. secondary schools. Arnold said he based his categories on literary quality and the complexities of the literary challenge, but Northrop Frye has suggested that Arnold relied heavily on the social-class sorting of the period:

> We begin to suspect that the literary value-judgements are projections of social ones. (Frye 1957, 22)

These Class I and Class II works established for English "a literary canon or established object to be known" (H. Adams 1988, 55; 1972), rationalized the organization of courses called English, and institution-alized "the authority of the teaching profession" (qtd. in Scholes 1992, 150). For a society desiring to establish national cohesion and to intro-duce the young to printed materials, the English class became a place for reporting and defining cultural traditions.

In addition to teaching national cohesion and new knowledge, teachers of recitation literacy also contributed to the sorting functions of schools during the post–Civil War years—by gender, by class differ-ences, by racial and ethnic groups, by achievement. This sorting in schools was part of a pervasive post–Civil War social response to the fear of disorder, a fear which enabled reformers to sort the poor into almshouses, the insane into asylums, and various classes of criminals into different types of prisons. First, teachers sorted their students by seating them in rank order by "achievement." This order often gov-erned the sequence of recitation:

> One end is called the head, the other the foot, of the class ... The teacher opens the book, which is of course Webster's *Elementary*, and turning to the lesson, pronounces the words, beginning at the head. If a scholar misspells a word it is given to the next one.... (Mi-nard 1905)

Second, teachers sorted by pushing some students out of school. The majority of those who stayed in school through high school were males, the children of whites, and usually from wealthy and profes-sional families, who, of course, often had the resources to buy their children books, tutors, and post-high school opportunities (Tyack 1974, 58). All of this sorting, of course, helped create enormous social in-equalities (Tyack 1974, 72).

By the 1880s, the intensive reading, the alphabet method, the spelling method, and the copying system of signature literacy had "died" (Robinson et al. 1990). It had been replaced by memorized ora-tions, oral pronunciation drills, dictation followed by copying, oral spelling bees (K. Goodman et al. 1988, 4), and extensive reading through "reading aloud" activities which "required the teacher to do little more than assign selections to be read and, if he chose, to correct the pronunciation of his students" (Finkelstein 1970, 49).[7] In general, by 1865, reading in K–12 became the "equivalent for oral expression," and this "central role of expressive oral reading in American reading in-struction remained steadfast throughout the nineteenth century" (S. Clark 1899; Robinson et al. 1990, 47). Olson has commented that oral readings and recitations did not mean that readers were being asked to get meaning from texts:

> Whether the reader understood was not emphasized, presumably
> because it was assumed that if you got the words, you got the
> meaning. (Olson 1986, 151)

The foundations for recitation pedagogy had been established almost fifty years earlier in U.S. colleges and universities, which produced many of the books and materials which later shaped recitation teaching in secondary and elementary schools.[8] For example, Ebenezer Porter's series of college rhetorics, published between 1819 and 1838, emphasized the importance of delivery as the source of textual meaning in recitation: "Emphasis is the soul of delivery, because it is the most discriminating mark of emotion. Contrast is among the sources of emotion" (Porter 1838; qtd. in Bartine 1992, 60).

When recitation teachers examined written samples from students, they paid little or no attention to the physical aspects of print, as had the handwriting "scientists" of signature literacy. Instead, they looked for complexity in other areas of language, such as omitted words, misspellings, punctuation errors, and so forth (Tuman 1992, 9):

> Comparatively few approach perfection, and a very large number
> are full of the most egregious blunders. Words are left out, words
> are misspelled, punctuation is omitted, capitals are omitted, and
> capitals are put in where they do not belong.... This comparison
> and others ... are sufficient to convince one beyond doubt that the
> French boy of eleven or twelve has gained materially over the
> American boy....(R. Brown 1915, 61)

The primary pedagogical difference between signature and recitation literacy appears to be that in recitation literacy, students were taught the procedure or ritual for giving oral readings or memorized oral reports as responses to formulaic questions, while students in signature literacy spelled words aloud or recorded their answers in a copying book during silent drills. Students during recitation literacy copied, too, but with a difference. They had dictation copying in which teachers first announced the paragraph which was about to be read, then orally dictated the sentences of the paragraph one by one while the students wrote the sentences down one by one, and finally collected the papers and marked the errors in spelling, punctuation, and so forth (R. Brown 1915). Sometimes teachers arranged dictated pieces in a sequence based on complexity. The goals of these writing lessons in recitation literacy were memorization, reporting of cultural facts ("words left out"), and use of the mechanics of expression ("punctuation is omitted").

Before Matthew Arnold, people were said to have *had* literature or the Bible through exercises like copying (Scholes 1992, 145), but after

Arnold, people were said to have been penetrated by literature or to have "imprinted" on literature by copying and recitation. The sensitivity and intelligence of this "penetration" or "imprinting" were usually reflected in one's oral recitation of a literary work. Says Arnold, "If we are thoroughly penetrated by their ['the touchstones'] power, we shall find that we have acquired a sense enabling us ... to feel the degree in which a high poetical quality is present and wanting there" (Super 1973, 9: 170; and qtd. in Bartine 1992, 19). Says Graff, "The assumption seems ... to have been that any gentleman of good breeding would naturally intuit the meaning of a literary work and, therefore, had no need to descend to interpreting the sorts of hidden meanings that became the staple of literature courses" during the later period of decoding literacy (H. Graff 1987, 129).

Thus, expressive oral reading or elocution assumed that "a properly receptive reader will experience" the powers of the text through the act of elocution (Dennis 1939, 1: 127; qtd. in Bartine 1989, 57), and, thus, oral readings were at once ways to memorize information, to assimilate the text as a delivered object, and to embed moral messages in the character of the reader. Porter, in fact, attacked efforts at Harvard and Cornell to replace elocution and recitation with lectures and discussions because he felt these approaches failed to anchor meaning in the personal character and moral spirit of the "readers" (G. Graff 1987, 32).

By the 1890s, signature literacy's emphasis on the Bible, alphabet books, silent spellers, and copying books had been replaced by texts emphasizing recitation skills and memorization of secular and nationalistic culture (Applebee 1974, 2–5; Clifford 1984, 491).[9] The original six-book reading series published by McGuffey during signature literacy (1836) emphasized alphabetic exercises, but the next McGuffey's reader, published in 1869 (McGuffey's *New Eclectic Primer in Pronouncing Orthography*), focused more attention on the mechanics of oral expression, especially the correspondence between sound and alphabet. The fifth McGuffey's reader, published in 1879, provided even more supplementary material on articulation, subvocals, inflection, aspirates and other "Elementary Sounds of English" (see Tuman 1987, 39; Applebee 1974, 16 [*n*14]). In summary, recitation literacy established textual meaning as familiar, formulaic, memorized, preannounced, delivered, and predefined by a small authoritative group of "men of letters." Recitation literacy also established that learning new meanings was an act of elocution in which messages were digested and assimilated. Recitation literacy, borrowing from classical and Biblical readings, also introduced two versions of a literal reading. A literal reading of books like the Bible or literature was a visualization or understanding of the metaphors and figures of speech organizing the book. A literal reading of a history text was a tracking of references to the real world (see Frye 1982, 57–65).

Composition studies took two forms during the recitation period. First, students were expected to copy essays composed and/or assigned by the teachers. Composition studies also included sentence diagramming, organized around Alonzo Reed and Brainerd Kellogg's *Higher Lessons in English Grammar and Composition* ([1885] 1894a) and *Graded Lessons in English* (rev. ed. 1894b) (Halloran 1990, 173). In general, the copying of forms in school grew out of the notion of the mind as having faculties which matched perfectly the modes of the external world—for example, description, narration, definition, and persuasion. One of the purposes of reading and writing was to imprint students on these inevitable forms, and copying enabled one to learn them. Of course, in these approaches, composition studies showed little interest in issues of invention and personal imagination (Berlin 1990).

The model of mind adopted by the pedagogy of recitation was John Locke's *tabula rasa*, or wax tablet model of mind, on which the modes of external experience were imprinted. In Locke's model, experiences are received through the senses, then imprinted on the mind, and finally processed through similarity and contiguity. John Locke's model of mind legitimized *all* people knowing things from their reading. This model was quite appealing to the nationalist spirit in the late nineteenth-century United States, where U.S. educators argued that they were not dependent upon European intellectuals or classical scholars to tell them the meaning of things. Locke's model of mind made possible this relocation of knowledge from Greek to English, from religion to secular life, and from an elite to everyman, and thus, during recitation literacy, knowledge was transferred to books written in English by authors located in the United Kingdom or educated in the classical tradition in the U.S.

Despite the importance Locke attached to experience, in schooling up until the end of recitation literacy, reading was a primary source of knowledge, and experience was secondary, or even tertiary, a status reflected in composition assignments. The idea of a specific research paper would have been without meaning in 1800 because prior to the reign of personal writing, teachers naturally assumed that the students had no choice but to write something transmitted and synthesized from their reading (see Connors 1987). Sharon Crowley has described how Locke's model of the mind was used to legitimize courses and textbooks organized around current-traditional rhetoric, in which the form of the written product was the dominant form:

> The emphasis on the composed product rather than the compos-
> ing process; the analysis of discourse into words, sentences, and
> paragraphs; the classification of discourse into description, narra-
> tion, exposition, and argument; the strong concern with usage
> (syntax, spelling, punctuation) and with style (economy, clarity,
> emphasis)….(Young 1978; qtd. as an example of Locke's influence
> in Crowley 1990, 12–13)

Given the fact that Locke's model of mind was an imprinting device, assessments of knowledge in that model turned to recitation tests. The earliest recorded effort to assess recitation literacy may have been a literacy test used in a Swedish parish from 1656 to 1669, in which parishioners had to recite from memory previously announced religious selections (D. Resnick and Resnick 1977). A later assessment effort, appearing in England's Revised Code between 1862 and 1897, required students in grades 1–5 to "read" aloud a brief passage selected from their textbook and required students in grade 6 to "read" aloud a paragraph from a newspaper or narrative. In the U.S., the most common tests of recitation literacy were the rhetorical, the spelling bee, and the immigration test. The first national measure of recitation literacy in the U.S. was the test established by the Immigration and Naturalization Service in 1891, which required potential citizens to recite the Pledge of Allegiance and, sometimes, other materials in English. The immigration test generally followed (and still does) the traditional question-answer pattern of a recitation lesson.

Another common recitation assessment was the "rhetorical," which was used by most colleges and many secondary schools. The University of Kansas, for example, required each member of the freshman, sophomore, and junior classes to appear "at least twice each year at a morning exercise in the hall" to present a speech or oral report to some students and faculty on a topic being studied in a class. The University of Missouri required that presentations be "before the whole body of students" (Russell 1991, 41–42). These oral reports and debates were apparently productive for many students, but professors sometimes objected to the recitation "load." One professor resigned from Yale in 1869 because of the burden of "*hearing* so many compositions" (qtd. in Russell 1991, 42; emphasis Russell's).

States began to use assessment data to establish goals for a minimum number of years in school for most citizens. By 1900, thirty-one states had passed compulsory education laws, and completion of the early elementary grades by all students had become a rough national indicator of minimum recitation literacy (Tyack 1974, 71). In 1897, Pennsylvania, for example, "set the literacy expected of a third-grade student as the standard for youth to qualify for work permits" (Clifford

1984, 475). Because of this emphasis on all students having some elementary schooling, public school enrollment tripled between 1840 and 1900, public expenditures on education increased nearly thirty-fold in real dollars, and the public share of total expenditures on education increased from less than one-half to more than three-quarters (Fishlow 1966, 420, 423).

The courts during recitation literacy also began to apply a new standard for measuring literacy. For one thing, people were expected to be able to write some. During signature literacy, signatures were adequate; but during recitation literacy, the courts ruled that signatures were no longer enough for contracts:

> That a person can write his name certainly does not fill the measure of the statutory requirement that the juror should be able to *write*. We think that he should be able to express his ideas in words upon paper with pen or pencil. (*Johnson v. The State* [Texas], 21 Texas Court of Appeals 1886; qtd. in E. Stevens 1983, 69)

All in all, the increasing supply of cheap, high-quality pencils, the rapid growth in the use of the typewriter, and the rapid growth of the U.S. postal system all suggested that people were writing more than they had during the signature literacy period.

In general, the schools did accomplish for many students the national goal of recitation literacy—that is, the completion of fourth or fifth grade, the memorization of a few pieces, an awareness of nationalistic values, the ability to write some, the enforcement of order, an exploration of notions of literal meaning (metaphorical and historical), and an awareness of English classics. In general, secondary schools remained an education for the elite. In 1869–1870, there were only about two students graduating from high school out of every 100 seventeen-year-olds. By 1910, that figure had increased to 8.8 out of every 100 (Snyder 1993, 55). "Only 732 pupils out of a total enrollment of 185,000 were seniors in high school in Chicago in 1894" (Tyack 1974, 57); and in 1890, about 220,000 students in the U.S. attended 2,526 high schools for an average of only eighty-six days each year (Cuban 1984, 25). But most people were enrolling in elementary school and were completing several elementary grades. By 1898, 71 percent of the people between the ages of 5 and 18 were enrolled in school, a 10 percent increase over the 1870 figure of 61 percent.

New students attending school and increasing numbers of recitations produced a demand for new ways to organize schools. Remember that recitation teaching began in the generally silent classrooms of signature literacy, with all of the teachers and students in one great hall or room where students silently copied lessons. But during recitation literacy, students recited reports aloud all the time, and sometimes they changed their seating order based on their recitation achievement. This method of organization sometimes required several teachers to take responsibility for different sections of the hall or the levels of achievement.

Having students at different grade levels in the same room, all reciting aloud from different works, created a pandemonium which forced school authorities in England in 1861 to debate the first major innovation in the public schools—separate, closed classrooms for different groups of students. In England, a Royal Commission appointed to study the issue agreed that there was a problem:

> The noise of 200 boys and four masters in the Upper School is so great that it is impossible for those at one end to hear what goes on at the other…and the great bulk of the division is learning nothing. (Cory 1897; qtd. in Reid 1987, 11)

But the Commission concluded that because noise served an important social purpose, the one-room schoolhouse should not be abandoned:

> It is necessary at the Bar, and in other careers in life, and in the Houses of Parliament, that much mental work should be done of all kinds, amidst many outward causes of distraction. (Reid 1987, 11)

Nevertheless, within a dozen years, separate classrooms began to become the norm as the needs of recitation teachers overwhelmed the policymakers. In these recitation classrooms, teachers often had forty or more students per room (Cuban 1984, 24). For example, the Quincy School, an early model of separate classrooms, had twelve classrooms holding fifty-six students each (Tyack 1974, 45), and the Chicago system assigned 123 teachers to teach 14,000 students grouped in ten elementary grades (Tyack 1974, 45–46), a load of over 100 elementary students per teacher or "classroom."

The acts of reciting passages aloud, giving reports aloud, summarizing a version of literal meaning (metaphorical and historical), learning to write some, learning diction, and learning to copy dictation were intended to socialize children from homes where one parent was home all day; to teach English to nonnative speakers; to socialize immigrants and natives into U.S. traditions; to overcome the shortage of printed materials in schools; to police the student population by teaching them "discipline"; and, according to many observers, to sort the population, even where segregation laws had been dropped, into segregated groups based on gender, economic class, and race or ethnicity. Most observers seem to agree that recitation literacy (1864–1916) served the needs of the emerging society where the Civil War, immigration, urbanization, and industrialization had weakened the bonds of shared information and shared values among people. In 1892, Charles Eliot argued that public education contributed significantly toward the "formation of habits" and to conditions in which "terrors have been disarmed, superstitions abolished…and civil order extended over regions once desolate or dangerous" (see Eliot's views in Krug 1961, 65).

But recitation literacy toward the end of the 1900s was not meeting the needs of a nation with increasingly centralized urban centers and large factories. Critics of the schools complained about the general meaninglessness of recitations of preannounced, familiar materials, and they began to call for a level of literacy in which citizens could read unfamiliar, unannounced materials using a new "scientific" approach to reading. One of the first major reports fueling these criticisms of the schools was Joseph Mayer Rice's series of articles attacking "the futility of the spelling grind" and the "meaningless verbiage" of recitation classrooms (Cremin 1961, 6; Tyack 1974, 82). Rice's criticisms were not that different from those of Matthew Arnold, who had served as a school inspector in England for twenty-four years and who had complained that the students understood very little of what they "read," even when they were reciting Arnold's touchstones (Tuman 1987, 46).

Many critics endorsed Rice's views. Colonel Francis Parker, a school superintendent and later director of the School of Education at the University of Chicago, argued that "the mere pronunciation of words, however correctly and readily done, is not reading…the main point… is this: Are the pupils led to get the thought?" (Mathews 1966, 106). In addition, Edmund Burke Huey, a widely respected educational psychologist, made a similar observation:

> Reading as a school exercise has almost always been thought of as reading aloud.…The consequent attention to reading as an exercise in speaking…has been heavily at the expense of reading as the art of thought-getting.…(Huey [1908] 1968, 359)

College faculty had challenged recitation literacy fifty years earlier when Edward Tyrell Channing, then a professor of rhetoric at Harvard University, turned his rhetoric or recitation class into a silent composition and reading class (Channing 1856, 17; Douglas 1976, 124). Douglas has called this challenge "a quite radically new view of rhetoric" in which the orator or man-of-recitation was being replaced by the reader or the man-of-letters (Douglas 1976, 116; Tuman 1987, 50). Why did Channing propose this shift in English studies? Says Douglas:

> Channing saw that, if the art of which he was a professor were to
> retain any credibility, it would have to be given an image more in
> keeping with the actualities of a society where opinion was more
> and more coming to be formed by the report and the article, rather
> than by the debate. (Douglas 1976, 124)

Even so, silent reading and written responses in class did not become
significant in K–12 schools until the 1920s, when a new decoding literacy for everyone emerged (Applebee 1974, 16 [n14]).

In 1892, near the end of recitation literacy, English and its collection
of interests in English literature, language, and composition became a
nationally recognized subject, certified as one of the nine main subjects in secondary schools by the National Education Association's
Committee of Ten, which was chaired by Charles W. Eliot, president of
Harvard University, and which was charged to recommend a new curriculum for secondary schools. The Committee of Ten organized separate conferences to define the nine different subjects, and the
Conference on English of the Committee of Ten met at Vassar College
in 1892 and defined the subject of English as "English language, English grammar, composition, rhetoric, and English literature" (Burrows 1977, 23). The key curriculum shift was the declaration that U.S.
public schools and even colleges were committed to studying English
literature and the English language, not Greek or Latin.[10] This declaration was, of course, a recognition of what had been slowly growing
throughout recitation literacy. The purpose of English was declared to
be (1) learning to express oneself clearly and (2) learning to understand others (Committee of Ten 1894). In addition, the Committee of
Ten placed its emphasis in secondary education on college preparation, not education for all students.

In summary, recitation literacy was introduced in 1864 as part of the
upheaval of the Civil War and the rise of nationalism in the U.S.; was
measured in citizenship tests; was institutionalized by a new organization of separate classrooms for different ages; was finally institutionalized in selections of English literature; and was taught by a pedagogy
based on association psychology, in which the mind, à la John Locke,
records the sensations and messages coming from experience and from
reading. Although self-reported literacy rose from 70 percent in the 1840
census to 80 percent in 1870 and to 93.8 percent in 1900 (Kaestle et al.
1991, 211), by the 1900s, people were beginning to criticize the schools
and recitation literacy for not doing enough. Within a few short years,
the report of the Committee of Ten was under attack for its limited view
of the high school curriculum, especially for its definition of the mission
of the high school as primarily preparation of students for college.

The history of recitation literacy teaches us once again that the graded classroom of thirty-five students is a social construction and that our present-day subject-matter organization around literature and the English (U.K.) language did not become national policy until the standards movement of 1911–1916. This construction was based on the social needs of the period, and it will be changed when our social needs change and when teachers and others can find the appropriate organizational forms for new forms of literacy. New forms of literacy are certain to produce changes in teaching, in the education of teachers, and in the role of school administrators. Teachers interested in class size should note that changes in literacy standards have had an impact on class size. Over the last hundred years, class sizes have been decreasing. I am convinced no public rhetoric on class size or any other topic of school reform will be effective until the public interest is spelled out in a specific match between social needs and reduced teacher loads.

This history of recitation literacy should also remind us that in our silent classrooms of textual decoding and analysis, we have lost some of our understanding of discourse as public performance. The following observation by David Russell on the recitation classroom is instructive:

> It must also strike us that the nineteenth-century classroom was a performance-centered, interactive place by comparison with the modern lecture classroom. The hour was taken up with students speaking, so much so that faculty complained that they had too little time for their own pronouncements. (Russell 1991, 39)

Today, in the 1990s, our schools need to examine once again the uses of forms of recitation in the contemporary English class. Robin Lakoff suggests that "there is evidence all around that as a culture we are contemplating—if we have not already taken—a leap from being written-oriented to being oral-oriented" (R. Lakoff 1982, 256). Certainly, for many of our students, the separation of the oral and the printed text is a violation of their authentic experiences of literacy. The fact is that recitation literacy created a form of secondary orality in which the oral comes from printed materials, not the face-to-face bonding of primary orality in oral literacy. This secondary orality, according to Ong, has become one of the dominant forms of communication in our television society. English studies in K–12 schools urgently needs to recognize recitation performance and visual media as two of the key "texts" studied in school.

One example of this kind of work in recitation performance is the experiment of Kristin Valentine (1992) at Arizona State University in her public speaking classes, where she assigns students the task of preparing a classroom recitation on research articles. She reports that the process of preparing for this recitation not only helps the reciter understand the article, but the process of hearing a recitation likewise helps the listeners understand it. Some students have taken the assignment one step further and added a second person, who at various points in the recitation presents a conversational translation of the recitation.

Another example of this effort to give recitation performance a prominent place in English classes is the recent work of John Dixon in the United Kingdom. Dixon has challenged the separation of reading from talking in the first Cox report on standards for teaching English (Cox 1988). Dixon recommends an emphasis on a performance model of reading in which reading is "a social act, involving the voices and the bodies of pupils who are interacting with each other" (Dixon 1994, 5). Says Dixon:

> A performance model makes explicit what the students are learning to use—their voices and their bodies—when they are reading aloud in-role....It foregrounds the roles of a director, and explicitly calls for the students to learn these. (Dixon 1994, 5)

Finally, says Dixon:

> Where a performance relies heavily on the spoken voice, as it frequently does in poetry, it's doing exactly what radio does. When a performance includes bodily as well as vocal signs, and costumes and settings (maybe with music or back-projected visuals), are all being responded to by the audience, this is exactly what the cameras and microphones are frequently working on in television. (Dixon 1994, 7)

It is essential to remember that some of the more rigid forms of early recitation literacy still persist in our classrooms. The secular catechism typical of signature and recitation literacy turns up frequently in Petrosky's study of classrooms:

Teacher: What kinds of books are on the back wall?

Student: Periodicals.

Teacher: No. Cox, what kinds of books are on the back wall?

Student: Fiction.

Teacher: What else, Misha?

Student: Biographies.

Teacher: If I wanted to know where George Washington was born, can I find that out from the encyclopedia?

Class: (*in unison*) Yes. (Petrosky 1990, 63)

Stuckey and Alston (1990) describe similar classrooms, observing that "at-risk students are rarely asked to do what their more privileged peers routinely do. That is, they are rarely asked to speak, to think, to plan, to collaborate, or to evaluate" (Stuckey and Alston 1990, 250).

It would be a mistake to conclude that this use of one form of recitation literacy in the 1990s accomplishes nothing. Petrosky notes that in the Delta, this literacy of recitation and basic skills helped solve that area's pressing problems of poverty and of "getting students out of the Delta and into post-secondary education or the military." Asks Petrosky, "Isn't that solution an indicator of a sophisticated literacy at work in a large social and political sense?" (Petrosky 1990, 65). The point is that this use of this form of recitation literacy in the 1990s may have accomplished something in the past, but it no longer accomplishes enough. There is a growing doubt that students will continue to be able to get out of the Delta with this kind of literacy. As noted earlier, for the first time in the history of the country, high school graduates are earning fewer dollars than their fathers (Murnane and Levy 1993).

Recitation was the last literacy period in the U.S. when teachers entered classrooms with unquestioned authority over knowledge. In a recitation environment, students often stood when teachers entered the room, nodded appreciatively when a teacher passed, and sat quietly when told to do so. A toe-the-line culture was possible because the teacher and his or her texts or works were the source of knowledge and moral authority. In the literacy periods which follow, authority begins to move from the teacher to the text and finally to various communities. Each shift of authority changes the forms of literacy, and these shifts in forms of literacy change forever the relationship between teachers and students. During recitation literacy, intelligence and literacy were associated with question-answer responses, with the eloquence and rhetorical skill of memorized recitations of authoritative texts, and with the student's composed and recited reports. By 1916, literacy was beginning to be redefined as silent reading and analysis.

Notes

1. Food was still made in the home for the home: "Though only a few miles from the center of the greatest metropolis in the land, Queens County and much of Brooklyn were still semi-rural in 1890, and many families were as dependent on small-scale agriculture as on the industrial or commercial employment of the men in the family....Manhattan itself was more bucolic than urban, and pigs and goats were often seen along the East River ... much of the care of urban livestock and gardens inevitably fell to women ... the majority of women

undertook a strenuous annual bout of preserving, pickling, canning, and jelly making, and most baking was done in the family kitchen. Among 7,000 working-class families investigated by the U.S. Bureau of Labor between 1889 and 1892, less than half purchased any bread" (Smuts 1971, 11–13).

2. Women are the second group of parents to leave the home to work. Men were the first.

3. Literacy standards in the U.S. have often been influenced by literacy standards in other countries. Similar trends of assimilation were underway in Italy and in France (D. Resnick 1991a, 22). Less than half the population of France spoke French in 1860, and no more than two or three percent of the population of Italy could speak Italian in 1860 (24). But in the late 1800s, both countries decided to mandate one language as a step toward national cohesion and assimilation. Says Daniel Resnick, "Public schooling in these nations lies on the ruins of buried dialects" (D. Resnick 1991a, 25). But the U.S., more than the two other nations, excluded other languages (25). Our contemporary language about "world-class standards" is, from one point of view, an expansion of the idea of the United Nations into our everyday lives and our educational forums.

4. There is good evidence suggesting "that literacy was boosted by the commercial aspects of urbanization, not the industrial aspects" (Kaestle 1985, 26). In other words, commercial and urbanization needs pushed the country toward recitation literacy.

5. Blair's book also helped "spread the rhetoricians' approach" to reading (Applebee 1974, 17 [n 27]). Both college and secondary classrooms used the book (Applebee 1974, 9).

6. Signature reading, such as it was, was intensive, very slow, and a distinct "contrast to the faster pace and casualness of mid-nineteenth century reading" (D. Hall 1983, 23).

7. This approach is reminiscent of what Goody found in some of the twentieth century's developing countries during the 1960s: "The elementary class is taught not to read but to recite, simply using the letters as mnemonics for what comes next" (Goody 1968, 222). Arithmetic in the recitation literacy period was primarily a form of the spelling bee, with students reciting such things as the multiplication tables. In high school or more advanced instruction, arithmetic evolved into a combination of reciting tables (addition, multiplication, and division), translating word problems to numbers on the chalkboard, and doing word problems on one's individual slate (P. Cohen 1982, 138). The use of the slate had two results. First, it saved money when compared to writing on paper, and second, it put a premium on memorizing and imprinting.

8. College instruction during recitation literacy appeared as follows:

> The division officer sits behind a sort of raised box or pulpit overlooking the whole . . . most of the officers call upon their men, by lot—drawing their names, haphazard, from a box which contains them—and so making each individual liable to be examined on every day's lesson. . . . In a Latin or Greek recitation one may be asked to read or scan a short passage, another to translate it, and a third to answer questions as to its construction, and so on; or all of this and more may be required of the same individual. The reciter is expected simply to answer the questions which are put to him, but

not ask any of his instructor, or dispute his assertions. If he has any enquiries to make, or controversy to carry on, it must be done informally, after the division has been dismissed. (G. Graff 1987, 32)

9. The dates of the overall pattern of instruction follow Gerald Graff (1987) here. Tuman (1986) suggests the recitation approach may have been on its way out by 1819. Tuman, it seems to me, is talking about colleges.

10. An article in *The Nation* shows that the debate was still raging in 1914 about whether Greek and Latin classics should still be required for a B.A. in college ("A New Battle of the Books" 1914, 315–16).

5 A Literacy of Decoding, Defining, and Analyzing: 1916–1983

> From 1918 through 1964, at least in the research reports focused on the teaching of reading comprehension, there were no studies that involved oral reading or other kinds of oral presentations as techniques for improving reading comprehension. (Robinson et al. 1990, 80)

During signature and recording literacy, the public did not generally endorse English and English literature as an appropriate subject for K–12 schools—in fact, in some places English literature was explicitly prohibited. But during recitation and report literacy, things changed. From 1860 to 1890, the percentage of high schools offering courses in English literature "rose from 30 percent to 70 percent" (Applebee 1974, 37). Finally, in 1894, the NEA's Committee of Ten named English literature as one of the nine subjects that should be taught in secondary schools, declared that high schools should serve primarily the needs of college preparatory students (Applebee 1974, 45), and decided that "elocution appeared to lie outside of the subjects which the meeting was convened to discuss" (qtd. in Burrows 1977, 23).[1] In other words, recitation was no longer the nation's minimum standard of literacy, and a subject called "English" was now a required experience for all secondary students.

English literature became an institutionalized requirement in U.S. secondary schools in 1894 when the National Conference on Uniform Entrance Requirements in English, an organization of colleges and universities, issued the Uniform Book List. The Uniform Book List, outlining the required readings for college preparation, was adopted again in 1900 by the College Entrance Examination Board and adopted yet again in 1907 by Eastern agencies that accredited high schools (New England Association Standing Committee on Courses of Study 1907, 559–75; Applebee 1974, 49–50). The Uniform Book List put the control of the high school curriculum in the hands of colleges and universities, named the required canonical works of English literature, named English a national subject, and, at the same time, mandated once again that secondary schools should focus their primary attention on college preparatory students.

In 1911, high school English teachers, revolting against the college controls exercised in the Uniform Book List, organized the National Council of Teachers of English and called for a new national effort to change the nation's definition of minimum literacy, insisting that high schools must recognize the needs of all students who, said NCTE, were being ignored and underestimated in the 1894 definition of English and literacy.[2] Charles Eliot, chair of the Committee of Ten, had, in fact, earlier predicted that the proportion of grammar school children incapable of pursuing geometry, algebra, and foreign language would turn out to be much smaller than imagined (Krug 1961, 67–68). In response to NCTE's revolt and to other concerns about the Uniform Book List, the NEA organized the Committee for the Reorganization of English, in 1917, chaired by NCTE's James Hosic, and the Committee on the Cardinal Principles, in 1918. The NEA charged these committees to examine once again what the nation's definition of literacy should be, especially whether secondary schools should be for *all* students.

These two committees, combining their commitment to equality with their belief in individual differences, essentially recommended a three-track system to bring all students into secondary schools, one track of English for college prep students, one for vocational students, and another for the general students. By 1994, the U.S. Office of Education was claiming that vocational schools served 20 percent of the population, college prep classes served another 20 percent, and general programs served 60 percent. USOE thought the generalist was being ignored: "We do not believe the remaining 60 percent of our youth of secondary school age will receive the life adjustment training they need and to which they are entitled as American citizens" (Applebee 1974, 144). In general, the college prep students were to be given Matthew Arnold's content, the vocational students were to be given occupational training, and the general students were to be given life-adjustment English.

The curriculum for these three tracks was first outlined between 1914 and 1916 by the American Psychological Association's project to prepare reading tests for draftees entering the army,[3] between 1915 and 1917 by the NEA's Committee on the Economy of Time in Education, and between 1917 and 1918 by the Cardinal Principles and the Hosic reports mentioned above. All of these projects defined English for "all" students as sequential reading skills, grammar skills, and some of the "basic" cultural information usually found in literature. Reading and grammar skills placed special emphasis on the decoding and analysis of parts of texts-as-objects. Thus, by 1916, the public had arrived at a new description of a three-track English program and a new national definition of basic, minimum literacy based on decoding and analytic skills.

But these policies were not adopted without an intense debate. Some reformers favored classrooms organized around the ideas of John Dewey, who advocated a social, civic literacy based on democratic transactions and aimed toward democratic participation and solutions of social problems. Still others, like Hugh Mearns and John T. Frederick, argued for personal growth and self-expression in which writing could be the therapeutic "doing away with maladjustments of personality" (qtd. in Kantor 1975, 18). Still others favored the ideas of Ellwood P. Cubberly, who advocated a decoding literacy based on industrial needs for efficiency and Frederick Taylor's notions of standardized work. James Hosic's *Report on the Reorganization of English in Secondary Schools* (1917), published by the Office of Education, attempted to find a midpoint among the influences of Dewey, Cubberly, and Mearns, describing the purpose of teaching composition, for example, as one effort "to enable the pupil to speak and write correctly, convincingly, and interestingly." "The first step toward efficiency in the use of language," said Hosic, "is the cultivation of earnestness and sincerity; the second is the development of accuracy and correctness; the third is the arousing of individuality and artistic consciousness" (Hosic 1917, 69–70).

In general, Cubberly won out, but not without a fight from people like Margaret Haley, who warned the 1904 convention of the National Education Association that the K–12 school reform debate was a struggle between two ideals:

> Two ideals are struggling for supremacy in American life today: one the industrial ideal, dominating thru the supremacy of commercialism, which subordinates the worker to the product and the machine; the other, the ideal of democracy, the ideal of the educators, which places humanity above all machines, and demands that all activity shall be the expression of life. (Haley 1904; qtd. in Tyack 1974, 257)

Haley, who helped establish one of the nation's first teachers' unions and who in 1916 became the first national organizer of the newly established American Federation of Teachers, warned that creating schools structured like factories could shift expertise in teaching away from teachers, where it was anchored during recitation literacy,[4] to the new administrators and the nonteaching bureaucrats of Cubberly's factory model of schooling. Haley decried

> the increased tendency toward "factorizing education," making the teacher an automaton, a mere factory hand, whose duty is to carry out mechanically and unquestionably the ideas and orders of those clothed with the authority of position, and who may or may not know the needs of the children or how to minister to them. (Haley 1904; qtd. in Tyack 1974, 257)

Dewey had a similar warning:

> If there is a single public-school in the United States where there is
> official and constitutional provision made for submitting questions
> of methods of discipline and teaching ... to the discussion of those
> actually engaged in the work of teaching, that fact has escaped my
> notice. (Dewey 1904; qtd. in Tyack 1974, 257)

NCTE leaders also pushed for Dewey's ideas, recommending in 1935 that the nation adopt *An Experience Curriculum in English* (Hatfield 1935) organized around Dewey's ideas. But Dewey, Haley, and NCTE were not able to stop the nation's adoption of Cubberly's definition of literacy and his model for organizing schooling. Dewey's ideas slowly disappeared from the few schools where they had been tried, and by 1944, Dewey's Progressive Education Association had closed its doors, and most of Dewey's notions about teaching and learning, although still discussed and debated, ceased to be a major influence in most public schools until the 1960s.

Decoding and analytic literacy differed from recitation literacy in at least six ways. The first difference was that decoding/analytic literacy defined reading as decoding and analysis of parts and, thus, required students to be able to understand materials they had not seen or heard before, unlike recitation literacy, in which students were only required to read (or recite) the preannounced materials. For example, World War I recruits were expected to show their reading ability by silently answering the following kinds of questions:

> The **pitcher** has an important place in **tennis football baseball handball. Cribbage** is played with **rackets mallets dice cards.** The **Holstein** is a kind of **cow horse sheep goat.** The most prominent industry of **Chicago** is **packing brewing automobiles flour.** The **topaz** is usually **red blue green.** The **Plymouth Rock** is a kind of **horse cattle granite fowl. Irving Cobb** is famous as a **baseball player actor writer artist. Clothing** is made by **Smith & Wesson Kuppenheimer B.T. Babbitt Swift & Co.** The **U.S. Naval Academy** is at **West Point Annapolis New Haven Ithaca. Rio de Janeiro** is a city of **Spain Argentina Portugal Brazil.**

From the point of view of the army recruits who were taught in the schools of recitation and reporting literacy, reading was largely the recitation of preassigned materials, and in recitation situations, people were generally not asked to recite or to read things they had not seen before. In addition, recitation tests were read aloud, not silently, and students got a chance to hear the public performance of others prior to their own performance. In the questions above, the first mass literacy test given in this country, recruits were asked, without any prior notice, to read silently the new questions or new materials and to answer them. For many of these recruits, these questions were unfair, the situation was unfair, and the assumptions were strange. This new army test, prepared by a project of the American Psychological Association, constituted a shift to a new method of "teaching" and "testing"—decode and analyze silently what you have not seen before and know the parts of the information requested—from *pitcher* to *cribbage* to *Chicago.*

Needless to say, the proposed change in the nation's definition of minimum literacy was accompanied by charges that students of U.S. schools could not read. One commentator, reviewing the results of the first national machine-scored assessment of decoding literacy in the U.S. (Kelly 1969, 35–36), reported, "An overwhelming majority . . . had entered school, attended the primary grades where reading was taught, and had been taught to read. Yet, when as adults they were examined, they were unable to read readily such simple material as that of a daily newspaper" (Burgess 1921; qtd. in Hofstadter 1959, 12).

This commentator seems to be criticizing the schools for not teaching reading, but my review of the evidence suggests that many of those draftees who went to school were taught to read the way traditional recitation literacy defined reading: reading is memorization, discussion, and recitation of preannounced passages. In 1916, draftees into the U.S. Army were encountering a new definition of reading: reading is silent decoding and analysis of the parts of unfamiliar materials. These recruits were criticized for not doing what they had never been taught to do. Recent attacks on schools for failing to teach students to read appear to be "déjà vu all over again" (to quote Yogi Berra, or was it Casey Stengel?). That is, contemporary students are being criticized for not being able to interpret or criticize texts, and yet they were usually taught reading as decoding/analytic literacy, a literacy which never stressed the criticism of texts.

The second difference between recitation literacy and decoding/analytic literacy was that decoding/analytic literacy dropped the recitation of whole passages and organized a bits-and-pieces interrogation of the student's mind. In both recitation and decoding literacy, "verbal exchanges between teacher and students still pivoted on questions asked by the teacher" (Cuban 1984, 132), but the formal recitation procedures of the nineteenth century, in which individuals recited from whole passages, were replaced by a questioning system in which the teacher attempted to discover orally or in writing the various parts and pieces which the students had in their minds (Cuban 1984, 132). Sometimes in decoding literacy, the teacher used a "socialized recitation" in which he or she asked groups of students some leading questions after which the students answered these questions while remaining seated at their desks (Cuban 1984, 132). This shift from oral recitations of whole pieces to oral answers about smaller bits meant that most classrooms began to seem like quiz shows focusing on small bits of information, not the memory dumps of whole pieces typical in many traditional recitation classes.

The third difference between decoding literacy and recitation literacy was the emphasis of decoding/analytic literacy on silent reading. Thorndike had proposed that "in school practice, it appears likely that exercises in silent reading to find answers to given questions, or to give summation of the matter read, or to list the questions which it answers, should in large measure replace oral reading" (Thorndike 1906, 329). Kelly has observed that "until the twentieth century there is hardly a mention of silent reading" (Kelly 1969, 152), and Robinson et al. have called the shift from oral to silent reading the most dramatic change in reading instruction in the eighteenth and nineteenth centuries in the U.S. (Robinson et al. 1990, 91). By 1923, Slama was reporting that "silent reading in the lower grades is now the most important problem confronting the primary teacher," adding that "heretofore, the main problem of the teacher was the teaching of oral reading" (Slama 1923, 142). Again, the difference between recitation and decoding/analytic literacy is easy to understand: in the recitation classroom, the sound of students reciting cultural messages; in the decoding/analytic classroom, the silence of students doing their written drills on word-attack skills and sentence analysis or giving short answers orally to questions.

The fourth difference was that decoding/analytic literacy was expected to give *all* students, usually tracked up through high school, the tools for analyzing the world and for achieving practical goals in either college or some other work after high school. In fact, as Applebee notes, W. Wilbur Hatfield, NCTE secretary/treasurer, warned NCTE leaders that "'unless it can be made clear, even to the practical mind,' that composition and literature achieve results 'commensurate with the time allotment' ... 'they will surely be replaced by subjects more obviously useful'" (Applebee 1974, 85). Thus, all students were expected to become basic readers, but the college prep students were expected to become advanced analytical readers in college prep English; the vocational students were expected to become informational readers in business English; and students in general English were expected to know the difference between connotation and denotation, between "subjective" and "objective" arguments, between "fact" and "opinion," between a main idea and its parts, between the concrete and the abstract, and so forth.

One result of decoding/analytic literacy for everyone was a new industry condensing and rewriting English classics into short pieces with simple words and short sentences. The *Reader's Digest*, for example, quickly became a major industry, and a rather astounding number of bestselling books were produced to teach the average person how to read—from Ezra Pound's *How to Read* (1931) to Mortimer Adler's *How to Read a Book* (1940). Adler's book was a national bestseller for over a year.

During decoding/analytic literacy, the number of American authors added to the booklists of English classes also increased. Early in the nineteenth century, American writers had started a revolt against the literary traditions of Great Britain. Edgar Allan Poe, Walt Whitman, Mark Twain, Emily Dickinson, William Carlos Williams, and many others had called for the use of common speech in literature and for new topics based on the American experience. This revolt continued into decoding/analytic literacy, when American literature started being offered as a course, usually in the eleventh grade.

Different ways of reading and different books to read eventually became different tracks and courses, and these tracks and courses sorted students inside schools, creating within the school program inequalities in race, ethnicity, social class, and gender (Wheelock 1992). Many students were pushed out, especially during the secondary school years. In fact, prior to the 1950s, many public high schools were proud of their large dropout rates because these rates were supposedly a clear sign of how intellectually "tough" their school was. But these "pushed out" students, who were the status symbols of schools in the 1920s and 1930s, became the "dropout" problems of the 1950s and the 1960s. From the 1960s onward, schools began experimenting with keeping all students in school through high school. The commitment of decoding and analytical literacy to bring all students into K–12 schools eventually extended to colleges, particularly through the G.I. Bills of World War II (1940s) and the Korean War (1950s).

The fifth difference between recitation literacy and decoding literacy was the treatment of language as an object to be analyzed into objective parts. Recitation literacy studied language as a transparent medium for delivering the nation's cultural heritage and for developing the character of readers. Decoding/analytic literacy treated language as a visible, opaque object which could be segmented into parts, separate from the responses of readers and from the intentions of the author. Recitation literacy emphasized the processes of elocution that made oral delivery visible, but decoding literacy emphasized language parts, "objective" methods of analysis, and a language about language:

> Fundamental to comprehension and composition in writing is the ability to analyze language as a system of bits and pieces in patterns. This analysis requires the use of metalanguage used to dissect language as an artifact. (Olson 1984)

This language about language included a body of knowledge about traditional, structural, and transformational grammars (Chomsky 1957; Chomsky 1965; Hunt 1965; O'Donnell, Griffith, and Norris 1967; Mellon 1969; O'Hare 1975); about reading as rules of phonology; and about text-level analysis (Robinson et al. 1990, 75). One essential change in decoding/analytic literacy was that a literal reading was distinguished from a reading of metaphors and figures of speech. Figures of speech were no longer considered a source for literal readings.

David Bartholomae has argued that these notions of the "objectivity" of text and the "objective reading levels" of readers produced a publication industry designed to match books with the "reading levels" of various types of readers. He gives as one example the work of Ruth Strang, one of Gray's students, who reported that an adult African American busperson ("N.T.") who had read *Mein Kampf,* Wells's *Outline of History,* Coon's *Measuring Ethiopia,* and Voltaire's *Candide* over a month or more had made "no attempt to separate his summary of what the author said from his own comments" (Strang 1942, 53). Strang concludes that this reader needs "help in getting a more adequate idea of what he reads ... For what does it profit N.T. to read if he gains from his reading only erroneous ideas?" (Strang 1942, 51). In other words, N.T. was judged not to be a competent reader because he inserted his ideas into the reading. Therefore, N.T. needed to be matched with different books at his proper level. Books at his level are presumably those N.T. would not need to comment on because the meaning was so obvious.

Literature, too, became an objective form to be analyzed and segmented. In 1917, influential Russian formalist Viktor Schlovsky published "Art as Device," which asserted that literary works were objects and that art was primarily structure or device, not a message (Eagleton 1983, vii). From the work of Schlovsky and others, decoding/analytic literacy created a literary language which dissected works into literature and nonliterature; into different traditions and historical periods; into different types of works and different types of heroes, narrators, symbols, and figures of speech; into a separation of linguistics from literary analysis; into a separation of rhetoric and literature—eventually separating linguistics and rhetoric from many English departments.

Shakespeare, Milton, and Matthew Arnold's other Class I works were still privileged during decoding literacy, but now these works were read/analyzed by formalists, not moralists, who, says Eagleton, "started out by seeing the literary work as a more or less arbitrary assemblage of 'devices'" and ended up defining a literary reading as an analysis of language forms—forms such as paradox, irony, image, sound, symbol, rhythm, meter, rhyme, metaphor, and character contrast (Eagleton 1983, 3).

The New Criticism of decoding/analytic literacy created a language for literacy in which one had to reject the "affective fallacy," in which meaning came from the reader's subjective feelings; the "intentional fallacy," in which meanings came from the "facts" of the author's life and private letters (see Wimsatt 1954, 3–18, 21–39)[5]; and what we might call the "message fallacy," in which the meaning of a literary work was assumed to be captured by paraphrases of a text's meaning (see Frye 1957, 77).[6]

This rejection of the information, the paraphrase, and the explicit moral messages of literary works was based on the claim that the function of various literary devices was to deform, estrange, violate, and defamiliarize ordinary language to such an extent that a literary meaning was "so ambiguous that it could not be debased and applied to any practical or dogmatic end" (Scholes 1992, 149).

The message fallacy insisted that good literature could not be a single, certain meaning. *Finnegans Wake,* for example, is literature because it simply cannot be read as a jigsaw puzzle in which all of the information is apparent at the end, and because it challenges us to learn to live with ambiguity. Eagleton says, "If you approach me at a bus stop and murmur, 'Thou still unravished bride of quietness,' then I am instantly aware that I am in the presence of the literary" (Eagleton 1983, 2). What social purposes were served by this approach to literature? Some literary critics argued that for college prep students, the complexities of the modern world required that human beings be capable of tolerating ambiguity in meaning and avoiding the hubris of certainty in meaning (Empson 1930). Of course, this uncertain meaning, reserved for college prep students alone, did not mean uncertain form. Form was always objective and clear.

This approach to literature served professional needs to protect literature from science. Literature needed to privilege the certainty and objectivity of form and the uncertainty and ambiguity of meaning because, according to I. A. Richards, the information of science was threatening to displace the authority of literature (Richards 1948). Wimsatt and Brooks insisted that "there could be no conflict for the good reason that there was no common ground on which science and poetry (properly understood) . . . could meet" because literature had certainty of form and science had certainty of meaning (Wimsatt and Brooks 1957, 626). Eventually, Richards's fear of information and paraphrase led him to privilege poetry as a "purer" literary form than either the novel or the short story, both of which Richards feared might have clear meanings, and led Wellek and Warren to restrict literature to fiction, which did not have a commitment to anything in the "real" world, as did science.

The separation of literature from physical science did not mean that literature was "unscientific." First, there was, as noted before, objective form. Second, Northrop Frye, the leading literary theorist during decoding literacy, claimed that literary criticism "is as coherent and progressive as the study of science," but, he added, that "the main principles of which are as yet unknown to us" (Frye 1957, 10–11). In the absence of these main principles, decoding and analytic literacy produced numerous literary forms focusing on types of writing (novel, poem, short story), types of heroes, cultural categories (American literature, English literature, literature of the Middle Ages), types of plots, and instances of metaphor, irony, and other literary devices. These kinds of topics, common in secondary school English courses into the 1970s, always claimed to be above immediate political issues and to be focused on universals of the human spirit.

This approach to literature as form was perfectly suited for a period in which English teachers wanted to make their work more "scientific," more "objective," more removed from metaphysics and the morality of recitation literacy—indeed, more Cubberly-like, more Taylorized. This objectification of literacy not only separated literature from physical science, it also separated literature from politics. Bruce Franklin has argued that this "scientism," "objectivity," and emphasis on form over content was perfectly designed for a profession wishing to ignore the political turmoil of the Russian Revolution of 1917, the rising proletarian literature and culture of the 1930s, the union movement of the 1920s and 1930s, the depression of the 1930s, the Harlem Renaissance of the 1930s, and the McCarthy period of the 1950s (Franklin 1970). One might add to this list the riots in African American communities in the 1960s and, finally, the dissent over Vietnam in the 1970s. To a very large degree, separation-from-the-world became the disputed norm for the teaching profession during decoding/analytic literacy, as professional groups attempted to protect themselves from public dissent and to maintain their tenuous professional status. By the end of decoding/analytic literacy, the separation of English from the world was no longer possible.

In the early days of decoding/analytic literacy, the separation of literature from messages left English without much of a subject for vocational and general students who, said administrators and school boards, wanted reading materials to help them in life adjustment and in vocational preparation. In the early days of decoding literacy, English courses for vocational and general students focused on guidance for everyday problems, including units on "Good Rules for Living," "Developing a Pleasing Personality," "Shame over Lowly Origins," biographies of canonical writers with "moral fiber" (Emerson, Milton, and so forth), and stories showing the moral imperative of history and democracy (*The Frontier, Obligations of a Democracy, War and Peace*). A few texts were added to the general English course to focus on specific vocational needs, including units on "How to Get a Job," "Good Work Habits," and Horatio Alger success stories showing how vocational skills and hard work paid off. By the 1950s, even most of these vocational and general English courses were focusing on reading of the parts—plot, setting, conflict, main character, genre.

This separation of reading for information from reading for a literary experience—always a tension throughout decoding/analytic literacy, particularly in secondary schools—eventually contributed to the separation of the International Reading Association from NCTE; to the separation of the Teachers of Speakers of Other Languages from NCTE; and finally to the separation of reading as a field from literary and humanistic studies. It took the whole language movement and its supporters to help establish once again some connections between the reading community and humanistic studies, and this happened because, by the end of decoding/analytic literacy, it was becoming obvious to everyone that even reading the newspapers these days is an interpretive activity. Simply segmenting works into parts was no longer enough.

Like reading, composition studies during decoding/analytic literacy began to drift away from literary and humanistic studies. Decoding/analytic literacy institutionalized in K–12 public schools a model of the essay adopted by the Royal Society of London in 1667 and elaborated on by George Campbell in *The Philosophy of Rhetoric* in 1776 (see Crowley 1990, 14, 55, 140–41). This model called for conciseness (do not waste words = efficiency), clarity (simplify the message), logic (ideas should have a rational connection), and no stylistic turns (see Sprat [1667] 1972). Notice that this way of writing is quite different from the forms celebrated in literature. Unlike compositions in recitation literacy, compositions in decoding/analytic literacy were silent events, focused primarily on the "product," not the audience, and certainly not the voice and elocution of the author. Says Crowley, "Indeed, some current-traditional textbooks frankly acknowledged students' nonidentity by insisting that they erase any textual marks of their presence, such as first-person pronouns" (Crowley 1990, 151). This model of the essay was, in fact, a model of the process of empirical science: start with a topic sentence or hypothesis, eliminate the first person, relate this hypothesis to prior knowledge in a novel way, present the implications of this topic sentence or hypothesis, present the tests or evidence supporting these implications, and then present the conclusion, possibly with an alternative hypothesis (see Olson 1994). Of course, in this definition of a composition, all that literary talk about an "unravished bride" simply did not belong.

Throughout decoding/analytic literacy there was a well-organized effort to keep composition studies in a relatively unimportant position within English studies. In colleges, the teaching of composition was assigned to low-paid graduate students, and literature courses were reserved for the full professors. This approach would not have worked, of course, without a theory which turned composition into a simple field of "techniques," requiring only low-level work. E. D. Hirsch was one of those who reiterated such a technical theory toward the end of decoding/analytic literacy, when pressure was building to do something about the position of composition in English studies:

> I infer that there are universal stylistic features in all good prose of every kind and that these features of good style are all reducible to a single principle: One prose style is better than another when it communicates the same meanings as the other does but requires less effort from the reader. (Hirsch 1977, 9)

Hirsch is arguing that composition, unlike literary studies, is a technical assignment to attain efficient communication and that a standard of writing quality and thus, readability could be learned in a few days:

> Our results to date suggest that an assessor can accurately score relative readability after a few days of practice. . . . This justifies a guarded optimism about the future of composition research and about its effectiveness in raising the competence of teachers and writers alike. . . . (Hirsch 1977, 190–91)

From the point of view of many composition theorists, Hirsch was trying to do to composition instruction what Frederick Taylor and Cubberly did to schooling—trivialize it by standardizing it, by turning it into a collection of techniques, and by destroying its connections to humanistic studies. Hirsch-like attitudes clearly succeeded in keeping writing programs marginalized in the literature emphasis of English classes throughout most of decoding/analytic literacy. Most K–12 studies reported that students did very little writing (A. Applebee 1981; Squire and R. Applebee 1968).

The sixth difference between recitation and decoding/analytic literacy is the way in which the two periods organized schools. Recitation literacy was embedded in a highly decentralized school system held together by shared values of national cohesion. Decoding/analytic literacy was embedded in a highly centralized system with regulations for establishing grade levels, for sequences of textbooks, for selecting tests for each grade level, and for describing sequences of instruction for each subject. These regulations were often the only cement that held together the many new intellectual communities of decoding/analytic literacy. I have already mentioned the tension between what composition programs tried to do and what literature programs tried to do. Because schools added new courses and new departments when requests were made, high schools became what Powell called the shopping mall high school in K–12 (Powell, Farrar, and Cohen 1985), and colleges became what Gerald Graff called "Let's-make-a-deal" institutions (see G. Graff 1987, 125–43). Schooling during decoding/analytic literacy was managed day-to-day by bureaucratic forms and processes, not issues of content. But, of course, this way of managing curriculum had an impact on content.

This centralized, bureaucratic pattern of school organization was promoted by Ellwood P. Cubberly, the first dean of Stanford's School of Education, who proposed in his 1916 text *Public School Administration* that K–12 schools should be like the factories of decoding/analytic literacy, complete with assembly lines of conditioned behavior. Cubberly's book, which George Counts called "the most widely read and influential book on school administration of our generation" (qtd. in Callahan 1962, 96), called for school decisions to be centralized in the administrative staff, for teachers to be defined as supervised workers, and for students to be defined as the products of a school-factory system.

One obvious result of this increased centralization was the dramatic increase in administrators. In their 1890 Middletown study, Robert and Helen Lynd found that only the superintendent did no teaching, but by 1924 they found "a galaxy of principals, assistant principals, supervisors of special subjects, directors of vocational education and home economics, deans, attendance officers, and clerks, who do no teaching" (Lynd and Lynd 1929, 210). The same pattern has been observed in colleges and universities.

Another result of centralization was the introduction of movable chairs and desks in K–12 schools (Cuban 1984). Movable desks made it possible for centralized management to vary class sizes and to establish classrooms wherever and whenever necessary. This change to movable desks did not necessarily produce more variation in seating configurations because teachers often followed the practice of marking "the floor where the furniture 'belonged'" (Mayher and Brouse 1986, 619). Some researchers have interpreted this behavior by teachers as evidence of teachers' resistance to change and innovation in curriculum, but it appears that for many teachers this marking practice may have been a last ditch effort to prevent increases in their class sizes.

Cubberly's centralization and the school-as-factory model would not have worked without some enthusiasm for centralized scientific management among education leaders. As early as 1911, the National Education Association's Department of Superintendents had expressed its enthusiasm for scientific management by charging the Committee on the Economy of Time "to eliminate nonessentials from the elementary curriculum" (K. Goodman et al. 1988, 14). This committee produced papers on standardized vocabulary by Robinson Jones, on minimum reading rates by S. A. Courtis, on graded texts by J. H. Hoshinson, and on principles of teaching reading by William S. Gray. This last paper contributed greatly to the development of basal reading materials (K. Goodman et al. 1988, 14–15) and ultimately to the development of teacher manuals to turn teachers into routine workers:

> A basic reader is really one part of a system for teaching reading. This system includes the basic books themselves, the workbooks that go with them, and the teachers' manual, which tells what to do with the textbooks, what to do with the workbooks, and also tells all the other activities a teacher should go through in order to do a complete job of teaching reading. (K. Goodman et al. 1988, 20–21)

The July 1912 convention of the National Education Association featured Taylor-like sessions on "By What Standards or Tests Shall the Efficiency of a School or System of Schools Be Measured?" "Progress in Standardizing the Measurement of Composition," "Standards of Measuring the Efficiency of Normal-School Students," and "The Principals of Scientific Management Applied to Teaching Music in the Public Schools" (NEA 1912). From 1916 to 1983, Cubberly's school-as-factory theory produced a continuing series of innovations in recordkeeping, machine-scored testing, specialists at various levels of management, and, by the 1960s, MBOs—Management by Behavioral Objectives:

> Educational objectives pinned to predictable, measurable student performance would offer a much-needed basis for measuring program cost against program effectiveness. Such cost accounting, in turn, would promote more effective allocation of existing resources among competing educational programs. (Lessinger and Allen 1969, 137)

Management by Behavioral Objectives grew out of the work of Franklin Babbit, professor of educational administration at the University of Chicago, who forty-five years earlier specified 821 educational objectives for K–12 schools. His list ranged from "ability to use language in all ways" to "ability to care for the hair and scalp" and "ability to care for the nails" (Applebee 1974, 83). By the 1960s, the care of the hair, scalp, and nails was no longer on the list of school objectives, and in its place were hundreds, maybe thousands, of small, measurable objectives for English instruction—all a monument to the ideas of Ellwood P. Cubberly and Cubberly's inspiration, Frederick Taylor.

Frederick Taylor's principles of "scientific management" and Cubberly's system for managing curriculum were also quite compatible with the measurement principles of Edward L. Thorndike, who argued that the teaching of reading and writing should be organized around "the essential elements" and that "whatever exists at all, exists in some measure" (Thorndike 1918, 16). Thorndike's book *An Introduction to the Theory of Mental and Social Measurement* (1904), which was called by Cubberly "the beginning of a new era in the study of educational problems" (Cubberly 1924, 186), called for teachers to break tasks into sequenced parts (Thorndike's law of readiness); to repeat each part frequently and sequentially (Thorndike's law of exercise); to present feedback in the form of a grade, a check, a smiling face, a star, or some other form of instructional M&M™ (Thorndike's law of effect); and to test things the same way they are taught (Thorndike's law of identical elements) (K. Goodman et al. 1988, 12–13). Thorndike's approach was perfectly suited to Cubberly's movement.

The shift to decoding/analytic literacy's centralized, objective testing using multiple-choice items and machine scoring was a ten-year process which culminated in the Army Alpha test of 1916–1917.[7] At first, there were a few experiments with analytic scales to measure writing achievement through the judgment of teachers, but teacher judgments were severely criticized for unreliability and unfairness in the sorting of students. One study showed a difference of 35–40 points on a 100-point scale among 142 different teachers across the country (Starch and Eliot 1912). These findings, plus the growing movement of scientific management, gave a high priority to new "objective," bias-free centralized approaches to assessment. The time was ripe for multiple-choice items for measuring English. According to Samuelson (1987, 118) and Madaus (1993), Frederick Kelly invented the multiple-choice item in 1914, and by 1916, the Army Alpha, a group-administered, multiple-choice test, was developed and ready to be given to draftees nationwide. By 1926, even the College Entrance Examination Board had adopted multiple-choice testing (Madaus 1993, 19), and in 1937, the College Board dropped the writing component of the Standard Achievement Test (Angoff and Dyer 1971).

Decoding/analytic literacy, through its emphasis on decoding unfamiliar, anonymous texts and its centralization of information, served the functional needs of the centralized city market, the centralized factory, centralized government, and the increasingly anonymous modes of discourse through which individuals interacted (Braverman 1974). Centralization and standardization were pervasive in society. They shaped the production of knowledge, of automobiles, and, yes, even of telephones. The Bell telephone would have disappeared, says Bruno Latour, if the Bell Company had not purchased Western Electric and made it the exclusive manufacturer for all of its telephone hardware (Latour 1987, 189).

By the early 1900s, the anonymous, modern corporation had become a recognized social entity which one could sue or tax—just as the state had once sued or taxed the family and other face-to-face groups in another age. Modern corporations, by relying upon centralized, anonymous texts directed at unfamiliar and often "standardized" audiences, expanded markets in all parts of the country. Even food production became increasingly anonymous and centralized. For example, the amount of butter produced by individual farms fell from nearly 100 percent in 1879 to 75 percent in 1899 and to 20 percent by 1939 (Braverman 1974, 275). In other words, industrial economics turned social needs like food into a processed product made in centralized factories, then sold by centralized food brokers, and finally purchased by centralized markets. The consumers of these products were increasingly people who organized their labor through centralized unions and other institutions.

The anonymous, centralized nature of interactions during decoding/analytic literacy, at least when compared with interactions during recitation literacy, helped change the definition of minimum "reading" levels in society. During recitation literacy, the courts attempted to protect those who could not read the literal meaning of unfamiliar texts. But in 1913, the courts ruled that "one who signs a contract is bound to exercise reasonable care and prudence to inform himself of its contents" (*Shores-Mueller Co. v. Lonning* 1913; qtd. in E. Stevens 1983, 78), and again in 1921, the court said the written contract overrode all prior oral negotiations (*Burns v. Spiker* 1921; qtd. in E. Stevens 1983, 78). These two court decisions were adopting decoding/analytic literacy as the legal definition of "reading"—a definition which legally required that people be able to decode for themselves the literal meaning of unfamiliar texts:

> Protection for the illiterate party to a contract became increasingly difficult within the context of an ideal free market economy. . . . During most of the nineteenth century, courts seemed to make an effort to preserve the rights of illiterate contracting parties and to protect these persons against abuses stemming from the inability to read and write. By the end of the nineteenth century, however, the emphasis had shifted. . . . Rather, it had become clear that the illiterate person was bound to inform himself and to take the initiative in securing a correct reading of the contract. (E. Stevens 1983, 79–80)

People were required not only to read the language of the law, but to read a *new* language of the law. By 1916, we find in legal discourse a style of logic and social practice quite different from that which was typical of legal discourse during most of recitation literacy. We find that "every phrase is technical and legal to an extent that often defies translation" (Johns 1904, iv), and we also find that "the struggle for clarity, the development of a specialist field . . . are constant themes in the analysis of the influence of writing on law" (Goody 1986, 147). This emphasis in law during decoding literacy on exactness of statement, clarity of definition, and a vocabulary of specialists was, of course, quite compatible with trends in reading, writing, factory production, and information processing throughout society.

In factories, the trends toward standardization required new forms of production and new systems for regulating production processes: "The development of automatic industrial controls from the 1920s on reflected the shift to continuous-process production in many industries and the emergence of systems-control methods" (Noble 1984, 59). Shaiken (1984) has shown that before the turn of the century, skilled workers had considerable power in the production process, but after Frederick Taylor's centralization and segmentation of functions, workers lost that power and became the interchangeable parts of a machine. Taylor's centralization and control of knowledge in the "new" factory eventually led to the development of thousands of electronic devices for storing, combining, and centralizing information. The UNIVAC, a data-processing computer, "was [first] sold to the U.S. Bureau of the Census in 1951, to CBS in 1953, and to General Electric in 1954" (Noble 1984, 51); likewise an analog computer for controlling automatic production was sold to Texaco's Port Arthur refinery in 1959, to Monsanto's Louisiana ammonia plant in 1960, and to B. F. Goodrich's vinyl plastic facility in Calvert, Kentucky, in 1960 (Noble 1984, 60).

In summary, the shift of economic activity away from the home, neighborhoods, and fragmented urban areas to centralized cities and factories meant that workers needed to be able to get literal, basic meanings from unfamiliar, anonymous materials in order to survive in a large corporation, a mass army, a large factory, and a mass communication system where newly printed materials appeared daily. To meet this social need for "basic reading," decoding/analytic literacy needed a model of mind which fit decoding/analytic literacy's assumptions. John Locke's *tabula rasa* model of mind had been an adequate foundation for recitation literacy because it focused the study of mind first on the patterns of knowledge imprinted on the mind through recitation and experience and second on the metaphysics of an internal "reasoner" or "writer on the mind"—what Gilbert Ryle called *the ghost in the machine* (Ryle 1949). This model of mind privileged a psychology of introspection (Wundt, Creighton, and Titchener 1896).

However, decoding/analytic literacy required a model of mind which rejected the metaphysics of an internal reasoner and which focused on observable, measurable, manageable data, and external behavior, not internal introspection. John Watson (1925) and later B. F. Skinner (1957) provided such a model of mind in behaviorism. In one sense, behaviorism ignored the mind altogether, and this was probably a good strategy at that time for a teaching profession which desired to proclaim its scientific status and its indifference to the political tensions of the period. And, of course, behaviorism worked as long as one was content with objective parts and "basic reading."

In the sixty-plus years between 1916 and 1983, the evidence suggests that the general population showed an overall increase in scores on tests that measured the decoding/analytic comprehension of unfamiliar materials. For example, Tuddenham (1948) reports that the scores of draftees increased 33 percentage points on the Army Alpha test between World War I and World War II (Kaestle et al. 1991, 85). During World War I, only about 45 percent of the recruits could read at what we have come to identify as a nine-year-old (or third-grade) level on the Army Alpha tests, but by World War II, that figure had risen to about 65 percent, and by the Vietnam War (Tyler 1990), to about 80 percent. These levels of reading are equally impressive when comparisons are made with other nations. From the data on a common reading test given in fifteen nations, it appears that the American educational system enables nearly three-fourths of its young people to attain a reading level that most other nations achieve only with a very select group (see Bracey's [1991] review of those not in school in other countries).

In 1992, over seventy years after *The Cardinal Principles of Secondary Education* (Kingsley 1918), the National Adult Literacy Survey (NALS) concluded that 95 percent of young American adults ages 21 to 25 could read at the fourth-grade level and about 80 percent at the eighth-grade level. In other words, for the general population, the goals of decoding literacy had nearly been achieved (see Kirsch and Jungeblut 1986; and also Kirsch et al. 1993, xiv–xv). Even during the hullabaloo about the SAT declines in the 1970s, children in grades 3 through 6 were scoring higher in literal comprehension than they had in nearly thirty years (Schrag 1986, 297).

These gains, however, were no longer adequate by the 1980s. Higher-order thinking skills were becoming essential for all students, but decoding/analytic literacy had not attempted higher-order thinking skills for *all* students. In addition, despite the gains of black students on tests emphasizing the skills of literal comprehension, the gap between white and black scores was still depressingly large in tests of higher literacy. By the 1960s, the problem of equal opportunity for all had become a visible, national issue:

> For without being an alarmist, I must say that when one considers the total situation that has been developing in the Negro city slums since World War II, one has reason to worry about the future. The building up of a mass of unemployed and frustrated Negro youth in congested areas of a city is a social phenomenon that may be compared to the piling up of inflammable material in an empty building in a city block. Potentialities for trouble—indeed possibilities of disaster—are surely there. (Conant 1961, 18)

In 1983, the publication of *A Nation at Risk* (National Commission on Excellence in Education 1983) opened up public debate once again about which standards of minimum literacy should be driving public policy in education. At the 1986 Carnegie Forum on Education and the Economy, the Berkeley Roundtable on the International Economy (BRIE) warned that survival in world markets depended upon a workforce with an education broad enough to enable workers to move flexibly among technological generations, adding that this kind of education is not specifically vocational and goes beyond the behaviorism and objectivity of decoding/analytic literacy's version of literal comprehension. In a similar message, *U.S. News & World Report* reported that, although conventional illiteracy—the inability to read a simple message in any language—had virtually disappeared in the United States, functional illiteracy—the inability to read and write at a level required to function in society—appeared to be increasing (Wellborn 1982). The national push for a new definition of minimum literacy was beginning.

In summary, decoding/analytic literacy was introduced as a new standard of literacy by a national reform report (see Kingsley 1918), was embedded in a network of national tests, was institutionalized in a factory model of schools, and was taught through a behaviorist model of the mind. Decoding/analytic literacy accomplished three important goals. First, it taught us a great deal about the forms of language—such things as new kinds of grammar and new types of literary texts, the way these forms could be separated from meaning, and the usefulness of operational definitions. Second, decoding/analytic literacy helped us enable most citizens to attain a basic reading level for handling texts in their everyday lives. Third, it introduced the concept of "objectivity" in mass reading by limiting the influence of author intention ("intentional fallacy") and the subjective responses of readers ("affective fallacy").

The history of decoding/analytic literacy teaches us a number of interesting principles about how literacy works. First, it reminds us that each shift in the nation's dominant form of literacy has been a battleground. Gerald Graff has observed, "If history, as it has been said, is a story in which the winners bury the losers, the modern curriculum could be said to be the story in which the battlefield is buried" (G. Graff 1992, 125). Our dominant form of literacy is always the product of an explicit public debate and contention, often an unacknowledged one. And the choices between one form of literacy and another are frequently implicit in other decisions, often located in obscure resolutions of technological, economic, and political differences. Finally, of course, the ultimate consensus is not the only one possible.

Second, the history of decoding/analytic literacy reminds us that the student, as well as the form of literacy, is a social construction. Recitation literacy defined reading as the memorization word-for-word of a preassigned or precomposed text. Imagine recitation readers who found themselves in the classes of decoding/analytic teachers who expected them to paraphrase unfamiliar materials on-the-spot, or imagine decoding readers who found themselves in the classes of recitation teachers who asked them to write down word-for-word from memory the materials they claimed to have read. In other words, reading and readers are social and historical constructions, and mismatches between readers and school literacy are likely.

David Bartholomae has noted that, during this period, "the problem of reading was thus conceived of as a problem residing primarily in books (they were too hard) and in readers (they were poorly prepared) and not in a system of production and distribution" (Bartholomae 1990, 14). Bartholomae's challenge, among other things, suggests that we could approach the problem of reading as a problem of created and encouraged opportunities in the culture: Are books generally available to all people? In other words, new opportunities in the culture could change our view of what reading is. If materials were generally available, for example, then we might have to worry less about our lesson sequences.

Third, the history of decoding/analytic literacy reminds us that competing forms of English can share a common model of literacy. In the 1960s, Chapter 1 English classes thought English should give more attention to the analysis of basic skills, and Project English classes thought English should give more attention to the analysis of literary form. Both were committed to a form of literacy in which language is an object for analysis, a series of devices and strategies operating like a machine with a hierarchy of parts, devoid of patterns of intention shaped by cultural interactions.

By the 1980s and the shift away from decoding literacy, English classes were struggling with a new conception of English in which cultural interactions were primary. Richard Lanham, for one, argued that decoding/analytic literacy's "dogma of clarity…is based on a false theory of knowledge; its scorn of ornament, on a misleading taxonomy of style" (Lanham 1974, 19). He suggested that "motive has always been the question of questions for Freshman Composition" (Lanham 1974, 134). Issues of motive obviously take us to purpose, social interactions, and culture, and, thus, Lanham's criticism of decoding/analytic literacy opens up the possibilities of a new standard of minimum literacy based on inferential comprehension and critical translations.

After nearly eighty years of drills, slot filling, and the listing of parts, a new standard of literacy and a new model of English are beginning to emerge. This new standard of literacy is expected to deal with a whole range of new social problems. By the end of decoding/analytic literacy, there were strong voices arguing that the old factories of standardized, routined labor could no longer produce the products necessary for a postmodern world. Furthermore, decoding/analytic literacy could no longer produce the meaning necessary for one living in a postmodern world. A new form of literacy was once again emerging as a social necessity.

The descriptions presented here of literacy teaching during decoding/analytic literacy are, I think, generally true. That is, decoding/analytic literacy was pervasive—yes, pervasive but not exclusive, generally true but not always true in all places. There have always been places of resistance, places of difference. These differences began to shape some of the new demands for a new definition of literacy. English classes—which during recitation literacy shifted from Greek and Latin models of literature to English models, and which during decoding/analytic literature shifted from exclusively English models to a mixture of English and American authors—now faced the issue of admitting to the core literature program such different voices as Toni

Morrison, Alice Walker, and Annie Dillard, to name just three. It took a special vote of the California State Board of Education in March 1994 to restore these three authors' works to the list of stories read in California's assessment of reading. This issue of divergent voices is only one of the many new issues of language and culture which now face the English teaching profession. These new issues are all being defined within an overall national movement for a new form of dominant literacy in public policy.

Notes

1. The English committee, established by the Committee of Ten in 1894 to define English as a course in K–12 schools, specifically established English as a subject in K–12 schools and named literature one of its parts. In addition, it specified the purposes of English:

> The main objects of the teaching of English in schools seem to be two: (1) to enable the pupil to understand the expressed thoughts of others and to give expression to the thoughts of his own; and (2) to cultivate a taste for reading, to give the pupil some acquaintance with good literature, and to furnish him with the means of extending that acquaintance. (Committee of Ten 1894; qtd. in Applebee 1974, 33)

2. The dispute between high school and college teachers within the growing English teaching community centered on whether colleges and universities were going to prescribe what high schools taught through an examination system requiring specific books, or whether colleges were merely going to advise the high schools through an accreditation system which recognized the many different roles high schools were expected to play. As a result of this dispute, college and high school teachers who supported an advisory approach organized the National Council of Teachers of English in Chicago in 1911, electing Fred Newton Scott from the University of Michigan as president and Emma J. Breck, English department head at Oakland High School, Oakland, California, as first vice president. This tension between a concern for local decision making focused on student needs and a concern for national standards continued to occupy English teaching professionals throughout the period of decoding/literal comprehension.

3. Between 1915 and 1919, the NEA Committee on the Economy of Time in Education issued a series of papers on minimum reading rates by S.A. Courtis, on graded texts by J. H. Hoshinson, and on principles of teaching reading by William S. Gray. The new national testing project was led by Edward Thorndike.

4. Because recitation was an in-class performance which could only be monitored, evaluated, and critiqued by those who were in class—that is, the teachers themselves—recitation was more teacher-centered than the Cubberly model of centralized curriculum.

5. "The design or intention of the author is neither available nor desirable as a standard for judging the success of a work of literary art" (Wimsatt 1954, 3).

6. Frye says that "the literal basis of meaning in poetry can only be its letters, its inner structure, and its interlocking motifs…All paraphrases abstract a secondary or outward meaning" (Frye 1957, 77).

7. See Chapman for a description of the bringing together of army and school psychologists (Chapman 1979, 119–41; noted in D. Resnick and Resnick 1985, 19).

6 The Transition to a New Standard of Literacy: 1960–1983

> The problem is not the inability to read … but the inability to read at a high enough level to function in an information-based society. We probably need literacy more now than we've ever needed it before. (qtd. in S. Taylor 1987, 29)

In 1989, at the Charlottesville Summit, when U.S. governors called for new standards of minimum literacy for all students, many commentators interpreted this call for new standards as a finding that the schools had failed to teach the traditional and basic literacy (decoding/analytic literacy) to most students attending school. However, there are at least five sources of data showing that the socioeconomic groups which have been in school since 1916 have had relatively stable reading rates and that more and more students who were formerly not in school, and who presumably could not read, have entered school between 1916 and 1983 and joined the growing number of people who have achieved decoding/analytic literacy. Let me repeat: During decoding/analytic literacy, decoding or basic reading achievement increased throughout the general population attending school. There is a minority of the population who need basic literacy desperately. But many of them have not been in school.

First, numerous tests of decoding/analytic literacy between 1940 and 1970 reported more and more people achieving literal comprehension in their reading (Farr, Fay, and Negley 1978). In 1982, the U.S. Bureau of the Census, which administered the English Language Proficiency Survey to 3,400 adults ages 20 and over, from a broad geographic and age distribution, reported that 87 percent of adult Americans scored above the functionally literate level (a score of twenty or more right answers on a twenty-six item review of information typically found on government forms and in descriptions of literacy standards based on literal comprehension) (U.S. Department of Education 1986). Between 1957 and 1971, the Iowa Tests of Educational Development, the SCAT, the tests of Science Research Associates, and the Metropolitan Achievement Tests all reported "general improvement" in reading comprehension (Stedman and Kaestle 1987, 19–20). In fact, the youngest cohort, those ages 16 to 24, is "the most literate" on these tests, suggesting that recent students in school are more literate in decoding/analytic literacy than were earlier ones (Stedman and Kaestle 1987, 35).[1]

Similarly, the 1993 National Adult Literacy Survey (NALS) reported that over 80 percent of young adults in the U.S. could perform the basic decoding literacy tasks of making matches between the text and information given, preparing responses to information, locating the time and place of a meeting on a form, calculating gross-pay-to-date from a paycheck stub, and locating information on a graph (Kirsch et al. 1993, 113–14, and see description of levels on 74–89). Finally, the Adult Performance Level survey, which in 1974 tested adults ages 18 and over on their basic skills in the five areas of occupational knowledge, consumer economics, community resources, health, government, and law, found that eighty percent of these adults were judged to be functionally literate (APL 1977).[2]

In addition, by the 1980s, most states were reporting above-average results on norm-referenced tests of decoding literacy in reading. Of course, these norm-referenced tests had defined "average" on the basis of sampling averages derived ten years earlier when people were generally reading at lower levels (Cannell 1987). The fact is "it takes a higher score now to hit the fiftieth percentile rank than it did in the previous decades" (Linn, Graue, and Sanders 1990; summarized in Berliner 1992). Berliner reports that the trends in SAT, MAT, and CTBS all show composite achievement at an all-time high point (Berliner 1992, 17). To eliminate the "Lake Wobegon Effect"—in which all states scored above average because of the increasing levels of decoding/analytic literacy in the general population—many testing companies renormed their tests in the late 1980s.

The recent redefinitions of reading are a second indicator of growing levels of literacy. In 1984, the National Assessment of Educational Progress (NAEP) acknowledged for the first time that different types of reading had different cognitive requirements. NAEP had acknowledged before that reading information was different from reading a poem, but they treated both a literary reading and a nonliterary reading as generic. In 1984, NAEP decided to say that the different score levels for reading—rudimentary, basic, intermediate, adept, and advanced—were qualitatively different acts and that basic reading was the old, decoding level, which is essentially bit-by-bit reading, and that adept reading is interpretive, which is close to the new standard which society now desires.

The NAEP attempt to define reading levels in a functional manner, one year after *A Nation at Risk,* was not a unique event. In 1992, in a report describing the literacy of those either getting unemployment insurance or entering a job-training program, the Educational Testing Service (ETS) proposed five levels of prose literacy, five levels of document literacy (bus schedules, charts), and five levels of quantitative literacy (Kirsch et al. 1993). ETS reported that 21 percent of the adults sampled were at the lowest level in prose literacy, 23 percent were at the lowest level in document literacy, and 22 percent were at the lowest level of quantitative literacy. In other words, almost 80 percent of the nation's adults were above the lowest level in all three areas. In addition, ETS found a direct correlation between education and literacy levels.

A similar shift in definitions of literacy took place in the preschool policies of the National Association for the Education of Young Children (NAEYC), which, in 1985, was stressing bit-by-bit, sequential learning (first objects, then letters), but one year later was proposing a more complicated, integrated approach (pictures, stories, words, and writing):

> Children need years of play experiences with real objects and events to enable them to understand the meaning of *symbols such as pictures and stories. . . .*
> *Pictures and stories should be used frequently* to build upon children's real experiences . . . *Some 4-year-olds and most 5's display a growing interest in the functional aspects of written language, such as recognizing meaningful words and trying to write their own names. . . .* (qtd. in McGill-Franzen 1993, 113; emphasis in original)[3]

High school graduation rates are a third indicator of achievement of decoding/comprehension literacy. In 1869–1870, only 2 percent of the seventeen-year-olds received high school diplomas (National Center for Education Statistics 1993, 30), in 1944, 42.7 percent, and in 1970, nearly 77 percent (National Center for Education Statistics 1993, 55). The 30 percent not graduating by 1970 were, nevertheless, going to school longer. In 1910, 76.2 percent of the population over twenty-five years of age had completed five years or more of schooling, but in 1980, 96.7 percent had accomplished the same goal. Among those 25 to 29 years of age, only 0.7 percent had fewer than five years of schooling by 1980, suggesting that almost everyone by 1980 was attending school throughout the elementary years. In 1890, only 3.5 percent of the nation's seventeen-year-olds were graduating from high school (Snyder 1993, 55). By 1980, 68.7 percent of the total population of the U.S. had completed high school (Grant and Eiden 1982, 16). And by 1990, 75 percent were graduating (Snyder 1993, 55).

The results of SATs and intelligence tests are a fourth indicator of the achievement of decoding literacy. Berliner shows, for example, that on

Wechsler and Stanford-Binet I.Q. tests, often given to top college students, average intelligence went up, not down, from 1932 to 1978 (Berliner 1992, 7-A). He also shows that the number of students qualifying for the Advanced Placement test increased from 90,000 in 1978 to 324,000 in 1990, and in addition, he further shows that the percentage taking the test tripled among Asians, doubled among African Americans, and quadrupled among Hispanics (Berliner 1992, 13). Finally, Berliner shows that when students are matched by high school rank and gender, SAT scores have increased one-third of a standard deviation between 1975 and 1990 (Berliner 1992, 13-A). In summary, then, these four indicators suggest that the public schools in the U.S. have achieved the reading goals of decoding/analytic literacy for nearly all and have *not* sacrificed the college bound or anyone else to lower levels of achievement. The problem, once again, is that now a new standard of literacy is needed.

Let's return to the question of the various ways in which literacy has been defined. Throughout the period of decoding/analytic literacy, there had been changes in the nation's definitions of functional and minimum literacy: three or more years of school was the definition of "functional literacy" of the Civilian Conservation Corps in the 1930s; fourth grade was the army's definition in the 1940s (Folger and Nam 1967, 126); and sixth grade was the definition of the U.S. Bureau of the Census in 1952 (U.S. Bureau of the Census 1953, 6–10). By the 1970s, some researchers were suggesting that functional literacy was the twelfth grade (Carroll and Chall 1975, 8; Stedman and Kaestle 1987, 23).

By 1985, several reports were claiming that students needed "higher-order thinking skills," not just years of schooling. But what are "higher-order thinking skills"? The National Assessment of Educational Progress (in three assessments in 1981) reported that 72 percent of seventeen-year-olds could correctly answer literal comprehension items, but that these same students were not able to undertake "explanatory tasks and problem-solving strategies and critical thinking."[4] Beginning in the 1970s, five studies attempted to determine what thinking skills were required for modern life. The first study examined the ability of sixteen-year-olds to read to understand and to fill out application forms (L. Harris 1970); the second examined the ability of sixteen-year-olds to read three types of materials—telephone dialing and rate information, classified housing ads, and classified employment ads (L. Harris 1971); the third examined the ability of seventeen-year-olds to read work passages, graphic materials (charts, maps, pictures), forms, and reference materials (Gadway and Wilson 1976); the fourth examined the ability of sixteen-year-olds to read ads, legal documents, instructions, and listings. And the fifth, the Adult Performance Level project (APL 1977), examined what was called "functional competence" in writing, computation, problem solving, and reading (Stedman and Kaestle 1987, 28–29).

These studies had two major results. First, they raised questions about the way functional literacy was being defined, questioning the validity of some tests in the workplace and schools which classified professionals as illiterate. After examining the data in which a few but not many professionals were classified as illiterates, Stedman and Kaestle concluded that "many people who do their jobs competently might not be able to negotiate airline schedules, Medicaid applications, or miles-per-gallon calculations" (Stedman and Kaestle 1987, 30). Although apparently agreeing that decoding/literal comprehension was no longer an adequate standard, these studies left unanswered questions about how a new standard of literacy should be defined and what should be taught in K–12 schools.

One way to examine the question was to study workplace needs and school programs. Everyone agrees that, in the U.S., the workplace does have an impact on schools (see Figure 8 and Table 2 in Chapter 3). In the 1980s, Lauren Resnick, John Seely Brown, Allan Collins, the Secretary of Labor's Commission on Achieving Necessary Skills (SCANS), and the American Society for Training and Development (ASTD) began a series of studies on the relationship between what is taught in school and what one needs to know in the contemporary workplace. Lauren Resnick, for one, found four critical differences between learning in school and learning in the contemporary workplace: (1) students in school work alone, and modern workers collaborate; (2) students in school cannot or do not use tools to get answers, but workers always use tools (computers, calculators) and various metacognitive shortcuts in their work; (3) students in schools solve problems which are organized for them and which have one right answer, but workers solve problems which are not organized for them and which may have more than one "right" answer; and (4) students in school use letters and numbers almost exclusively to solve problems, but workers use a wide range of sign systems (L. Resnick 1987, 13–20).

Collins, Brown, and Newman, examining similar differences, found that in those workplaces with apprenticeship programs, "cognitive and metacognitive strategies are more central than either low-level subskills or abstract conceptual and factual knowledge," the latter being more important in traditional schooling (Collins, Brown, and Newman 1989, 455–56). In addition, John Seely Brown found that file clerks "constantly invent new work practices to cope with the unforeseen contingencies of the moment," and that "these 'workarounds' enable an all-important flexibility that allows organizations to cope with the unexpected" (J. Brown 1991b). To teach these metacognitive strategies and workarounds, Resnick, Collins, Brown, and Newman proposed that schools should use a model of learning called "cognitive apprenticeship," which views learning as an apprenticeship in a collaborative process of model fitting or negotiations, not as an individualized assimilation of decontextualized, separate, isolated skills—the latter being typical of learning during decoding/literal comprehension.

In yet another study of which skills were needed in contemporary workplaces, the Secretary of Labor's Commission on Achieving Necessary Skills (SCANS 1992) identified five new competencies and foundation skills "to enable postmodern citizens to enjoy a productive, full, and satisfying life":

(1) *resources*—workers schedule time, budget funds, arrange space, or assign staff;

(2) *interpersonal skills*—competent employees are skilled team members and teachers of new workers...negotiate with others to solve problems or reach decisions...work comfortably with colleagues from diverse backgrounds...responsibly challenge existing policies and procedures;

(3) *information*—they...interpret quantitative and qualitative data... convert information from one form to another...are comfortable conveying information, orally and in writing;

(4) *systems*—workers should understand their own work in the context of the work of those around them; and

(5) *technology*—[workers are capable of] selecting and using appropriate technology, visualizing operations using technology to monitor tasks (SCANS 1991, 11–13).

Finally, the American Society for Training and Development (ASTD), a nonprofit, professional association representing 50,000 practitioners and researchers in the field of human resource development, interviewed more than 400 experts to identify the skills needed in the workplace. This study identified sixteen subskills within the following seven skill groups: learning how to learn; basic competencies in reading, writing, and computation; communication skills; adaptability skills in problem solving; developmental skills in self-esteem and motivation; interpersonal skills; and leadership skills.

Some studies focused on future trends in job needs, not present needs; the prediction was that the majority of U.S. workers would have to become information workers. By the 1970s, almost 40 percent of U.S. workers were already in that category, and for many of them, this may have meant little more than inputting ("typing in") data. One study shows 30 percent or more of the population in categories of clerical/sales, professionals, and managers (S. Rose 1992, 20). The U.S. Department of Labor reports that in one pool of workers, "45 to 65 percent consider[ed] reading, writing, and math skills as very important" in their jobs (U.S. Department of Labor 1993, 94). But the category of information worker appears to be undergoing radical change as the convergence of information technologies like electronic mass media, print communications, and computing has created new kinds of jobs in the digitizing of information (Bailey 1988). These new jobs, dealing as they must with the blurred distinctions among various types of information like numbers, words, pictures, sounds, and even tastes and odors (Beniger 1986, 25), appear to require workers with not only new kinds of processing capabilities, but also new kinds of interpretation skills.

The studies by SCANS, ASTD, Brown, Collins, Resnick, and Beniger are quite consistent with each other in their conclusions and with my own observations of the new skills required of workers in the new NUMMI plant in Fremont, California—where workers must learn how to work in teams, how to learn, how to problem solve, and how to use an increasing range of tools (see the review of findings in Chapter 1). But how pervasive are these new skills in the workplace? Some observers argue that the "higher-order skills" at NUMMI are so rare in the U.S. workplace that teaching them to students could flood the job market with overqualified workers. In fact, in one radio program, Louis Harris reported that 75 percent of the 402 companies he sampled were not organized to use the new skills identified by groups like SCANS.

Braverman (1974) has been arguing a related point for some time, saying that traditional industrialization has, in fact, decreased the skill demands of most jobs, not increased them—that, in fact, contact with a machine does not necessarily require greater skill in a job, an assumption behind the Bureau of the Census statistics on job skills since the 1930s (Braverman 1974, 428–30). Braverman points to the work of Ivar Berg, showing that educational "achievements" have already "exceeded requirements in most job categories" (Braverman 1974, 441; Berg 1971, 14–15). Levin and Rumberger (1983) make similar claims, reporting that more jobs are expected to be available in eating and drinking establishments than in high-tech industries. Stern (1983) adds that the total number of new openings for computer operators, programmers, systems analysts, and computer mechanics combined is expected to be less than the number of new jobs for janitors. Glynda Hull has shown that workplaces are not using the higher-order thinking skills of most workers and, in fact, appear to be using new technology to de-skill jobs and exploit workers (Hull 1993, 31).

But Braverman, Stern, Levin, Rumberger, Hull and others are describing the present situation in most traditional factories, not what could be or should be (Marshall and Tucker 1992). Levin (1987) argues, for example, that factories need to be reorganized to include more collaborative work. Ira Magaziner (1992) warns that U.S. factories and service companies have been dumbing down their jobs for the last fifteen years to fit what he calls the underskilled graduates of U.S. schools and that, as a result, 70 percent of the economic growth (GNP) we have experienced in the last fifteen years has come from selling U.S. companies to foreigners, not from productivity. Magaziner has argued that U.S. factories and companies must stop dumbing down jobs or else lose out in international competition. Similarly, Bailey warns that managers who want to use technology to de-skill jobs are pursuing a strategy which will not work in the postmodern production environment, which will exhibit an increased consumer demand for variety and an accelerated pace in both technological and market change (Bailey 1990, 44). Both Magaziner and Bailey are calling for the restructuring of the workplace.

But, of course, restructuring has not as yet happened on a wide scale. Even literacy programs introduced into the workplace are often organized around decoding/analytic skills. Gowan describes a workplace literacy program that asked African American entry-level workers at a large, urban hospital to write and read about "Dust Mopping, Daily Vacuuming, Damp Mopping of Corridors and Open Areas" and so forth. These workers resisted this program, one saying "I felt I already knowed that" (Gowan 1990, 262). Even companies which attempt to reorganize often do not recognize that in the culture of the new translation/critical literacy, the workers must be part of the planning and implementation process. Darrah describes the failure of the team concept at one company where this team innovation was simply announced and mandated, creating the impression that the company did not believe in worker involvement in planning. Afterward the company blamed the workers for the failure of the idea, claiming the workers lacked the necessary skills (Darrah 1990; see Hull 1993, 29–30). The development of translation/critical literacy requires a context in which workers can influence the way work is done. Glynda Hull warns, "We must ask…in what contexts and under what circumstances this literacy will be empowering" (Hull 1993, 44).

Within the English teaching community, there are those who are skeptical about using the workplace to rationalize the teaching of English. But there appears to be a close fit in our new information society between what schools offer and what work, citizenship, and personal growth require (see Figure 8; see also Beniger 1986, 23). As noted earlier, in a recent Educational Testing Service/Office of Education survey of adult literacy in the U.S. (Kirsch et al. 1993), the more schooling the adults had, the higher their literacy rates were. Seventy-five to eighty percent of those performing at the lowest level of literacy had 0–8 years of schooling, and only 1 percent of these adults with 0–8 years of schooling were in the top two levels of literacy on a five-level scale. Furthermore, those at the lowest level of literacy reported median weekly earnings of $230 to $245, compared with $350 for those in the middle level and $620 to $680 for those at the top level. In addition, those at the lowest level reported working only 18 to 19 weeks during the previous year, and those in the middle and top levels reported working 34 to 44 weeks. Schools have some responsibility for helping young people to develop the skills they need to get jobs in future workplaces, and it is generally agreed that translation/critical literacy represents that future.

Of course, needs in the workplace are not the only reason for changing our nation's standard of literacy from decoding/analytic literacy to a new translation/critical literacy. Changes in the complexity of citizenship in modern democracies are another reason—maybe a more important reason. In an essay written almost forty years ago, R. P. Blackmur charged that teaching decoding/analytic literacy was an inadequate standard for the schools in a contemporary democracy, arguing that understanding the literal meanings of printed materials was not enough for citizens in an age with a plethora of print and visual media. He observed that as long as citizens believe that "saying so makes it so," modern media could be used by despots to control populations—even in a so-called democracy (Blackmur 1955). To maintain a democracy in the modern world, citizens must, according to Blackmur, be able to infer, to critique, to interpret, and to translate the intentions behind words. Even those who take a much more skeptical view of school accomplishments and industrial needs have acknowledged that literacy standards for all students must change to meet the demands of modern citizenship:

> Even if the workplace is not truly demanding more reading ability, we shall nonetheless need much better reading skills across the entire population if we are to survive and improve as a democratic society in an increasingly complex age. (Stedman and Kaestle 1987, 42)

A third social need, maybe more important than the needs for either citizenship or the workplace, is the need for personal growth, particularly the possibility of individual empowerment through participation in culture and critique of that culture. Literacy is one way to provide for the students the mechanisms they need for their personal growth. One of the key problems for individuals who are considering their own place in the world is the way change penetrates all places, everywhere, and turns those places into homogenized offshoots of a worldwide industry and technology, thereby threatening the efforts of individuals to understand their own identity in the world. This homogenization is increasing its speed of diffusion, from the 150–200 years required for the steam engine to spread throughout a population to just 15 years for the transistor (Schon 1971, 24). As a result, says Schon, "a large Spanish city has less the character of a Spanish city than of a modern, industrial city anywhere" (Schon 1971, 25). The issue of diversity, then, is partly an issue of preventing the total homogenization of our culture, of using literacy to protect cultural roots from total destruction.

Another key part of this new curriculum of personal growth is the development of a caretaking sensibility in which every student is asked to assume at least some mentoring responsibilities. That is, one's individualism and personal development depend upon the support of networks of families and mentors, and at present, there are not enough available family members and mentors to go around. Daniel Patrick Moynihan has suggested that, without these "mentors" and a caretaking sensibility, our nation may be the first to forget how to care for its children, given the fact, among other things, that, more and more, both parents must work and more and more caretaking units have collapsed. The collapse of families, says Moynihan, threatens opportunities for healthy personal growth. He reports that thirty years ago 1 in every 40 white children was born to an unmarried mother (Moynihan 1994, 13), but today that figure is 1 in every 5. In some communities, the figure is 2 out of 3. Teaching young people how to care for younger children and seniors could help meet a number of social needs, including the need to expand opportunities for literacy. By asking students to assume new roles for public service in the community and in schools, schools could help expand the social capital available for the support of young people's personal growth. In summary, translation/critical literacy, like other literacy movements, is intended to help solve a range of human problems (see Figure 8).

For many students, translation/critical literacy will not help them in their lives without an accompanying improvement in equity and equal opportunity. Basic problems of equal opportunity threaten the opportunity of large numbers of children to get jobs and to participate in civic events. Ethnic minorities still lag behind the general population averages in academic achievement, even though some improvements have been made. The difference in white and black school enrollment rates for those five to nineteen years of age narrowed from 23 points in 1900 to 7 points in 1940; by 1991, the enrollment rate for five- to nineteen-year-olds was 93 percent for blacks, whites, males, and females, with little difference among the groups (National Center for Education Statistics 1993, 6–7). Finally, between 1971 and 1984, the National Assessment of Educational Progress (NAEP) achievement gap between black and white students was reduced. In 1971, about one-third of the black students at age nine lacked even rudimentary skills. By 1988, this figure had been reduced 16 percent (Applebee, Langer, and Mullis 1987, 23). In 1975, only 7.99 percent of black students and 13 percent of Hispanic students, age seventeen, were at the adept level in reading. By 1988, 16 percent of black students and 20 percent of Hispanic students, age seventeen, were at the adept level (Applebee, Langer, and Mullis 1987, 24). Berliner reports similar gains on the SAT (Berliner 1992, 13a).

Despite these gains, adequate levels of equity have not been achieved in the U.S. We need a new approach. In the 1960s, the *Brown v. Topeka* decision of 1954 was used to argue a legal theory of equity based on access to schools, but access to schools often proved to be a deceptive and disappointing path to equity. People of color were admitted to all schools, but many of them often found that the schools they attended were funded at levels far below the levels at other schools. In the 1970s, California's *Serrano v. Priest* suit (Serrano, the plaintiff; Priest, the state treasurer) defined equity as equal public dollars, a tolerable public-dollar gap between one school and another. This theory, too, often proved to be a deceptive and disappointing path to equity because public dollars were "equalized" at a lower level—everyone became equally poor in the public schools—and additional private funds were put into "mainstream" schools through local foundations and the private contributions of parents. All of this created new forms of financial inequality, even though the dollar gap of public dollars going into different schools was reduced to a legally acceptable level.

Today, in the 1990s, a new legal theory of equity is beginning to emerge—one based on learning opportunity. This adequacy theory of equity is not a pipe dream. This theory says that proof of an equal educational opportunity in schools should be the evidence that the student has had the literacy experiences in school necessary to enter the world as a functioning citizen, thinker, and worker. Notice that this theory of equity does not argue either the dollar gap or access. An Alabama state court ruled in 1993 that the K–12 school system in Alabama is unconstitutional because it does not provide "students with an opportunity to attain sufficient skills to compete with students throughout the world" and does not provide "sufficient understanding of the arts to enable each student to appreciate his or her cultural heritage and the cultural heritage of others" (*Alabama Coalition for Equity, Inc., et al. and Alabama Disabilities Advocacy Program, et al. v. Jim Folsom, Governor and as President of the State Board of Education;* Decision: June 9, 1993, by Eugene W. Reese, Circuit Judge). As Manno observes: "Helen Hershkoff call[ed] the decision 'a landmark because it recognizes that children have a right not only to an equitable education but also to an adequate education'" (Manno 1993, A-14). Notice that this right to adequacy means a right to a curriculum content that helps students become functional workers and citizens.

What evidence would be needed to prepare a court challenge based on a learning opportunity or adequacy theory of equity? The first type of evidence would be the kinds of tasks assigned in an English class, and this type of evidence might require, first, a collection device in the classroom—say, a portfolio—and second, a description of standards or curriculum targets considered to be adequate—something to show that writing persuasion, for example, is a necessary experience for all students who hope to have an equal opportunity. The standards project of the National Council of Teachers of English and the International Reading Association, funded in part by the MacArthur Foundation and assisted by the College Board, is one such effort to describe that content. This book is intended to be a research review of some of the possible foundations for a different kind of content in the K–12 curriculum in English and the English language arts.

In summary, past literacy practices have served different national goals, different markets, different contracts, different tools, and so forth. It is clear that the K–12 teachers of the United States are being asked to aim for a new standard of literacy for *all* students and that this new standard, like others from the past, results from a convergence of new insights into texts, new models of learning, and new national needs—in this case, the new demands of contemporary economic problems and the workplace, the new demands of pluralism and diversity in our democracy, and the new demands for new supports for personal growth. What are some of the features of this new standard of literacy? That is the subject of the chapters which follow.

Notes

1. "If one takes age into account, more of the tests show gains than declines, whereas many others show approximately equal performance rates...Our educated guess is that schoolchildren of the same age and socioeconomic status have been performing at similar levels throughout the twentieth century" (Stedman and Kaestle 1987, 18). This statement does not, of course, cover those who are not in school.

2. In *The Literacy Hoax: The Decline of Reading, Writing, and Learning in the Public Schools and What We Can Do about It,* Paul Copperman (1978) claimed that people were declining in their reading ability. Two groups of researchers have identified key flaws in Copperman's thesis. First, the variation in number of years in school, reported by Fisher (1978, 9), may account for the variations in scores in Copperman's data, not the educational program at a particular time (see Kaestle, et al., 1991, 11). Fisher concluded that, in fact, present-day eighteen-year-olds were doing better than the number of years in school would typically predict, thus suggesting that programs have not declined in recent years. In addition, Stedman and Kaestle found that Copperman's argument was not supported by the results of functional literacy tests which Copperman failed to cite (Stedman and Kaestle 1987, 34–35). In fact, Kaestle et al. point to results on the Survival Literacy Study and the Reading Difficulty Index to show that "Copperman's argument was also contradicted by the results of the other functional-literacy tests" (Kaestle et al., 1991, 111).

3. NAEYC recommended in 1986 that children be introduced to stories, not kept away from them. This is similar to the shift from 1971 to 1979 by the High Scope Curriculum—from saying "reading and writing...are not attempted" to saying that "[the preschool teachers should respond] to interest in letters, sounds, and words . . . and whenever there is an opportunity, encourag[e] children to look at books and 'read'" (qtd. in McGill-Franzen 1993, 113).

4. NAEP elaborated on these results, saying that students seem satisfied with their initial interpretations of what they have read and seem genuinely puzzled at requests to explain or defend their points of view. As a result, responses to assessment items requiring explanations of criteria, analysis of text, or defense of a judgment or point of view were, in general, disappointing. Few students could provide more than superficial responses to such tasks, and even the "better" responses showed little evidence of well-developed problem-solving strategies or critical-thinking skills. The net result is that most school-age children have acquired basic skills by age nine, and over 70 percent have attained literal and inferential comprehension by age seventeen (NAEP 1984, 29).

7 The Event-Based Features of Translation/Critical Literacy

[T]he critics of the god Thoth, the inventor of writing, . . . did not realize that the written word is far more powerful than simply a reminder: it recreates the past in the present, and gives us, not the familiar remembered thing, but the glittering intensity of the summed up hallucination. (Frye 1982, 227)

In this chapter, as we shift from the history of literacy policy to a description of contemporary literacy policy in the U.S., several points need to be restated.

1. Changes in literacy practices are always accompanied by changes in what data from the world need to be visible, stable, transportable, and combinable (see Latour 1987, on science in action). The visible, combined data become for us a text which triggers memory, as in recitation literacy; or a text which becomes an analyzable object, as in decoding/analytic literacy; or a text which becomes a revisable hallucination, as in our new translation/critical literacy. These texts enable us to construct necessary pictures of events in the world.

2. In this book, "literacy," as a term, does not represent a distinction between print and nonprint practices; rather, it is a term referring to a set of sanctioned communication practices with assigned political authority and social status given to selected sign systems—for example, oral and written reports, visual marks and gestures, fingers and tokens (for counting), pictorial and alphabetic texts. A form of literacy always includes many social practices.

3. In the first six chapters, this book examines the history of public-policy literacy in the U.S. Public-policy literacy is reflected in the curriculum and assessment policies of schools, the required entry tests of various institutions and jobs, and the policy statements of government spokespersons. In the U.S., the literacy of public policy is always dominant across the country, if not in particular locations, and it always shapes the subject matter of schools in unique ways.

4. New literacy practices are always added to a culture's range, old literacy practices rarely or never disappearing. In addition, every literacy practice has a rich intercultural history. One can, for example, trace many features of decoding/analytic literacy to Luther and Descartes and from them to the Middle East (Arabic numbers and an alphabetic system), Asia (the graphite pencil), and elsewhere.

5. *Most people know how to use more than one form of literacy in appropriate circumstances, and most people have at one time or another resisted a form of literacy.* Resistance to a form of literacy is one way to protect local and family practices from intervention and possible elimination by other literacies.

6. *A form of literacy is often closely linked to teaching methods, to occupational practices, and to citizenship practices.* One's way of teaching, one's way of working, and one's way of engaging in citizenship convey an attitude and habit of mind toward texts typical of a particular form of literacy. Therefore, methods of teaching and occupational practices are always a reflection of a form of literacy, and debates about teaching methods are often debates about which occupational practices and, thus, which form of literacy should dominate in schools.

7. *Each form of literacy has its own version of context.* Recitation literacy in schools had what Bernstein calls "the cover of the sacred" (Bernstein 1990, 86), but decoding/analytic literacy in schools initiated "a truly secular form born of the context of cost efficiency" (Bernstein 1990, 86). For recitation literacy, the oral performance always "contextualized" print. For decoding/analytic literacy, the text was separated from oral performance, turning the reader and writer into a silent individual located in a private study. The definition of reading and writing as private and silent is a startling contrast to reading in ancient Israel, where reading was a public, collective, oral activity located in two primary contexts—in the synagogue or the House of Study and in the court. "In contrast," says Boyarin, "there are two privileged social sites for the practice of reading in Europe in Late Antiquity, the Middle Ages, and the Early Modern period: the study and the bedroom" (Boyarin 1993, 19). The shift from the public and oral to the private and silent was observed by Saint Augustine, who believed that one got meaning from written texts by hearing those texts performed and interpreted within a community but who watched with amazement as the great Catholic bishop Ambrose read in silence: "when he was reading, he drew his eyes along over the leaves, and his heart searched into the sense, but his voice and tongue were still" (*St. Augustine's Confessions* I: 272).

8. *A form of literacy is usually associated with issues of nationhood.* English language study during recitation literacy was largely the study of English grammar as an imitation of Latin and Greek models in the literature of Great Britain, but language researchers during the early days

of decoding/analytic literacy shifted their attention to English as it was actually spoken in the United States. Fries prepared a taxonomy of English sentence types based on letters he collected (Fries 1940; Marckwardt and Walcott 1938; Pooley 1946), and in the process, introduced notions about levels of usage in U.S. English.

After almost seventy-five years of decoding/analytic literacy's dominance over literacy practices in the U.S., we are now observing the emergence of translation/critical literacy as the literacy of public policy. Translation/critical literacy's emerging dominance is the result, among other things, of new kinds of occupations, new relationships to the state, and a new market-oriented pedagogy—each of which has reconceptualized knowledge in the subject of English as embodied, distributed, negotiated, situated, and designed (see Figure 25 in Chapter 15).

In the world of this new literacy, various codes within event-based discourse have become ways to contribute to culture, to establish personal identity, to exert power and influence, and to get employment. In decoding/analytic literacy, one knows something by analyzing the autonomous parts of generic language—from phoneme to word to sentence—and in the new literacy, one knows something by using and observing language in situated events. The event-based curriculum echoes in some ways the experience curriculum of sixty years ago, in which the curriculum was "a body of guided experiences paralleling present and future out-of-school experiences" (Hatfield 1935, 9).[1] But there are several key differences. One difference is the fact that "out-of-school experiences" have changed dramatically. Workplace experiences are not so prefabricated and predictable, and citizenship experiences are more often encounters with multiple differences of perspective (gender, class, race, ethnicity). A second key difference is that employee development, training, and explicit study have been added to the participatory experiences of work sites and citizenship. Thus, in contemporary "real-world" work, we find that people have institutionalized both learning-by-doing and learning-by-drawing-back-from-the-world for explicit instruction and practice. The world has become too complicated for an exclusive commitment either to learning-by-participation or to learning-by-explicit-study.

What are the elements of event-based discourse in English studies? Event-based discourse has

1. a *self* who plays the role of *writer/speaker* encountering the question, "Who has the right to speak or write?";

2. *tools* which distribute problems and about which one asks, "How does this tool shape my thinking? Who gets access to tools?";

3. an *event-based language and text* model about which one asks, "What code do I use to represent my thoughts? What are the parts of language?";

4. an *audience/reader* about whom one asks, "What are the interpersonal relationships in the language? Who has the right to read or to listen?";

5. a *set of cognitive processes* about which one asks, "What strategies are important?";

6. a *set of ideas or concepts* about which one asks, "What are the relationships between texts and concepts? What topics are allowed or not allowed?"; and

7. a *performance* (book, speech, action) of consumption (reading or listening) or production (writing or speaking) about which one asks, "What is the purpose? How is this performance described in the classroom and in distant centers of calculation?"(See Figure 25, pp. 286–87.)

The writer/reader is actively engaged with a set of tools—some of them external hardware and software and others internal metacognitive strategies and dialogic innerspeech—in three kinds of negotiations: (1) cultural/social negotiations, involving collaborative or resistant interpersonal constructions between *self* as *writer* or *reader* and various *communities* of audiences and authors; (2) cognitive negotiations, including computational processing of language for specific skills like spelling, and modular or representational processing of language for skills like phonemic and syntactic awareness; and (3) conceptual negotiations, involving text-to-text relationships in an area of knowledge. In all of these negotiations, the student fluctuates between believing (translation) and disbelieving (critical) (see Elbow 1986), between appreciation (translation) and criticism (critical), between participation and observation.

Performance requires that classrooms, workplaces, and citizenship projects take place in a tool-based environment, making distributed knowledge possible—having a publication center for production of participant work (graphics, printing, binding) and having a plan for distribution of student work (including displays throughout the school).

This emphasis on performance and participation should not obscure the fact that event-based discourse requires both writing and editing, both reading and revising, both participation in discourse events and time-out periods for explicit study of texts and language. Sometimes schools and workplaces are not able to provide participation in discourse events for students and employees who have not learned some information, processing skills, or social interactions. In order to participate, students, for example, often need explicit practice in the sounds of language, technical conventions, figures of speech, sentence combining, or unraveling a plot on a time line. Lave and Wenger (1991) found that butchers, midwives, and many others cannot learn *only* through participation and involvement in a "real-world" event in postmodern workplaces. These workers, too, must have time set aside for drill and practice.

Students, then, must experience in schools what Jean Lave has called situated, legitimate, peripheral participation, in which students alternate between participation and observation, use of language and study of its forms. Lave has described how these two learning activities— participation and observation—combine "the two characteristics of *invisibility* and *visibility:* invisibility in the form of unproblematic interpretation and integration into activity, and visibility in the form of extended access to information"—in other words, the observation and practice of visible parts of practice (Lave and Wenger 1991, 103).

There is a contemporary tension between parents who want more drills and practice in specific skills in English, something closer to decoding/analytic literacy, and parents who want more participation in literacy events, something closer to translation/critical literacy. Those parents whose lives and jobs are organized around the traditional prefabricated jobs of decoding/analytic literacy and those parents whose lives and jobs are organized around the new problem-solving and information-processing jobs of translation/critical literacy are often not in agreement about what the schools should do. Today, when the federal government is offering incentives to many businesses to introduce translation/critical literacy into the workplace, parents caught in the middle of this transition fear that their children may be denied what students need for work and citizenship. Lisa Delpit (1986) has suggested that the absence of explicit teaching and practice may hurt the disadvantaged but may not hurt the students of the upper middle class, whose parents can provide explicit teaching at home or hire tutors and outside teaching help. In addition, some publishers who have invested heavily in materials for decoding/analytic literacy, which emphasizes explicit study, have inflamed parental fears by charging that some programs for the new literacy—for example, whole language— have failed to include a balance of participation and observation in their programs.

This public debate makes clear that we need a concept that links event-based discourse, including its fluctuation between participation and observation, and the beliefs and attitudes of different groups—different ages, genders, economic classes, occupations. Halliday, Hasan, and Bernstein, according to Lemke, collaborated "to forge this missing link" between school and community, in what Bernstein called "code, or later, semantic coding orientation" (Lemke 1995, 27; see Bernstein 1971). The codes of different occupations, for example, help explain how the events in discourse represent different social relations, different cognitive strategies, and different ideas. Tannen (1990) has pointed to gender differences in the code of event-based discourse, Smitherman (1977) has pointed to racial and ethnic differences, and Bernstein has pointed to differences in the different occupational classes.

Each of these codes and their impact on English teaching are examined in this book. But special emphasis is given to workplace and citizenship codes. Why? Translation/critical literacy represents a market-oriented pedagogy, a distinct break from the moral and religious traditions of recitation literacy and from the traditions of universal knowledge in decoding/analytic literacy. Unlike decoding/analytic literacy, a market-oriented knowledge opens our schools to our communities:

> Historically, urban schools have been located in the centers of entrepreneurial activity but largely insulated from such activity. One of the consequences of breaking the boundary between the world of school and the world of enterprise could be that urban working-class pupils, black and white, will have opportunities to demonstrate entrepreneurial intelligence and achievement that has found no legitimate place in the schooling of the past. Thus the principle of market exchange and of enterprise does have a potential for breaking the culture of academic failure long associated with urban working-class schools. (Grace 1995, 224)

It seems clear that different occupational groups now use different codes which are based on different assumptions about literacy. Some production workers have adopted the beliefs, attitudes, and code of translation/critical literacy, others have retained the code of decoding/analytic literacy, and a very few still retain the code of signature literacy. Some managers have adopted the managerial code of translation/critical literacy, while other managers have retained the managerial code of decoding/analytic literacy. In summary, a new social class of information workers, professional service workers, lawyers, and scholars have also adopted the code of translation/critical literacy.

The point is that if schools do not introduce the students to the codes and literacies of power, then schools will become part of the process of socially transmitted inequality. Bernstein has suggested that, in schools, the discourse of pedagogy has a code which helps students learn the discourses of power or else prevents them from learning those discourses. What are the primary features of pedagogical codes? Codes, says Bernstein, vary in *classification* and *framing*. Classification codes build weak or strong boundaries between school and home, teachers and students, school knowledge and everyday knowledge. Framing establishes strong or weak control on the part of the teacher or school (Bernstein, 1971). Bernstein (1975) argues that weak classification and framing—what he calls invisible pedagogy—were institutionalized in British infant schools to serve the interests of a new middle class who were employed in the professional serving of persons, an occupation requiring flexibility and openness (Bernstein 1975, 122–23, 136). These professionals socialized their children into this invisible pedagogy at home, but the children of traditional production workers had no such socialization and were left without what they needed—a visible pedagogy of explicit instruction in the new flexibility, with strong classification and framing.

Notice the similarity in the visible-invisible distinctions of Bernstein and Lave. Both are saying, I think, that participation alone creates an invisible pedagogy and that explicit instruction creates a visible pedagogy (see Cazden 1995). Both are also saying that participation and explicit teaching are present in successful educational settings. In addition to his findings about the importance of the visible pedagogy of explicit teaching, Bernstein has reported that "[i]t would appear that the invisible pedagogy carries a beneficial potential for working-class children" (Bernstein 1975, 127). The basic challenge for teachers in translation/critical literacy is, according to Cazden, "how to achieve flexible competencies from explicit teaching" (Cazden 1995, 162). The answer, I claim, is to be found in the workplace where translation/critical literacy is used. There we find a fluctuation between flexible participation and explicit teaching. Many novice workers may now and then need the explicit teaching of drills from recitation or decoding/analytic literacy in order to understand the parts of participation in translation/critical literacy. I have had students for whom "Write an essay on a controversial topic of your choice from your reading" is too vague, too invisible. These students need to be told, "Write 500 words on why Oakland High is the most beautiful place in the world." This is a visible topic they can resist with a proposal of their own (and they do!), revealing their own opinions, their own topics. To teach the new literacy, teachers need a multiliteracy awareness of the different codes needed by students to learn the new codes of power in translation/critical literacy.

Let me review once again why translation/critical literacy has become essential in the workplace. Xerox™, for example, faced a big problem in the 1980s when increasing numbers of customers were complaining that the new Xerox™ copiers were "unreliable." The old Xerox™ copiers had been simpler machines, and the instruction manual, often chained to the machine, had provided a specific solution for anything that might go wrong. The first models of the new Xerox™ copiers used the same "idiot proof" approach to instructions as the old machines, but the new copiers had many new functions, faster speeds, and new complexities which the old generic manual seemed unable to anticipate. The result: many dissatisfied customers. Xerox™ decided that the new Xerox™ machine had become too complicated for the generic, prepackaged directions of the old machine and decided to try a new approach:

> Instead of trying to eliminate "trouble," we acknowledged that it was inevitable. So the copier's design should help users manage trouble—just as people manage and recover from misunderstandings during a conversation. This means keeping the machine as transparent as possible. . . . (J. Brown 1991a, 107)

Xerox™ dropped its prepackaged manual with generic solutions for predetermined troubles and shifted to several small screens with diagrams showing the operations of the machines at any moment and with short messages indicating many possible problems. This redesign, which cost less than $20 in parts, changed the user of the machine from one who follows the directions for targeted problems at every step to one who translates visual screens into possible solutions and then tries out (and criticizes) a solution or two.

This small change in the Xerox™ machine is typical of what happened in factories throughout the world as assembly lines became technologically more complicated and ceased to have a fixed, prepackaged, technological solution for all production problems. Einar Thorsrud of Norway, P. G. Herbst of Norway, Fred Emery of Australia, Kenneth Benne of the U.S., and Ronald Lippett of the U.S. have all reported that the solutions to problems in reorganized, modern factories require, first, flexibility in the way a problem is understood or coded; second, on-line, situated decision making; third, collaboration, criticism, and negotiation; and fourth, the engagement, commitment, and personal enthusiasm of workers who must be involved in the negotiation, translation, and criticism of production-line problems at every step (Wirth 1987, 64).

The NUMMI plant in Fremont, California, GM's Saturn plant, the Harmon Auto Mirror Company, and many other workplaces in the

U.S. have all reorganized their production systems to achieve these four features. These companies reduced the number of separate job categories in their factories, thereby increasing the need for worker flexibility and situated solutions; increased the information, strategies, and ideas workers should know, and, at the same time, increased on-line decision making and control; increased the involvement of workers in planning, thereby increasing engagement across boundaries of authority and craft; and developed new teams on the plant floor, thereby giving workers new collaborative responsibilities. In other words, in our most advanced factories, the fixed, generic solution appears to have been replaced by the processes of a new event-based, idea-driven form of literacy. Of course, these changes have not happened everywhere or possibly even in most places (Hull 1993)—but they have happened in many places, and, most observers predict, they must happen, in time, in virtually all places.[2]

Changes in a form of literacy, which is what happened in the reorganization at NUMMI, require changes in many parts of a culture, from the processes of the Xerox™ machine to the processes of factories and civic forums, not just changes in ways of reading and writing. The changes in the practices of NUMMI workers are a particularly interesting example of a radical literacy change. It is essential to remember that the NUMMI reorganization took place with the *old* workers, not the new ones—with, in other words, the workers whom many had blamed for the failures of the old plant and who were, according to some, too illiterate to work in the new plant. The education of these workers in new ways of problem solving was, to the surprise of some, a relatively easy process because the new NUMMI culture valued and encouraged these ways of thinking in the workplace. In addition, the change was relatively easy because the union (United Automobile Workers) at the NUMMI plant helped oversee the hiring process, planned the design of the plant, and organized the orientation of the workers. Without the involvement of the workers in the processes of planning and implementation, most plant reorganization efforts are doomed to failure (see Hull 1993, 38).

The need for a new form of literacy is not just a workplace issue. It is also a citizenship need. Before the 1960s, U.S. public schools generally accepted the notion that U.S. society was homogenous and universally normative. Ethnic identities, for example, were considered "recessive, readily explained by the immigrant experience, but essentially transitional," on their way toward nationalization as cultural differences became assimilated into the "melting pot"—into a generic Universal model of "Western man" (Moynihan 1993, 27). That kind of assimilation or nationalization no longer works. Why? First, our nation's family myth of two parents has been shattered by a recognition that 20 percent or more of our contemporary families are headed by a single parent. Second, our nation's gender myth of male and female roles has given way to a recognition that gender roles and marriage and bonding arrangements can vary a great deal. Finally, as a result of decentralized media, including the collapse of centralized media control by three major television networks, our nation's ethnic myth of homogeneity has been shattered by the growing visibility of our nation's ethnic diversity on television news, on radio talk shows, in do-it-yourself publications, and so forth.

The evidence of this diversity is everywhere. Thirty percent of the students in U.S. schools today are classified as non-European people of color. Over 90 percent of the K–12 students in Detroit, Washington, D.C., and Baltimore are African Americans. Soon, the majority of K–12 students in California and Texas will be people of color. The percentage of students coming from homes with a non-English language as the first language is estimated to be above 20 percent in U.S. schools, and most of these students speak an Asian or Hispanic language. Roughly 31.1 percent of children under age eighteen are from a racial minority group: 15 percent of the students in U.S. schools are African Americans, 11 percent are Hispanic Americans, and approximately 5 percent are Asian Americans. By 2010, it is estimated that 38.2 percent will be minority. Roughly, 16 percent of U.S. students will be African American, 19 percent Hispanic, 7 percent Asian, and 1.5 percent Native American (Hodgkinson 1992, 5, 17).

There is a growing recognition that this diversity is here to stay. For example, in 1978, the U.S., for the first time, recognized that defendants who did not understand oral English had a right in criminal and civil actions to "interpretation services" (de Jongh 1992, 11). This right to interpretation was denied under the previous assumptions of immediate assimilation. In another example, young people who formerly accepted the Ellis Island myth of assimilation and universality have started to define themselves in terms of their cultural roots. For example, "African American" is now the label of choice for 55 percent of young blacks 21 years of age and under, for 37 percent of those 31–40 years of age, and for 29 percent of those 40 and over (Smitherman 1993). In other words, the vocabulary shift from "Negro" to "Black" in the 1960s has now been replaced by the shift from "Black" to "African American," a label emphasizing specific cultural roots in Africa and the United States.

These differences, of course, do not necessarily produce a functioning nation—witness the fragmentation and civil war of Yugoslavia in 1993. The fundamental dilemma facing contemporary citizens in our culture of recognized differences is how do we sustain a commitment to a common set of democratic values, to a common set of U.S. traditions, and at the same time sustain a respect for pluralism and diversity—how do we establish "linkages" between one view and another and make it possible in our English classes "for people inhabiting different worlds to have a genuine, and reciprocal, impact on one another" (Geertz 1983, 161). "And for that," says Geertz "the first step is surely to accept the depth of the differences; the second, to understand what these differences are; and the third, to construct some sort of vocabulary in which they can be publicly formulated" (Geertz 1983, 161).

English classes have a major responsibility for helping to create a public discourse which, while acknowledging different perspectives, constructs a shared, intercultural understanding across boundaries. In other words, our new translation/critical literacy must emphasize both translations—speaking across boundaries—and critiques—recognizing the strength of differences within and across those boundaries. In the reading of literature, for example, texts need to be paired with other texts from the same period, bridging across different materials, and paired with contemporary texts, bridging across time.

In summary, then, contemporary students need to situate their problems within the complexities of postmodern identification (gender, being one), within the new Xerox™ machines, within reorganized factories, and within increasing civic trends toward democracies with a variety of voices represented. Now, let's review how research in learning and language has taken us in the same direction as industrial reform. Lashley (1951), as early as 1948, warned that behaviorism's *isolation of parts* simplified the complexity and apparent disorganization of thinking processes. In other words, it organized complexity for us, but it ignored those larger patterns in the mind which seemed to add complexity but which dictated the forms of language, music, and athletics in actual performances and thinking in contexts. By the 1980s, most English language researchers were beginning to assemble a literacy organized around event-based discourse, culminating in a series of research studies focusing on social construction (Bruner 1978), cognitive construction (Emig 1971), and idea or text construction (Prawat 1991).

First, let's examine the social negotiations between the self/writer and audiences/readers (see Figure 25 in Chapter 15). Bruner, in the late 1970s, rejecting Chomsky's innate language acquisition device as being "simply false," called for an understanding of the social *construction* of knowledge as a way to understand language learning (Bruner 1978, 44). Social construction in language learning has been described as an initiation into communities of learners (Atwell 1987)

and into discourse/disciplinary communities (Bizzell 1992; Bartholomae 1985); as a shift from isolated language behaviors to "whole language" (K. Goodman, Bird, and Goodman 1991); as a shift from
isolation of parts to *integration of parts* (Iran-Nejad, McKeachie, and
Berliner 1990, 515); as a process of scaffolding for novices (Collins,
Brown, and Newman 1989; Langer, 1992); and as participation in cultural conversations (Applebee 1994), in literacy events (Heath 1986a,
1986b, and 1986c), in communicative events (G. Graff 1992), and in
acts of resistance (Giroux 1983).

Many scholars have observed that social construction seems to initi-
ate or socialize students into discourse communities without regard for
the individual inclinations of the students. Bizzell, like others, says that
the possibilities of resistance can be maintained even while students engage in social construction in schooling (J. Harris 1989; Bizzell 1992),
and even while these same students experience communal pressures.
She insists that human resistance to a community and other larger cultural frames is one key source for new ways of thinking about problems:

> As long as human beings are masses of contradictions, then, the
> power of a discourse community, no matter how culturally domi-
> nant, can never be total. Someone will always be ready to exercise
> what David Bartholomae has called a "rhetoric of combination"
> (1985), bringing opposition into jarring contact that generates a
> new idea. (Bizzell 1992, 235)

Any process of social construction within event-based discourse is
certain to have an impact on the fashioning of self. Writing and reading
are, after all, acts of self-definition. Gregg Sarris remembers that while
sitting in the UCLA library, reading a transcription of Kashaya legends
for the first time, he began "to realize that it wasn't necessarily the case
that 'university people weren't Indian and what was Indian wasn't in
books.'" He realized that through his participation in literacy events,
"he was himself becoming 'a university person who is Indian'" (qtd. in
Boyarin 1993, 7). A sense of self creates, of course, the possibilities of
empowerment. It also creates, among other things, the possibilities of
alienation.

Second, research in decoding/analytic literacy tended to examine
language as a product or object, but by the 1960s, studies in cognitive
processing had begun to explore either computational skills or representational "playing around." It is extremely important to distinguish
in cognitive processing between computational processing, which
functions like a computer (linear, binary), and representational processing, which functions like playing around in an area. Computational
rules produce the specific skills of spellings, sound-letter correspon-

dences, and syntactic transformations, and representational processing produces awareness about an area (Bereiter 1995). Of the five hundred studies prior to 1963 that are cited in George Hillocks's *Research in Written Composition* (1986), only two even indirectly studied the information-processing strategies used by students in writing. By the end of the 1970s, however, more and more processing studies were being undertaken, including three particularly influential ones: Emig's (1971) interview study of the writing processes of eight sixteen- and seventeen-year-old students who were interviewed about their writing processes after school; Donald Graves's (1975) study of the writing processes of seven-year-olds and eight-year-olds observed writing in class; and Flower and Hayes's (1980) study of the writing processes suggested by student talk-alouds while students were writing.

Other studies like these produced such strategies as Miller's chunking strategy for remembering (G. Miller 1967), Bruner's planning and guessing strategies (Bruner, Goodnow, and Austin 1956), and various executive controls for monitoring, checking, and guiding actions (Flower and Hayes 1981). It is important to remember that these cognitive strategies help students solve such important problems of information processing as the "bottleneck" (Broadbent 1958), the limits of "mental power," the limits of "processing space," the limits of "attention span," and the limits of the "executive-processing span" (Case 1985).

Near the end of decoding/analytic literacy, most research on the English sentence used a computational model of information processing, extending Chomsky's theory of transformational grammar into classroom practices. Chomsky, rejecting structural grammar—which Searle called verbal botany (1972, 16)—had proposed a transformational model of syntax (Chomsky 1957) which attempted to recapitulate the history of the sentence from kernels to surface structure.[3] This idea inspired a number of studies of how sentences are generated and combined, including Kellogg Hunt's (1965) study of syntactic combinations in the early grades and John Mellon's (1969) and Frank O'Hare's (1975) studies of sentence-combining exercises in secondary schools. Extending the findings of these studies, Francis Christensen (1967) and William Strong (1973) developed an extensive classroom composition program using syntax as a foundation for studying the relationships among sentences, paragraphs, and larger units of discourse. John Mellon's transformational sentence-combining activities could be said to teach computational or specific skills

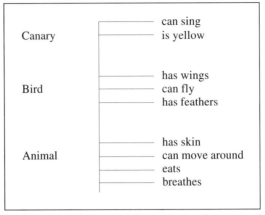

Fig. 9. Schemata for processing speed (from fast at the top to slow at the bottom). (Adapted from: Collins and Quillian 1969, 241. Used by permission of the Academic Press.)

(Mellon 1969), and Strong (1973), Christensen (1967), and Joseph Williams (1989) could be said to teach representational skills.

Sign shifting is a critical part of representational processing. A. M. Collins and M. R. Quillian (1969) suggested over twenty years ago—and it has since been confirmed (R. Anderson and Pearson 1984)—that the direct information one experiences every day is more readily available in memory than abstract information covering the same experiences. They proposed the schemata in Figure 9 which tells us that making decisions about whether information is true or false will take longer for the information that is lower on the scale. What is quite interesting about this scale is that the information at the top tends to come from actual, hands-on experiences with canaries, the middle tends to come from looking at pictures, and the bottom comes from verbal classifications of many types of animals. In other words, this scale is an example of how sign shifting can be used to process information faster (see Chapter 10). The ability to shift from the verbal description to the hands-on experience helps one to remember and use information.

The learning of general awareness skills, which is not well understood, has been confirmed in many areas of human learning. Esther Thelen, a developmental psychologist, has suggested that children do not learn walking and reaching by adding up or building up one part of an action at a time—what one would expect of a specific skill in a computational approach—but by being introduced to a broad range of models or representations of walking and reaching, then by trying out and exploring a few models, and finally by being immersed in a selected model. This skill of general awareness appears to be encouraged by a criss-crossing or immersion approach to learning (Prawat 1991). In other words, the child learns the general skill of walking or reaching awareness and then selects. The child's way of walking or reaching eventually combines common core characteristics from the selected model or representation and some of the child's individual inclinations (Thelen 1990), as the child works from the model to the parts.

In neurology, Rosenfield has argued that memory has a similar dependence on models—that, in fact, past events are reconstructed as a whole story or set of meanings and are not stored in the brain as a fixed record or trace of small parts which add up to a story automatically, one part added to another part and these parts then added to another part (Rosenfield 1988, 192–93). The act of remembering is the act of exploring various wholes and working from a possible whole to the parts, from the parts to a possible whole. One finding seems to be that practicing of parts makes more sense when models of whole performances are everywhere apparent, and participation is everywhere available.

Although social construction and cognitive processes have received considerable emphasis in our thinking about event-based discourse, ideas have been often ignored (Bereiter 1994). Neisser (1976) noted that what we ask about information-processing systems is how they process information we have, not how they develop the new ideas of an interpretive framework. As Bereiter observed about cognitive-processing theories, "It seems to be generally agreed that there is no adequate cognitive theory of learning—that is, no adequate theory to explain how new organizations of concepts and how new and more complex cognitive procedures are acquired" (Bereiter 1985, 201). One way to interpret this comment by Bereiter is that too many cognitive-processing theories have tried to psychologize everything and, in the process, ignored the use of conceptual knowledge to construct new ideas. Discourse events must have two kinds of ideas—first, textual ideas with a clear, functional purpose ("I am after Justice," "I am hungry") and, second, literary ideas which can themselves become tools for thinking and accomplishing purposes (Prawat 1993). Frank Smith has called the first kind of idea the *"Can I have another doughnut?"* theory of language learning (F. Smith 1988, 7). The second kind of idea includes, in English, truth, irony, plot, and ambiguity—the distinctive ideas of an area of study. This second kind of idea is often called disciplinary knowledge.

In summary, then, translation/critical literacy is organized around a language model of event-based discourse in which readers and writers fluctuate between participation and observation and in which various language codes link events to beliefs and attitudes in society (see Figure 25, pp. 286–87). These codes and the perspectives they represent are a central part of the subject of English in translation/critical literacy. This model of language contrasts sharply with that of decoding/analytic literacy, in which language was organized as a generic hierarchy of parts from phoneme to word to sentence to paragraph and to larger forms of language. Event-based discourse examines the same parts and wholes but within the changing relationships of self, tool, sign systems, speech events, mode, stance, and style.

In translation/critical literacy, all ways of saying have silences and exuberances; each language is saying something that another language "tends to pass over in silence." José Ortega y Gasset says that he was "left stupefied" by the claim of Meillet that "[e]very language . . . expresses whatever is necessary for the society of which it is the organ" (Ortega y Gasset 1963, 246). The fact is that society may need to say something for which it has only silences. One way to find different ways of saying something, a different combination of silences and exuberances, is shifting signs, speech events, modes, and stance—matters which will be discussed in the following chapters.

Let me illustrate how event-based discourse might look in schools, beginning with examples from an elementary school lesson on heat and a high school lesson surveying a community (Figure 10). In the elementary classroom of Deb O'Brien, students began the study of heat one spring day by describing in their journals the sources of heat:

> Heat came from the sun, they wrote. And from our bodies. But when Owen spoke about the heat in sweaters, everyone else agreed. Sweaters were *very* hot. Hats, too. Even rugs got "wicked hot." (B. Watson and Konicek 1990, 681)

O'Brien suggested that by putting thermometers inside these things, the students could find out whether heat comes from sweaters, hats, and rugs:

> Christian, Neil, Katie and others placed thermometers inside sweaters, hats, and rolled up rug. When the temperature inside refused to rise after 15 minutes, Christian suggested that they leave the thermometers overnight. After all, he said, when the doctor takes your temperature, you have to leave the thermometer in your mouth a long time. Folding the sweaters and hats securely, the children predicted three-digit temperatures the next day.
>
> When they ran to their experiments first thing the next morning, the children were baffled. They had been wrong. . . .

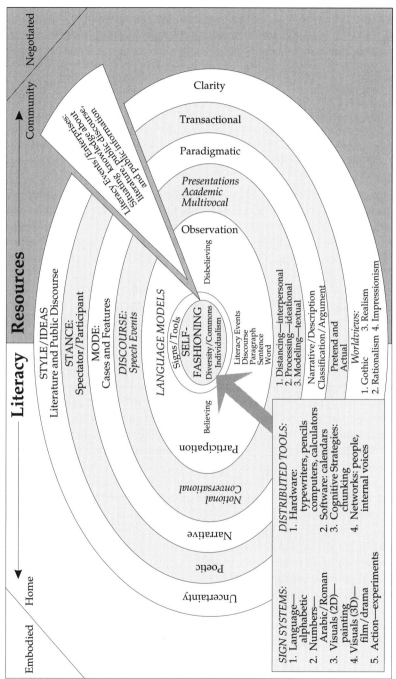

Fig. 10. Cognitive resources.

> The children refused to give up. "We just didn't leave them in
> there long enough," Christian said. "Cold air got in there some-
> how," said Katie. And so the testing went on. (B. Watson and Kon-
> icek 1990, 681)

Notice that these children are constantly translating from one overall structure, theory, or model to another. For example, remembering
attics and cars, some of them said that closed spaces were hot:

> How could you test that? O'Brien wondered. Neil decided to seal
> the hat, with a thermometer inside, in a plastic bag. Katie chose to
> plug the ends of the rug with hats. Others placed sweaters in clos-
> ets or decks. ... (B. Watson and Konicek 1990, 682)

The teaching here is significantly different from recitation/report and
decoding/analytic approaches in two ways. First, it does not treat information as primarily a memorized selection (recitation) or as a list of
parts (decoding/literal comprehension) or as a list of sequential strategies (information processing). Deb O'Brien could have had students recite a selection about the dynamics of heat or complete ditto sheets on
the parts of a thermometer or follow a prefabricated checklist of strategies and processes. Of course, information can be presented in this way
when it helps students make the transition from one form of literacy to
another and when it helps clarify essential information. But in O'Brien's
classroom, students are primarily negotiating and translating several
variables at once, continuing their negotiations for some time, making
translations from one model to another, and dreaming up unexpected
reasons for which they are rewarded, even reasons that may prove
somehow wrong. The purpose of the event is clear; the focus on ideas is
primary; the social interactions are built-in; cognitive processing is evident, including an intersection between home and school theories about
heat; and there are numerous opportunities for performance.

Another example of a translation lesson involves students in interactions with their local community, in a lesson I used at Oakland High
School in Oakland, California. In this event-based discourse, students
conducted surveys on their own topics while traveling on BART trains
running back and forth between Richmond and Fremont, California
(Dandridge et al. 1979). The students selected their own topics, constructed at least ten questions which probed the topic, and crafted a
few background questions on the respondents—age, sex, ethnicity, and
so forth. The students piloted the surveys on each other before taking
them into the world.

The survey has all the elements of event-based discourse. First, *ideas.*
Some students surveyed family issues: Who were the favored children
in the family? Others surveyed opinions on matters like parenting, skin
color, dating, and drugs, and still others probed contemporary contro-

versies like nonsmoking areas and gangs. Second, *social construction.* Almost all of the BART customers, most of them adults, wanted to be interviewed—in fact, they seemed to feel they had an obligation to negotiate their opinions with these young people. As they interacted with these adults, all of the students gained confidence in their abilities to engage in social construction. Self-fashioning could almost be observed as they learned to assert their authority as data gatherers and to play the role of learners. The students were often leading the adults through the survey and the issues, and, at other times, adults were leading the students through the survey and the issues. Finally, some students acted as mentors and expert guides for novice interviewers. These novices would stand and watch an expert student at work before attempting an interview themselves. Third, *cognitive processing.* The interviewing, drafting, editing, and redrafting engaged the students in challenging cognitive processes. Fourth, *performance.* The end result of the project was a published survey, complete with charts and data, which was distributed through the classroom library.

Neither teachers nor schools—or for that matter, any social scientist—can avoid classifying and evaluating responses based on some theory of development. Forms of literacy are always expressed in terms of individual development in schools. What is the theory of development underlying translation/critical literacy? For decoding/analytic literacy, development was a linear process moving through predetermined stages of development at particular ages. Children were either on-target, behind, or ahead of their predicted developmental goals. For translation/critical literacy, development represents emerging "zones of possibility" rather than a predetermined, linear process (Engestrom 1993, 69). These "zones of possibility" change as the student moves from egocentric to public audiences in social construction; from undifferentiated ideas and forms to differentiated and integrated forms and ideas; from social dependence and scaffolding to independence and selected collaboration; from conscious steps to automatic, tacit, and self-reflective strategies. In translation/critical literacy, these combinations produce portraits of development quite different from those portraits from stage, linear theories. In the new translation/critical literacy, students are being asked to learn five things about knowledge in event-based discourse:

1. knowledge must be embodied because the self has to be an *active* reader and writer, not a passive receiver of information;

2. knowledge must be distributed because the technology of hardware, software, metacognitive strategies, and networks has proved essential for postmodern problem solving;

3. knowledge must be negotiated through social construction, cognitive processing, and concept construction;

4. knowledge is situated in speech events, signs, mode, stance, and style, and each situation shapes knowledge in particular ways; and

5. knowledge, in order to be knowledge, must have a design or structure which distinguishes it from information and which connects it to the codes of social formations.

There are those who insist that groups like NCTE should never put forward a specific literacy policy for adoption as public policy. These educators believe that all literacies should have equal footing in schools. The free self—free to choose any curriculum and any school—is the goal of these educators. Bernstein has warned us to beware of choice proposals in public schools: "[T]he explicit commitment to greater choice by parents and pupils is not a celebration of participatory democracy but a thin cover for the old stratification of schools and curricula" (Bernstein 1990, 87). In other words, choice carried too far does not improve agency for students. Instead, it disempowers students, leaving them uninformed about the discourses of power.

One final comment about Donald Graves's lament that bad things seem to happen to good ideas. During a major transition between two forms of literacy, each form of literacy, the old and the new, attempts to reshape new ideas in its own image. Process approaches to writing, for example, got reshaped by a decoding/analytic literacy into segmented steps in which mapping and drawing became prefabricated sequences in the writing process. In the framework of decoding/analytic literacy, the recursive nature of writing got lost, the child's construction of the topic was ignored, and the opportunities for resistance and individual expression were eliminated. These issues of purpose and intention are not lost, however, when process approaches are placed within a framework of event-based discourse, the basic framework or unit of analysis in translation/critical literacy. One possible way to stop bad things from happening to good ideas is to place those ideas, from the very beginning, within an appropriate overall framework for literacy and for English. Now let's turn to some of the structural principles of *translation/critical literacy*, beginning in the next chapter with self-fashioning.

Notes

1. *An Experience Curriculum in English* was prepared by the Curriculum Commission of the National Council of Teachers of English in the early 1930s

(Hatfield 1935). Applebee has suggested that one reason the experience curriculum failed to take hold in the schools was that it lacked a clear set of structural principles. I am arguing that event-based discourse has a set of structural principles.

2. This issue of whether workplaces will use "higher-order skills" was raised by Kenneth Goodman at the 1993 NCRE (National Conference on Research on English) meeting in Pittsburgh. After Lauren Resnick's speech describing the use of higher-order skills in the workplace, Goodman asked, "Where do we find numerous jobs of this type? If so, why are so few of these jobs available and why are so many low-skill jobs available?" (K. Goodman 1993). In fact, low-skill factories ignore the high skills workers have. Darrah says one skill recognized by the workers and ignored by the supervisors in one traditional plant was the skill of learning to explain decisions in such a way as to "establish their plausibility should they later be challenged" (Darrah 1990; qtd. in Hull 1993, 35).

3. Chomsky argued that structural grammar put the sentences "John is easy to please" and "John is eager to please" in the same classification (subject-linking verb-modifier) based on surface structure, but, said Chomsky, the two sentences were entirely different kinds of sentences, one in which John is the receiver of the action in its kernel structure and the other in which he is the agent.

8 Embodied Knowledge:
Self-Fashioning and Agency

Binet's daughters exemplified individual differences in mental and personal styles, Watson's children were proper behavioral products, Piaget's infants were active constructionists, and Skinner's daughter dwelt happily in the baby box. Thus, children of behavioral scientists are not only their fathers' biological progeny but their cultural inventions. (Borstelmann 1983, 34)[1]

The American historian Elting Morison tells the story of Sims, a young naval officer who attempted to introduce into the Navy a new technology of continuous-aim firing, which all tests proved could sink more ships without increasing costs. But the Navy resisted, not because the technology was not better—it was—but because the new technology would have radically changed the roles and status built into the Navy's specialized, highly trained gunnery team, which was organized around the old technology of a heavy set of gears. In the new technology, any new recruit could quickly learn to operate the gun. Eventually, a direct order from President Theodore Roosevelt forced the Navy to change, and with this change came the elimination of the old firing team with its patterns of status, authority, and self-identity (see Morison 1966, 27–38; Schon 1971, 31–32).

Similar changes of status, authority, and self-identity accompany changes in literacy. A form of literacy is *always* a form of self-fashioning. The first question to be asked about a form of literacy, in fact, is "who, among the totality of speaking individuals, is accorded the right to use this sort of language (*langage*)? Who is qualified to do so? Who derives from it his own special quality, his prestige . . . " (Foucault 1972, 50). Luria, believing that the collective activity of the communist revolution would change identity and literacy levels, tried to probe these changes by asking his Uzbekistan subjects, "What sort of person are you?" and "What are your shortcomings?" He got responses like "I have only one dress and two robes, and those are all of my shortcomings" and "How can I talk about my character? Ask others; they can tell you about me. I myself can't say anything" (Luria 1976, 148–50). These responses represent an interesting range of attitudes. The first respondent is fashioning the "self" as equivalent to the material objects she owns ("How many dresses do I own?"), and the second is denying the possibility of public reflection about the self ("How can I talk about my character?"). These respondents are fashioning their selves in terms consistent with some forms of literacy, but not in terms consistent with the "higher forms of literacy" which Luria was looking for.

The important relationship between a form of literacy and a form of self-fashioning has been suggested by many researchers. When the Wolof child in Patricia Greenfield's experiments was asked whether two beakers in a typical Piagetian conservation experiment had the same amount of water or different amounts and why, the child replied, "It's not the same [because] you [the adult researcher] poured it" (P. Greenfield and Bruner 1973, 374). Jerome Bruner, who had studied populations like the Wolof children, recognized that this child's explanation of difference was one that "we had not seen before among American children, although Piaget reports one example in a Swiss four-year-old" (P. Greenfield and Bruner 1973, 374). Bruner concluded that this child was attributing to the adult researcher some magical powers "made possible by realism in which animate and inanimate phenomena occupy a single plane of reality" (P. Greenfield and Bruner 1973, 374).

This kind of reasoning, Bruner argued, is rarely found among schooled children, who learn the key distinction between human processes and physical phenomena, who learn in school to recognize their own ability to act and to sort out problems. For example, among Senegalese children who had been to school, either in the bush or in the city, not one instance of such reasoning was found. Greenfield and Bruner predicted that if the role of the Wolof child were changed by having the Wolof child pour the water instead of the researcher, the child's answer would change because the child would know that the researcher did not change the physical substances. Bruner was right:

> And so it turned out to be. The experiment was done again; everything remained basically the same with one exception: this time the child did all the pouring himself. . . .
> Among the younger children, two-thirds of the group who transferred the water themselves achieved conservation, in contrast to only one-quarter of the children who had only watched the experimenter pour. Among the older children, the contrast was equally dramatic; eight in ten of those who did the pouring themselves, as compared with slightly less than half of the others, achieved conservation. (P. Greenfield and Bruner 1973, 375)

Price-Williams has argued that Greenfield and Bruner's results do not reflect a schooled versus unschooled difference, but they do reflect a difference among cultures in the definition of self. Price-Williams reported that his Tiv children, instead of using the passive-self definition of Greenfield's Wolof children, almost always reacted with an authoritative definition of self:

> These subjects would spontaneously actually perform the operation themselves. . . . Furthermore, they would reverse the sequence of operations. . . . (Price-Williams 1961, 302)

Because of a cultural difference in self-definition, so the argument goes, the Tiv children in Nigeria in general, schooled and unschooled, had all reached conservation by age eight. Of course, children from other cultures may only learn to fashion an authoritative self in school, and in some cultures, children may never do so. The essential point is one that Ruth Benedict made fifty years ago:

> The vast proportion of all individuals who are born into any society always and whatever the idiosyncracies of its institutions, assume, as we have seen, the behavior dictated by that society. (Benedict 1946, 235)

Because the self is deeply influenced by cultural practices—because some cultural situations teach children to take risks and to define themselves as authorities and others do not—there ought to be many hints in anthropological and historical studies of shifting theories of the self within the same culture, between cultures, from one historical period to another (Harre 1984, 29). In fact, many different social constructions of the different selves of babies, children, adolescents, adults, students, senior citizens, and others have begun to emerge in historical and anthropological studies. Heath reports, for example, that some communities (Roadville) use stories to reaffirm the commitment of individuals to community, while other communities (Trackton) use stories to "set out the individual merits of each member of the group" (Heath 1983, 185). In addition, some communities (Roadville) allow only stories which are factual and have little exaggeration, and other communities (Trackton) encourage exaggeration and fiction, often developed around a "real event" (Heath 1983, 187–88). The latter obviously encourages the imaginative self and the former does not. These cultural differences can have profound effects upon the individual's capacity to imagine a different self and to create the fiction of a different self which can be fashioned and tried out.

Some cultures have taken great pains to deny the possibility of a particular self altogether. Although Saint Augustine acknowledged that man had an "inner turn" and a will to control inclinations toward sin (C. Taylor 1989, 131–35; Mauss 1985, 1–25), he thought a person was not capable of changing the world or of fashioning a new self. In fact, Augustine issued the medieval dictum to avoid self-fashioning: "Hands off yourself.... Try to build up yourself, and you build a ruin" (Greenblatt 1980, 2).

Until Sir Thomas More, according to Stephen Greenblatt, the self in England was a fixed entity held in place by family and tradition, but after Sir Thomas More, the sixteenth century's new secularism (1550–1700) created a more flexible approach to self-fashioning. René Descartes, for one, opens his first *meditation* with the ultimate commitment to self-fashioning: "I will therefore make a serious and unimpeded effort to destroy generally all my former opinions" (Lafleur 1951, 15). How was this to be done? Descartes proposed that the individual self could control individual introspection through rules of reason, through various instruments for measuring influences numerically, and through various procedures for organizing problems. Although Descartes's notion of the self led to the Enlightenment's richer conceptions of freedom, responsibility, and self-mastery, Descartes's self also led to atomistic thinking, a separation of the self from history and culture, an exploitation of nature, an emphasis on individuality, and a redefinition of the self as the sole owner of intellectual property.[2]

Different selves can also be found in the different forms of literacy within the U.S. Signature literacy constructed the student self as a passive, silent mental muscle sitting at a desk bolted to the floor, engaging in mental exercises like copying, while waiting for the teacher to provide the advice of a moral policeperson. Recitation literacy, on the other hand, constructed the student self as an "empty vessel" into which the teacher, sitting on raised platforms and playing the role of information authority, poured knowledge. The wax tablet brain of this recitation self absorbed lectures and recitations and then poured out this "knowledge" in recitations which were organized around the nuances of elocution and "good character." Finally, decoding/analytic literacy constructed the student self as a factory worker who needed to have his/her schoolwork managed, segmented, and organized around prefabricated assembly lines of intellectual work.

Each of these approaches to literacy produced particular responses from students. In decoding/analytic literacy, when students were asked to summarize information, they hesitated to depart from the wording of the text and relied upon verbatim or "copying" skills (A. Brown and Day 1983). Many elementary students, according to Annemarie Sullivan Palincsar, were "fairly strong decoders but had little comprehension or recall of what they had read" (Palincsar 1994). Some decoding/literal comprehension students in high school, when interviewed, typically thought that learning was a conduit from which the passive learner, a container, received information or strategies from an active teacher for later silent, word-for-word, strategy-by-strategy reproduction (Reddy 1979; Iran-Nejad 1990). These students were typically described as exhibiting widespread docility (Sizer 1984, 34), and as showing a "general picture of considerable passivity" in literacy events (Goodlad 1984, 113).

Translation/critical literacy, on the other hand, requires an active, meaning-making self. Knowledge in this new literacy is embodied in the actions and lives of students. Let's start with the risk taking of the first grader who, reading aloud from a text in which Johnny was sent to a home for *orphans*, first pronounces the word "or-puns" and, later, after reading that Johnny had no parents, pronounces the word "or-funs." Literacy in the case of this first grader who shifts from "or-puns" to "orfuns" is a form of courage, of risking mistakes, of a willingness to risk a guess, to propose a hypothesis or guesstimate, and to try another hypothesis or guesstimate if necessary. One of the purposes of English and English language arts in the new translation/critical literacy is to teach students to develop confident selves with the courage to engage with difficulty.

Sheridan Blau (1981) has argued that one way to learn to risk mistakes is to learn to continue the struggle, to be selves, for example, with the courage to read difficult literature in our English classes:

> Who among those of us who admire Faulkner felt able to read his demanding prose in the first days or first 20 or 30 pages of our acquaintance with him? If we have come to read him with interest and delight, it is because, in spite of the difficulties we once experienced, we continued in our struggle to understand him until his old-fashioned language, his unfamiliar cadences, and his convoluted syntax became as familiar to us as the voice of a trusted, if somewhat eccentric, old friend. (103–4)

Blau argues that the courage to tolerate ambiguity and to confront difficulty distinguishes the expert from the novice in literary readings:

> Often, the difference between a student and a literary critic is that what the student encounters as a reading problem and sees as evidence of his own insufficiency is, for the critic, an occasion for an essay on a problem in reading a particular text. It is our willingness to confront such problems and our courage in working them out— not our defenses against having them—that define and exemplify our literacy and represent the mode of disciplined attention which we are responsible for passing on to our students. (103–4)

How are students to learn these forms of courage and self-fashioning? First, within the classroom of translation/critical literacy, teachers need to model the roles and operations of thinkers and learners for those students who are new participants in academic studies. Mike Rose describes how one of his teachers helped him learn how to cope with difficulty by modeling a person thinking aloud, struggling with difficulty, reasoning like Hegel:

> As he laid out his history of ideas, Mr. Johnson would consider aloud the particular philosophical issue involved, so we didn't, for example, simply get an outline of what Hegel believed, but we watched and listened as Don Johnson reasoned like Hegel and then raised his own questions about the Hegelian scheme. He was a working philosopher, and he was thinking out loud in front of us. . . .
>
> *The Metaphysical Foundations of Modern Science* was very tough going. It assumed not only a familiarity with Western thought but, as well, a sophistication in reading a theoretically rich argument. It was, in other words, the kind of book you encounter with in- creased frequency as you move through college. It combined the history of mathematics and science with philosophical investiga- tion, and when I tried to read it, I'd end up rescanning the same sentences over and over, not understanding them, and, finally, slamming the book down on the desk—swearing at this golden boy Johnson and angry with myself. . . .
>
> We worked with *The Metaphysical Foundations of Modern Science* for some time, and I made my way slowly through it. Mr. Johnson was helping me develop an ability to read difficult texts—I was learning how to reread critically, how to tease out definitions and basic arguments. And I was also gaining confidence that if I stayed with the material long enough and kept asking questions, I would get it. That assurance proved to be more valuable than any particu- lar body of knowledge I learned that year. (M. Rose 1989, 49–51)

In this kind of teaching, the English teacher is showing how knowl- edge is embodied—how a literate self behaves, talks to oneself, ques- tions difficulties, admits difficulties. Many years ago, Gordon Pradl suggested that teachers should model first-time reading in front of the class by reading and discussing a poem which the teacher had not read before, and recently Paul Rabinowitz has suggested that English class- rooms must become places where both teachers and students are fre- quently reading something together for the *first* time. This willingness to risk first-time readings together in English classes helps model a self with a willingness to risk, with a tolerance for ambiguity and uncer- tainty—both requirements for living in our postmodern world.

Sometimes students come to class with cultural assumptions that stand in the way of their efforts to develop a new model of the self. These students remind one of the Malay linguist, who, after struggling to translate Emerson into Malay, finally concludes, "The problem is that only God could talk like that" (Becker 1992). In Malay, "talking like God" is hubris, and honorable selves do not attempt to talk like God. Copying Emerson's sentences may, in fact, be a kind of hostile act toward the sacred. Of course, in the U.S., learning to talk like Emerson is one way to learn to influence others and to fashion the self as an authority—of course, learning to influence others and fashioning the self as an authority are acceptable social intentions in the culture of the U.S.—and, indeed, it is one of the aims of translation/critical literacy. But without a different model of self and a different worldview, one cannot expect the Malay to feel comfortable talking like Emerson.

Celie has a similar problem. The young Celie in Alice Walker's *The Color Purple*, hanging on to life, dares not use the first person in her letters to God. She is incapable of any direct personal involvement in a conversation with God because God's authority is overpowering to her and because she lacks the confidence in herself and her personal relationship with God to use "I" in her "conversations" with God. How are students like Celie or the Malay linguist to learn to explore other models of self in English or English language arts classrooms?

One of the key ways to explore other models of the self is participation in regularly scheduled *cultural conversations* (Applebee 1994) in English classes, conversations which explore common issues and individual choices in literature and public discourse. The first key strategy in these cultural conversations in class (written reviews, discussions, projects) is an adequate selection of culturally and historically conscious literature which enables the class to focus on issues of gender, ethnicity, race, and so forth from an insider's point of view at different times and places. Sims (1982) has noted that many literature books labeled multicultural do not have an insider's perspective and, thus, do not introduce students to the typical historical, cross-cultural experience in the U.S. The second key strategy in these historical, cultural conversations is Peter Elbow's "believing and doubting game," which essentially assumes that learning to do anything is, first of all, a task of pretending to do it: One learns to read by first pretending to read, one learns to understand by first pretending to understand, and one learns the point of view of others by playing the game of believing other points of view and/or doubting one's own. Elbow gives several practical suggestions for how this game works: "a five-minute rule" in which no criticism of an idea is permitted and people request "Tell us more"; role-playing the position of another person, carrying the idea into other areas; and taking a position of resistance to one's own idea, arguing, for example, against a text one likes. Elbow developed the believing and doubting game from an insight he had about cultural conversations in the English class:

> When a reader is telling what she sees in a text or what happened
> to her in reading, the writer and the other readers must not just
> shut up; they must actively try as hard as they can to believe her—
> to see and experience the text as she does. This may be our only
> hope of seeing something faint that is actually there which she is
> particularly good at seeing but the rest of us are ill suited to see.
> (Elbow 1986, 259)

While playing the believing and doubting game, we practice, says
Rorty, "redescription" in which we develop a willingness to translate
"our vocabulary of moral deliberation in order to accommodate new
beliefs" and "to expand our sense of 'us' as far as we can" (Rorty 1989,
196).[3] Stanley Fish argues that conversion to new beliefs is likely to be
somewhat accidental self-interest and is not likely to be the result of
cultural conversations or translation exercises—what Fish calls "empa-
thy exercises" based on "a special empathetic muscle" (Fish 1994, 217).
But the practical effect of these positions, in my view, is the same because Fish, like Rorty or Elbow, believes that we must keep the conversation going, even among those with different vocabularies, and, of
course, one can discover things about one's self-interest by *attempting*
to describe another's point of view. Through the continuous practice of
these redescriptions or translations, students can learn the possibilities
of fashioning other selves and of constructing what George Steiner
calls "alternities of being" (Steiner 1975, 473).

One of the requirements of these cultural conversations is that
democratic principles must be followed. Democratic principles are not
up for amendment. Students will not be allowed to cut off the hands of
those with whom they disagree; they will not be allowed to prohibit
women from speaking no matter how respected such practices might
be in another culture; and they will not be allowed to attack another
person with personal name-calling, despite the fact that some groups
honor this practice. This goal in English of establishing a cultural conversation based on democratic principles has become, for many, one of
the central goals of English and English language arts, an effort to prepare citizens for engagement in productive public discourse (see
Faigley 1992, 71–74).

Another requirement of these cultural conversations in English is that
choices should not be forced and consensus should not be overstated. Students at various times in schooling are in a subconscious search for "mutuality" which connects them to others and which holds off the crisis of
making choices from many selves and alignments (Erikson 1968). Joseph
Harris argues that we too often project in our cultural conversations a
view of our classrooms as monolithic learning communities. Instead, he

says, "one is always *simultaneously* part of several discourses, several communities, and always already committed to a number of conflicting beliefs and practices" (J. Harris 1989, 19).

One of the purposes of the believing and doubting game is to practice balancing individuality and commonality, our "objectivity" and our "subjectivity." Our postmodern view of self borrows from Descartes the notion that "a characteristic feature of human social life is our ability to view ourselves and our practices as objects in the world, and from different perspectives" (Hammersley and Atkinson 1983, 234); but at the same time, our postmodern view of self borrows from Montaigne the view that we are subjective, embedded in our own contingent circumstances of history and social relations. The challenge is to balance, not deny, both individual insight and collective consciousness, to satisfy, not deny, some of the claims for our individual, "minimal self" (Lasch 1984), and some of the claims of our collective self "caught in dailyness, in consumerism, in survivalism" (Greene 1986, 235). This balance of our individuality and commonality is one of our most serious modern challenges to self-fashioning—"to define ourselves by locating ourselves among different others" (Geertz 1983, 234), to learn the arts of the contact zone (Pratt 1991), to search for mutuality amidst the threatening uncertainty of many selves (Erikson 1968, 219).

Let me illustrate this tension between believing and disbelieving and between individual needs and social needs with a lesson on Brontë's *Wuthering Heights,* in which we begin with Brontë's efforts to fashion a self to tell her story. Brontë has several self-fashioning problems to face, one being the fact that she was a Victorian woman who was discouraged from talking about passion in public. To get the public voice she needs, Brontë puts between herself and the reader first the culturally "acceptable" male, Lockwood, who tells the story to the reader, and second the culturally "safe" nurse Nelly Dean, who tells much of the story in a moralizing, hush-hush, nurse-like manner to Lockwood and to the public reader who listens in. Brontë essentially uses Lockwood and Nelly Dean as spokespersons to tell her story to the public because Nelly and Lockwood provide "safe" and "acceptable" public selves, allowing Brontë to put forward otherwise questionable material.

This technique of using the conversational views of Lockwood and Nelly Dean, says Mark Schorer, leads Brontë to discover something about her story and herself. She discovers, says Schorer, the limits of Cathy I's and Heathcliff's unconventional point of view (Schorer 1964,

14–15). At the point of that discovery, halfway through the novel, Brontë drops Heathcliff, who disappears into the background, and drops Cathy I, who dies. Brontë then turns the story toward Hareton and Cathy II. In Mark Schorer's reading of *Wuthering Heights*, Brontë had to translate her visions of passion into the conventional language of Lockwood and Nelly, and in doing so, Brontë discovered the limits of her vision of passion. In other words, technique became discovery.

Now, a quite different translation is also possible. In this other translation, Brontë is forced by sexism within the culture to adopt Lockwood as the spokesperson and to abandon the novel she wanted to write (and should have written) about the passion of Heathcliff and Cathy I. This gender translation of Brontë's predicament changes substantially the meaning of *Wuthering Heights* and suggests that instead of Schorer's triumph of reason, one could find in Brontë's pages the defeat of feminist feeling and intuition. Yet another translation of *Wuthering Heights* could adopt the point of view of the marginal figures in the novel, examining the silences of people of dark color or old people and translating the novel into the perspective of a person of dark color or a person of age.[4]

Playing the believing and doubting game about such matters will take some students into alternatives they feel they must resist. In *Storm in the Mountains*, Moffett (1988) suggests that *agnosis*, a kind of "blocking of consciousness" (236) is a malady so strong in some people that its preconceptions can "override almost any amount of contrary information given in the text" (171–72). Moffett acknowledges that *agnosis* is widespread—everyone resists knowledge at some time—but he believes that *agnosis*, when it becomes a way of life, "cut[s] life off at its very roots" (182).

Moffett's position has been challenged by Bogdan, who argues that in the poetics of need, people may block the consciousness of others to maintain their fragile identity: "when identity is fragile," we sometimes maintain our identity by "maintaining an enemy" (Moffett 1988; qtd. in Bogdan 1990, 131). Bogdan suggests that there is in the classroom a tension between social needs for social pluralism and individual needs for individual marginality:

> A narrower range of identification is more consonant with the poetics of need, and a wider range is more consonant with the poetics of pluralism. The literature curriculum needs to accommodate both, so that literary literacy signifies the feeling of coming to know the truth about oneself and the world (engagement) and getting distance on that feeling (detachment). (Bogdan 1990, 143)

One way to accommodate those individual needs for separation and special identity is to provide a network of clubs both in and out of school. These clubs, safe houses, discussion groups, and meeting places inside and outside of school can protect some of the concerns of individuals with special needs (see Pratt 1991; McLaughlin, Irby, and Langman 1994). Outside of schools, these safe houses have in the past taken the form of women's reading and writing groups (the Tenderloin Women's Writing Workshop, the Saturday Morning Club of Boston), male self-improvement groups (the New York Garrison Society), and numerous other groups engaged in self-fashioning projects. However, after-school activities (chess clubs, Latino Student Alliance) have actually almost disappeared in many schools, as schools ceased to be safe for after-school meetings or lost essential funding, and as programs like NCTE's experience curriculum (Hatfield 1935) lost support in the schools. But self-fashioning in the new translation/critical literacy requires both the cultural conversations in the classroom, using the believing and doubting game, and a rich array of school clubs organized around particular interests. During decoding/analytic literacy, English as an autonomous subject, separate from culture and history, could ignore club programs as irrelevant to the core responsibility of schools. In translation/critical literacy, that position is no longer possible. English teachers have a professional responsibility to encourage a rich array of clubs and activities inside and outside of school. This could mean, as David Berliner (1994) has proposed, that Elementary and Secondary Education Act (ESEA) funds should be spent on these club activities outside of school.

Translation/critical literacy also calls for new roles for students in schools. Our present roles for the young grew out of past literacy periods—what Mead calls a postfigurative culture—in which change was so slow that "grandparents, holding newborn grandchildren in their arms, [could not] conceive of any other future for the children than their own past lives" (Mead 1970, 1). In this situation, the old were guides to the young. By the middle of decoding/analytic literacy, parents began to feel that children had to learn from peers, not elders— what Mead calls a co-figurative relationship (Mead 1970, 59–60). But by the end of the decoding/literal comprehension period, parents were beginning to feel "their children's age-mates [were] moving in ways that [were] unsafe for their own children to emulate" (Mead 1970, 91), and, as a result, says Mead,

> We must, in fact, teach ourselves how to alter adult behavior so that we can give up postfigurative upbringing, with its tolerated configurative components, and discover prefigurative ways of teaching and learning. . . . We must create new models for adults

who can teach their children not what to learn, but how to learn
and not what they should be committed to, but the value of commitment. (Mead 1970, 92)

In this new prefigurative relationship, students must be taught to be
leaders, teachers, and guides, including learning the commitments
these roles require.

One of the courses which students must teach to other students is
how to go to school. Other countries appear to spend considerable
time teaching students how to go to school, stressing both individual
needs (food, learning needs, choices of classes, recreation, school materials, social life) and collective needs (group demands, acceptable
behavior in class and in hallways, diminishing ethnic tensions, civic
responsibilities in the school and community). Teachers in Asia, according to Stevenson, teach students explicitly "minor details of behavior that often are left to chance in our own culture" (Stevenson and
Stigler 1992, 91). These details of behavior include how to organize
desks, how to take notes, how to collect the necessary articles for pencil boxes in first grade, how to show the steps in one's answer, how to
interact in class, and so forth. Notice that each of these routines starts
with the assumption that a self can be fashioned for the classroom.
With training, older students could teach this kind of material to
younger students.

Another teaching role for students is the role of guide for adults.
Students should have some experience working in an adult environment outside of school where they would be required to answer questions and offer guidance to adults—an information booth at a hospital
is one example. This experience should be a school requirement. In
schools, students can play administrative roles (reporting attendance,
reading bulletins), counseling roles (chairing safe house meetings), assistant roles at faculty meetings, and teaching assistant roles in courses,
in grade-level or department work, and, of course, in the reading and
writing in the classroom where identity negotiations are taking place
(Brooke 1991). Finally, of course, the young can play critical leadership
roles in a rich array of clubs.

It is important to remember that this new teaching responsibility is
not only necessary for self-fashioning in school, but for effectiveness in
the workplace. When one looks at the NUMMI plant, one is struck by
the fact that in restructured workplaces, teaching has become one of
the basic skills, primarily because there are only a handful of basic jobs,
and workers must move around to meet the production needs of the
plant. In this new plant, everyone needs to know how to teach something to others.

In addition to teaching and leadership roles, another important self-fashioning activity for students is the writing of several kinds of personal narrative. Harre observes that "knowledge of one's own history as one's own is a condition for the sense of personal identity" and "an important part of self-knowledge" (Harre 1984, 265). One essential narrative is the personal literacy biography. By examining the literacy boundary between home and school, these personal literacy histories help explain family understandings of literacy events—the father who recounts his own problems learning to read, the mother who remembers reading as memorization, the sister who remembers how a bad grade made her feel. These personal literacy histories invite students to reflect about, to protest, to put forward the literacy tensions between home and school. In his autobiography of his own literacy, Keith Gilyard says, "I know that I, had I been asked in, say, 1964, could have told someone something about this clash between cultures, this problem of being Black and attempting to cope with the instruction offered in a school controlled by those of another background" (Gilyard 1991, 10).

In her book on multicultural education, Helen Fox tells the fascinating story of Shu Ying's conflicts over what literacy means:

> In my own class in academic argument, Shu Ying, a new student from Taiwan, has approached me with a similar request: that I allow him to miss the first hour of every class and give him an extra half-hour of one-to-one conference time every week to make up for it. Clearly, this is a proposal for which he needs to make a convincing case. But how does he design his argument? He does not simply tell me his reasons in a straightforward way, polite but assertive, to the point so as not to waste my time. Instead, he silently shows me his schedule, waiting for me to notice that his Chinese class conflicts with the first hour of my course. He does not advance crucial information, but waits until I ask for it—that all other sections of the writing course are closed and that he needs my course this term in order to get into the intellectual meat he has been waiting for, the classes in philosophy and history that he could take in his sophomore year. He does not mention these facts or his own personal wants and needs partly out of deference to my status as his instructor and partly out of simple politeness, which requires that he not insult my intelligence by telling me directly what I could figure out for myself.
>
> Besides these strategies of polite omission, Shu Ying has been doing me schoolboy favors, erasing my blackboard after class, asking my advice about other courses he is taking, working to establish a relationship that would leave me feeling obligated to bend the rules for him. His strategies for arguing his point, effective in his own society—and who knows, maybe effective with me, too—are far from a model for the first assignment in the political science

class; they are not the moves that in the U.S. context would "naturally structure" an argument. In fact, what seems natural to Shu Ying is strangely reminiscent of what he has been doing on some of his papers—leaving out some of the obvious, or seemingly obvious, points that he needs to make a convincing case. And this, of course, is the reason he needs to take my class, even though in many respects his English writing skills are superior to those of many of my U.S. "mainstream" students. (Fox 1994, 12–13)

These cross-cultural conflicts over issues of literacy are not limited to composing and persuasion techniques. Recently, a father called NCTE and complained that his son, who was born in India and who was educated in elementary school in India, had recently gotten a bad grade in an Ohio English class that was studying parts of speech. It seems that the teacher was asking students to sort various nouns into three buckets—one for person, one for place, and one for thing. The Indian student had to decide what to do with *horse*, and he knew from his religion and his experiences in India that *horse* could not be a *thing* or a *place*. Therefore, he called it a *person*. WHAM! He got a bad grade. In the Ohio English class, *horse* was a *thing*. The story had a happy ending, I might add, because Dennis Baron did a commentary on the issue on American Public Radio, and the principal of the school in Ohio used Professor Baron's commentary as the framework for a schoolwide assembly on cultural diversity.

The writing of personal literacy histories is, according to Louise Z. Smith, editor of *College English*, emerging as a new area of literacy scholarship:

> *College English*'s articles by Cheryl Glenn of *The Book of Margery Kempe* and by Janet Eldred and Peter Mortensen on literary narratives in G. B. Shaw's *Pygmalion* are the first that I know of to treat canonically literary representations of the acquisition of literacy ... This seems to me to be a particularly rich field of inquiry, not only because it offers us new ways to read Kempe, Chaucer, Shaw, and Toni Morrison, but also because it offers students opportunities to write about their own acquisition of literacy, broadly defined....(L. Smith 1993, 79)

Another important self-fashioning project for English classes is the personal life history focusing on the beliefs and experiences of the student. These autobiographies written in English classes should be placed within the context of one's family biography, including the voices of others in the family, voices of friends and co-workers from the workplace, and voices from the community, creating the self as "ensembled individualism" (Heath 1990, 301). In this assignment, students must be taught how to interview others and how to weave these voices together into a coherent personal story. Bruner's description of one family auto-biography is a very instructive example (Bruner 1990, 125–36), and the autobiographical project of Bartholomae and Petrosky is another (Bartholomae and Petrosky 1986). If possible, students should leave behind at the school at least one product (drawing, writing) which is catalogued in the school library, complete with library number.

The student portfolio, in which the student displays what he or she knows and is able to do, is yet another valuable self-fashioning project in English and English language arts. For the past two years, I have been working with several hundred teachers nationwide who are attempting to develop an alternative assessment model for English and English language arts which is organized around classroom portfolios.[5] For the student, this project becomes equivalent to a publication project, one in which the portfolio displays the student's overall picture of growth, including the reading of a range of books and materials, the writing of a range of pieces, and so forth. To make clear what the individual pieces contribute to the overall picture, the student must prepare an index of the materials, an introductory letter explaining the contents, some pieces reflecting on strengths and weaknesses, and captions attached to each piece that explain what the selection shows. After reviewing numerous portfolios from different kinds of classes as well as the teachers comments on these portfolios, I have become convinced that the portfolio may become a new genre in English classes to display translation/critical literacy skills and, at the same time, may become one of our primary instruments for examining student self-fashioning in the classroom (see Yancey 1992; Graves and Sunstein 1992; and Murphy and Smith 1990).

Self-fashioning requires the growth of self-consciousness and an increasing awareness of the differentiation of roles one can play. In one sense, this awareness of self, growing out of an increasing differentiation of roles, parallels an increasing awareness of subject matter, growing out of an increasing segmentation of English into literature, public discourse, modes, speech events, and so forth. The integrated literacy experiences of elementary schools later become the segmented and interdisciplinary experiences of secondary school English. These subject-matter developments aim for effectiveness in work and citizenship, but self-fashioning aims for habits of mind and heart—for commitments to truth, to justice, to tolerance. Thus, in self-fashioning, we find the tension between the differentiated and the integrated self, just as in our language models we found a tension between teaching practices focused on literacy events and a body of knowledge focused on modes, speech events, and so forth.

One last comment: First, the assumption that students can write coherently about themselves often suggests that the self and its family history have a delivered, unified coherent shape when, in fact, English may be the place where students attempt to invent a coherent story for what is otherwise unclear and uncertain (see Faigley 1992, 126–29). Second, in an age focused on the historical and the collective, the notion of self-fashioning and agency may seem remarkably out of place. A closing comment by Stephen Greenblatt seems appropriate. At the conclusion of his book, *Renaissance Self-Fashioning*, he says, "I want to bear witness at the close to my overwhelming need to sustain the illusion that I am the principal maker of my own identity" (Greenblatt 1980, 257). This is undoubtedly the view of our students. Schools should be reorganized to teach self-fashioning as a habit of mind, and this should make them better students and more confident individuals.

In summary, the self-fashioning features of the new curriculum for translation/critical literacy include (a) an after-school program of clubs, teams, events, jobs in the community, funded through ESEA; (b) an orientation at the school, describing the commitments and school habits necessary to attend class; (c) the preparation of students for assignment to administrative, teaching, and tutoring responsibilities; (d) modeling by teachers of new learning and uncertainty; (e) the writing of an autobiography by students; (f) the writing of a family literacy history by students; and (g) the development of a portfolio assessment system in the classroom.

Notes

1. This relationship between a learning theory and the fashioning of self is also evident in the way research approaches in experimental psychology have fashioned the rat. At Berkeley in the 1950s and 1960s, there were stories around Tolman Hall about Hull rats, Tolman rats, and Strawberry Canyon rats. Clark Hull used a T-maze which tended to privilege rats who got on down the road. Tolman's open-strip mazes favored rats who looked around and checked things out. Bruner says that Tolman and his students favored open-strip mazes in a rich visual environment rather than the closed-in alley mazes favored by Hull at Yale: "The Californians wanted their animals to have access to a wider range of cues, especially spatial ones outside the maze. Tolman's theory, not surprisingly, ended up likening learning to the construction of a map, a 'cognitive map' that represented the world of possible 'means-end relations.' Hull's ended with a theory that treated the cumulative effects of reinforcement in 'strengthening' responses to stimuli" (Bruner 1990, 103). And no one liked Strawberry Canyon rats, who were wild but who were believed to be smarter than either Tolman rats or Hull rats: "Animals growing up 'in the wild' in the

9 Distributed Knowledge: The Technology of Translation/Critical Literacy

> Instead of focusing exclusively on the technology of a writing system and its reputed consequences . . . we approach literacy as a set of socially organized practices which make use of a symbol system and a technology for producing and disseminating it. (Scribner and Cole 1981, 236)

We are, says Nancy Cole (1990), facing at this moment in our history a tension or transition from one conception of educational achievement to another. This book argues that this historical moment is a transition from decoding/analytic literacy to translation/critical literacy. During decoding/analytic literacy, cognition was defined as a hierarchy of isolated, universal skills which are acquired through school drills, exercises, and sequenced assignments. In translation/critical literacy, cognition is defined as a skill which is acquired and shaped by participation in socially organized practices.[1] These practices are organized around particular goal-directed contexts (producing a class newspaper, conducting a community survey), with specific domains of knowledge (English, history, mathematics), including technologies (computers, writing groups) and roles for participants (types of audiences, speakers, readers, and so forth). The domains of knowledge include style (ideas and themes), stance (literary or nonliterary), sign systems (actions, visuals, and language), and the roles for participants, including self-fashioning, speech events, modes, and style. Technologies are the subject of this chapter.

During decoding/analytic literacy, the schools proposed to teach *all* students in different tracks—one for vocational goals, one for college entrance, and one for the interests of the general student. The Smith-Hughes Act (1917) established separate vocational classes in secondary schools, the College Board created a system of tests for the college bound, and machine-scored tests separated the general students into remedials and those at or above grade-level norms. The tracking system of decoding/analytic literacy kept more students in school, but it separated and isolated many parts of the curriculum. The tracking system of decoding/analytic literacy, for example, often placed technology exclusively in the vocational track. Students in

157

business English, for instance, tended to have all the typewriters, adding machines, dictating machines, and copying machines while college prep and general English students tended to have only pencils and paper. The technologies of translation/critical literacy, which are discussed in this chapter, are intended for *all* students.

Schools during decoding/analytic literacy defined intelligence as the manipulation of symbols and strategies within the individual mind, and within this definition of literacy, schools developed a set of cultural practices to monitor individualized work. For example, in schools, group work was discouraged, group skills were not "counted" in accountability reports, cheating "rules" specifically prohibited the use of particular tools like calculators and spell checkers to solve problems in class, and "talking to others" was prohibited in all assessment situations that measured intelligence and achievement. Translation/critical literacy modifies all of these practices, granting special emphasis to the importance of students becoming literate in all the various manifestations of "technology," from group work to using computers, from thinking strategies to writing-to-learn.

We begin our biological existence, of course, with a set of biological tools—eyes, ears, limbs—and with an innate representation of our world through given sign systems. We extend our eyes, ears, and limbs with tools we hardly notice—hardware tools like pliers and saws, cognitive strategies like prewriting and chunking, software tools like posters and calendars, and networking tools like people who help us. Our primary hardware tools are now things like computers and fax machines, and our software tools are things like Gantt charts, calendars, datebooks, Post-Its™, and numerous other paper supports for planning and self-management. Our cognitive strategies are used for, among other things, remembering (such as chunking) or for seeing (such as squinting) or for simplifying and predicting. In addition, our new networking tools of other people facilitated by e-mail and other computer networks also help us to see, to remember, and to solve problems. We internalize these exchanges with these other people, and this internalized "talk" becomes a way to take with us those internalized voices for remembering and solving problems.

The key difference between early decoding/analytic literacy and the newly evolving translation/critical literacy is that decoding/analytic literacy stressed the importance of working alone without the help of either other people or various tools, and the new translation/critical literacy stresses the importance of collaborative work with people and tools. This change in attitude toward collaborative work took place in two steps. First, during the last twenty years of decoding/analytic literacy (1963-1983), when information processing and the computer model of mind began to dominate, collaborative work became important as a scaffold and support for students learning new material. Both Bruner (1976) and Langer (1989) called this reliance on others "scaffolding." Scaffolding first takes place during what Vygotsky (1978) called proximal development, shortened to Zo-Ped by Griffin and Cole (1984), in which the student is grappling with new ideas at the frontier of his or her learning and needs to lean on tools and other people to get help in internalizing those new ideas. When ideas are adequately internalized, the student can work alone, adding numbers mentally, for example, that were formerly totaled with a calculator or with finger counting, or writing out the words formerly prompted by external questions from helpful mentors. Notice that in this view, the student works with others when acquiring a new skill and works alone when the skill is acquired, and the writer or reader has matured. Translation/critical literacy introduces a modified model of the mature reader and writer in which that mature reader and writer sometimes collaborates, sometimes works alone (see Table 3).

The expert reader or writer can and often does work alone, but he or she also often needs to work in a collaborative setting in order to solve particular kinds of problems. These problems are at the frontier of society's cognitive efforts and are often interdisciplinary—problems like a crisis in environmental protection, where needs to protect the environment must be balanced against needs to produce goods and services, or problems like a crisis in ethnic diversity, where needs to protect the diversity of the population must be balanced against the needs for common commitments, joint efforts, and standardized ways for sharing information.

To secure the necessary collaborations for solving these special kinds of problems, the expert reader and writer will need to have a repertoire of hardware tools, software tools, external/internal mentors, and cognitive strategies. One of the new responsibilities of schooling is to teach students how to acquire and organize a network of tools and then how to distribute problems to those tools (Perkins 1990). Ann Brown (1990) proposes a jigsaw assignment in which different members of a group have different parts of a problem. The networks of tools used in the classroom must reach beyond its four walls. Editing groups and other forms of collaborative learning in the classroom can contribute to a model of the autonomous classroom, separate from the world-at-large.[2] Through mentors and activities outside of school and through computer networks, classroom interactions should expand to interactions

Table 3. Novices and experts.

The Novice Reader/Writer	The Transitional Reader/Writer	The Expert Reader/Writer
External lists which help External adults who help External peers who help External talking to others and to self	Available computers to use Talking to oneself aloud Writing notes to oneself External adults with clues	Internalized lists Internalized voices Internalized strategies
Learner has proximal development (scaffolds for help)	Worker does collaborative/ distributive work	Worker works, individually and collaboratively

with different views in local communities, in regions, in national networks, and in international settings.

Teachers who fill their classrooms full of technology must consider the ideological impact of these tools. Think about the clock for a minute. It seems that the clock began in the twelfth century to help Benedictine monks keep track of the seven periods of devotion during the day (Postman 1993, 14), but by the fourteenth century, Lewis Mumford reports, the clock had an impact on whole cultures: "The mechanical clock made possible the idea of regular production, regular working hours and a standardized product" in industrial factories (Mumford 1934; qtd. in Postman 1993, 15). By 1916, the idea of the clock had made possible the standardized measurement of time, the standardized assembly line in standardized management, and finally the concept of segmented processes in decoding/analytic literacy. The clock, then, had a major ideological impact on people's lives.

The computer will have a similar impact. Many city newspapers now distribute their newspapers free on computer networks, and many of these newspapers encourage readers to write to them on computers. One result is that letters to the editor can now appear the day after a story appears, making them more timely and a part of the ongoing civic discussion about an event or problem. These computer newspapers also change reading habits. It appears that people browse a great deal with printed newspapers but substantially less with computer newspapers. What impact does this technology have on our reading? Are these technologies reducing the amount of time we allocate for reflection while reading?

It has long been the standard view that ideas beget tools. For example, Maxwell's law of electromagnetism is said to have been used by unknown toolmakers and engineers to produce oscilloscopes. But Anna J. Harrison, former president of the American Association for the Advancement of Science, has suggested that this single direction of influence—from science to tools—should be challenged:

> It is true that science drives engineering and technological innovation, but it is equally true that both engineering and technology drive science. The three processes, science, engineering, and technological innovation, are synergistic. Each is dependent on the other two; each supports the other two. (Harrison 1984, 940)

There is a growing body of research showing that Maxwell's "discovery" could be told the other way around—that is, a tool helped generate the line of inquiry leading to Maxwell's discovery, just as clocks helped generate the ideology of the assembly line. If ideas come first, then Galileo's mental "invention" of ideas should be given more importance than the telescope, which was simply used to implement Galileo's ideas. If the tool is given more importance, then John Lippeeshey, a Dutch spectacle maker, should be honored as the first important initiator of what became Galileo's thoughts. The issue here is critical in schools because if tools are treated as though they were a secondary matter—a possible concern after one has ideas—then ideas do not require tools, and tools are not purchased by the school.

It is now clear that tools themselves expand our cognition (Engestrom 1987). They may teach us a problem-solving pattern or connect us by telephone or computer network to people who can help us solve problems, or they may reshape our ideas or teach us cognitive strategies which become the mental residue left over from the use of hardware tools (Salomon, Perkins, and Globerson 1991; Bereiter and Scardamalia 1987; Salomon, Globerson, and Guterman 1990). For example, a computer outlining program may be teaching one how to use outlining for improving the organization of an essay. In summary, then, every student must have available a full range of tools in order to have the opportunity to be able to generate a full range of thoughts and to have a complete opportunity to show what he or she can do.

Many people still believe that tools lead to the dumbing down of intellectual tasks, but various studies show that, although tools may de-skill or dumb down a particular activity, tools do not necessarily de-skill or dumb down the entire intellectual system surrounding a problem. Lauren Resnick has described how new tools change the social distribution of skills but do not necessarily change the total intellectual requirements of the system:

> With each of these changes in technology, compasses in effect became "smarter," and the user needed successively less skill. But the total system lost no intelligence or knowledge. Instead, some skill and knowledge passed out of the hands of compass users and into the hands of compass designers and their products. (L. Resnick 1987, 14)

For example, Puluwat sailors needed to be able to read the stars, the waves, and the winds in order to be navigators, and because they internalized maps of the heavens and of the winds, they were able to "start with any island in the known ocean and rattle off the stars both going and returning" (Gladwin 1970, 131). Says Hutchins, "The Micronesian navigator's toolbox is in his mind" as he stands in the boat and watches the stars pass overhead or the colors of the sea pass by the sides of the boat (Hutchins 1983, 223). But, says Hutchins, the modern navigator of translation/critical literacy is in a different position: "When a navigator takes a compass bearing on a landmark from the bridge of a boat, he is over the sea surface looking down on the position of his craft in a representation of the real local space" (Hutchins 1983, 207). For this last navigator, the skills of navigation were redistributed when maps, the compass, and the gyroscope were invented, taking some skills from the sailor-navigators and distributing those skills to new tools and other people (L. Resnick 1987, 14). At the same time, this redistribution created new skills for reading the new instruments, the new maps, and the new ways the weather was reported.

Thus, new tools almost always create the need for new skills in the system surrounding a problem. Sailors who started without maps had to learn to recode information about wind and stars as geometric calculations in order to match the codes of maps with latitude and longitude, and later, sailors with a magnetic compass had to recode compass readings to compensate for degrees of variation between magnetic north and true north on the simple compass (Dunlap and Shufeldt 1969). Still later, when the magnetic compasses made this computation automatically, navigators had to have the necessary new skills to read this new magnetic compass and to calculate the direction of sighting (L. Resnick 1987). And even later, the gyrocompass provided both the computation and the direction of sighting, but new skills were required to read the gyrocompass.

Many schools have limited the use of tools because they have feared the dumbing down of the tasks the schools teach; for example, the spell checker is believed to undermine the teaching of spelling, and the calculator is believed to undermine the teaching of arithmetic. What schools have not noticed is that new skills are needed—are, in fact, authorized in school—when machines like spell checkers and calculators help carry out old tasks. Schools have also failed to notice that some knowledge cannot be known without some tools. The decision to have or not to have a wide range of tools is not a casual matter. Schools, then, need to purchase a wide range of tools, to distribute some of the basic skills of decoding/analytic literacy to hardware and other tools, and to have students organize their cognitive abilities into a mental toolbox of various strategies for complex problem solving.

What are the tools, hardware and software, that people use? To examine the range of tools that people use, I asked 253 teachers how they used various tools in their lives. They reported the use of clocks, telephones, faxes, computers, calculators, stoves, refrigerators, thermostats, pumps, cars, hoes, hammers, pliers, shovels, and the usual collection of hardware tools. They also reported using an interesting array of software tools like calendars and lists. Many of these software tools come from our postmodern stationery stores: schedule books, time savers, memo pads, office flow charts, reference guides, books on time-management systems, and of course, Post-Its™—the essence of modern devices for the regulation of self and others. Who would have imagined that postees could become a million dollar business? These changes in our local stationery store are only a small indication of the revolution that has taken place in our software tools for cognitive problem solving and remembering.

One teacher reported tacking on the inside of the front door of her house a note listing everything she needed the next day for school. This note and its regular location became a tool for enhancing her memory. An elementary teacher described how she gave the children handkerchiefs to hold out into the air when they danced on the playground so that they would have an image of their bodies moving through space. The handkerchief, thus, became a tool for imaging the movement of one's body and, thus, helped amplify for the students the body patterns they were trying to imitate. Another teacher reported inventing a "thumbs-up, thumbs-down" language to communicate to her students when to pay attention ("thumbs up") and when to quiet down ("thumbs down"). Another teacher reported putting a clothespin in her shoe to remind herself of what she needed for school when she put on her shoe the next morning. Another used a rubber band around the wrist to remember a particular task.

Many teachers reported using the refrigerator door in the kitchen as the central information display of family messages and reminders. In fact, most teachers with families identified the refrigerator door as an institutionalized communication center for the entire family. Each of the tools above—the handkerchief, the clothespin, the rubber band, the refrigerator door—is an example of an *everyday* software or hardware tool used as a cultural amplifier of memory and/or as a postmodern device for the regulation of self. Students need to hear how people use everyday tools to organize their lives, and yet not one teacher reported asking students to review the various tools used around the home to regulate family life and to help people look smart.

To get a review of the third tool, cognitive strategies, I asked these 253 teachers (who also did the beaker test in Chapter 10) to try to memorize fourteen random letters and then to report what internal strategies (no pencils allowed) they used to memorize these letters. Forty-two used such cognitive strategies as visualizing a page on which the letters appeared or visualizing a room in which things beginning with the letters were located. Eighty-one used *action* devices—for example, simply repeating the letters over and over (three did not participate). But 127 others turned the letters into words, sentences, or stories and recalled the letters by recalling the words, sentences, or stories with which the letters were connected or chunked (as first letters or whatever). In other words, the most common cognitive tool for overcoming the limits of memory is the chunking of a small thing into a larger network of meaning coded in letters and numbers. The first thing to notice about these recalls is that they are coded in three basic sign systems—action, visuals, and words.

Teachers, however, did report teaching writing strategies like visual mapping, written notes, and dividing a writing task into parts (M. Myers and Gray 1983, 19-33); reading strategies, such as questioning, skipping, guessing, and chunking; and math strategies, such as working backwards, simplifying problems through metaphor, charting problems, and visualizing problems in images (California State Department of Education 1985, 31). When I asked teachers whether or not they explicitly taught students how to use chunking for memorization, not one of these teachers remembered explicitly teaching students the cognitive tools of chunking through the sign systems of repetition (action), visualization, or words.

In addition, only one of the teachers reported teaching students various methods for displaying problems visually, particularly three types of logic diagrams—Venn, Marquand, and Ramus. Venn diagrams, for example, were invented in 1880 by John Venn, an English logician and lecturer in the moral sciences at Cambridge, in order to show relationships in a syllogism. The rectangular graph was invented in 1881 by

Allan Marquand, then at Johns Hopkins, to show relationships of several variables at one moment (M. Gardner 1982). Long before Venn and Marquand, Ramus, in 1546, introduced the dichotomized table in which each term had its opposite and generated two other contrasting terms at a lower level in the hierarchy (Ong 1983, 200)[3] (see Figure 11). The Ramus chart for generating contrasting terms was thought by many at the time to be essential for serious thinking. Recently, Johnson and Thomas have proposed that concept mapping is an essential feature of technology education for today's workplace (S. Johnson and Thomas [in progress]).

Two other strategies are also worthy of emphasis. The first is the use of metonymy, simile, metaphor, and analogy to map our experiences onto language (G. Lakoff 1987, xiv), and the second is the use of verbalization, nominalization, and modification to translate information between actions and objects and between foreground and background. Each of these strategies, like the hardware tools described earlier, has become a conventionalized cultural tool for discovering and expressing nuances of meaning. More on these strategies later.

In addition to the use of hardware tools like computers, software tools like Post-Its™, and cognitive strategies like figures of speech, most people also use external networks of "mentors," experts, and collaborators to help them solve problems and look smart. Although many of the teachers acknowledged that the phrase "I was networking" felt strange and alien to them, they also acknowledged the growing necessity of this social practice in their everyday lives. Several teachers reported the consistent practice of calling friends to get help with problem situations. Learning the social and intellectual skills to work in a team on a problem and learning to develop a network of others who can be a resource to help one solve problems—these have become, as SCANS (1991) and other studies have indicated, a key part of postmodern literacy. The teachers interviewed recognized that mentoring and collaboration must be established in the classroom, but many of these teachers also recognized parental and administrative concerns about what all of this means in terms of traditional cheating and individual work. One persistent question from teachers was how does collaborative work get graded?

Another key tool in our postmodern tool kit for translation literacy is internal talk, and this tool grows out of networking and collaborating with others. When I asked the 253 teachers to explain how they regulated themselves, one teacher described "talking herself out of bed," and another described "talking herself through her day." These expressions suggest the power of internalized discourse as a tool for self-regulation,

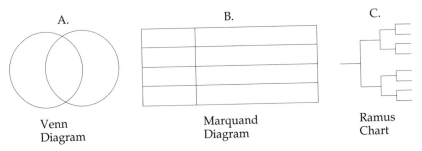

Fig. 11. Three diagrams.

problem analysis, and self-discovery. Internal talk, which, like other tools, is a social construction, has to be explicitly taught or suggested. This became clear to me in my teaching at Oakland High School when I found that not all students use internal talk for problem solving and that many students were not even aware that it existed. The individual student's situation may be very similar to that of Saint Augustine's, in my earlier anecdote, when, for the first time, he saw his teacher apparently reading something without moving his lips (Steiner 1975, 2). Saint Augustine was astonished, given the fact that always before "readers" had moved their lips and that the printed page was often thought of as a "talking" page. Saint Augustine speculated about whether Saint Ambrose was merely "preserving his voice" or "recruiting" his mind, concluding that Saint Ambrose's heart "searched out the sense" while "his voice and tongue were at rest" (*Confessions* 1956, 86). This was a new way of being literate.

Piaget confronted a problem similar to Saint Augustine's while he was studying children who, at particular stages of development, stopped talking aloud to themselves. He speculated that children started with egocentric speech—that is, they talked aloud to themselves—and later they stopped all talk to themselves as they became less egocentric and began talking instead to peers and even adults. Vygotsky, on the other hand, argued that this external, egocentric talk did not stop, as Piaget had suggested, but instead became internalized as internal "voices" for self-regulation, for the internalized talking of oneself through problems and even for talking oneself through memory retrieval or through the reconstruction of events. In the zone of proximal development, the talk of the other people and even talking aloud to oneself supports or scaffolds the learning of children with questions, suggestions, and other conversational exchanges. When children are able to internalize these conversations, they have made an advance in their development. But they need to know, as Piaget and Augustine at first did not, that internalized talk is a recognized cultural tool.

Even after one learns something by storing it in memory, one may still need the external or internal voices to retrieve or reconstruct the memory. For example, in early memory problems, a child often goes through extended dialogues with mentors and supportive others in a collaborative effort to construct memory (the following is a paraphrase of Wertsch 1986):

> *Mother-to-child:* "Where did you lose your gloves?"
> *Child:* "I don't know."
> *Mother:* "Did you take them to school?"
> *Child:* (Shrugs)
> *Mother:* "Did you have them on the bus?"
> *Child:* "Yes."
> *Mother:* "Did you have them when you entered class?"
> *Child:* "No."
> *Mother:* "Did you have them when you got off the bus?"
> *Child:* "Yes."
> *Mother:* "Did you ..."
> *Child:* "Oh, I remember. I left them on the bench at the bus stop."

Vygotsky argues that these social and external voices become internalized as psychological and internal voices. Years later, when the child is an adult, the child replicates this exchange in order to remember where he or she parked the car, left a fountain pen, dropped a coat: "Did you park near the entrance? Did you walk upstairs to get out of the parking lot? Did you...." In this approach, memory is an internal language exchange which recategorizes and translates events, a retelling which "stumbles" across the coat, the pen, the car.

In advanced Western countries, talking to oneself is valued only as long as one does not move the lips. Moving one's lips while talking to oneself is considered a form of senility or mental retardation or "uneducated" behavior in the United States. The fact that people look smart in the West by hiding the fact that they are talking to themselves appears to be unknown to many young people who, of course, rarely see people moving their lips. In my survey, I asked the 253 teachers whether or not they explicitly taught students how to use "talking to themselves" for self-regulation and problem solving. Two said they had done so, and these teachers taught internal "talk" in front of the class by demonstrating it, by "talking aloud to themselves" as they solved a problem. I am recommending that all teachers share similar uses of internalized voices with their students. Make internalized talk visible.

The importance of learning to talk to oneself is one of the reasons that students should assume some of the teaching roles in schools. Apparently, while teaching, students learn one of the most effective tools for solving problems, the "self-explanation effect" (Van Lehn, Jones, and Chi 1992). Webb (1989) and Van Lehn (Van Lehn, Jones, and Chi 1992), for example, report that published studies on small peer groups indicate "that giving explanations almost always improves learning, whereas receiving explanations is seldom correlated with increased learning" (Van Lehn, Jones, and Chi 1992, 54). Several researchers have reported studies showing that successful students are those who studied problems by explaining problems to themselves (see in Van Lehn, Jones, and Chi 1992, 2). Assigning students to work on projects in teams is one way to encourage students to learn how to explain things to others and to themselves.

These new patterns of distributed intelligence present new challenges for the classroom teacher. One challenge is collaborative writing. Ede and Lunsford (1990) report that their collaborative writing project revealed to them many of the problems that collaborative writers face. For one thing, the single writer writing one piece is the favored model. For the classroom teacher, of course, the first problem is how to grade the work. Do both writers get the same grade? The question itself reveals the competitive framework in which school writing takes place. The challenge to the teacher is to design some opportunities for collaborative writing. This kind of assignment helps develop the habits of mind necessary for distributive work.

The new literacy, then, requires that students learn to use a wide range of tools, including hardware like computers, software like lists, cognitive tools like figures of speech and predicting, networks of people, and internal talk. Thus, one looks smart in the contemporary world by having a distributed network of tools that helps in solving problems—what some have called "distributed intelligence." The creation of one's own customized, distributed system is one of the first requirements of a thinking person in this postmodern age so that we are never without necessary tools if we need them. Schools can help teach this distributed habit of mind by assigning students, first, to editing groups for writing assignments; second, to teaching and tutoring roles; third, to study groups for exam preparation; and fourth, to project groups for project assignments. In addition, each student should be assigned to prepare a personal directory of community and personal resources for problem solving (people, libraries, computer networks), and each year students should update this directory. In addition, in English, students should be explicitly taught the use of particular tools (knowing how to use the computer network, knowing how to use the library and research resources) and how to develop their own tool kits and work stations. Without an awareness of tools, without the experience of using them, and without the practice of developing one's own distributive system, students will not have what they need to participate in the new translation/critical literacy.

Notes

1. A very interesting confirmation of this assumption that literacy is shaped by the practices of culture is the study of student achievement in reading and writing by the International Association for the Study of Educational Achievement (Purves 1973; Purves and Takala 1982). Purves reports that in responses to literature, students in Belgium and Italy emphasized the form (structure) and impersonal aspects of texts, whereas students in Chile, England, and Iran emphasized the content and personal aspects of text. In a study of writing samples from fourteen countries, students from Israel and Australia tended to emphasize their personal thoughts and feelings, and students from Nigeria and Finland tended not to mention their thoughts and feelings. Purves concludes, "From these results one should infer that a part of literacy training in a society is learning to be a member of an interpretive community that helps bind that society together" (Purves 1987, 219). In reading, Purves comments that U.S. students are weak in expository reading but "seem to join the symbolic-moralitic interpretive community that has characterized U.S. readers since the landing of the Pilgrims" (Purves 1984, 106). Some of these same differences in attitude can be seen in Sarah Freedman's (1994) contrast between English instruction in the U.S. and Britain.

2. Lisa Ede and Andrea Lunsford (1990, 91) have suggested that collaborative writing is marginalized in a society stressing the autonomous self as author.

3. Johnson and Thomas propose three types of concept maps: hierarchical, web, and chain (Johnson and Thomas [in progress]). Notice that this proposal comes from a vocational education study, not a study of English or a cognitive experiment. Johnson comes from the Department of Vocational and Technical Education, University of Illinois at Urbana-Champaign, and Thomas is from the Division of Home Economics at the same university. My point is that English teachers could benefit from a broader view of literacy, one that pays attention to what people do in the workplace.

10 Negotiated and Situated Knowledge: Translating among Sign Systems

> To ask whether the geometry of Euclid is true and that of Lobatchévski is false, is as absurd as to ask whether the metric system is true and that of the yard, foot, and inch, is false. Transported to another world we might undoubtedly have a different geometry. . . . (A. Miller 1987, 23)

The different forms and social uses of literacy described in the first five chapters of this book were often a translation from one set of sign systems to another: face-to-face orality gave special status to oral and kinesthetic signs (like handshakes and nods); signature literacy privileged visual images; and decoding/analytic literacy gave special emphasis to silent alphabetic and numerical signs. Sign shifting always produces new ways of knowing: Helen Keller's shift from actions to words to express her desires ("Water!") (see Keller 1954); Uncle Toby's shift from maps to models to describe his battlefield experiences in Sterne's *Tristram Shandy*; the shift of stories from ballads to drama to attain status; and Professor Bijker's shift from pictures to models to save Rotterdam—each shift generated new knowledge by translating from one sign system to another (see Latour 1987).

And each shift served a social purpose. Ballads, which "had an inferior status" in pop culture, gained a new intellectual respectability when they were translated into dramatic "tragedies of private life" (R. Cohen 1984), and Lillo and John Hughes helped this intellectual respectability along by calling these dramas "an extension of Aristotle's notion of tragedy" (R. Cohen 1984). Professor Bijker's translation of maps and pictures of the Rotterdam Harbor into an automated, scaled-down, 3D model in his garage enabled Bijker to tell the Port Authority of Rotterdam, with a high degree of reliability, the kind of dam which could control flooding (Latour 1987, 231). A similar approach was used by Watson and Crick to translate X-rays into a proposed Tinkertoy™ model of DNA, a model which won them the Nobel prize.

Within the lives of individuals, these different sign systems follow a developmental pattern, according to Piaget. He argued that all children go through four universal, developmental stages, beginning with sensory-motor knowing and action signs (0-2) and then crossing the great divide into letters and numbers (Case 1991). Using his stage theory of ideas and development, Piaget was able to predict with much success what children should know and be able to do at different ages. But in follow-up research, more and more subjects did not perform as predicted, and the basic assumption that Piaget's epistemology was genetic, beyond cultural influence, began to be challenged.

First, some children appeared to understand some concepts too early, and some adults understood too late. Conservation of number, for example, was found at ages 5-6, when the children's only logic at that age, according to Piagetian theorists, was supposedly one-way functions (Case 1985, 236). Second, teachers began to be able to "teach" students to do better in Piagetian problems like conservation (Gelman and Gallistel 1978), an improbable overcoming of genetics. Third, some children began to demonstrate an understanding of a concept in some tasks but not in others, and, in fact, the correlations of performance from task to task in individual students were often "low or insignificant" (Case 1991, 6). Finally, some cultures seemed to have different sequences of development (Gudschinsky 1979).

To solve problems like these, Piaget introduced the notion of *decalage*, which helped rationalize some of the slippage between what was predicted by Piagetian theory and what actually happened. But the notion of *decalage* failed as an explanation of the inconsistencies in Piaget's data because *decalage* became not the exception, as originally intended, but "the rule in studies of cognitive development" (H. Gardner 1983, 21). As a result, neo-Piagetian revisionists like Robbie Case argued that any given concept can have several different levels of meaning or understanding, each distinctive, and that "any given type of concept or ability—including conservation and decentration—can be acquired at almost any age. What varies with age is the level of understanding," not the concept itself (Case 1985, 240).

Notice that in Case's revision of Piaget, *concept* and *level of understanding* are no longer the same thing, and, in addition, *sign systems* and *levels of understanding* are more closely related. Thus, sitting on a chair and visualizing a chair are different *levels of understanding* the unchanging *concept* chair, and these different *levels of understanding,* sitting and visualizing, are, of course, two different *sign systems* for talking about a *concept.* Each *sign system* is, of course, distinctive in the sense that each *sign system* is silent about some matters related to the *concept* and exuberant about others.

Although early studies by Frederic Bartlett (1932) showed that multisign encoding is an efficient way to remember, Bruner was the first to propose that Piaget's stages of development—sensorimotor, representational (preoperational and operational), and formal—could be reconceived as different sign systems or forms of representation—enactive (actions), iconic (visuals), and symbolic (letters and numbers). Bruner suggested that each sign system emerged at different times during the first two years of life as tools to solve problems—at 6, 12, and 18 months (Bruner et al. 1966, Chapters 1 and 2)—but these notions of sign systems as universal stages of development were not supported by subsequent research. For example, Gudschinsky (1979) reported that European children, ages 6-12, recognized geometric forms first, words next, nonsense syllables third, and pictures of familiar objects last. These children seem to follow a sequence almost the opposite of Piaget's stages. Although Bruner's predictions about stages of sign system development were not confirmed by later experiments, his general view of the importance of sign systems as mediators of knowledge was confirmed in a number of studies (Case 1991; H. Gardner 1983). Bruner's view, in fact, inspired new interpretations of Vygotsky's work in which domains of knowledge became culture's way of organizing sign systems for use.

Throughout the early twentieth century, humans were assumed to receive sensory information unmediated from the environment and, thus, in general, to respond in a similar fashion to events coded in quite different sign systems (Engestrom 1987, 74). Later, during decoding and analytic literacy, the alphabet and numbers became privileged as the complete way to know something, and other sign systems, like action and visual perception, became simply incomplete ways for knowing what the alphabet and numbers have already told us.

At the same time, in animal studies, sign systems were not considered an important variable, but in the 1970s evidence began to accumulate which showed that both classical and operant conditioning could no longer assume that sign systems made no difference in the relationship between animals and their environment:

> Rats could not associate visual and auditory cues with food that made them ill, even though they could associate olfactory cues with such food....
>
> The same kind of pattern was discovered in experiments in operant conditioning. Rats readily learn to press a bar for food, but they cannot learn to press a bar in order to avoid an electric shock. (J. Gould and Marler 1987, 75)

One interpretation of the evidence above was that sign systems shape our experience of the environment in quite different ways and are, thus, different ways of knowing. One critical kind of evidence for significant differences of knowing among the different sign systems is the fact that students have many difficulties shifting from one sign system to another. For example, experiments show that test "performance is highest when the symbolic form of the problem as given corresponds to the symbolic forms of the response required" (Shavelson, Carey, and Webb 1990, 695).[1] In other words, if visual problems require visual responses and if language problems require language responses, performance will be higher than when sign systems do not correspond. Switch the sign systems—visual to language, and language to visual—and performance is lower.

Another line of evidence which suggests that sign systems are significantly different ways of knowing is the growing body of evidence that there are distinct mental frameworks for sign systems within the neocortex. As Allport says, "Overwhelming evidence has accumulated for the existence of specialized neurones, responding selectively to particular (often quite abstract) invariant properties of the sensory input," such as touch, sight, sound, and so forth (Allport 1980, 28). Howard Gardner, Jerry Fodor, and Michael Gazzaniga, using evidence from transfer studies, argue that each sign system has a frame of mind which operates according to its own rules and exhibits its own processes (Fodor 1983; Gazzaniga 1967; H. Gardner 1983). Gardner, in fact, has proposed that there are distinct multiple intelligences—spatial, linguistic, musical, mathematical, and social (H. Gardner 1983, 283)—and Jackendoff (1994) has proposed innate, separate, universal grammars for music, language, and visuals.

This independence of sign systems within the brain has been confirmed in a number of studies showing that "simultaneous use of external information through multiple sensory channels" learning in diverse local sites and sub-systems of the nervous system "is the rule" (Iran-Nejad 1990, 584) and that these systems are "not necessarily conversant internally" (Ledoux et al. 1977; qtd. in H. Gardner 1983, 283). In Gardner's studies of adult brain damage and child prodigies, giftedness or damage in one part of the mind appeared to have little or no effect on another part (H. Gardner 1983, 50–51). Finally, of course, we return to Robbie Case, who started as a Piagetian committed to universal, cognitive processes and who lately has concluded that a theory about how children represent problems in sign systems at different ages may be of more importance than a theory about procedural complexity within a sign system (Case 1991, 97). This does not mean that there are not general cognitive processes.

The fact is that people can achieve a level of understanding in one sign system and not another and can know a basic concept in different sign systems simultaneously. Let me illustrate this point with an experiment I conducted with 253 teachers in eight different situations across the country. First, I gave the 253 teachers a problem adapted from De Bono (1968, 79–80) and Case (1975, 78):

> [*The problem as described to participants in the experiment*:] Two beakers have different pure substances in each. The one on the left has pure *wine*, and the one on the right has pure *water*. A tablespoon of pure wine is put into the beaker on the right (pure water) and stirred. Then a tablespoon of this mixture of wine and water from the beaker on the right is put into the beaker on the left, what remains of the pure wine. *The question is:* which beaker, the one that began as pure wine or the one that began as pure water, has more impurity (mixture of the other substance) in it, or do the two beakers have an equal amount of impurity? Remember there are no tricks. All conditions are true by definition.

In the first step of this experiment, I presented the same problem in three different translations to over 200 teachers. In the first presentation, I labeled the beakers as *Blox* (wine) and *Obnib* (water); in the second presentation, I labeled the beakers as *Beaker A* (for wine) and *Beaker B* (for water); and in yet another presentation, I labeled the beakers *Wine* and *Water*. The sequence of the terms was scrambled so that each set (*Wine/Water, Blox/Obnib* or *A/B*) was presented in first position to approximately one-third of the subjects, who numbered 81, 87, and 85 in the three groups. The subjects were asked to rank which terms made the problem easy to understand.

Three-fourths of the teachers (198) reported that the labels *Beaker A* and *Beaker B* made the problem easier for them than the other two labels—*Wine/Water* or *Blox/Obnib*. The reason teachers gave for this preference is that the labels *A* and *B* enabled them to separate the problem from immediate, everyday narrative contexts in which *Wine* and *Water* and things like *Blox* and *Obnib* were associated with food, thirst, and other data from everyday life. These everyday associations interfered with understanding the problem.

However, 37 of the teachers liked *Blox* and *Obnib* better than *Wine* and *Water* or *A* and *B* because most of these subjects thought *Blox* and *Obnib* made the problem sound like science fiction or fantasy or some other unusual or exciting event. However, this change made the problem threatening or difficult for many of the 198 teachers because some of them thought that *Blox* and *Obnib* were liquids which they were expected to know but which they did not know. Eighteen others did not like either change, deciding to stick with *Wine/Water*. In summary, most of the teachers (three-fourths or 198) found that labeling *Wine* and *Water* as letters (*A* and *B*) made the problem more understandable or more translatable because most people find that an alphabetic or an algebraic coding of problems helps them escape immediate events and enables them to analyze events as a mathematical or decontextualized problem to be solved.

In the second step of the experiment (maybe at this point you should reread the problem), I asked the subjects (253) to give me their answers to the question "Which beaker, *A* or *B*, has the most impurity?" Remember: we first mixed some of A in B (B is on the right) and then mixed some of the combinations in B into A. The question was then asked another way: "In other words, we have mixed the pure ingredients of the original two beakers, and now we want to know which beaker got more of the other ingredient mixed in, creating some unequal proportion of impurity in the two beakers or creating impurities of equal proportion in Beakers A and B." Sixty-eight said that the beaker on the left (*A, Wine, Blox*) *had more impurity*, 116 said that the beaker on the right (*B, Water, Obnib*) *had more impurity*, and 37 said that the two beakers had the *same amount of impurity*. Thirty-two did not answer. I will examine these 32 later. (You should know that I experimented with this large number in order to get a class [32] who would not participate.) At no time in any of the trials did this overall pattern of responses change. Most people thought Beaker B had more impurities. The correct answer is, of course, *the same*. Thus, 37 were correct, and 184 were wrong.

I then asked selected subjects in the group (those who raised their hands) to explain their answer to me in writing and then orally. Selected subjects from the 116 who selected the beaker on the right (*B, Water, Obnib*) explained that the beaker on the right received a pure tablespoon of the other substance and that the beaker on the left (*A, Wine, Blox*) received a mixture of both beakers, not a pure tablespoon of one substance. Therefore, according to these selected subjects from the 116, the beaker on the right had more impurity or mixture of the other substance. These selected subjects organized the problem as a contrast between two sequential events and concluded that the beaker on the right had more impurity because it had received a pure dose and the left beaker had not. These subjects described the experiment as if it were an experience in which they swallowed doses of different liquids at two different times, and their body knowledge told them that the first swallow had pure *A/Wine/Blox*. These selected subjects are, of course, correct in their contrast between the two events as long as one assumes that these two events are separate blocks of experience, as if one were contrasting two separate places, two separate recipes, or two separate bodily experiences.

However, the problem requires a solution in which the events are sequential *and* interact. What is returned in event-2 must be subtracted from event-1. Thirty-one of the 37 who got the right answer (*same*) explained how they captured this interaction and solved the problem with algebraic letters and numbers—in other words, with what Piaget called formal operations, with what Patricia Greenfield calls schooled behavior (P. Greenfield and Bruner 1973, 375), or with what David Olson calls "rules of logic for deriving implications" (Olson 1977, 277). As I will show later, these subjects used mathematics to escape their view of the problem as a chronological narrative with two fixed, separate events.

In the third stage of this experiment, three different ways to solve the beaker problem were presented to the teachers (216) who gave one of the wrong answers to the problem. These teachers were asked to indicate which solution helped them understand why the correct answer was *same*. In the first solution, which coded the problem as an action simulation, 16 teachers were given two pairs of cups with an equal amount of BBs (25) in each, one set of 25 BBs colored red and the other set of 25 BBs colored green. This action solution was only given to 16 of the 184 teachers because the experimental conditions (16 cups, 16 sets of BBs) were too complicated for most of the situations in which the problem was presented. The remaining teachers had the action solution described to them.

The 16 teachers worked together in pairs as they moved a specific number of red or green BBs from one beaker to another (see Figure 12). They found that they always ended up with equal proportions of red and green BBs in the two beakers as long as they moved the same number of BBs each time. Thirteen of the 16 reported learning why the answer was *same* by this action manipulation of the BBs. The remaining 3 simply said, "I don't get it." Of the 200 teachers who were simply told about the action solution, only 8 teachers out of these 200 teachers reported that this action solution, when described to them, revealed to them why beakers *A* and *B* had the *same* amount of impurity. Action solutions seem to be an effective way of knowing as long as people participate in the action and are allowed to interact with others. Simply imagining an action is not as effective as actually doing it. No surprise here.

In the second solution, coding the problem as visual signs (color and shape), the two beakers were presented as sections of colored paper, and the solution was presented as three visual steps (see Figure 13). In the first step, the red-papered Beaker A had a tablespoon section cut out of it, and this red-papered tablespoon section was placed over the green-papered Beaker B. The second step placed a tablespoon with a combination of red and green paper over Beaker A, which had the

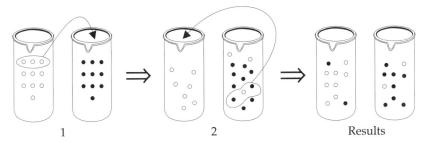

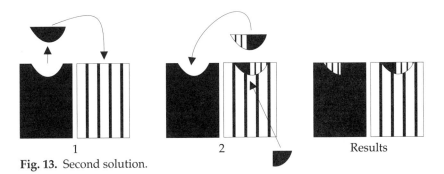

1   2   Results

Fig. 12. First solution.

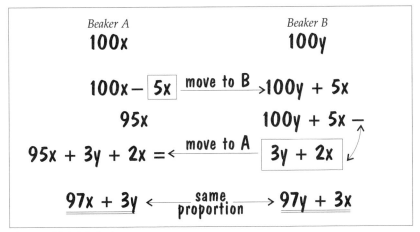

1   2   Results

Fig. 13. Second solution.

Beaker A	Beaker B

$$100x \qquad\qquad 100y$$

$$100x - \boxed{5x} \xrightarrow{\text{move to B}} 100y + 5x$$

$$95x \qquad\qquad 100y + 5x$$

$$95x + 3y + 2x = \xleftarrow{\text{move to A}} \boxed{3y + 2x}$$

$$\underline{97x + 3y} \xleftrightarrow[\text{proportion}]{\text{same}} \underline{97y + 3x}$$

Fig. 14. Third Solution.

First step: Which terms make the problem understandable?

Step: Wine/Water: 18   Blox/Obnib: 37   A/B: 198

Which beaker has more purity or is the same?

	Can't Answer	*Left beaker* 1. Wine 2. Blox 3. A	*Right beaker* 1. Water 2. Obnib 3. B	Same (Totals)	No. who learned by solution
2nd step	32	68	116	37	37
3rd step (action solution)	41	52	102	58	*21 (action)
4th step (visual solution)	41	26	74	112	54 (visual)
5th step (symbol solution)	41	3	5	204	92 (symbol)

*Of the 21 learning by an action solution, 13 actually did the action solution with BB's and 8 only heard the solution described.

Fig. 15. Results summary: Responses in the beaker experiment.

green section cut out of it. The third step compared the size of red paper in the Beaker B tablespoon to the size of green paper in the Beaker A tablespoon. The result was the same. Fifty-four teachers found that this visual solution explained to them why the amount of impurity was the same (see Figure 15).

In the third solution, which used only letters and numbers, the amounts in Beaker A and Beaker B were recoded as 100x (A) and 100y (B). Then, five units (or 5x) were removed from Beaker A (100x was reduced to 95x) and moved to Beaker B (100y became 100y + 5x). In step two, Beaker B, which now was 100y + 5x, had five units removed—in this instance 3y and 2x, although any combination equaling 5 will work. Thus, Beaker B was reduced from 100y + 5x to 97y + 3x. In step three, the 3y and 2x from Beaker B are added to Beaker A, which had 95x left. Thus Beaker A now has 97x and 3y. Notice that now there are 100 units in each of the two beakers, and that the proportions of x and y are the same (see Figure 14):

Beaker A: 97x + 3y
Beaker B: 97y + 3x

Ninety-two teachers reported they understood the answer after examining the solution above with numbers and letters.

Although a few (21) teachers understood the solution by encoding the problem in a simulated action sign system of BBs and paper cups, and although many teachers (54) understood the solution when the problem was encoded in a visual sign system of drawings and colors, the largest number of teachers (92) understood the solution when the problem was recoded as a sign system of letters and numbers. Thus, letters and numbers, again, seem to be an efficient way for most people to code events for solving problems of logic and proportion (see Figure 15). But the 92 who finally understood had had the experience of trying the problem in other sign systems. Half of the 92 said that the trials in the other sign systems helped because shifting sign systems kept the problem from being repetitive.

It is important to examine for a moment the additional 41 teachers who could not understand the correct answer even after the action, visual, and letter-number solutions were presented. Some of these 41 teachers appear to have been like the 32 teachers who were not able to do the problem when it was presented as a *Wine/Water* contrast in step two. Remember, these 32 explicitly complained that the problem was impossible, pointing to potential problems in their everyday narrative experiences:

"Was it red or white wine? I think the water content is higher in white."

"Some of the water will drip off the teaspoon and make the actual amounts unequal."

"Water evaporates, I think more than wine. They can't be equal."

"A person can't measure out amounts exactly alike by just putting in a spoon."

"The wine was pure, and the other was not. So that beaker got more mixture."

"Alcohol can never be pure, and wine is alcohol."

"You really shouldn't mix water and wine."

"The water is no longer water, and the wine is no longer wine."

Some of the 41 presented similar explanations of their problems. These responses and others like them show that some of the 41 teachers in step five and most of the 32 teachers in step two found it impossible to treat the problem as a paradigmatic problem in which the beginning conditions were true by definition—in other words, they could not or did not, in Donaldson's terms, treat the problem as a purely linguistic formula (Donaldson 1979). Some even insisted on treating the problem as a *conversational* event emphasizing social relations ("I thought you were playing some kind of joke").

Twenty-one of the 32 teachers who did not do the second problem for the reasons listed above stayed on the sidelines throughout the other steps of the problem. The other 20 did the problems, missed the point, and offered an explanation. Most of these teachers did not, in other words, find an adequate way to code the problem. For them, the problem was unanswerable or, possibly, avoidable. I say "avoidable" because many people, teachers and students alike, often use strategies like these to avoid doing a problem. The "fear" of being wrong in these situations creates an incentive to find explanations for not doing the problem. One surefire way to avoid a problem is to discredit the problem for everyone. Some teachers were obviously "afraid" to enter the problem and needed whatever rationale they could develop to discredit and avoid the problem. Notice that I have added for this last group quite a different explanation for the various problems these teachers had with the problem. I am suggesting that these teachers had such an uncertain fashioning of themselves as school learners that they literally could not release themselves or give themselves over to believing in the problem as a valuable experiment. They feared the impact of failure on their sense of self.

The beaker experiment illustrates why Piaget needed a theory of *decalage*. In fact, the experiment itself is similar to Piaget's conservation problem with one small, fat glass and one tall, thin glass. The teachers who got the answers wrong were obviously beyond the Piagetian age at which the conservation concept develops, and yet in this problem many of them could not conserve. Furthermore, many people could conserve or understand the problem in one sign system, say the visual, but not in another. Thus, one might argue that various forms of the concept conservation can be learned in different sign systems at many different ages, the conclusion Bruner reached nearly thirty years earlier.

Twenty-four of the 92 teachers who understood the problem after it was presented as a letters and numbers solution reported they still did not believe the answer to be true "in real life." That is, these 24 understood the symbolic solution of numbers and letters, even agreed that it was correct, many reporting a "shock of recognition" when the symbolic solution was being worked out on the chalkboard. But in their more everyday world of experiencing substances like *Wine* and *Water*, these 24 teachers reported that *B* "still seemed to feel like the right answer." Several teachers reported similar results with other kinds of problems. For example, one reported knowing the code for the aerodynamics of flying jets, but this person still could not believe that such heavy objects could actually be held up by air molecules passing over the wing. This tension between "knowing the answer" and "feeling otherwise" is an interesting example of people caught between sign systems of letters and numbers and the sign systems of action and embodied experience.

Sometimes sign-system problems are related to problems of translation from one mode to another—say from the narrative to the paradigmatic (see also Chapter 12). Some teachers reported "knowing" the right answer in a letter or numerical code but needing the action or visual codes to help them "believe" the answer of letters and numbers. In other words, the narrative experience of hands-on manipulation in action solutions not only helps some people understand mathematical solutions to problems but also helps other people to believe the paradigmatic, mathematical answer they get with letters and numbers. In fact, from this series of experiments, I got the impression that many of those who calculated the solution with letters and numbers went back to visuals and the hands-on BBs to see whether they could confirm or "believe" the answer in another sign system. This is like counting on your fingers to make certain your addition on paper is correct. The point is that *getting a right answer* may not be the same as *knowing the right answer* (in the sense of "believing"). Thus, *knowing* has two meanings as a result of translating from one sign system to another. One may need to *know* an answer (experience the answer) in two meanings or two sign systems in order to *know* it completely.

The sign system least understood, almost never used in schools, and yet critically important for understanding, is the body knowledge of the action sign system of direct experience. Hands-on action knowledge and other bodily ways of coding experience were given little status in decoding/analytic literacy and its cognitive theories organized around computerized models of information processing. However, Mark Johnson (1987), Neisser (1976), Dreyfus (Dreyfus et al. 1983), and Prawat (1991) are among those many researchers who are arguing that abstract knowledge—for instance, a sign system like numbers and letters—"is rooted in [the] physical experience" of actions and visuals (Prawat 1991, 6). In other words, to solve the problems of translation/critical literacy, we need to give new status to action/body knowledge and visual sign systems.

In one of his well-known experiments, Luria tested the ability of unschooled farmers to solve the following problem: "In the far north all bears are white: Novaya Zamyla is in the far north. What color are the bears there?" The farmers generally answered that they did not know. One commented, "We always speak only of what we see; we don't talk about what we haven't seen" (Luria 1976, 109). Luria concluded that these farmers could not think "logically" (114–15). Scribner and Cole (1981) replicated this experiment with other participants, got similar results, and then interviewed their participants, asking them the reason for their answers. Scribner and Cole found that instead of thinking illogically, these participants simply insisted on testing the assertion in a different sign system—in the act of actually going north and looking at the color of the bears. In other words, they did not wish to answer the question within the decontextualized linguistic sign system of the syllogism without testing the idea in the action system of direct experience. Scribner and Cole note that these farmers had not been to school where syllogistic thinking within a decontextualized linguistic sign system was taught as the norm. These farmers, then, were not guilty of being stupid; they were simply guilty of not using and not "understanding" the sign systems valued in schools.

In another example of the importance of body knowledge, students who did well on textbook problems in physics could not apply the laws and formulas learned in school in the hands-on, action sign system of actual physical events (L. Resnick 1983, 477). These students were given the following problem (this is my paraphrase of the problem found in McCloskey and Kargon 1988, 51):

> You swing the yo-yo around your head and then let it go. Draw the trajectory of the yo-yo, putting an X at the point where you let go.

Their responses are shown in Figure 16. These students knew from their physics textbooks that objects continue in a given direction until they are acted upon by a force, but, as their drawings of an actual physical event show, the students did not "know" how the numerical-letter knowledge of the text looked in hands-on, body-knowledge contexts like the yo-yo problem. The correct diagrams were those like (B) in Figure 16. Where did the incorrect diagrams come from? What "logic" did the students use to produce the incorrect "picture"? One possibility is that the students imagined themselves turning and turning like the yo-yo. In this kind of experience, one cannot stop one's body from turning right away—thus, the curve rather than the straight line in the right answer. In this last instance, therefore, students may be letting hands-on, body experience produce the wrong answer. The point is that the ability to shift sign systems becomes essential to "test" one's assumptions.

Yet another example of body knowledge that shapes one's concept of something is the conduit metaphor for writing in which writing is

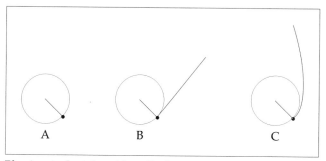

Fig. 16. Physics students' problem. In the yo-yo problem, the students are to assume that in (A) the string broke or else the students let go of the string. The correct diagram in such a case is (B). The students tended to draw the incorrect answer (C). (Source: McCloskey and Kargon 1988, 51. Used with permission.)

treated as the transportation of physical material, not as an interactive enterprise. The conduit metaphor—that is, information is hauled like freight on the highway of writing—assumes a body/action sign system in which the reader is a container, the writer is another container, and something is taken from the writer and sent to the reader (M. Johnson 1987). Students who choose body metaphors like the conduit metaphor to understand writing have often been mystified by the requirement to "interact with the audience in one's writing." Body knowledge tells them that writing is *the delivery* of information from one place (the speaker or writer) to another (the listener or reader). In these last two instances, body knowledge metaphors have not been particularly helpful first for understanding the physics problem and second for understanding a process like writing.

But in other situations, body knowledge is very helpful. The operations of new CNC machines are recent examples of the growing necessity for a partnership of body knowledge and other sign systems in the new "amalgam of vocation[al]-technical knowledge and abstract, academic knowledge" (Scribner 1987):

> Although these new machines actually cut metal in the same way that traditional lathes and milling machines do, the process of set-up is carried out by symbolic command rather than by manual manipulation. In addition, there is the whole skill of programming. Some firms have recognized that employees with machining knowledge may become more effective programmers. One machinist-programmer commented that in order to program you have to "see" the program from the point of view of the machine: "When you write a program, you have to put yourself pretty much on the machine. You have to visualize the action, the

tool movement. If you don't write in every step of the movement, the machine will crash into itself."[2]

The argument being outlined here is not only that sign systems are a way of knowing, but that knowing something in several sign systems is often essential. In the Scribner paragraph above, knowing something hands-on is probably a necessary partner to knowing something in the letters and numbers sign systems of a computer program. Scribner is suggesting that hands-on experience in the use of various machines may be a prerequisite to becoming an effective programmer of computers which run those various machines.

There is considerable reliance on bodily experiences in "out of school" problems, especially experiences which integrate objects, visuals, and actions. One example is the Weight Watchers'™ attempt to solve the problem of 3/4 of 2/3's of a cup of cottage cheese.

> The problem solver in this example began the task muttering that he had had calculus in college and then, after a long pause, suddenly announced that he had "got it!" From then on he appeared certain he was correct, even before carrying out the procedure. He filled a measuring cup two-thirds full of cottage cheese, dumped it out on a cutting board, patted it into a circle, marked a cross on it, scooped away one quadrant, and served the rest. Thus, "take three-quarters of two-thirds of a cup of cottage cheese" is not just the problem statement but also the solution to the problem and the procedure for solving it. Since the environment was used as a calculating device, the solution was simply the problem statement, enacted. At no time did the Weight Watcher check his procedure against a paper and pencil algorithm, which would have produced 3/4 cup x 2/3 cup = 1/2 cup. (Lave, Murtaugh, and de la Rocha 1984, 89)

Another example of shifting from numbers to an integration of objects, visuals, and actions occurred in the study funded by the military to find a better way to train people to become experts in electronics. The military asked for the study because the military could not function with the 80 percent failure rate of traditional programs. The study found that the traditional electronics classes started with books only— using language and numbers—then gave paper and pencil tests on the content of the books. The results: failure of 80 percent of the applicants.

Drawing upon evidence that experts in electronics depended upon hands-on experience with objects and equipment, researchers hired by the military decided to design an experimental course which started not with books, but with flashlights, table lamps, curling irons, portable radios, tape recorders. The students in this course, working in groups, examined how each object worked as a system, beginning with action (taking it apart), the visual system (the pattern of parts and wiring), and then words and numbers (written explanation of how the system operates). The researchers reported that the students, who would otherwise have failed, learned basic electronics (Sticht 1992).

Body knowledge is not the only sign system often ignored by decoding/analytic literacy. Visual sign systems are another. The importance of learning how to turn objects of the world into a visual sign system is evident in the way dairy preloaders in a dairy warehouse manage to open boxes efficiently, without leaving too many half-opened boxes strewn about. Dairy drivers place their orders for products in terms of numbers of units—how many pints of skim milk, how many half pints of cream, how many quarts of milk. The preloaders confront mixed numbers on the order form and cases sitting in the warehouse. The cases in the warehouse are translated into a visual design, like an abacus:

> I walked over and I visualized. I knew the case (holding 16 cans) I was looking at had ten out of it, and I only wanted eight so I just added two to it.... I don't never count when I'm making an order. I do it visual, a visual thing you know. (Scribner 1992, 107; see also Scribner 1984)

> These milk packers . . . used a base-ten system (from experience with counting and writing numbers) and also a base-four system learned in their activities as product assemblers. The "mere learning" of how cases were organized, what they look like when half or a quarter full, the number of units in multiple cases, etc., allowed for the performance of a mental math virtuoso.... (Nunes 1992, 137)

Another example of the recoding of objects as visual patterns is the inventory system of young candy sellers on the streets of Rio de Janeiro (Saxe 1988b). These children, attempting to make a profit and still have enough money to buy another order of candy, must mark up the prices for street sales in the midst of Brazil's rapidly changing triple-digit inflation. Furthermore, to get wholesale prices, the children are forced to buy many boxes of different types of candy, each with a different street value (1988b, 1416). In summary, these children, who are reportedly unable to use or to decipher the standard mathematical system of their culture, must keep their costs clearly coded, must sort the candy into types, must subdivide the amounts, and must reprice items frequently, often several times a day as inflation changes values. These calculations appear to require adding, subtracting, dividing, and an understanding of ratios and fractions, numerical skills which some children do not learn until they have attended several years of school.[3]

These unschooled Brazilian candy sellers accomplish these calculations by relying on an integration of objects and actions. A first grader named Marcos, for example, determines his prices by separating the types of candy into different sections of his candy box and by assigning sequenced numerical values to groups of candy in different locations in the box (Damon 1990, 35–38; Saxe 1988a; 1988b). Thus, after purchasing his candy wholesale, Marcos has to rebox ten groups of candy with three bars in each group. Then, he assigns an amount to each of the ten groups, the total representing the purchase price plus profit plus recalculations to add inflationary changes. When the child looks in the box, the child is looking at candy reconceptualized and recoded as stacks of money.

Most people appear to have similar systems for recoding problems. A friend of mine has described for me how a fifth grader used sign shifting to solve the following problem:

> A child had four peanuts, and her mother gave her some more until she had eleven. How many did her mother give her?

The fifth grader counted out four peanuts and put them in her left hand. Then, she continued counting, reached eleven, and made a pile with those in her right hand. Then, she put aside the four peanuts in her left hand and began counting the number in the pile near her right hand. Finally, she announced "seven" and, thus, solved the problem. Penelope Peterson (1988, 10) has described many examples like this, showing how students use many forms of sign shifting to solve math problems.

The child's work in Figure 17 is another example of the importance of sign shifting. The child started with the drawing and then worked back and forth between the drawing and the writing.[4] There is substantial evidence that children use drawing as a scaffold for their writing and that early writing becomes a way to translate one's drawing (Dyson 1993). In these situations, writing often appears to precede one kind of reading—the child translating from drawing to writing and then translating the initial writing into a reflective reading. A similar example of sign shifting is the work of the student who wrote the letter in Figure 18, first mapping the letter and then writing the letter. Mapping allows the student to get some ideas flowing before having to undertake what, for this child, is the more difficult task of writing.

Adults working on research projects also find that recoding information can be a powerful tool for discovery and knowing. Latour (1987, 224–25) has suggested that shifts from one sign system to another, especially from action systems to visual maps, print, and numbers are part of an overall effort to own information as a source of power. Thus, information is first made *visible* (stars become bearings), then *mobile* and *portable* (stars are turned into maps and drawings on paper), then *stable* (stored in

Fig. 17. Example of sign shifting.

libraries and placed on long-lasting paper), and, finally, *combinable* (maps are standardized so they can be combined). In the process, discoveries are made. One example of this discovery process through sign shifting is Galileo's translation of *time*, an invisible entity, into *distance*, which could be drawn on paper as a geometric, mathematical proof. This is *not* just a recoding or substitution. These sign shifts "reconstruct those properties" and give us a different interpretation (Olson 1994, 221).

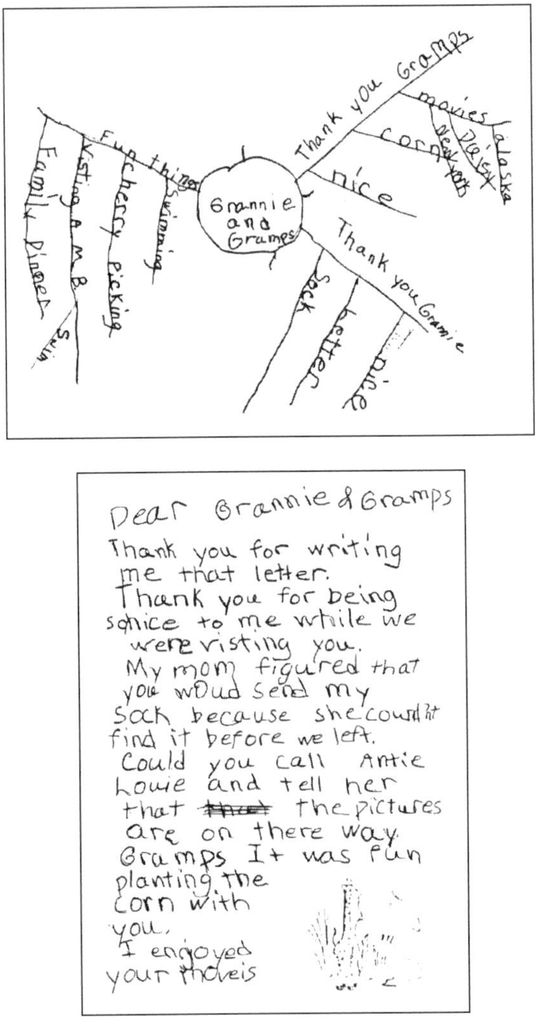

Fig. 18. Mapping the letter. (Source: Buckley and Boyle 1981, 197–98. Used by permission of the Bay Area Writing Project.)

In the chapter on tools, we have already seen how recoding stars and ocean currents into maps and compass calculations expands one's cognition (Engestrom 1987). These changes also change our views of ourselves—say, from the role of travelers to the role of explorers: "Only after print and extensive experience with maps ... would human beings, when they thought about the cosmos ..., think primarily of something laid out before their eyes ... ready to be 'explored.' The ancient world knew few

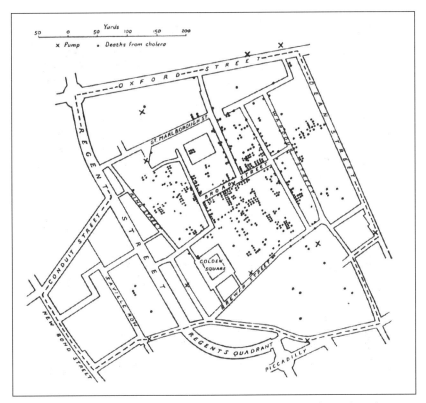

Fig. 19. Visuals as research tools. The map of a section of London that was drawn by John Snow in 1854 showing cholera deaths and water pumps. It is often used as a landmark in epidemiology. (Source: Tufte 1983, 24.)

'explorers,' though it did know many itinerants, travelers, voyagers, ..." (Ong 1982, 73). In another example of sign shifting as discovery, in Figure 19, the dots code deaths from cholera, and the X's mark water pumps. The visual pattern enabled John Snow to estimate in 1854 the relationship between the water contamination and cholera (Tufte 1983, 24). Although modern computers have increased the use of visualization as a research tool, very few English classes encourage students to make use of this capability—or simply to visualize their ideas, to study the way ideas change when they move from columns to a bar graph, from a pie chart to prose, from a photograph to prose description.

Because sign shifting has become one of the required habits of mind for postmodern life and for translation/critical literacy, English studies and the English language arts, K–12, should include translations from

Table 4. Sign shifting.

Subject	Alphabet/ Discourse	Action/Words	Action	Visual	Visual/Spatial	Film/Sound
1. Shirley Jackson's *The Lottery*	Read *The Lottery* (short story)	Rewrite *The Lottery* as a play/TV show	Act out scenes from *The Lottery*	Design ad for TV play	Design setting for one scene	Filmed interviews on responses to story
2. Mark Twain's *Huck Finn* *Tom Sawyer*	Read *Huck Finn* and *Tom Sawyer* (novels)	See musical *The River* ("Huck Finn" musical). Write one scene for play on Huck Finn	Act out scene from play	Draw detailed map of Huck's travels down the river	Design detailed setting for one scene	Write a 3-minute TV ad for the play *Huck Finn*
3. Fall of Icarus	Read the poem (Auden, Ovid)	Rewrite poems as stories	Read story aloud	Discuss painting *Fall of Icarus* (Brueghel)	Contrast two Icarus paintings	Filmed panel discussion on poems
4. Steinbeck's *Chrysanthemums*	Read Steinbeck's *Chrysanthemums*	Write scene for TV drama of *Chrysanthemums*	Act out scene from TV drama	Discuss Grant Wood's *American Gothic*	Design detailed scene for TV adaptation	Write a 3-minute TV ad for "The Lottery"
5. Brontë's *Wuthering Heights*	Read the novel	See the movie. Write one scene for the play *Wuthering Heights*	Act out one scene from play	Draw detailed map of Grange and Heights	Design lot and room layout of *Wuthering Heights*	Filmed interviews on responses to *Wuthering Heights*

one sign system to another as an essential part of the curriculum. These translations in English studies should include translating words into action—"acting out" scenes from stories, poems, and dramas—and translating novels to films, reports to speeches, paintings to descriptions, descriptions to maps, maps to models, ideas to talk-show panels, novels to time lines, newspaper reports to charts, statistical summaries to essays, essays to a series of still photographs, definitions to pie or bar charts (see Table 4). This means that students in English and English language arts classes need to begin to give substantially more attention to various media, particularly television and film.

This need for attention to media is particularly apparent in our secondary composition programs, where a number of researchers are beginning to present interesting models. Barbara Morris continues to publish interesting studies on the structure of media, and Glynda Hull is one of the few composition researchers I know who is experimenting with multimedia compositions in her university composition classes. Brian Reilly has developed an outstanding portfolio project using video and CD-ROM at Bell High School in Los Angeles, while several teachers in the literacy unit of the New Standards Project are using visuals, sounds, and print in their portfolio reports on student work. These are just a few of the efforts to expand the sign systems we use within the domain of K–12 English and English language arts.

Notes

1. "Performance was highest for the numeric/algebraic problem that required a numeric response...and for the word problem that required a verbal response.... Performance was lowest for the numeric/algebraic problem that required a verbal response...and for the word problem that required a numeric response.... The results of both studies suggest that varying the symbolic form of the problem given and of the response required will provide more information about students' understanding than will varying one or neither of these factors" (Shavelson, Carey, and Webb 1990, 695).

2. Sylvia Scribner wrote this paragraph to describe a CNC project proposal which was later funded and for which she was the principal investigator. After her death, her graduate students and colleagues completed the CNC project. One of the publications from that study reports the following conclusion, a confirmation of Sylvia Scribner's earlier hypothesis:

> Our study showed that the knowledge and skill associated with CNC machining (e.g., the use of a specialized code, the specification of coordinates in space) do not exist independently of mechanical machining knowledge and skills for any machinist learning CNC.... Much of the information used in the process of traditional

11 Negotiated and Situated Knowledge: Translating among Speech Events

> The stupendous reality that is language cannot be understood unless we begin by observing that speech consists above all in silences. A being who could not renounce saying many things would be incapable of speaking. And each language represents a different equation between manifestations and silences. Each people leaves some things unsaid in order to say others. (Ortega y Gasset 1963, 246)

In the 1970s, while organizing dozens of K–12 writing assessments for the Bay Area Writing Project, I noticed that the students just below the passing point were almost always writing what I would call *conversational* prose. Because of this nagging consistency, I undertook a research project to explore what kinds of speech events appeared to be shaping written composition and what kinds of ratings schools were giving compositions based on different speech events. What I found was not all that surprising. First, I found that the top scores in all writing assessments were given to writing samples based on *presentational* speech events and that lower-half scores were given to either *conversational* writing or *acquisition* writing. Acquisition writing received low scores because it lacked fluency, including motor coordination. *Conversational* writing received low scores because, according to those who scored papers, it was "too personal." In a series of follow-up interviews, I found that many of these *acquisition* and *conversational* writers thought they were doing the right thing. *Conversational* writers thought they were writing in an honest, warm, engaging way, and *acquisition* writers thought they had spelled everything right. So what went wrong? What went wrong, of course, was that, among other things, they picked the wrong speech event to shape their discourse (M. Myers 1982b).

This happens all the time. Let me illustrate the point with a story broadly paraphrased and borrowed from Margaret Donaldson, one which she borrowed from Ziff. Two men are sitting in a football stadium, waiting for the big game to begin. The first man asks, "Do you suppose anyone can get through all that security and get in the game free?" The second man says, "No." The first man says, "Gotcha. The coach will get in free" (paraphrase of Ziff 1972; source story in Donaldson 1979, 69).

Why do some people think this is a funny story? This story is not funny—in fact, it makes no sense—unless one realizes that the first man instantiates an *academic* speech event by asking an academic question, and the second man assumes this is a *conversational* exchange. Not realizing that the situation was a test or *academic* speech event, the second man responds with a *conversational* exchange in which social relations are cooperative and words like "anyone" are approximations. The joke is that the second man guessed wrong about the speech event.

This kind of joke is played on Piaget's subjects all the time. In one standard task, a child is shown two parallel rows of ten pennies and asked to judge whether the two rows contain the same number of pennies or a different number. Then, one of the rows is lengthened or shortened, and the child is asked again whether the two rows have the same number of pennies or a different number. Typically, children say that the two rows no longer have the same number of pennies. Donaldson and McGarrigle (1974) suggested that this incorrect answer resulted more from the child's misunderstanding of the speech event than from the child's misunderstanding of numbers and the words "all" and "more."[1]

They observed that in these experiments, the experimenter establishes a *conversational* relationship (or speech event) with the subject before, during, and after asking, "Are they the same or different?" Because the child interprets the experimental question as part of a *conversational* speech event in which one is not asked exactly the same question twice without a good social reason, the child says the two rows do *not* have the same number of pennies. Donaldson says the child gave an inappropriate answer to these Piagetian questions because "the child has not learned to distinguish between situations where he is supposed to give primacy to language, and situations where he is not" (Donaldson 1979, 69).

Giving primacy to language is, of course, the practice in *academic* speech events, not in *conversational* speech events where social variables are primary. In academic events, one gives primacy to the language of *same* and *different*. In *conversational* speech events, one gives primacy to social relationships with the experimenter or partner. What do you do when someone rearranges something in front of you and then asks, "Are they the same or different?" Imagine watching someone rotate the tires on your car and then having that person ask you whether the number of tires was the same or different. The rules of *conversational* sociability and approximation lead many people to interpret the question as a social request for "different." Thus, the child gives an approximate social answer, and, like the man at the football stadium, finds himself or herself caught in a "gotcha." What the child got wrong, once again, was the speech event. Our estimate of the speech event in which our speech is embedded, then, can make a big difference in the way we judge appropriate responses.

However, except for studies of levels of usage, variations among speech events were generally ignored by teachers and language researchers during decoding/analytic literacy. What mattered to teachers and language researchers of decoding/analytic literacy was Chomsky's universal syntax, not contextualized points of view ("I" or "he"), hesitations ("ah"), particular modifiers ("sorta"), and other matters of special interest in social interactions. Of course, everything Chomsky asserts about the biology of syntax can be true and still tell us little or nothing about speech events. Toward the end of decoding/analytic literacy, teachers and language researchers turned for language models to Piaget, who believed there were universal, basic structures like time and space underlying all problems, and who, like Chomsky, believed that various forms of mental development reflected these universal structures of knowledge. Thus, for Piaget, like Chomsky, the highly contextualized speech event was not a matter of interest.

Bernstein challenged Piaget's assertion of universal structures for *all* knowledge by examining how specific speech events shaped information and how students learned to distinguish among the rules of different speech events. In his experiments, asking children to tell the story contained in a sequence of pictures, Bernstein found that working-class children responded with an "involved" perspective: "They're playing football and he kicks it and it goes through there" (Bernstein 1972, 167). Middle-class children, on the other hand, responded with a "detached" perspective, drawing explicit attention to details in the sequence: "Three boys are playing football and one boy kicks the ball and it goes through the window" (Bernstein 1972, 167).

In my reading of Bernstein, the middle-class child's use of the speech-event conventions of explicitness—for instance, saying "Three boys are" instead of "They're" and "it goes through the window" instead of "it goes through there"—indicated the middle-class child's mental ability to create a detached, decontextualized context for problem solving, and, thus, to create an academic speech event. The reason these middle-class children differed from working-class children in their ability to create the detached context could be traced, said Bernstein, to the differences between the contexts and conventions created and authorized by middle-class and working-class families. That is, middle-class families encouraged the detached context and elaborated codes of academic speech events, and working-class families did not. Furthermore, because academic speech events were given high value in school, a child's middle-class background ended up being given high value in school.

A similar finding was reported by Patricia Greenfield, among others, in a series of studies examining Wolof children from Senegal who were given an array of pictures and objects and who were asked to put together those that were most alike. She asked the children, "Why do you say (or think) that thus and such are true?" Schooled Wolof children responded, as had schooled American children previously, by explaining why they grouped together pictures of an object with the actual object itself. But unschooled Wolof children responded "with uncomprehending silence" (P. Greenfield and Bruner 1973, 372).

Greenfield then changed the question from "Why do you say or think these are alike?" to "Why are these alike?" To this second question, the unschooled Wolof children responded. Greenfield concluded that unschooled Wolof children showed in their response to the first question that they "lack Western self-consciousness" because they "[did] not distinguish between their own thought or statement about something and the thing itself" (Greenfield and Bruner 1973, 372). In other words, she, like Bernstein before her, recognized that within the norms of schooling in the U.S. and the U.K., the failure to stand outside the immediate question is evidence of a literacy deficit. This is particularly true within the conventions of decoding/analytic literacy in the U.S., where the ability to decontextualize events—to stand outside the event, and ask "Why do I think?"—is equivalent to being literate.

The key point here is that Greenfield's assumption "that context-dependent speech is tied up with context-dependent thought, which in turn is the opposite of abstract thought," is both correct and incorrect (P. Greenfield 1972, 169). Greenfield is recognizing that some speech events and their contexts do shape our ways of knowing, but she treats "abstract thought," as decoding/analytic literacy always did, as independent of context. I want to shift the terms of this discussion to the assumptions of translation/critical literacy in which all knowledge is context-dependent. Abstract, academic language is made so, in part, through the rules or cultural conventions of academic speech events. Unlike decoding/analytic literacy, where decontextualization defined "high" literacy, the new translation/critical literacy assumes that all knowledge is contextualized, that all speech events require interpretation, and that *hermeneutics* exist in all discourse, not just in textbooks or religious documents or middle-class families. Even *conversations* do not have "ready comprehension," no more so than a lecture or a textbook.

This means that the tests of truth accepted by a culture and the relations among people will vary from one context or speech event to another and that knowing the different styles of problem solving from one speech event to another is a key skill in postmodern literacy. First, a word about speech events. The speech event is one way to describe context—sometimes called a shift of register (Halliday 1978)—and English classes are the places to learn how speech events work. Let me warn the reader that I have just established a second foundation for the argument of this book. In the previous chapter, I suggested that sign-system experiments show that people learn things simultaneously and sometimes separately in different sign systems; that knowing something in one sign system does not mean that one knows something in another sign system; that one's knowledge of something can be "deepened" by knowing something in several sign systems; and that moving from one sign system to another is an act of translation in which one leaves out some things and adds other things to one's understanding of a general concept. In fact, one might claim that sometimes the translation of a concept from one sign system to another actually produces a different mixture of sign systems. Now, I am about to make a similar argument about speech events.

I am also about to argue once again that Vygotsky's notion of proximal development has sometimes been misinterpreted in schools (see Chapter 7), where it is often assumed that one leaves behind some ways of speaking. The point of the zone of proximal development is that one turns to various kinds of scaffolds and supports for learning something new, like a "scientific" concept. These supports and scaffolds can be a variety of things—*conversational* speech events, lists, visual and action sign systems, dictaphones and computers. For example, to know about "gravity," one may need to describe gravity to others in *conversational*, spontaneous speech events while at the same time learning to talk about gravity in the monologue language of *academic* speech events. When I can translate "gravity" from one speech event to another easily, from the *conversational* to the *academic* within my own head, working alone, then I have internalized not only the two ways of speaking, but also two versions of the concept itself. I do not now leave *conversational* speech events behind. In fact, I have internalized two related but different concepts, one in a *conversational* event and another in an *academic* event.

Vygotsky suggested many years ago that *spontaneous*, everyday concepts, which are embedded within *conversational* speech events, and *scientific* concepts, which are embedded within *academic* speech events, should be learned in a parallel and converging fashion because translations between the two forms of language contribute to learning (Vygotsky 1962). In other words, just as sign shifting may help students learn difficult concepts in multiple versions, speech-event shifting may help one learn a concept in multiple versions. Many years ago, L. P. Benezet proposed teaching math in *conversational* settings and delaying arithmetic instruction in *academic* contexts, which require exact answers (Shanker 1987). Benezet reported that he had improved the math scores of students by beginning mathematical study with *conversational* language in which heights, lengths, areas, distances, and the like were estimated in conversational interaction. Then he turned to math in academic events.[2]

An interesting example of speech events shaping mathematical responses occurs in Lave's study of the arithmetic skills of adults doing everyday shopping in supermarkets and taking paper-and-pencil tests covering integers, decimals, fractions, addition, subtraction, multiplication, and division. Lave, who followed shoppers while they were doing their *conversational* shopping and gave them an *academic* test in the parking lot at the end, found that shoppers gave better mathematical responses during *conversational* shopping in the supermarkets than they did while taking the *academic* tests:

> Their scores averaged 59% on the arithmetic test [in *conversational settings*], compared with a startling 98%—virtually error free—arithmetic in the supermarket.
> The first puzzle is the virtually error-free performance by shoppers who made frequent errors in parallel problems in formal testing situations. The other puzzle is the frequent occurrence of more than one attempt to calculate in the course of buying an item. Shoppers carried out 2.5 calculations, on the average, for each grocery item that served as an occasion for arithmetic. . . . (Lave, Murtaugh, and de la Rocha 1984, 82–83)

The rules of speech events played a critical role in these results. *Academic* speech events like those in which formal tests are embedded require definitive, hierarchical, well-composed answers, all of which discourage the guessing and estimations typical of *conversational* speech events. In the *conversational* grocery shopping above, the subjects made many guesses and many approximations, attempting an average of 2.5 calculations for each problem. One of the approximation strategies used in Lave's study is called gap-closing, in which numbers are rounded off to simplify calculations and comparisons. One shopper, examining American Beauty Noodles at 64 ounces for $1.98 and Perfection Noodles at 32 ounces for $1.12, rounded off these numbers to fifty cents per pound and sixty cents per pound, concluding "there is a difference":

> *Shopper:*   "Yeah, that is. That's two dollars for four pounds (*referring to the American Beauty elbow noodles*). . . . That's 50 cents a pound, and I just bought two pounds for a dollar 12, which is 60 [referring to Perfection Noodles]. So there is a difference. (Lave, Murtaugh, and de la Rocha 1984, 88)

In other words, the shopper used the *conversational* rules of estimation and approximation to determine that Perfection Noodles cost more. It is probable that the shopper felt the "academic" test did not allow for these kinds of guesses because the norms of *academic* language and testing call for neatness, certainty, and speed. *Conversational* problem solving is much more casual. But notice that *conversational* processing of information can provide a support for the development of *academic* thinking. In fact, in this grocery shopping example, it is clear that the *conversational* rules allow young learners to guess, make mistakes, and correct first efforts.

One of the first major research studies of speech events is Luria's study of problem solving among peasants in Russia almost fifty years ago. Starting with the assumption that different contexts produce different tests of truth and that revolutionary, collective activity forced people to organize information more formally and not to depend upon face-to-face relations and *conversational* language for problem solutions, Luria decided to study whether the collective action of the Russian Revolution created opportunities for Russian peasants to learn to solve problems in such *academic* speech events as formal tests of classification.

To test this hypothesis, Luria's researchers gave a classification test to an unschooled peasant who was first given the group (*ax-sicklehatchet*) and then asked to pick an object from a second group (*saw-ear of grain-log*) which would be in the same class of objects as those in the first group. The desired response was *saw* from the second group to go with the tools (*saw* with *ax, sickle, hatchet*) in the first group. What Luria got was the following:

> *Subject:*   The saw belongs here. If you've got an ax you definitely need a saw. A saw also goes well with a hatchet, but for the sickle you need an ear of wheat. [Luria comments that this person groups things *"in terms of practical, situational thinking."*]
>
> *Researcher:*   You have to pick only one thing that will fit in with the first three.
>
> *Subject:*   My first choice is the saw, then the ear of wheat.
>
> *Researcher:*   Which would be more correct?
>
> *Subject:*   If I've got to pick only one, it'll have to be the saw. But then I'd have to take out the sickle and put in the log. You need

a sickle for an ear of grain and a saw to saw a log. Then you have to split it with an ax. [Luria comments that the subject *"persists in the use of situational thinking."*]

Researcher: But the whole first group has to be alike, the same kinds of things.

Subject: Then I'll take the ear of wheat, because we need wheat most of all. [Here, says Luria, the subject *"employs attribute of necessity."*]

Researcher: But could you pick the ax, sickle, and saw?

Subject: No, the ear of wheat has to be near the sickle and the saw has to be next to the ax. [The subject, says Luria, again uses practical, situational thinking.]

Researcher: But all these are farming tools.

Subject: Sure, but each one's connected with its own job. [Luria notes that the subject *"acknowledges the possibility of categorical classification but considers it immaterial."*]

[The subject is then given the series of *tree-ear of grain* to match with one of the following: (*bird-rosebush-house*).]

Subject: There should be a house next to the tree and the flower [ear of grain]. [Luria says that here the subject uses a *"practical scheme of grouping."*]

Researcher: But is a house really like a tree in any way?

Subject: If you put the rosebush here, it won't be of any use to a person, but....(Luria 1976, 71)

In the experiment above, the subject consistently embeds the problem and the answer in everyday narrative contexts, which is a typical way of organizing things in informal, *conversational* exchanges. The subject acknowledges that all the items can exist as a class of farm tools, but he or she rejects classification-for-the-sake-of-classification and, thus, rejects the method of organization typical in many *academic* speech events.

Remember, Luria's "interviews" were being conducted in a local gathering place for drinking and social, *conversational* interaction. Many of the subjects seemed to be upset by the researcher's attempt to shift the context of the Russian tearoom from social conversation embedded in informal events to classification-for-the-sake-of-classification and other practices typical of more formal speech events. One subject, when told by the researcher, "Try to explain to me what a tree is," responds, "Why should I? Everyone knows what a tree is, they don't need me telling them" (Luria 1976, 86). The researcher, of course, is focusing on the "primacy of language" (to use Donaldson's term) by asking for a definition of a tree just to get a definition—an instantiation of an *academic* speech event—and the subject appears to be resisting the researcher's question as a social intrusion, as possibly an effort to undermine the possibilities of social relations in a *conversational* speech event. Luria found that those young Russian peasants who had been involved in the new Russian collectives—and, thus, in large collective groups with school-like, academic settings—could quickly shift from *conversational*, social events in the tearoom to the classification-for-the-sake-of-classification of the academic speech events, in which the researcher assumed the role of dominant instructor/questioner and gave the subject tests. Luria concluded that the collective experience of the Russian Revolution had helped create the cultural and historical situation necessary to teach Russian peasants the forms of literacy typical of *academic* speech events. Notice that Piaget's experiment and Luria's study are both examining what happens when someone is placed in a *conversational* event—a teahouse or a one-to-one clinical setting—and then is expected to follow *academic rules* in a response. Obviously, those who resisted did so for good reasons.

Remember, a speech event, as defined here, can be oral or written. A *conversational* speech event can be a written letter, a written memo, an oral exchange face-to-face, or an oral exchange over the telephone. There are those who have argued that the oral-writing distinctions are more important than speech-event distinctions. First, Eric Havelock (1963) and, later, Jack Goody and Ian Watt (1968) argued that the essential cultural requirement for academic literacy is writing, learning the differences between the oral and the written, not learning the differences among patterns of *academic* speech events, whether oral or written. In fact, Havelock, Goody, and Watt insisted that oral language "is hostile to the expression of laws and rules" (Havelock 1978, 42-43) and that the "analysis involved in the syllogism, and in other forms of logical procedure, are clearly dependent upon writing" (Goody and Watt 1968, 68). Logic and syllogistic thinking was, they said, clearly not possible in oral form.

Using this same line of argument, Olson concluded that only writing taught people how to objectify information by teaching them how to operate within the boundaries of sentence meaning as an explicit problem, "to entertain sentence meaning per se rather than merely using the sentence as a cue to the meaning entertained by the speaker" (Olson 1977, 277). Hildyard and Olson found that readers, when compared with listeners, paid more attention to sentence meaning and were more accurate in their recall (Hildyard and Olson 1982, 32). In other words, so this argument goes, writing of any kind turns language into an object and creates the detachment necessary for academic thought. Within decoding/analytic literacy, this assumption meant that oral language was *not* important for academic thinking, and, in fact, one of the major changes in translation/critical literacy is a new recognition of the importance of oral language in academic thinking.

By the 1980s, substantial evidence was beginning to suggest that exposure only to writing does not *always* lead to higher scores on Western-style tests of abstract, classification tasks and logic problems. Scribner and Cole found that the Vai who write letters all the time in Vai script did not do any better on these Western-style tests of logic and classification than the Vai who could not write:

> Our results are in direct conflict with persistent claims that "deep psychological differences" divide literate and nonliterate populations (see Maheu 1965). On no task—logic, abstraction, memory, communication—did we find all nonliterates performing at lower levels than all literates. Even on tasks closely related to script activities, such as reading or writing with pictures, some non-literates did as well as those with school or literacy experiences. We can and do claim that literacy promotes skills among the Vai, but we cannot and do not claim that literacy is a necessary and sufficient condition for any of the skills [logic, classification] we assessed. (Scribner and Cole 1981, 251)

In the Scribner and Cole study above, some Vai children learned to write Arabic in academic settings in schools that usually focused on reading and memorization of the Koran; some Vai learned outside of any school the written Vai script used for writing personal letters and lists; some Vai learned to write English in government schools for the purpose of academic work in economics and political science; and some Vai did not learn to write at all. These groups were given various tests. Two groups—the Vai who wrote personal letters and the Vai who did not write—did not significantly differ in their results on tests of logical reasoning. But those Vai who learned to write academic English in a Western-type school did show significantly higher scores on these tests of classification, logical reasoning, verbal explanations, and so forth. The essential point here is that, among those who could write, the Vai who did academic writing in school did better on academic tests than the Vai who wrote personal letters in Vai script outside of school (Scribner and Cole 1981, 132–33, 251–54). The point is that learning to write in daily affairs does not substitute for learning to write in schools. Postmodern literacy cannot be separated from postmodern schooling.

Thus, learning to write may not help one do much academic work, but learning to write and speak in academic prose in academic contexts will probably help. Scribner and Cole say, "Our evidence leaves open the question of whether conceptional or logical skills are promoted by expository text." But they add, "If our argument that specific uses promote specific skills is valid, we should expect to find certain skills related to practice in written exposition" (Scribner and Cole 1988, 69). To some degree, what we call "higher-order thinking skills" in school is a form of *academic* discourse or way of speaking or exposition in a particular scholarly context and is not embedded in *conversational* speech events like personal letters and conversations which occur both in and out of school. This hypothesis also suggests that higher-order skills or academic language is only one way of thinking, not the only way or even the most effective way in all situations. Scribner spent the last years of her life studying problem solving in places like dairies, and she concluded that these casual, *conversational* settings have distinctive problem-solving strategies which we know nothing about, but which are distinctly effective.

Over the past fifteen years, Olson, Goody, Scribner, and Cole have moved closer together in their views. Olson, after claiming in 1977 that written texts simply mean what they say, without reference to such matters as illocutionary force in speech events, now says, "I would now admit that texts always mean more than they say. What a text means depends upon not only the sense of the expression as specified by the grammar and lexis, but also on the illocutionary force" (Olson 1994, 158). Scribner and Cole, who started by proposing that writing and literacy did not have "general cognitive effects" (1981, 132), modified their views in the last half of their study, as noted above. Finally, Goody, who found oral language hostile to logic, has modified his emphasis on oral-written differences (Olson 1994, 43). What matters to Goody and others is "literate discourse; whether spoken or written is of less significance" (Olson 1994, 43).

The point here is *not* that oral-written differences do not matter at all. Learning the conventions of written language is one of the things children must do to be able to enter both *conversations* through the mail and *academic* speech events through articles. But writing conventions *alone* are not an adequate foundation for thinking and talking the way academics think and talk. English classes must focus on both writing conventions and the conventions of speech events. Notice that the shift from an emphasis on writing to an emphasis on speech events brings oral and written language together in English classes. In fact, in our age, with its mixture of oral and written forms, the oral has been influenced by written materials—what Ong calls "secondary orality" (Ong 1982). This bringing together of the oral and the written, composition and rhetoric, is exactly what a number of composition theorists have been recommending.

Many K–12 English classes are also beginning to give serious attention to many of the variations within speech events—studying the *conversational* styles of men and women (Tannen 1984), the mix of *conversational* and *presentational* speech events in courtroom testimony (R. Lakoff 1990), and the differences among *academic* papers in different academic settings. In general, speech and rhetoric need to return to the K–12 classroom for English language arts. We need, says John Dixon, a performance model of reading and writing (Dixon 1994).

In summary, then, one way to learn what we call higher-order thinking skills is to learn to shift from one speech event to another within oral and written forms and to learn to talk and write in academic speech events. Talking in an academic event may mean "reading" printed materials because participants in academic conferences literally "read" their typed manuscripts. That is the way an academic event works. I have already mentioned the work of Kristin Valentine (1992) and others at Arizona State University in Tempe, who have their students "perform" or read aloud published articles in academic journals, including both quantitative and qualitative studies. Some of these performances include speech-event translations, a first reading in the language of the *academic* speech event and a second reading or translation in the language of a *presentational* or *conversational* speech event.

Speech events always take place within larger communicative events like the marriage ceremony, the shopping excursion, the reception, the convention, and so forth; and, of course, within the speech event, there are different kinds of speech acts and different kinds of sentences. A speech act is just that, an act—a command, for example, which takes the form of a question ("Will you close the window?") or a direct command ("Close the window."). A speech act is always a small unit within a speech event.

What are the different kinds of speech events, and what kinds of translations from one event to another shape our thinking? The four major categories of speech events are outlined in Figure 20: (1) *notational* events like roll calls or grocery lists; (2) *academic or ritual* language events like the words of the marriage ceremony or academic research papers; (3) *conversational* events like jokes, letters, and social exchanges; and (4) *presentational* events like toasts, magazine articles, editorials, and political speeches. There is a fifth speech event, now emerging, which I will call the *multivocal* speech event. This speech event challenges the boundaries of the other four speech events by mixing different speech events. For example, the conversational voices of students are mixed with the presentational registers of teachers. More on this challenge later.

	THE FOLLOWING ARE SAMPLES OF THE FOUR SPEECH EVENTS IN WRITTEN FORM:

The Notational Event	8 tablespoons butter 1 bunch green onions, chopped ½ cup finely chopped parsley 2 small ribs celery, chopped 3 tablespoons flour
The Conversational Event	Hi — Did y-hear? Yes! Sue talked to H̲I̲M̲ and 👁 watched (You know it) and 👂 listened. And Some!!! Say, did you see Law and Order last night, and that new one??? Take a hike, I guess. Bye
The Presentational Event	*The person in my life who made a great impression on me was a friendly strongheaded man, Mr. Hamish Glenn, who lived next door to me. He was a man, rather old, about 85 or so. He was a grandfather figure to me. I called him Grandpa Hamish.*
The Academic Event	Two of the most fundamental themes in modern psychology are evident in Lawrence Kohlberg's widely known work on moral judgment. The first theme is the "naturalistic" argument that the development and expression of human behavior reflect spontaneous constructive processes characteristic of life in general. The naturalistic theme owes its modern impetus mainly to Jean Piaget but was also expounded by J. M. Baldwin, Heinz Werner, and John Dewey. The second theme. . . .[1]

Fig. 20. Samples of speech events. ([1]Gibbs 1977, 43.)

What are the features of these different speech events? First, *notational* events or lists have the restricted purpose of memory retrieval or reconstruction, and to accomplish this purpose, lists eliminate all words, speech acts, and sentences establishing a rhetorical relationship with an audience. The list or notational speech event is a way to avoid personal agency and rhetorical entanglements in either a writing or an oral situation, and it has one primary speech-event purpose—to record and to remember. Hayden White, commenting on the *Annals of Saint Gall* (one of the early "historical lists"), asks, "What kind of notion of reality led him [the author] to represent in the *annals form* what, after all, he took to be real events?" (White 1981, 6). White suggests that the annalist writes the historical list because he or she does not wish to assert that history makes a story and does not wish to assert any personal authority. However, the annalist does wish to record things and to remember. In everyday situations, the *notational* event takes the form of recipes, roll calls, telephone directories, auctioneering, announcements at athletic events, grocery lists, bus station schedules, and so forth. *Notational* events are, then, oral and written lists for remembering and recording— not for explaining or asserting, although lists have implicit connections.

The other three speech forms—*conversations, presentations,* and *academic events*—attempt to do more than simply record experience. These three forms assert personal agency and attempt to reproduce an event through three kinds of relationships: *tenor* or *distancing* relationships (the interpersonal relationship between the speaker and the audience/reader); *field* or *processing* relationships (the ideational relationships between the speaker and the subject); and *modal* relationships (the textual relationships between the speaker and text conventions) (Halliday 1978, 33; M. Myers 1982b). These relationships establish what Bakhtin calls "the speech plan," so that from the very first words, listeners "sense the developing whole of the utterance." This "whole" governs the relationships of all participants, speakers and listeners alike, whether the speech event is oral (speakers and listeners) or written (writers and readers) (Bakhtin 1986, 78).

First, let's examine distancing, tenor, or speaker and audience relationships. One way to establish distancing is person—first ("I"), second ("you"), or third ("it"), the latter being a way to avoid close personal relations. *Conversations* emphasize close, personal relations and camaraderie, not the professional bonding of *academic* discourse around third-person "objectivity." *Conversational* discourse aims for subjectivity in interpersonal relations, using first person ("I") and a direct address ("you") to achieve that aim. For this reason, the logical, definitive information typical in *academic* speech events is often considered antisocial and inappropriate in *conversational* speech events. Luria's interviews illustrate such an antisocial intrusion, and, in fact, some of the subjects objected to Luria's introduction of *academic* material into their conversational setting.

Let me describe the way *conversational* speech events shape writing in the social notes written by students in school. One way to derive the rules of the social note is to contrast the discourse of the social note with the discourse of the typical *presentational* essay in composition texts. The *presentational essay* has such features as the clear thesis sentence and the marked conclusion. Students will discover, of course, that when the social note is rewritten with a clear thesis sentence and a marked conclusion, the social note becomes antisocial. The junior high school social note has its own set of consistent "rules" calling for fragments, for a series of exclamation points (!!!), for capitalized words (YOU), for parenthetical expressions.[3] These practices exist for a reason. They help establish the close interpersonal relations and approximate processing which are the *conversational* foundations of social notes. So far, I have been talking about the standard rules for conversational speech events across the country. Social notes, in my observation, use pretty much the same "rules" from Portland to Orlando. But invented spelling, when it is added to the conversational rules, creates the sound of local dialect in the writing, and these dialects differ. Sometimes students use invented spelling in their conversational writing because they do not know any better. But sometimes students use invented spelling to assert their local identity as a resistance to national norms. In a similar fashion, President Clinton did this during the 1992 campaign, using his Arkansas dialect and jokes to assert his resistance to "Washington politics."

Academic speech events have a different set of practices. Increased distancing of interpersonal relations, one of the critical features of an academic speech event, can be established in scientific/academic speech events by changing to the third person:

> Everybody wants to put things in the third person. So they just say, "it was found that." If it's later shown that it was wrong, don't accept any responsibility. "It was found. I didn't say I *believed* it. It was found." So you sort of get away from yourself that way and make it sound like these things just fall down into your lab notebook and you report them like a historian . . . Of course, everybody knows what's going on. You're saying, "I think." But when you go out on a limb, if you say "it was shown that" or "it is concluded" instead of "we conclude," it should be more objective. It sounds like you are taking yourself out of the decision and that you're trying to give a fair, objective view and that you are not getting *personally* involved. Personally, I'd like to see the first person come back. I slip into it once in a while. "We found." Even then I won't say "I." I'll say "we" even if it's a one-person paper. Can spread the blame if it's wrong [laughs]. (qtd. in Gilbert and Mulkay 1984, 58–59)

Second, ideational relationships, processing, and field are established in *academic* speech events through, among other things, the processing rules of syllogistic reasoning and nominalization. Nominalization takes several forms, each form increasing the "rank" or embeddedness of the nouns. For example, *The child continued growing* becomes *The continued growth of the child is interesting.* In this example, nominalization or the shift from verb to noun embeds action ("continued growing") as a noun or object ("continued growth"). Let's consider another example, this time from the writing of Stephen Jay Gould: "He [Darwin] insisted *that any complex Cambrian creature must have arisen from a lengthy series of pre-cambrian ancestors*" (see Halliday and Martin 1993, 38–39) is translated into a noun group/phrase at the end of the sentence: "yet the peculiar character of this evidence has not matched Darwin's prediction of *a continuous rise in this complexity toward Cambrian life* (Halliday and Martin 1993, 39). In this example, Darwin, who started as an active agent ("[Darwin] insisted"), becomes transformed into a prediction ("Darwin's prediction"), and the complex creature who *"must have arisen"* turns into a *"continuous rise in this complexity."* The change here is both a change from verb to noun and also a change in rank—from the beginning of the sentence ("He insisted") to the end ("Darwin's prediction of"). Nominalization (from a verb to a noun) and changes in rank (from a clause at the beginning of a sentence to a noun phrase at the end) are pervasive in *academic* speech events (Halliday and Martin 1993, 39–43), and one result of this nominalization and change in rank or embeddedness is the increasing non-negotiability of knowledge. These nominalizations, embedded ever more deeply as rank decreases, begin to grow more and more into objects which the reader cannot control. Halliday and Martin stress this point: "You can argue with a clause but you can't argue with a nominal group" (Halliday and Martin 1993, 39).

Through logical procedures, *academic* events attempt to project a method of skepticism and doubt and to control, if not eliminate, the possibilities of personal interactions. The tests of truth in *academic*/ritual speech events were, first, a claimed confirmation from differing sources, which is sometimes called triangulation, and second, a validation of the documents and evidence used for evidence, establishing the dates and authors of documents used as evidence and establishing the general acceptance of the selected cases as somehow typical of the population under consideration. Of course, both the adequacy of the triangulation and the typicality of the data are continuing matters of debate within research communities. In any case, the key point in an *academic* speech event is to keep personal involvement invisible:

> A style is adopted in formal research papers which tends to make the author's personal involvement less visible.... This formal appearance is strengthened by the suppression of references to the

> dependence of experimental observation on theoretical specula-
> tion, the degree to which experimenters are committed to specific
> theoretical positions, and the influence of social relationships on
> scientists' actions and beliefs. (Gilbert and Mulkay 1984, 47)

The development of the *academic* speech event, now common in the composition texts of K–12 schools, can be dated from 1667 when the Royal Society of London, believing that the advancement of science depended upon the use of "the English language as a medium of prose," called for writing with a mathematical clarity, a plainness of style, and an absence of digression and of stylish swelling and amplifications (Sprat [1667] 1972, 56; Olson 1977, 269). One of the first uses of this proposed essay form as an academic method was John Locke's *An Essay Concerning Human Understanding* ([1690] 1962). Locke's essay "differed notably from the predominant writing style of the time," which emphasized personal flourishes and point of view (Olson 1977, 269). Ellul reports, "An uninitiated reader who opens a scientific treatise on law, economy, medicine or history published between the sixteenth and eighteenth centuries is struck most forcibly by the complete absence of logical order....It was more a question of personal exchange than of taking an objective position" (Ellul 1964, 39, 41; qtd. in Olson 1977, 269).

These documents, then, were based on conversational speech events. *Conversational* events use approximations and fragments to create exploratory knowledge and to establish close interpersonal relationships between speaker and listener. *Conversational* speech events emphasize approximations of information (*sort of, kind of*), not the exactness of statement found in *academic*/ritual speech events, because in *conversations,* knowledge is a social, informal construction. Therefore, information is often incomplete and parenthetical, always negotiable, always open to interaction. The following example illustrates the differences between *conversational* and *academic* processing of information and the impact of these differences on thinking:

> "If a person has a quarter, a dime, and two cents, how much money
> must this person borrow from a stranger in order to purchase a 60-
> cent ice cream cone?" Two of the three students answered "a quar-
> ter," but the third argued strenuously that the correct answer was
> "twenty-three cents." (L. Resnick 1993).

In this example, the third student ignores the *conversational* situation in which people emphasize social relations and process information with approximate or rounded-off amounts and instead proposes to process information with definitive amounts. As a result, the third student's answer violates the goal of sociability typical of *conversational* events, but accomplishes the goal of exactness typical of *academic* events. However, the other two students propose the approximate answer of "a quarter," which follows the *conversational* rule of approximation and abides by the primary social purpose of the *conversational* speech event, avoiding any unnecessary intrusion on strangers. Schooling and *academic* speech events, of course, call for exact answers and for detached distancing between speaker and listener/reader, and in this kind of event, "twenty-three cents" is the right answer, even though the answer does lead to antisocial intrusions. The point I am making here is that math problems are not just matters of learning numerical signs. In this speech event, the interpersonal relations and the conventions for information processing help shape the mathematical response.

Another example of the way *conversations* and *academic* events shape problem solving comes from Myron Tuman's problem in which a person has "two coins that equal fifty-five cents, and one of them is not a nickel. What are they?" Tuman provides the following analysis:

> The key to responding correctly to this question has to do far less with innate intelligence than with one's general understanding of the literate use of language....Assuming the good faith of the questioner, we interpret this question as telling us that the "one" coin that is not a nickel is either coin. The trick, and hence the secret to responding correctly, is to adopt an entirely different psychological stance. No longer can we assume the good faith of the other party; we are not engaged in conversation. (Tuman 1987, 21)

In most *conversational* situations, people adopt the *conversational* assumption that a social interchange is underway, not a test or logical speech event. Thus, the struggle of *conversationalists* for a social answer eliminates a nickel as one of the possibilities. When *conversationalists* understand that this is a test and *not* a *conversation,* they understand the primacy of language in the situation and that exactness, not social ability, is called for. Of course, the answer, then, is a fifty-cent piece *and* a nickel. This instance is essentially the same problem as the two people at the football game in the opening to this chapter. In both cases, if the participant aims for exactness, not sociability, the participant gets the answer right.

Between the *conversational* and the *academic* speech event stands the *presentational* speech event, a middle ground of popular culture and public discourse. *Presentational* events emphasize personal authority and personal knowledge, but not social purposes. The knowledge in *presentations* is definitive and hierarchical, but it is not institutionalized, not loaded with the in-group language of *academic* speech events or the neighborhood dialects of *conversational* speech events. Instead, *presenta-*

tional speech events are public discourse, directed toward the general community, free of the requirements of disciplines, professional societies, and *academic* institutions and, therefore, available for iconoclastic assertions and polemics. *Presentational* speech events are also free of the conventions of neighborhood and family *conversations*.

Most of the time *presentational* discourse leans upon narrative and the personal authority and credibility of the author. *Presentational* speech events do not have the institutional status of *academic* speech events because they have not yet organized the appropriate *academic* institutions for certifying knowledge. But they have become important sources for public opinions and insights. When *presentational* events enter *academic* communities, they often struggle to find institutional support. One recent example of this struggle is the effort of some early ethnographic approaches, not yet institutionalized, to find a secure position within some research communities.

Modeling features are a third trait of speech events. One modeling feature of speech events is space. *Conversations,* for example, can come in short segments, but in *conversations* one attempts to fill up the space on the paper or the time bracketed for *conversational* exchanges. Empty space in written *conversational* speech events conveys an unfriendly attitude; long silences in oral conversations can have the same effect. Imagine an $8\frac{1}{2}''$ x $14''$ piece of paper with one sentence on it: "Hi, Mom!" The solution in *conversational* writing is to reduce the space by using postcards, memo pads, and so forth.

In *academic* speech events, bibliographies and citations are a key modeling feature. These bibliographies and citations are, of course, part of academic discourse's effort to suppress personal involvement and agency. In *academic* events, author agency is reduced or "set aside" or "disguised," and alternative explanations are highlighted in order to sustain the Cartesian "rule" or "myth" of doubt and objectivity. In addition to reducing personal agency, bibliographies and citations distribute credit and recognition to other practitioners in the field, and this helps build constituents in support of an idea. The bibliography, in fact, becomes a device for establishing the existence of a formal body of knowledge.

Speech events differ significantly in the modeling features they use in diagrams. *Presentational* speech events use drawings, photographs, charts, diagrams—all sorts of visual coding of information. But *academic* speech events have strict rules about which visuals, if any, are allowed. The Modern Language Association's *PMLA,* for example, does not encourage diagrams. Both *presentational* and *academic* speech events will allow subheads, but *conversational* speech events will not.

Academic speech events often use a colon in the title, but the other events rarely do so.

When information is moved from one speech event to another, it undergoes radical changes. For example, notice the different claims in the examples below of *academic* and *presentational* speech events, all reporting the same information (Fahnestock 1986, 287; the emphasis is mine, except where noted):

> (1) *We favor the hypothesis that* sex differences in achievement in and attitude toward mathematics result from superior male mathematical ability, which *may* in turn be related to greater male mathematical ability in spatial tasks. This male superiority is *probably* an expression of a combination of both endogenous and exogenous variables. *We recognize, however, that our data are consistent with numerous alternative hypotheses.* Nonetheless, the hypothesis of differential course-taking was not supported. *It also seems likely that* putting one's faith in boy-versus-girl socialization processes as the only permissible explanation of the sex difference in mathematics is premature. (Benbow and Stanley 1980, 1264; emphasis is Fahnestock's)

> (2) The authors' conclusion: "*Sex differences in achievement in and attitude toward mathematics result from superior male mathematical ability.*" (D. Williams and King 1980, 73)

> (3) According to its authors, Doctoral Candidate Camilla Persson Benbow and Psychologist Julian C. Stanley of Johns Hopkins University, *males inherently have more mathematical ability than females.* ("The Gender Factor in Math," 1980, 57)

> (4) Two psychologists said yesterday that *boys are better than girls in mathematical reasoning,* and they urged educators to accept the possibility that something more than social factors may be responsible. ("Are Boys Better at Math?" 1980, 107, col. 1)

The first comes from an *academic* event in a research journal, and the other three come from *presentational* events in the popular press. Notice how the three samples from *presentational* events personalize the claims ("the authors' conclusion" in number 2) and then remove all of the scientific hedges and qualifications for the claim. The speakers in the *academic* event acknowledge that "our data are consistent with numerous alternative hypotheses," but they also are willing to say they "favor" a given hypothesis. *Presentational* events often use metaphors like "boys have a math gene" to make the point clear, even though the statement is not exactly representative of what the researchers reported. Of the three versions, *Newsweek* makes the most sensational claim in its assertion that males have "superior male mathematical ability." *Time* simply says "more mathematical ability," and the *New York Times* says "better." The *academic* speech event in the first version, however, points to a combination of "endogenous and exogenous variables," leaving various alternatives as the conclusion, an approach which obviously limits the popular appeal of *academic* writing.

Let's examine how an *academic* event emerges in two drafts and a final version of an article on RNA written for an *academic/ritual* community. This examination follows generally (but not *always*) the analysis suggested by Greg Myers (1985; 1990). Selections from the drafts (versions I and II) and the final version (version III) appear in endnote four.[4]

In versions I and II, the author actively searches for similarities or homologies and says so: "a search is being conducted for sequence homologies," (vers. I, l. 1) and "our work will continue to identify examples of these homologies by searching for them" (vers. II, l. 6). But in version III, the search for similar sequences disappears and is replaced by a situation in which "from all species of organisms studied," there emerges "stretches whose base sequences are identical" (vers. III, l. 1). Thus, the drafts shift the perspective from a personal search for a pattern to a pattern emerging from the data, as if the pattern were the result of the data itself, not the personal agency of the author. This shift in the author's role, from an agent who is searching to an observer who is watching, is called "objectivity" in the norms of most *academic* communities.

The same thing happens when the author says in the first version that "the purpose is to search for evidence of common origins" as an explanation of molecule similarity (vers. I, l. 3), but says in the second version that "a common evolutionary origin" emerges from or is suggested by the data (vers. III, l. 3). Again, the author ceases to be an active agent whose "purpose is to search" and becomes an observer watching "a common evolutionary origin" emerge. Finally, in the third version, after personal agency has been removed, not one but two explanations are said to be emerging from the data—"shared functions" and "common origins" (vers. III, l. 3). Thus, the first draft's active search for common origins as the only explanation of the data disappears, and common origins is presented as one of two possible explanations for the emerging data. The practice of presenting an alternative hypothesis to explain data is, of course, a common practice in *academic* speech events, where it is important for the speaker to maintain the Cartesian rule of doubt and skepticism.

Similarly, in the first version, "a model is proposed for the evolutionary origin" for molecules (vers. I, l. 4), but in the second version, a model is no longer proposed. Instead, a pattern seems to emerge from the data: the data "patterns suggest a common evolutionary origin for two classes of molecules" (vers. II, l. 3). Again, in the shift from "a model is proposed" (by the author) to data "patterns suggest" (a model emerging from the data), the role of author as agent is reduced or eliminated, and the role of author as "objective" observer is increased. In the third revision, by line 8, the model is gone altogether and in its place is the need for "continued identification" or more research (vers. III, l. 8). This version says that the possibility of an evolutionary or ancestral model emerges from the "overlapping set of homologies" in the data and that more research is needed to reconstruct the RNA "that is ancestral to both tRNA and rRNAs" (vers. III, l. 8). In summary, these revisions shift the discourse away from a form close to the *presentational* speech event, where the author's personal agency is explicit, to an *academic/ritual* speech event, where the author's personal agency appears to disappear.

In addition to *lists, conversations, presentations,* and *academic* speech events, our postmodern world appears to be establishing the conventions for yet another kind of speech event in which the introduction is a beginning but not necessarily a thesis; is *multivocal* and not a single point of view; and is, thus, a mixture of several speech events. Richard Ohmann has been suggesting that in the postmodern speech event, the author lets the thesis evolve from the author's initial questions and proclaimed confusion, thus letting the audience participate in the discovery (Ohmann 1971), a kind of mixing of *conversational* and *presentational* events. In addition, David Bartholomae has suggested to me that we teach students how to mess things up, to reveal the multivocal situation around most questions.

What social purpose does the *multivocal* speech event serve? There is a growing skepticism toward the all-encompassing academic functions of the traditional *academic* speech event and its claims of nonpersonal evidence and of a clear, certain conclusion. One example of this challenge comes from feminist critic Diane P. Freedman, who says, "I thought I should be prepared for my days as citizen—study English or attend law school, or both. I hadn't yet recognized that as a woman I was alienated by both tradition and temperament from conventional argumentative discourse" (D. Freedman 1992, 3). The issue appears to be whether there are some verifiable scientific facts or findings, which require *academic* speech events, and some topics, riddled with uncertainty, which require a *multivocal* speech event that invites questioning and negotiations (see Halliday and Martin 1993, xiii). Halliday and Martin argue that the non-negotiability of the traditional *academic* speech event may be an obstacle to solving problems in many intellectual areas:

> A radical expansion in the areas of textual and experiential mean-
> ing potential is bought at the interpersonal price of decreasing ne-
> gotiability, since down-ranked meanings are relatively difficult to
> challenge. This problem is something that needs to be seriously
> addressed as science discourse moves into a century in which it
> has to negotiate in new ways with both discursive and non-dis-
> cursive resources....(Halliday and Martin 1993, 41)

This charge from Halliday and Martin is similar to Bakhtin's proposal for a multivocal project to challenge traditional genres (Bakhtin
1986). How might a *multivocal* speech event be organized? Freedman,
Thomas J. Farrell, and others call for the *"female* mode—a style [which
is] associative, nonhierarchical, personal, and open-ended" (D. Freedman 1992, 3), and which "seems at times to obfuscate the boundary between the self of the author and the subject of the discourse" (Farrell
1979, 909), following "the shifting perspectives of the writer's mind,"
not a pre-designed format (Huber 1987, 356). Ohmann has called for a
discourse which attempts to "lower the barrier between speaker and
audience" and to emphasize cooperative efforts in which a speech
event is a "joint movement toward an end that both writer and audience accept" (Ohmann 1971, 66).

Ohmann argues that classical rhetoric—part of what I am calling de-
coding/analytic literacy in K–12 schools—"assumed that the speaker or
writer knows in advance what is true and what is good," but in the
"newer view"—what I am calling translation/critical literacy—"rhetoric
becomes the *pursuit*—and not simply the transmission—of truth and
right" (Ohmann 1971, 66). Therefore, "canny persuasion actually threatens good rhetoric" (Ohmann 1971, 66). In a similar plea, Gibson calls for
a modern style in which the speaker "knows his limits" and "admits the
inevitably subjective character of his wisdom" (W. Gibson 1962, 105). In
translation/critical literacy, secondary schools will need to experiment
with various ways of constructing a rhetoric that has the personal exploration of conversations, the clarity of presentations, and the evidence of
academic discourse.

In order for secondary schools to begin to introduce *multivocal*
speech events into their composition programs, we must have more
models. One example of the *multivocal* speech event is "Cross-Curricular Underlife: A Collaborative Report on Ways with Academic Words,"
which alternates between the views of Susan Miller and five under-
graduates (S. Miller et al. 1990). Richard Gebhardt, former editor of *College Composition and Communication,* says that CCC "may have invented
this genre" with this Miller article in February 1990 (Gebhardt 1993,

95). As other examples, Gebhardt points to "Portfolios and the Process of Change" by Marjorie Roemer, Lucille Schultz, and Russel Durst (December 1991), and to "On Blocking and Unblocking Sonja: A Case Study in Two Voices" by Beverly Lyon Clark and Sonja Wiedenhaupt (February 1992), the latter involving the voices of teacher and student.

In general, writing programs in K–12 schools have not given enough attention to the cultural impact of speech events. For example, *conversational* speech events have been treated in many writing programs as a neutral, transparent device for developing personal growth and for liberation from the detached relations in which much of school prose takes place. But *conversational* talk can go wrong in classrooms because some cultural groups find a conflict between the rules for speech events in their own culture and the rules for *conversations* in classrooms. The typical speech events of some California Hopi, for example, place the teacher at a distance and in the authority position typical of speakers in *academic* or *ritual* speech events. The close, personal, teacher-student relationships produced by *conversations* run counter to the cultural assumptions of the Hopi, making *conversational* discussions between these students and teachers a deeply troubling event for such students.[5] The insistence of the Dartmouth Conference (Dixon 1975) that the primary purpose of school language should be personal growth is, thus, deeply contrary to the linguistic assumptions of the Hopi—and other ethnic and cultural groups, I might add. The Lisa Delpit statement in this area is well worth rereading (Delpit 1986).

Another example of Dartmouth's limitations is the assumption that expressive *conversational* language is nonpolitical. Much of the discussion of talk in the classroom has ignored the fact that *conversational* speech events, even among native speakers, have a political impact. For example, *conversational* speech events are used by some people as a political strategy to stifle explicit expressions and to hide explicit political positions. My students at Oakland High School in the 1960s struggled to tell me more than once how they saw government officials and others use *conversational* speech events to produce the facade of sociability and equality among participants, thereby disguising the actual lines of personal and institutional authority.[6]

In the 1960s, public authorities in Oakland, California, often sponsored neighborhood kaffee klatches for discontented citizens, surrounding them with *conversational* language, and often using *conversational* discourse at public meetings to produce approximate, vague realities, thereby hiding clear, uncomfortable assertions. In such a *conversational* event, the person who wants to present a clear thesis statement is made to feel antisocial or even deviant. Furthermore, because *conversations* follow the rules of transitory discourses, the *conversational* speech event often leaves behind no records or institutional memories. In fact, anyone asking to tape-record *conversational* events at one of those Oakland kaffee klatches would have been considered antisocial.

Conversations can be used, then, to depoliticize events and to marginalize those who attempt to express explicit hypotheses, hypotheses which run counter to efforts to use social bonding to hide difference. President Clinton, for example, uses his community conversations for their appropriate purpose—to depoliticize issues—and, furthermore, he needs to get out of Washington, D.C., to find those *conversational* settings which can be televised nationwide. The Dartmouth Conference seemed to assume that expressive and *conversational* language were neutral forms, generating personal growth. To some degree, as noted earlier, Dartmouth's language policy may have been used by many as a language policy for ignoring the political revolutions of the 1960s.

However, James Britton was right when he said that *conversational* speech events are very useful for learning. The use of approximations and collaborations in *conversational* settings often help students learn because the rules of approximations allow "error," brainstorming, and transitory or draft texts in which everyone, whether speaker or audience, shares collaborative responsibility for what is said. In such situations, because no one individual is held responsible, speakers can say whatever comes into their heads, thereby "greasing" social relations, decreasing responsibility for error, and creating situations in which students, through conversational talk, stumble across ideas:

> I don't get the story. If she loved him, why did she leave? Yes. She could have stayed. Probably. But say she stayed. Would she have turned him in. Yes. Probably. So life is not simple I guess. (Eighth grader's learning-log response to a story; M. Myers 1982a)

In this learning log, the student demonstrates how conversational talk—what appear to be parts of an internal dialogue written down—leads to discovery, a recognition of the story's ambiguity. One of the key differences between translation/critical literacy and decoding/analytic literacy is that decoding/analytic literacy focused on writing as communication—the delivery of information to another person—and translation/critical literacy focuses on writing as both communication and exploration/discovery.

In summary, the rules for logic and knowledge are dependent upon the speech event in which logic and knowledge are embedded. The logic of one situation is not the logic of another. The working-class child in Bernstein's data (see the early portions of this chapter) might have wondered why anyone would refer to the presence of the picture when the researchers were present and could see it for themselves. The problem for Bernstein's working-class children may have been that they thought the question was in a *conversational* context, like Donaldson's children. Bernstein's children did not recognize that a game was being played in which an *academic/ritual* event was being instantiated. What these children needed to know to get the answer right were the rules of the event, not some general principles about observation, abstraction, decontextualization, or elaboration.

Richard Ohmann warns that the argument that working-class children cannot decontextualize has been used as an argument for static social status, in which people of different classes are sorted into different types of fixed-context users, thus restricting *academic/ritual* literacy to particular social groups. Ohmann argues that people have a style "choice at every point" as they move from one speech event to another: "The participants *create* the social relations of each encounter, in addition to inheriting them" (Ohmann 1982, 17). Thus, contemporary schooling must begin with the assumption that one's cultural setting is not a prison. Literacy is a way of developing areas of choice and, therefore, overcoming limits within parts of one's culture. It is the essential task of schools to make students aware of their choices of speech events and the results of the speech events they choose. The key point here is that each way of speaking is a way of thinking, and each way of thinking makes a contribution to our awareness of the world and our ability to liberate ourselves from some of our own perceptions.

Notes

1. "Speech event" is a term borrowed from Dell Hymes, who says the speech event is our largest rule-governed language unit (Hymes 1974, 52). A theory of speech events gives us a theory of context in which "all our utterances have definite and relatively stable, typical forms" (Bakhtin 1986, 78). Bakhtin also uses the speech event as a central rule-governed form.

2. Benezet's experiment is similar to those allowing invented spelling (estimations) at the beginning of writing.

3. Teachers who attempt to have students write a grammar of the social note need a supply to give to the class. Students do not like analyzing their own. The supply is available from the lockers of junior high students on the last day of school.

4. The following are selections from an author's revisions as he attempted to get his article accepted by a research publication (from a study by Greg Myers 1985, 240–44):

Version I:

(1) *A search is being conducted for sequence homologies* and for homologies of the reverse complementary sequences among tRNAs and rRNAs....

(3) *The purpose is to search for evidence of common origins* of these classes of RNA.

(4) *A model is proposed for the evolutionary origin* of the protein synthetic mechanism that predicts a common origin of the different classes of RNA.

Version II:

(1) *Ribosomal RNA is peppered with tracts that are homologous* with regions found among the different transfer RNAs. . . .

(3) *Their distributions and patterns suggest a common evolutionary origin* for two classes of molecules. . . .

(6) *Our work will continue to identify examples of these homologies by searching for them among a variety of organisms.*

(7) *The search was prompted by a model for the origin of a[n] . . . RNA molecule....*

(10) *The model suggested the existence of homologies....*

Version III:

(7) *A large minority of tRNAs from all species of organisms studied have stretches whose base sequences are identical or nearly so* to stretches found in rRNAs.

(8) *Factors contributing to these matches might be shared functions at the RNA or DNA levels, or common origins.*

(9) *The occurrence of an overlapping set of homologies ...suggest[s] that their continued identification should permit the reconstruction of an RNA that is ancestral to both tRNAs and rRNAs.*

5. Professor Tom Gage, of Humboldt State University's English department, called this problem to my attention in a personal communication.

6. During one break from a bargaining table, one teacher-colleague bellowed out, "When is this conversational [expletive deleted] going to stop and get down to business." My experience at bargaining tables is that those who are marginalized and relatively powerless—whether white, black, Hispanic, Asian, or whatever—are generally more confrontational and resistant to the neutralizing effects of *conversations* at the bargaining table.

12 Negotiated, Situated, and Embodied Knowledge: Translating among the Modes

Mind is primarily a verb. It denotes all the ways in which we deal consciously and expressly with the situations in which we find ourselves. Unfortunately, an influential manner of thinking has changed modes of action into an underlying substance that performs the activities in question . . . This change of ways of responding to an environment from which actions proceed is unfortunate, because it removes mind from necessary connection with the objects and events. . . . (Dewey 1931, 263–64)

As previous chapters have shown, translations from one sign system to another (Chapter 10) and from one speech event to another (Chapter 11) have become ways for one to know something which one might not otherwise know. For example, translating words about continents into maps of the continents may, for example, help one understand the plate theory of floating continents, and translating *conversational* events into *presentational* events may, for example, help one understand historical relations which get lost in conversations. But translations among different media and sign systems (words, pictures, numbers) and among different speech events (conversations, lectures) are not the whole story. As Dewey notes above, translations among the modes are also a way of knowing, and sometimes a given period of literacy will, as Dewey notes, emphasize one mode and exclude others. Dewey argues that in the 1920s, the beginning of decoding/analytic literacy, the emphasis was on knowledge as timeless, static, "objective" objects, separate from the verbs of narratives in time.

As a result, during decoding/analytic literacy, the paradigmatic essay—argument and exposition—became the privileged way of writing. Narrative was used in elementary schools as a developmental necessity, but secondary English classes rarely designated narrative writing as a critical way of knowing. Narrative writing, both fiction and nonfiction, was assigned to creative writing and other marginal options, and secondary English classes spent most of their time teaching the expository essay or argument and using literature or public issues as the topics. But in translation/critical literacy, there has been a change. Some facility with shifting among the modes has become part of the curriculum, and one result of this flexibility is that narrative forms assume a new importance, a new status as a way of knowing. Almost any instance of discourse can have several sign systems, several speech events, and several modes all present within the same discourse, but except in some multimodal and multivocal cases, only one sign system, one speech event, and one mode are usually positioned by the speaker or writer as primary. For example, the primary sign system could be visual in silent movies, but the discourse might also include subtitles. Furthermore, an *academic* speech event might insert a *conversational* event, such as a joke, but still remain primarily academic. So, too, the primary mode of a piece of discourse could be argumentation, but this discourse could also include narrative or descriptive material. Pure modes are rare in practice, but this does not mean that the categories of modes are difficult to identify. Ralph Cohen has put it this way:

> Naming a text a "novel" or a "non-fictional novel" ... pins down what is unpinnable.... Genre-naming fixes what is necessarily unfixable, encloses in boundaries that which crosses boundaries. Nevertheless if we think of people instead of maps, we know that border crossings are common practice in some countries (like our own) and that the reasons for such crossings are social and economic....The point is that if texts cross borders or boundaries, they must have borders or boundaries to cross....(R. Cohen 1984; qtd. in Bleich 1988, 117)

The way we describe the types of writing in English is, at this time, a contested area. The National Assessment of Educational Progress (Applebee et al. 1994) identifies three types: *information,* which focuses primarily on the subject; *persuasion,* which focuses primarily on the attitudes of the reader; and *narrative,* which focuses primarily on the imagination of the writer. Kinneavy (1971) identifies four types: *expressive,* which emphasizes the *writer;* the *referential,* which emphasizes the *subject;* the *literary,* which emphasizes the *text;* and the *persuasive,* which emphasizes the *reader.* What Kinneavy calls "literary" is called "narrative" by NAEP, and some of what Kinneavy calls "referential" is called "information" by NAEP. Many states do not include imaginative writing at all among their lists of primary types. To sort some of this out, I want to argue that the various types of writing have three primary methods of organization: distance to audience (Moffett 1968; Moffett et al. 1987); stance, literary or nonliterary (Rosenblatt 1968); and mode or arrangement of subject matter, either progressive, static, or nonlogical (D'Angelo 1975) or synthetic or paradigmatic (Pepper

1942). Distance to audience is covered in speech events (Chapter 11); the literary and nonliterary are covered in stance (Chapter 13); and arrangement is covered in this chapter on modes.

In translation/critical literacy, there are five primary modes: the *expressive, narrative, descriptive, expositive/definitive,* and *argumentative.* The expressive mode, which was not typically recognized as a mode in the school writing of decoding/analytic literacy, is a "free" association of impressions such as taking a word-association test, expressing feelings in an "emotional moment" (exclamations of joy, expletives of anger), engaging in private "freewriting" on memories, "free talking" about one's response to a text or an event (Britton et al. 1975; Britton 1970). The expressive mode also occurs in art (Eisner 1982), where it has been described as "more raw and sensuous … as if an inhibitory mechanism has been released and the patients can now give freer vent to their most primitive, least disguised feelings" (H. Gardner 1982, 323).

The expressive mode has a new importance in translation/critical literacy in the teaching of literature, where the expressive, following Britton's model of literary response, shapes the student's initial response to literature (Britton 1970). In fact, the expressive is widely recognized as a mode which serves the purposes of discovery and learning (Macrorie 1980; Murray 1987). Several states have begun to list the expressive mode as one of the forms which states will assess—for example, the California Assessment Program. However, the expressive mode in some districts has become a contentious issue. There are some parents who object strongly to inquiries from teachers about "How did this line of the poem make you feel?" or "What are your feelings about the character's choices?" Those parents, many of whom also object to what appear to be the violence and entertainment values of many schools, feel that these questions inquire into private beliefs, which schools will display and then allow other students to ridicule. The fears of these parents, who are usually described as conservative or fundamentalist, are quite similar to the fears of left-wing radicals in the 1950s, who did not want schools inquiring into the private feelings and beliefs of their children and then displaying these beliefs publicly in the classroom. These left-wingers feared that in the McCarthy atmosphere of the U.S., their children would be ridiculed as being un-American.

A second criticism of expressive questions is that they take teachers away from the academic goals of schooling and into the province of mental health professionals (Blau 1994). It is one of the interesting turns of history that when experimental psychologists began to recognize the importance of affective motivations in cognitive knowledge, they drifted closer to their clinical colleagues and, ultimately, made teachers vulnerable to charges that the teachers were abandoning their traditional cognitive goals. Not so, of course. Feelings are one crucial way we engage with events and texts, and this engagement is a critical part of our commitment to "make meaning" out of the text or event in front of us. Furthermore, says Sheridan Blau, feelings are a key responsibility of the arts in K–12 schools:

> Works of art, including literary works, and especially lyric poems, address themselves to the feelings of readers and have traditionally been justified…for the contribution that the experience of such works makes to the refinement and deepening of a student's capacity to feel. In an age and public culture that is nearly saturated by films that terrorize the imagination, by emotionally abusive popular music, and by media that numb feeling by celebrating violence, one can only pray that the schools continue to teach literature for its capacity to help students respond feelingly to the intellectually complex, subtle, and morally significant representations that are constructed by literary texts. (Blau 1994, 7)

As I finish this chapter, a California judge (Judge Robert O'Brien, Superior Court of Los Angeles, May 10, 1994) has ruled that the "feeling" questions in California essay exams on literature did *not* illegally violate the state's privacy law (*N. Greenfield et al. v. Los Angeles Unified School District* 1994), but by the time the Court gave its opinion, the California State Board of Education had dropped the word "feeling" from all of its essay exam questions. The struggle over this issue is not over.

The four other modes group themselves into two larger sets of language patterns and, in fact, into the two major approaches to philosophy, the *paradigmatic/analytic* and *narrative/synthetic*. These two major patterns shape the way we determine the meaning of words (R. Anderson and Nagy 1990); the way we make decisions (Kahneman and Tversky 1973); the way we organize knowledge (Pepper 1942); and the way we establish the truthfulness of statements (Bruner 1985). If we use the synthetic approach to determine a word's meaning, then we are more like Wittgenstein in our approach in that we are using cases and exemplars to organize knowledge and to illustrate a word's meaning. In this synthetic approach, which includes the modes of narration and description, we merge the parts of experience into stories and images focused on the character of events that occurred, not in the laws which they may exemplify (Pepper 1942, 141–50).

If we use the paradigmatic approach of tightly organized part-whole relations to determine meaning, then we are more like the classical logicians in that we use a list of specific features to outline a word's meaning. In the paradigmatic approach, which includes exposition and argument, we segment experience into parts, features, laws, or regularities. The paradigmatic, says Bruner, "verifies by appeal to formal verification procedures and empirical proof" by using a set of features as proof, and the synthetic or narrative establishes the "truth-likeness or verisimilitude" of an event or act by using cases and exemplars as proof (Bruner 1985, 97).

In the paradigmatic mode (definition/exposition and argument), one knows the meaning of a word in the way one knows the boundary between Illinois and Indiana, the exact location being a set of features or coordinates determined by measures agreed upon by the community. Say Anderson and Nagy, "A biologist trying to come up with terms—say, at the mid-levels of a biological taxonomy—is essentially trying to impose a grid on a conceptual domain" (R. Anderson and Nagy 1990, 716). The grid is the result of an agreement within the community of biologists. In both cases, the exact features are not, one should remember, a casual matter because the tax collector uses location features to tax some people and not others, and biologists use category features to establish categories and to distinguish between one living thing and another.

Although the paradigmatic approach works for the tax collector and biologist, the paradigmatic or grid approach does not always work for everyone. It does not work very well, for example, for the person who delivers mail to areas where "the region is sometimes simply counted as part of the city, even though it may not be physically contiguous" or may not be included in legal definitions of the city (R. Anderson and Nagy 1990, 716). In this scattered-points situation, the case or narrative is often used to mark a boundary. People say things like, "The town ends out there somewhere near that house" or "That house probably marks the area in the next town." The boundary in these instances is determined by cases, not by specific notational indicators of a boundary grid.

There are many everyday categories where cases or prototypes, not features, are more usable definitions. Rosch and Mervis (1975) found that when they asked people to list the characteristic attributes of twenty different items in six large classes (20 items in *furniture, chair, sofa, table, dresser*, and so on), the twenty items in each of the six large classes rarely shared even one feature in common. Because not even one feature could be used to define these categories, a paradigmatic approach to classification would not work. In classical paradigmatic categories, remember, features are common to *all* items in the category. People defined Rosch's categories by agreeing on a case or prototype for the category (*car* for *vehicle, chemistry* for *science, apple* for *fruit*), not a list of features.

There are numerous instances where narrative and paradigmatic approaches are both used. In their studies of everyday decision making, Kahneman and Tversky (1973, 237–51) found numerous examples of narrative approaches. In one study, Kahneman and Tversky told subjects that they were going to hear descriptions of people and be asked to guess whether the person described was a *lawyer* or an *engineer*. The subjects were also told that the description to be read was randomly selected from a sample of 100 in which 70 were *lawyers* and 30 were *engineers*. The description was then read: "Jack is a 45-year-old man....He is generally conservative, careful, and ambitious. He shows no interest in political and social issues and spends most of his free time on his many hobbies, which include home carpentry, sailing, and mathematical puzzles" (241). Most subjects labeled the description *engineer*, and they did this despite the 70/30 odds favoring *lawyers* in the pool of descriptions.

A paradigmatic approach to proof in this case would have focused on the statistical probability of a given answer. *Lawyer*, of course, is the statistically appropriate or paradigmatic answer, given the 70/30 distribution. But a synthetic/narrative approach to proof focuses on "everyday realism," or narrative logic in which the features "conservative" and "no interest in political and social issues" are typically associated with the case or narrative of an *engineer*. Coherence, lifelikeness, typicality—all narrative measures of truth—suggest in this case that *engineer* is an appropriate answer, not *lawyer*. Kahneman and Tversky have replicated these results with many other pairs.

Where exactly do the modes come from? An increasing number of researchers are suggesting that the narrative and paradigmatic modes are essentially biological in origin, each meriting the status of a "natural kind" (Bruner 1985, 97). Jakobson and Halle (1956, 53–82), examining studies of brain disorders and impairments, found that particular types of disorders or impairments appear to disable either narrative or paradigmatic ways of knowing. Patients with brain disorders or impairments who lose their use of paradigmatic styles because of aphasia can still use a narrative style of association when asked to tell their associations with various objects. For example, they can associate *knife* with *fork*, *table* with *lamp*, *smoke* with *fire*—all narrative associations based on actual cases and events—but they have trouble associating *car* with *vehicle*, *knife* with *dagger*, *furniture* with *chair*—all paradigmatic associations based on a set of features to establish categories of objects.

Another kind of evidence for the biological origin of modes comes from George Lakoff's (1987) argument that the root metaphors for all modes grow out of bodily experiences. This is, of course, part of the general position of translation/critical literacy that thought is not a transcendent, universal process but is situated and, in the case of the modes, embodied. For example, the *narrative*, which is historical, evolutionary, and rooted in the life cycle of an organism, is our habitual way of mapping our experiences and information along a time line, and description is our habitual experience of mapping an image with up-down, left-right, and foreground-background distinctions. Narrative time lines and descriptive images are the way we live in our bodies. A third bodily experience is the container experience in which we sort things—for example, for eating, "taking" things into the container of the body and leaving other things out. This third bodily experience becomes our habitual sorting out of similarity and difference to create containers of the similar and related. These similarity/related containers become our metaphorical map for organizing information into the expository or definition mode.

The image or descriptive mode is organized as foreground-background, up-down, left-right, and part-whole structure—say a description of a particular scene—or as a radial structure with a prototype or case at the center of the structure and variations and other examples surrounding the prototype or case, offering illustrations from the periphery. Exposition, on the other hand, uses linear order with a hierarchical structure from up to down and radial structures with the prototype at the center and a list of features surrounding the prototype, each feature a part of the whole prototype. Exposition may compare and contrast two or more linear orders or two radial structures with different features.

A fourth bodily experience is combat, pulling in a given direction, a tug-of-war between two things, a push of several parts toward one goal, and a pull away or resistance to an idea. Walter Ong suggests that physical combat was first turned into games and "metaphors," or dramas, of ceremonial combat and then turned into the "metaphorical" combat of oral rhetoric (Ong 1981, 120). This mapping of mechanics with cause-effect, source-goal, pushing-and-pulling, and resistance to a given force onto discourse produces the mode of argument, persuasion, and editorials. The acts of persuasion and argument push and pull their rhetorical force toward a concentrated point, often using the four-stage strategy of introduction, methods, results, and discussion (Medawar 1964).

George Lakoff and Mark Johnson (1980) have also suggested that within these four modes, which use our experiences to map the structures of our discourse, there appears to be a consistent pattern of values. For example, in the narrative mode, the time lines for our experiences seem to value "first" and "ahead" over "second" and "behind," and in image or description, "up" is valued over "down." In definition or exposition, "in" is valued over "out," and in argument, "push" is valued over "pull." The source for these apparent values is not all that clear, but one can imagine a number of experiences in which "up" is always better than "down," and "ahead" is always better than "behind."[1] Gerald Edelman has argued that Lakoff's embodied categories with their embodied values match very closely Edelman's notions of brain structure. Edelman states flatly that the computer model of the brain does not work and that a new model is needed:

> The structural crisis, which I described in detail in my book *Neural Darwinism*, are those of anatomy and development. Although the brain at one scale looks like a vast electrical network, at its most microscopic scale it is not connected or arranged like any other natural or man-made network. As we have just seen, the network of the brain is created by cellular movement during development and by the extension and connection of increasing numbers of neurons. The brain is an example of a self-organizing system. An examination of this system during its development and of its most microscopic ramifications after development indicates that precise point-to-point wiring (like that in an electronic device) cannot occur. The variation is too great. (Edelman 1992, 25)

Embodiment as a source of wiring in the brain is, however, a promising alternative to computer models which deliver point-to-point wiring at birth. Edelman's work, which proposes wiring based on embodied experiences, provides "an essential biological underpinning for many of their [Lakoff's and Johnson's] proposals concerning the importance of embodiment to grammar and cognition" (Edelman 1992, 252). Embodiment helps to provide a biological alternative to Chomsky's innate structures.

How might embodiment work in grammar? The four basic everyday experiences with which we map our modes are also used to map our verbs: narrative actions (*walking* in time), descriptive images (something in space *is* up/down/left/right/beautiful), definition containers (something *is* a fruit or vegetable), and combative arguments (someone *pushes* or *pulls* something toward a goal) are all ways of talking about how different verbs shape our discourse. For example, we learn how to turn the experience of *walking* into an active verb ("run"), which generates a particular kind of sentence (see Table 5).

Calling the verb "a little despot," Pinker remarks, "one cannot sort out the roles in a sentence without looking up the verb" (Pinker 1994, 113–14). Fillmore agrees. In Fillmore's frame semantics (Fillmore 1982), the verb "saw" produces the scene or semantic frame with an agent ("*He* saw") and an object ("He saw *it*"), and the verb "gave" produces

Table 5. From body experiences to verbs.

BODILY EXPERIENCES	EMBODIED SCHEMA/ CONCEPT STRUCTURE	KNOWLEDGE STRUCTURE	MODE STRUCTURE	VALUES IN STRUCTURES	ASSOCIATED SENTENCE STRUCTURES
1. Sorting out what to eat	1. In-out schema/ concept of container	1. Categorical forms (in container)	1. Definition/ Exposition (container)	in = good out = bad	SVLSC/SVLM She is the writer. She is wise.
2. Walking somewhere (narrative relation)	2. Kinesthetic path-goal schema/time-line concept	2. Linear/ organism (on time line) knowledge	2. Narrative/ story (kinesthetic time line)	ahead = good behind = bad	SVIOO/SVO/ SVM He ran home. He hit the ball. He gave her the ball.
3. Putting beads on a string (association relation)	3. Beads schema/ association/ link concept	3. relational/ associative knowledge (on a string)	3. Expressive (associative) mentioned	mentioned= good Not mentioned = bad	Association list crime/dime/lime

4. Breaking/ taking part of something/ putting it back (metaphorical)	4. Part-whole schema/ hierarchical concept	4. Hierarchical knowledge/ mechanistic knowledge (part of whole)	4. Persuasion/ Argument (push-pull/ part-whole)	push = good pull = bad	SVOM(a)/SVOOc She thought the tree a maple. She thought the book funny.
5. Pushing and pulling	5. Push-pull schema/ combat concept	5. Debate knowledge Thesis-anti-thesis (pushing)		whole = good part = bad	
6. Looking up and down	6. up-down schema/ hierarchical concept	6. Verticle knowledge (at the top)		up = good down = bad	SVLM It is green.
7. Looking forward and backward	7. Foreground-background schema/depth concept	7. Highlighted knowledge (in spotlight)	5. Description (image up-down/ foreground background)	foreground = good background = bad	SV<SC The apple is a fruit.
8. Looking at center and periphery	8. Periphery/ schema center/ concept	8. Radial knowledge/ Image structure (in set)		center = good periphery = bad	

the same cast of characters, plus an indirect object or the receiver of the object ("He gave Bill the ball.") *Saw, gave,* and *run* might be said to generate narrative structures (or vice versa), but *is* generates exposition or description (or vice versa). *Thought,* on the other hand, seems to generate persuasion or argument (or vice versa) (see Table 5). The essential point to be made here is that sentence study in this lexical approach begins not with sentence patterns but with the lexicon or vocabulary, particularly the verb (see Table 5), and particular verbs appear to share with particular modes a common origin in embodiment. Lakoff calls this approach to grammar "cognitively based grammar," as opposed to transformational grammar, semantic grammar, or generative grammar (G. Lakoff 1987, 462). Clearly, cognitively based grammar's emphasis on idealized models of cognitive structure—what I am calling the modes—brings grammatical structure and mode structure together (see Table 5).

The fact—let's assume that it is a fact—that these modes of narration, description, exposition, argument, and possibly the expressive have a biological or bodily foundation does not mean the cultural context doesn't exert a major influence on the uses and shape of these modes. In Edelman's embodiments, our experiences "grow" our brains. Foucault (1970, 17–25) has argued that the Enlightenment shifted our methods of knowing from a structure based on time (narrative) and space (description) to a structure based on the parts of a container (exposition) and the parts of a debate (argument). According to Foucault, the Enlightenment divided things into parts, and these parts were turned into units with arithmetical relations based on some system of notational measurement (Foucault 1970, 51–58). Why did these changes occur? Some allege that the analytic parts and numerical relationships of the paradigmatic modes of containers in definitions and exposition and the push-pull of arguments saved the seventeenth century from the metaphysical chaos then created by basing political and scientific knowledge on narratives about the creation of the world.

Whatever the reasons, the growing status of the paradigmatic occurred in all areas of knowledge. One fascinating example of this shift from the narrative to the paradigmatic occurred in the eighteenth-century debate in chemistry between Antoine-Laurent Lavoisier and Pierre-Joseph Macquer (W. Anderson 1984). Essentially, Macquer organized chemistry around stories and analogies—in other words, the narrative and descriptive modes—and Lavoisier organized chemistry around methods of measurement, analysis of parts, and the push-pull mechanics of hypothesis testing—in other words, the paradigmatic modes. At the end of this debate, Lavoisier's paradigmatic approach won out, and as a result, the language of eighteenth-century science ceased to be personalized and became highly institutionalized.

Eventually, the paradigmatic and its institutionalized scientific language for paradigmatic features became the dominant form of knowledge during decoding/analytic literacy in the United States. Even literary criticism began to look more like paradigmatic feature analysis than narrative responses, and the essay began to look more like argumentative analysis than narrative reflection. But by 1973, we seemed to have learned as a society that the paradigmatic could not solve all of our problems, primarily because it could not handle some types of postmodern complexity:

> As the complexity of a system increases, our ability to make precise yet significant statements about its behavior diminishes until a threshold is reached beyond which precision and significance (or relevance) become almost mutually exclusive characteristics. (Zadeh 1973, 28)

The postmodern complexity of the present period of translation/critical literacy seems to require new roles for the synthetic/narrative modes. These modes are now at least equal to the paradigmatic/analytic as a source of knowledge. One example of this increased status of narrative ways of knowing is the increased use of Zadeh's fuzzy-set prototype theory in various areas of postmodern life. Zadeh's work, for example, has fundamentally changed the way many problems are solved in electrical engineering, an area which has traditionally been dependent upon classical paradigmatic logic—*on* or *off*, *A* or *B*, one feature at a time. For instance, the image on the traditional television tube has been organized around a paradigmatic list of features, and these features have been adjusted by the viewer, one at a time, until the image has all the features the viewer wants. Recent TV sets (Sony's Triniton XBR, for example) are no longer organized around a list of features, but instead are organized around exemplar or case images with a set of features. In this fuzzy logic or narrative habit of mind, the image of the tube is electronically checked every 1/60 of a second against a database of forty exemplar (narrative) images, each exemplar or case representing a different model of perfection. The tube makes adjustments to some features in the selected exemplar, ignores others, and attempts to attain a "close," but not perfect, match of the features in one of the selected prototypes or exemplars of screen images. This approach requires that one have a theory of exemplars. In writing, this takes the form of exemplars for different genres, and in reading it *should* take the form of exemplars for different genres of reading (reading *USA Today* on the morning bus; reading research reports in preparation for a city council presentation). Reading has yet to develop such genres.

This use of a narrative fuzzy-logic and prototype theory is now being applied to automatic transmissions, elevator management, video camcorders, bank loans, and stock portfolios. In stock and loan problems, narrative cases of expert judgments are created for various loans and investment situations in which experts weigh the results of variables, which are always somewhat contradictory. Again, these new computer programs are matching to cases and exemplars of expert judgments, not just reviewing a list of paradigmatic features or rules (McNeill and Freiberger 1993, 217).

New science has also become increasingly dependent upon narrative knowledge to anchor its findings. Thomas Kuhn, in fact, has argued that in the "disciplinary matrix" holding together the body of knowledge of a contemporary scientific community, it is the cases and exemplars which are the most critical: "More than other sorts of components of the disciplinary matrix, differences between sets of exemplars provide the community fine-structure of science" (Kuhn 1970, 187).

Cases and exemplars have also started to play a role of increasing importance in various professions. Some occupations have typically focused on the case or exemplar, and others have focused on laws or features. For example, the crafts of wallpapering and upholstery have typically sold their products by showing paradigmatic features of wallpaper and fabric, but the occupations of baking and architecture have typically sold their products by showing narrative exemplars of a finished product—the cake, the cookies, the completed house or office. Law was at one time a feature profession, teaching young lawyers a list of laws; it shifted to a case-study profession. A similar shift has been underway in business for at least fifty years, beginning with Harvard Business School's decision to shift from features and principles to a case-study approach in the study of business.

Education, too, has begun to give new status to narrative ways of knowing. Although education continues to have more than its share of arguments about whether educational understanding should be based on a set of features and laws (formism and definition) or on cases and exemplars (contextualism and description), the recognition of the importance of diversity, individuality, and complexity in educational contexts has led to an increasing use of narrative case studies to capture the "truths" of the classroom, truths not revealed by the statistical patterns of paradigmatic proof. Frederick Erickson, for one, urges that teachers make extensive use of narrative ways of knowing in order to discover the essential patterns of teaching:

> Practitioners can learn from a case study even if the circumstances of the case do not match those of their own situation.... The results of interpretive research are of special interest to teachers.... Teachers

> too are concerned with specifics of local meaning and local action; that is the stuff of life in daily classroom practice. (Erickson 1986, 153, 156)

There has been a growing status accorded to narrative ways of knowing in research in English education. Mike Rose's personal narrative is an essential foundation for his *Lives on the Boundary* (1989), winner of NCTE's David H. Russell Award in research in 1989, and the same is true of Joseph Harris's 1989 Braddock Award-winning article, "The Idea of Community in the Study of Writing" (1989), and Nancy Sommers's Braddock Award-winning essay, "Between the Drafts" (1992).

Some fields show an increasing tension between the narrative and the paradigmatic. The creation of score categories in writing assessment has involved a continuous tension between score categories based on features and score categories based on exemplars or cases (M. Myers 1980). The creation of categories in biology has fluctuated between the pheneticists who want to organize taxonomies around cases and overall role, function, and form, and the cladists who want to organize taxonomies around the features of today's species (S. Gould 1983, 363–64). In writing assessment, different modes produce different scores for papers, and in biology, different modes produce different categories for animals like zebras (see G. Lakoff 1987, 119).

The work of Eleanor Rosch (1973; 1977; 1978; 1983), an experimental psychologist at the University of California-Berkeley, has given us an excellent picture of how prototype or narrative proofs work in our everyday categories. For one thing, narrative and descriptive ways of knowing, which are more open, more individual, more inclusive categories without either-or boundaries, are, nevertheless, categories which have clearly agreed on structures. People understand quickly which exemplar or case defines which category. Using lists of six words in eight categories (*bird, vehicle, fruit, science,* and so forth), Rosch asked 113 students to rate on a scale of 1 (high) to 7 (low) the degree to which each of six cases defined a given category. For instance, in the *science* category, *chemistry* got the highest rating (1.0) as a case or exemplar defining science, and *geology* got the midpoint rating (2.6). In the *vehicle* category, *car* got the highest rating (1.0), and *boat* got a midpoint rating (2.7). Most amazing was the amount of agreement about what prototype or case defined each of the eight categories. For example, all 113 students ranked *chemistry* as the perfect exemplar of *science* and *car* as the perfect exemplar of *vehicle* (Rosch 1973, 112–13).[2]

This 1973 experiment "took only 10 minutes," say McNeill and Freiberger, "yet [it] had an impact which society has still to absorb" (McNeill and Freiberger 1993, 84). For one thing, Rosch's findings confirmed the position of Lofti Zadeh (1978) that human categories and syllogisms often have a narrative fuzziness that does not fit the categories of classical, paradigmatic logic. In Zadeh's terms, the classical syllogism should be rewritten with a narrative fuzziness: *most* men are vain; Socrates is a man; thus, it is *likely* that Socrates is vain.

In Rosch's terms, many categories should be redefined with cases and exemplars. The prototypical *bird*, for instance, is something like a *robin*, which produces sensible results in *bird* sentences more often than *chicken* or *ostrich* or numerous other choices. *Chicken* is closer to the central prototype (or is a stronger member of the set) than the *ostrich*. *Ostriches* and *penguins* are clearly members of the category *bird*, but their rankings as members are not as strong as the rankings for *robins* or *seagulls* or *chickens*. The point is that some narratives or cases are better representatives of a given category than other cases or narratives (Rosch 1977; 1983; G. Lakoff 1987, 45).

In addition, some categories have clearer boundaries than others. Remember that some kinds of things like *birds* can be well known in either the narrative or paradigmatic modes, depending upon whether one intends academic or everyday uses. In everyday categories, the bird category typically has a clear boundary, but there are other, quite different categories like *bachelor* and *tall man* which always have somewhat fuzzy boundaries. In classical, paradigmatic logic, which uses a set of features, one could attempt to determine who is a bachelor by answering such paradigmatic questions as "How old is a bachelor? Sixteen? Twenty-one? Thirty?" In a narrative or case approach, we could use a narrative case to suggest the meaning of "bachelor" (see, for example, Fillmore 1977). Guess which one works in everyday life and literature?

In decoding/analytic literacy, which approached categories primarily as a set of paradigmatic features, not as prototypes, categories were arranged in a hierarchy, with parts adding up to objects and with objects arranged in hierarchical fashion along a ladder beginning with the concrete and leading to the abstract. Thus, some parts added up to *dining-room chair* and the parts of *dining-room chair* added up to the larger category of *chair*, and the parts of *chair* and *sofa* added up to the larger, superordinate class of *furniture*. This approach, as noted earlier, created the very useful superordinate categories of most paradigmatic studies. Most students learned their science on this ladder of abstraction.

But these hierarchial categories based on paradigmatic features and parts have not proved particularly useful for some kinds of everyday work and many of the complex problems of the humanities. For survival in these situations, people need information at a much more human level. For example, people use exemplars to tell them what a tiger is because adding up the parts takes too long and leads to one being the tiger's lunch. But this raises the question of what people typically use as their basic category for objects—*lawn chair, chair,* or *furniture*—which are different points on the ladder of abstraction. It turns out that *lawn chair* is too specific to be very useful as a category, and *furniture* is too abstract to be useful. Furniture cannot be seen, except as something more concrete. The basic level of most categories—and the source of most prototypes—is the *chair* level. Thus, most of our category systems have three vaguely bounded levels forming a hierarchy—the subordinate level (*lawn chair*), the basic level (*chair*), and the superordinate level (*furniture*)—and the prototype or narrative case tends to come from the midlevel, which has everyday survival value. However, paradigmatic approaches to classification tend to privilege the superordinate categories (*furniture*) (Rosch 1983).

Thus far, this discussion has assumed that the two ways of knowing, *narrative* and *paradigmatic*, can be used at any time on any material. To test whether I could get narrative and paradigmatic representations of the same material, I asked 274 teacher-subjects to read the following paragraph and to write an explanation of what the paragraph means:

> The procedure is actually quite simple. First you arrange things into different groups. Of course, one pile may be sufficient depending on how much there is to do. If you have to go somewhere else due to lack of facilities that is the next step, otherwise you are pretty well set. It is important not to overdo things. That is, it is better to do too few things at once than too many. In the short run this may not seem important but complications can easily arise. A mistake can be expensive as well. At first the whole procedure will seem complicated. Soon, however, it will become just another facet of life. It is difficult to foresee any end to the necessity for this task in the immediate future, but then one never can tell. After the procedure is completed one arranges the materials into different groups again. Then they can be put into their appropriate places. Eventually they will be used once more and the whole cycle will then have to be repeated. However, that is part of life. (Bransford and Johnson 1973, 400)

Twenty-three of the subjects, almost 10 percent, quit reading after a line or two, and the reason they gave for quitting is that they did not "know what was happening." In fact, one person said, "I didn't finish because it was nonsense." I want to suggest that most humans who have not assimilated "school habits" or who have not adequately fashioned themselves as meaning makers tend to avoid failure experiences by quitting. Notice that this is very similar to what happened to two dozen people in my beaker experiment in sign shifting (Chapter 10). School teaches people to fashion themselves as meaning makers and to have faith that they can get meaning out of what at first appears to be nonsense. The average unschooled person, however, does not continue reading nonsense.

The second important pattern in the data was that among those who kept reading and making guesses, some 68 percent (172 subjects) of the readers produced narrative guesses such as "organizing the morning mail," "washing my dishes," "cleaning my cluttered desk," or "doing my laundry," and 31 percent (83 subjects) of the readers produced paradigmatic or thematic guesses such as "the beliefs of one's philosophy of life," "the hum-drum quality of daily living," and "ways to solve problems." The responses of 2 percent (6) of the subjects were classifiable as "kept looking for the solution to the problem." In summary, the modes do appear to be ways in which people organize things, even in the most everyday circumstances.[3]

The developmental patterns of modes often start with the *list* or *conversational* speech event and then evolve into the *presentational* and *academic*. For example, novices who are attempting to write narratives for the first time often organize their narratives as *list speech events*—one-thing-at-a-time sequences of small, unchunked bits—because they have not achieved cognitive automaticity. The list approach is a common novice approach to all of the modes, just as in ballroom-dancing lessons, I used the *list event* to organize ballroom lessons as a one-part-at-a-time sequence. The novice use of the list speech event to organize narrative looks very much like the following[4]:

> The daddy works in the bank. And mommy cooks breakfast. Then we get up and get dressed. And the baby eats breakfast and honey. We go to the school and we get dressed like that. I put coat on and I go in the car. And the lion in the cage. The bear went so fast and he's going to break the bear back, in the cage. —*Eliot M., 2 years, 11 months* (Applebee 1978, 37, 59)

Another example of the novice use of the list speech event to organize narratives comes from Sarah Michaels's analysis of the narratives and descriptions presented by children during oral sharing time in elementary schools (Michaels 1986, 94–116). In most elementary schools, sharing time is a marked *presentational* speech event in which the children are asked to share with the class a narrative about an event or a description of an object or place. Children are expected to follow two "rules" which govern all expertise in all of the modes except the expressive and which are typical rules of *presentational* and *academic* speech events—stay on one topic and pick something "important" in some way to the audience.

When children do not follow these two rules, the other children and the teacher ask for and demand explanations: "What is your story?"

"What are you describing?" "How many of them rocks is she gonna show us?" "Tell us things that are different." In addition, children are expected to follow the rules for sharing time—to answer questions that arise ("Was the water cold?") and to hold the floor for a short time ("Others are wanting their turn"). One child (Deena) told the following narrative:

Deena: Um...I'went to the bēach / ..'Sûnday /
       ānd /'to MacDônalds /
       and to the pârk /
       ...and / ..I'got this for my / ..bìrthday / /
       ...My'mother bought it fôr me /
       ...and um / ...Ì hād / ..um / ..tẁo'dollars 'for my 'birthday
       and I 'put it 'in hére /
       ...and I 'went to' where my frîe-nd /
       ..named Gî Gi /
       ...'I went over to my grandmother's'house with her /
       ...and um /.....Ŝhe was on my bāck /
       and'I / ..and 'we was walkin' aro̧und /
       ...by my house /
       ..and um / ...'she was hêâ-vy /
       She ⌈was in the'sixth or'seventh grade / /

Teacher: ⌊OK I'm going to stop you. I want to talk about things that are really really very important. That's important to you but tell us things that are sort of different. Can you do that? And tell us what beach you went to. (Michaels 1986, 108–9)

Here, again, like the earlier Applebee example from Eliot, is a narrative told within a list speech event with an expressive string of associations held together with the word *and* and a loose time line. The child has attained some fluency, but the teacher attempts to move the child to one topic ("And tell us what beach you went to") and to selectivity or importance ("That's important to you, but . . ."). At the end there is a lingering sense of failure and frustration on the part of both the child and the teacher, the teacher not understanding the list event and the expressive mode that the child was using and the child not understanding which event and mode were called for.

The story below is an example of a transition from the speech event and the expressive mode to the list narrative to the narrative embedded in conversational and presentational speech events:

Davy Crockett he was walking in the woods, then he swimmed in the water to get to the other side. Then there was a boat that picked him up. Then he got to the other side. He went into the woods. He was in the place where Indians made. The Indians came and got him. Then pretty soon he got loose. The Indians let him loose. —*Kip P., 4 years, 9 months* (Applebee 1978, 65)

In the story below the child presents what qualifies as an *expert narrative.* According to Applebee, Vygotsky (1962) calls this form "concepts" because the child shows that he/she does understand the concept of narrative organization along a time line, organized as a presentational event with a topic focus:

> There was a boy named Johnny Hong Kong and finally he grew up and went to school and after that all he ever did was sit all day and think. He hardly even went to the bathroom. And he thought every day and every thought he thought up in his head got bigger and bigger. One day it got so big he had to go live in the attic with trunks and winter clothes. So his mother bought some goldfish and let them live in his head—he swallowed them—and every time he thought, a fish would eat it up until he was even so he never thought again, and he felt much better. —*Tracy H., 5 years, 8 months* (Applebee 1978, 66)

The long-maligned, five-paragraph essay is an example of novices using a five-step list to learn to write something like an argumentative essay: first, an introduction or thesis; then three proofs; and finally a conclusion. Notice that a student could use the novice approach while writing the argumentative essay and not use a novice approach while writing narrative. In other words, a person could write expert narratives, even using flashbacks and other variations of time lines, and still write novice arguments using five-paragraph essays. I know that many of my friends in the writing projects will object to my giving legitimacy, both historical and developmental, to the five-paragraph essay, but I think its survival value tells us that it has some useful social function and, therefore, deserves our serious consideration as a form of literacy. In summary, then, the five modes of *expressive, narrative, description, exposition* (or *definition*) and *argument* are primary ways of organizing our experiences, and these ways go through a *novice* period in which the *list speech event* is used to organize each one.

To attain at least a minimum level of translation/critical literacy, students must learn how to use all of the five modes (*expressive, narration, description, definition/exposition,* and *argument*) and how to shift easily among them. In addition, translation/critical literacy encourages experiments with modes as a way to find an appropriate form and voice for discussing particular kinds of contemporary problems. Jane Tompkins, for example, has objected to argumentative, academic writing organized as "the showdown on main street" in which writers aim for the "moral advantage" over adversaries, "the moment of murderous-ness" (Tompkins 1988, 589–90). She has called for forms of argument which are nonadversarial.

Others have called for a mixing of modes. One example is Donald McQuade's Chair's address to the 1991 Annual Convention of the Conference on College Composition and Communication, in which he brought together the story of his mother's sickness and his own concerns about his profession's ways of knowing (McQuade 1992). Yet another example is the mixing of instructor-exposition and student-narrative in Beverly Lyon Clark's and Sonja Wiedenhaupt's case study of Sonja's development as a writer (Clark and Wiedenhaupt 1992). And another recent example is Anthony Petrosky's speech/article on his experiences running a research lab for the National Board for Professional Teaching Standards (Petrosky 1994). Petrosky shaped his discourse around a mixture of the narrative and argumentative modes—his narrative describing a deteriorating relationship between a husband and wife and his argument outlining the issues which led to contentious differences between Petrosky and the NBPTS staff. Mode mixing, like the sign mixing and speech-event mixing (multivocal speech event) mentioned before, is becoming an interesting way to explore and to communicate ideas in an age of ambiguity and uncertainty.

Finally, of course, in translation/critical literacy, we are proposing to restore narrative and storytelling to a high-status position as a way to learn and to construct knowledge. The writing of case studies, descriptions of exemplars, ethnographic stories, and literary narratives needs to become a central part of our English classes. One of the jobs of English is to develop the cases and exemplars which will help us understand some of our human problems. This is essential in an age that recognizes that narrative cases can anchor our knowledge and understandings in ways that paradigmatic features cannot. In addition, in the English of translation/critical literacy, we need to experiment with a range of modes and the shifting of modes within the same speech event and topic (see Table 6). Decoding/analytic literacy's emphasis on the purity of the modes and on the centrality of the paradigmatic as a source of knowledge will not help us solve many of our problems of work, citizenship, and personal growth in this age of translation/critical literacy.

(For Notes, see page 242.)

Table 6. The genres: Modes x speech events.[1,2,3]

Speech Events	The Modes: The Cognitive Dimension—What are the cognitive ways we organize "knowledge"?				
	Expressive Mode	The Synthetic Mode — Prototype Categories, Case Knowledge		The Paradigmatic/Analytic Modes — Classical Grid Categories, Feature Knowledge	
What are the social ways we organize knowledge?	Organizing with "Free" Associations EXPRESSIVE (Nonlogical)	Organizing with Time Line NARRATION (Logic Progressive)	Organizing with Spatial Image DESCRIPTION (Logic Static)	Organizing with Types, Sets or Containers EXPOSITION (Logic Static)	Organizing Parts toward Thesis ARGUMENT (Logic Progressive/ Repetitive)
What are the social dimensions? What are the audience (interpersonal), subject (ideation), text (textual) relationships in discourse, the degrees of formality, the point of view of the narrator?	*To associate* things, focusing on expressive purpose, using freely whatever comes to mind. Emphasis on writer's feelings.	*To recount* factual events or tell fictional stories (events), focusing on an historical purpose, using cause-effect process, time line, kinesthetic experience arranged over time. Emphasis on subject references.	*To describe* and portray with an ethnographic purpose, using contextual details to focus on image arranged in space at a moment in time. Emphasis on subject references.	*To define* forms and types, focusing on definitions and categories, using container experience to compare and contrast, to divide things into parts. Emphasis on subject references.	*To argue*, to persuade, focusing on systems of proof, the part-whole machine/hypothesis of input and output, causes and effects, reasons and results. Emphasis on reader's feelings.
Notational Speech Events: The discourse of lists of things. *Point of view:* often not noted	Clinical word-association test, a "stream" of associations.	List of events, calendar, steps in a *recipe*, simple directions, chronological grocery list, roll call listed by birthdate.	Classified want ad, police wanted poster, résumé, census statistics, weather statistics.	Types, grocery list, notes toward report, clustering ideas, telephone directory, stock market, tables, list of type of things, the reading of the list of dead at a memorial, the message on a tombstone.	Proverbs, maxims, predictions.

Conversational Speech Events: The discourse of close social relations and common sense. *Point of view:* "I" (INFORMAL) →	Pouring it out to a friend; "letting it all out" in a personal journal.	Anecdotes, gossip, joke, an informal biographical sketch, social exchange over sequential steps in a procedure, personal letter with story, some fairy tales, sharing time, stories, dinner-time conversation.	Casual descriptions of place, informational travel ads, personal letters describing someone in context.	Journal or diary reports, learning logs and memos describing definitions of things, types of things, categories of things.	Personal letter of opinion, informal letter to editor, a draft of problem solutions, an informal debate.
Presentation/Public Speech Events: The discourse of public issues. *Point of view:* "I" and "He/She" (MORE FORMAL) →	Public "confession" on Oprah, public monologue about one's feelings about an issue.	A biographical event, myth, auto-biographical incident, a fable, policeman's accident report, newspaper reports of events, an elaboration of direction/procedures.	Newspaper description of weather damage; a magazine sketch portraying a person or place.	Magazine report on world economy or elections showing types of voters or businessnesses. Report on heroes in novels.	Formal letter to editor, editorial, proposed solution, analysis of reasons for an event, movie review, evaluation of a candidate, a commentary on reasons.
Academic Speech Events: The discourse of specialized knowledge. *Point of view:* "He/She" and "It" (FORMAL) →	N/A	Academic history paper, books on chronological procedures of historical research.	Ethnographic study of place. Research report from Geertz or Becker or Margaret Mead	Technical summaries, summary of laws or types, Popper's world hypothesis (four types of hypothesis), Botany studies, Chomsky's syntactic structures.	Papers from disciplines: social science thesis—proof cause-effect scientific summary of results, philosophical argument, political theory on trends and reasons.

[1]The expressive has no publicly "accepted" form in academic speech events.
[2]The examples in the cells are forms of discourse/writing shaped by speech events and modes.
[3]References: speech events (Hymes 1974; Moffett 1968; M. Myers 1982b); modes (R. Lakoff 1990; Pepper 1942; D'Angelo 1975; Kinneavy 1971).

Notes

1. Lakoff's claim that the modes grew out of our bodily experiences is not that different from Stephen Pepper's fifty-year-old claim in *World Hypotheses* (1942) that the modes were a universal way of organizing the world. Pepper proposes that there are four primary ways to organize hypotheses about the world: organicism, which is like time lines and narrative; contextualism, which is like image and description; formism, which is like containers and definitions/exposition; and mechanism, which is like push-pull and argument. He argues that the four have the following relationships in philosophy:

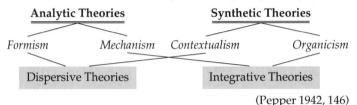

(Pepper 1942, 146)

2. Rosch later clarified "prototype" to mean a case judged to have a high "degree of prototypicality." She said, "Only in some artificial categories is there by definition a literal single prototype" (Rosch 1978, 40).

3. My experiment is a variation on a classic reading experiment by Bransford and Johnson (1973).

4. Applebee, following Vygotsky, calls this form "complexes" or "unfocused chains." This selection comes from Eliot M., 2 years, 11 months (Applebee 1978, 63). The category "complexes: unfocused chain" comes from Vygotsky (Vygotsky 1962).

13 Negotiated and Situated Knowledge: Translating between Stances

Although conception without perception is merely *empty*, perception without conception is *blind* (totally inoperative). (N. Goodman 1978, 6)

During recitation literacy, Matthew Arnold gave the highest priority to the moral meaning of the cultural touchstones of literature and generally ignored issues of literary form. But by the 1930s, during decoding/analytic literacy, Cleanth Brook's New Criticism was emphasizing form in literary studies and resisting any reference to "extrinsic" meaning, either the reader's experience or the author's intention and experience. By 1965, the College Board's Commission on English was warning that both New Criticism's emphasis on a close reading of form and Arnold's emphasis on moral meaning were "killing" the reading of literature in secondary schools:

> The pernicious practice of converting every literary work into a moral homily is perhaps the abuse most frequently committed. But the Commission believes that no discussion, no study, no reading of any work is complete without some consideration of possible extrinsic meaning, meaning that brings that work directly against the reader's own philosophical convictions and experience. It may be ironic that, after so many years of complaint about teachers who taught the moral instead of the work, warning should now be given against the incompleteness of any study of literature that avoids this consideration. But the Commission believes that "close reading" may as readily sterilize the study of literature as moralizing once stultified it. (Commission on English 1965, 72–73)

The Commission called for a balance, which has become the special project of the new translation/critical literacy. To achieve this balance, translation/critical literacy has, in part, shifted the focus of literature classes from types of texts to types of readings interacting within structures of texts.

The first major proposals for shifting the focus of literature from types of texts to types of readings were made in 1937–1938 by D. W. Harding and Louise Rosenblatt. Harding proposed that the socially constructed roles of onlookers, hearers of gossip, and spectators were the roles played by readers engaged in a literary or poetic reading, and the socially constructed roles of participants, transactors, and activists were the roles played by readers engaged in nonliterary readings. In Harding's view, these two kinds of reading or roles could be applied to the same text, just as in everyday settings, such as a construction site, one could play the role of spectator and produce an aesthetic "reading" that focuses on patterns of laborers and machines or play the role of participant and produce a nonpoetic reading that focuses on information about the construction (Harding 1937). In the former, one might observe the shape of the landscape and the potential form of a new building, but in the latter, one might estimate how much dirt was being moved each hour by laborers and machines.

Around the time that Harding's article on spectator/participant roles appeared, Louise Rosenblatt's *Literature as Exploration* (see Rosenblatt 1968) also appeared. Like Harding, Rosenblatt suggested that the difference between the literary and the nonliterary is a difference of stance during reading, not a difference in types of texts. She also emphasized that a difference in stance is not a difference between subjectivity and objectivity. Harding's spectator/participant distinction tended to describe the literary reading as one in which the reader stood back from events, but Rosenblatt's distinctions emphasized the "lived" experience of literary and aesthetic events and the observed information of nonliterary events. She insisted that, in most texts, "no hard-and-fast line separates efferent—scientific or expository—reading on the one hand from aesthetic [or poetic] reading on the other" (Rosenblatt 1978, 35). For this reason, she called each encounter with a text a "unique event":

> Since each encounter between a reader and the text is a unique event, it is not possible to simply look at the text of Gibbon or Emerson or, to cite a more recent work, Loren Eiseley's *The Immense Journey,* and assign it a particular place in the spectrum. But we know that texts like the ones cited above tend often to produce literary experiences that fall somewhere in the middle of the continuum. (Rosenblatt 1978, 35–36)

Rosenblatt concluded that "a reader has to learn to handle his multiple responses to texts in a variety of complex ways, moving the center of attention toward the efferent [nonliterary] or aesthetic [literary] ends of the spectrum" (Rosenblatt 1978, 37). Harding's distinction between spectator and participant roles was a key issue at the Dartmouth Conference in 1960, when the U.S. and the U.K. gathered together to define "What Is English?" After Albert R. Kitzhaber opened the conference by proposing that English be defined as the triad of language, literature, and composition studies, James Britton, who was the respondent to Kitzhaber, countered that the center of English as a subject should be the spectator or literary role in the reading and writing of the English language. Furthermore, said Britton, the development of this spectator or literary role contributed to a key responsibility of English—the personal growth of the students (Britton 1970; Dixon 1975)—because by learning to play various spectator or literary roles, students would learn to give shape to their own lives.

Rosenblatt also argued that the process of shifting back and forth between the poetic or spectator reading and the efferent or participant reading developed in students' habits of reflection and imagination, which could help students engage in social choices in public discourse.

> The emotional character of the student's response to literature offers an opportunity to develop the ability *to think rationally within an emotionally colored context.* . . . The reading and discussion of literature can contribute greatly to the growth of such habits of reflection. (Rosenblatt 1968, 227–28)

> When there is active participation in literature—the reader living through, reflecting on, and criticizing his own responses to the text—there will be many kinds of benefits. We can call this "growth in ability to share discriminatingly in the possibilities of language as it is used in literature." But this means also the development of the imagination: the ability to escape from the limitations of time and place and environment, the capacity to envisage alternatives in ways of life and in moral and social choices, the sensitivity to thought and feeling and needs of other personalities. (Rosenblatt 1968, 291)

In an extension of Rosenblatt's notions of literary reading as lived events, Walker Gibson argued that readers who were engaged in a literary reading had to become different "mock readers" when they read different works of literature (W. Gibson 1950, 266). In a good book, Gibson said, "We assume, for the sake of experience, that set of attitudes and qualities which the language asks us to assume"—in other words, we agree to play the role of mock readers assigned by the work—but a bad book "is a book in whose mock readers we discover a person we refuse to become" (W. Gibson 1950, 265, 268). In an extension of Gibson's distinction, Stanley Fish suggested that the roles adopted by readers were shaped by the interpretive communities in which readers and writers live and that these roles become the standards we use for saying a book is good—we accept the role of the mock reader—or if the book is bad—we reject the role of the mock reader (Fish 1994). Thus, Fish argued, a literary reading is always historically and culturally contingent, expressing an expression of an interpretive community's attitude toward individual gender, class, racial, ethnic, national, and age issues at a particular moment and in a particular place.

In general, then, Harding and Rosenblatt in the 1930s and Gibson and Fish in the 1960s outlined an approach to literature which characterizes translation/critical literacy today. First, the new translation/critical literacy defines reading as an event in which the reader's translations shift the reader's role from spectator to participant, from a literary reading of an experience to an informational reading of a commodity within the same text and within the same reading. Texts in this new critical literacy are arranged on a continuum representing the kind of reading they typically receive, and a literary work is, then, a work which typically, but not exclusively, receives a literary reading. Second, in high schools especially, texts should be read in their historical setting.

How are the contexts of reading defined? Modes are one way to describe the contexts or purposes in which readings take place. Britton, for instance, emphasized the importance of the expressive mode as the initial response to literature. Britton et al. (1975) argued that the expressive reading was the root of both transactional and poetic readings and that readers, after beginning with the expressive, may or may not branch into poetic and transactional (nonpoetic) stances. Sheridan Blau (1994), among others, has argued persuasively that initial feelings and emotional reactions to what we read and experience must become central, important matters in our English classes ("It was too hard!" "I loved that one scene!" "Why did they go?") and that the expressive mode is the place to start. There are many young readers who must begin with their feelings in order to develop ideas about what they read. But this is *only* a beginning.

In addition to the expressive mode, the narrative and descriptive modes provide a context for reading, what Scholes calls reading the text *within* the text (Scholes 1985, 24). In a narrative reading, one might identify the historical setting of the story, make a map of the setting and indicate locations of various scenes, and in a descriptive reading, one might contrast the descriptions of two people or two places in the story or two contrasting descriptions of the same place or person within the text. The emphasis in this kind of reading is on comprehension (Scholes 1985, 27).

A third context for reading is the appreciative or expository reading in which we place one text *upon* another text (Scholes 1985), examining how two stories by the same author are alike, or how two stories by different authors in the same historical setting are different or alike, or how critical viewpoints in the texts might differ. We could contrast *Huck Finn* as a novel with *Huck Finn* as a musical, for example, examining what gets lost in the translation (see Probst 1984 and Beach and Marshall 1991 for other ways of organizing a text-on-text literary reading).

In the argumentative mode or critical reading, we use text *against* text, the reader using one text or framework or historical period to resist another (Scholes 1985). In English departments in recent years, these resistant readings have produced many perspectives for resistance to traditional readings—gender, ethnicity, class, and so forth. For example, a feminist reading of Conrad's *Heart of Darkness* resists the text that we have come to think Conrad wrote, revealing how a point of view at a particular point in history denigrates women throughout the story (Sullivan 1991). This kind of reading or context, like all of the others, is not limited to English departments. It is part of our public discourse. Recently, I received a letter from the National Rifle Association protesting NCTE's award to a children's story about Peter Rabbit (see Figure 21). The NRA argued that the story, in which Peter Rabbit is chased by Farmer Brown, privileges the point of view of the rabbit and denigrates the point of view of the hunter. The NRA was reading against the grain of the typical reading of the story, in an argumentative mode, and in doing so revealed some of the values of the story itself.

In literary readings, students participate in the lives of fictional others (narrative), reflect on and understand the values of place (description), retell the stories of characters in different situations (expository), and read against the story in some way (argumentative). In nonliterary readings, readers judge the lifelikeness and/or "accuracy" of information in the plot (narrative), the coherence of the descriptions of place (description), the reasonableness of evidence of conflict between this author and others (definition), and the biographical and cultural disputes surrounding the work at the time of its creation and since (argument). In summary, the context of our readings can be organized through the modes, beginning with the expressive and proceeding through the narrative, the descriptive, the definitional, and the argumentative (see Table 7).

A second approach to context, in addition to mode, is the institutional location of the text or its form. Nelson Goodman (1968) was one of those who changed the question from "What is art?" to "When is art?" by placing objects in different institutional settings. He argued that the institutional context of a reading radically changes the way we read the same text, event, or object. For example (and what follows is my interpretation of Goodman), we can "read" a rock, in at least five different institutional contexts. In the first institutional context, a rock is used to block the back wheel of a car, basically a nonliterary/aesthetic context. In a second institutional context, the rock is moved inside the house and used as a door jamb; again, generally, a nonliterary/aesthetic context but inviting some literary or aesthetic response. The rock is then moved to a third institutional context, the center of a front-room coffee table, calling for a mixture of aesthetic and nonaesthetic readings. The rock is then moved to a fourth institutional context, onto a pedestal in a local art museum, creating a wholly aesthetic context. And, finally, the rock is moved to a fifth institutional context, a glass case in the local historical museum, primarily a nonart context focused on information (some museum theorists will object here).

In these five institutional contexts, the "reading" of the rock shifts from a transactional, nonart reading to a poetic reading and then to a nonpoetic reading. The question is how does the rock "look" in each context or, put another way, how is the rock "read." To develop the particulars about how the rock might be read, I asked students in two of my classes at the University of Illinois at Urbana-Champaign to describe their readings of the rock in five different institutional contexts. These are some of their responses:

> (1) *blocking the tire of a car:* "the ragged rock is heavy enough to block the tire"; "the rock is flat against the tire"; "the rock may not be big enough to block the tire"; "the rock is flat enough on the bottom to stay in place." *Relevant Features:* weight to block tire and shape to fit against tire and to stay stable on the ground.

> (2) *blocking the door:* "the rock blocks the door on its flat side and adds a natural feeling"; "the rock is heavy and has to be moved to close the door"; "the rock does not scratch the door"; "the rock does not mark the floor while blocking the door"; and "the rock is too big for blocking the door, but it has an interesting color and makes a conversation piece at the front door when people come in." *Relevant Features:* shape to block door, size, edges, color.

> (3) *the coffee-table object:* "the rock has interesting colors"; "the rock has a sharp edge reflecting light"; "the rock is a little too big for the table"; "the rock has a patterned texture which people like to touch"; "people like it"; "the rock may be a family memento from the Missouri vacation of 1979"; "the rock has a shape which is aesthetically pleasing"; and "the rock holds down magazines and seems to have a face emerging out of one side." *Relevant Features:* size holds down magazines, color gets our attention, size may be too big for context, texture important, face seems to emerge, may be a history artifact, people respond to it, may be an object to trigger an imaginary story.

> (4) *the rock on the pedestal in the middle of a room in an art museum:* "the rock has an interesting symmetry and balance"; "its weight is planted, holding the earth down"; "the rock has a sharp edge which twists into a flat edge"; "the rock reminds me of a small sculpture in a Chicago museum"; and "the rock has colors which change as the light changes in the room from the sun-

August 25, 1992

Miles Myers, Executive Director
National Council of Teachers of English
1111 Kenyon Road
Urbana, IL 61801

Dear Mr. Myers:

I am writing on behalf of the National Rifle Association of America's nearly three million members to belatedly express our outrage at the reprehensible decision of the National Council of Teachers of English (NCTE) to honor Arnold Adoff with the 1988 "Award for Poetry for Children."

Although this honor is awarded for an author's collective works, Adoff's editorial negligence and ignorance are clearly evident in his 1985 "The Cabbage are Chasing the Rabbits." His repeated characterization of hunters as "hateful" presents an impressionable audience with an inaccurate and downright slanderous description, based on the narrow opinion of one individual, of a 20 million person segment of society. Such characterization displays remarkable prejudice against a group of society with different values than the author's, a surprising attitude considering the other titles Mr. Adoff has written or edited. Furthermore, Mr. Adoff completely disregards the legitimacy of an American heritage, steeped in tradition, and very influential in rural America as well as other portions of society, which is responsible for the restoration of wildlife populations over the past century, and committed to their conservation in the future.

That an individual would write such material is not surprising. But for a 110,000 member organization representing America's teachers, ostensibly dedicated to education and the pursuit of knowledge through open-minded consideration of a wide array of ideas and information, to endorse this material designed for highly impressionable children, and even honor its author, is shockingly close-minded and highly irresponsible. Furthermore, presentation of such a distinguished award to an individual with a personal agenda against those with dissimilar values is a shameful commentary on your organization, and a disturbing precedent for our educational system.

I sincerely hope that the NCTE will adhere to a more socially responsible and ethically stringent set of criteria when considering candidates for the next Award for Poetry for Children.

Sincerely,

James Jay Baker
Executive Director

Fig. 21. Letter from the NRA.

Table 7. Using the modes to organize poetic and transactional readings.

THE SOCIAL GOALS OF RESPONSES	USING THE MODES TO ORGANIZE A READING	SHORT STORY AS POETIC EVENT	SHORT STORY AS TRANSACTIONAL EVENT
GETTING THE GIST OF THE STORY, COMPREHENDING/ INTERPRETING MEANING	**I. Expressive Reading** Expressing initial response *Text in Self* *"Telling initial feelings"*	How do you feel about the incident?	N/A
	II. Narrative Readings Creating Text in Text (Time line)	Tell this story from the point of view of another person in the story.	What is the time of day at the beginning of the story? Summarize the plot. Where does this story take place?
	III. Descriptive Reading Creating Text in Text (Space)	Substitute "old" for "elderly" in "I know that elderly man." What is the impact of the change on the story?	Contrast the descriptions of the two people or the two places.
EVALUATING/ REFLECTING ABOUT WHAT IS IMPORTANT IN THE STORY, COMPARING TEXTS	**IV. Exposition Reading** Creating Text on Text (two comparable texts compared and contrasted)	Compare and contrast the choices of the two heroes. How does the structure of the poem X change the emphasis found in poem Y?	What are the historical settings or biographical details of the two heroes (as shown in the three novels)?
CRITIQUING TEXTS, USING TEXTS TO SOLVE SOCIAL PROBLEMS	**V. Argumentative (Resistant) Reading** Placing Text or Worldview or Critic against Text	What is your argument against the view presented in the story?	Explain why Critic A is right about the story and Critic B is wrong.

light." *Relevant Features:* symmetry, balance, edges twisting into flatness, changing colors.

(5) *the rock in a glass case in a historical museum:* "the rock's colors show that the rock has minerals found in Arkansas"; "the rock's flat edge makes it likely the rock was used as a tool"; "the rock was dated at 6,000 B.C."; "the rock was found in New Mexico." *Relevant Features:* mineral content, use as tool, age, location.

Differences among the preceding responses represent differences of readings between aesthetic contexts and informational or nonart contexts. In the first context (blocking the tire), the rock gets a nonart reading, completely. In some places, such as the coffee table, the rock gets both an art reading ("The rock has interesting colors") and a nonart reading ("The rock holds down magazines"). The nonart reading on the coffee table seems to take several shapes—for example, the instrumental uses of the rock ("The rock holds down magazines") and the historical references ("The Missouri vacation of 1979"). If the historical references are personal ("a family memento from . . . 1979"), then the reading moves closer to the center, between the poetic and the transactional. Also, again on the coffee table, the rock is read as an imaginative creation with a "face emerging," suggesting a poetic reading. The reading in the art museum is clearly poetic/aesthetic, and the reading in the history museum is clearly informational.

What are the differences between these art and nonart readings? First, the language of art has *density*—what Judith Langer (1989; 1992) calls horizons of possibility—and the language of nonart has *notationality* (N. Goodman 1968)—what some call clear references. Literature is primarily a way of reading in which readers are asked to enter multiple frames of reference, especially imaginary worlds in which they are invited to play roles. In one sense, a literary reading is one in which the text is always read as fiction, even reading nonfiction as fiction—turning a newspaper report into a drama, an editorial into a push-pull game, letters to the editor into a personal narrative (Culler 1975, 128). When one is reading for aesthetic *density,* any variation from a pattern may be of critical difference or significance ("The rock has a sharp edge") because within the language of art, one has to contend always with these multiple frames of reference.

When one is reading for *notationality* in the nonpoetic reading, one follows closely the *notational* rules of measure and order within a *notational* system. Notational measures are matters like counts, dates, numbered lists, weights, locations, alphabetic listings, and distances, all of which narrow the references and limit the information framework of the object. For example, in "The ragged rock is heavy enough to block the tire," "heavy enough" is notational because it has a reference point and, thus, a measure for weight. That is, if the rock is "heavy enough" to block the tire, it must have a particular weight relation to the car. Notice that we have no notational system for "ragged" as used here in "the ragged rock" because, in general, we have no notational system for measuring or ordering raggedness. "Ragged," of course, could be changed to a non-aesthetic or notational reading of the rock by simply saying "ragged enough to cut paper," which provides an empirical, notational measure for "ragged": Does it or does it not cut paper?

Barbara Herrnstein Smith is sympathetic toward Goodman's effort to destroy "the deeply entrenched dichotomy between the cognitive and the emotive" (N. Goodman 1968, 247), but Smith believes, like Rosenblatt and others, that in the process, Goodman "obscured a quite validly conceived distinction, namely that between nature and art" (B. Smith 1978, 11). Smith argues that "the speech of men in nature and history is distinct from the language of art" (B. Smith 1978, 67), and she presents the following obituary notice, revised as a poem, to make her point:

> Albert Molesworth
> Eighty-seven years old,
> Owner of the nation's largest
> And most prosperous potato farm,
> Died yesterday
> At his home in Idaho
> He left
> > no
> > > survivors.

She argues that when the text above is structured as a poem, not as an obituary notice, "literary interpretation is understood to be the purpose" (B. Smith 1978, 75). Barbara Herrnstein Smith argues that what is true of the poem is not true of nature and history. Nature has no poetic intent, no literary form, she says, and, thus, nature does not invite a literary or aesthetic reading. Man must organize nature into art. In other words, the rock does not in itself invite a poetic reading, sitting in its natural surrounding. In nature, we probably give the rock a nonpoetic reading, reading size, type, age, location. But when we frame the rock by placing it on a pedestal in an art museum, we are revising the rock for a poetic reading, just as Smith revised the obituary notice to invite a poetic reading. The context of a work, then, is the form and location of the work—a poem, a short story, and a novel being three literary forms or contexts students should understand and a history, an essay, or a syllogism being three nonliterary forms students should recognize. One of the challenges of English and English language arts in translation/criti-

cal literacy should be experiments with different kinds of readings, poetic and nonpoetic, of the same plot materials by changing the location
or form of the materials, the *rock* experiment being but one example.
The assumption of translation/critical literacy is that stance shifting is
a helpful way of refining one's knowing.

Let's try another example. We can read Figure 22 either as an aesthetic object or as a nonart transactional object. If we read Figure 22 as a
report of an electrocardiogram test, placed in a hospital context, then
we read the line in the language of *notationality* and nonart. In the notational, nonart reading, the only properties of the sign that matter are
the dips and peaks, which are conventionalized *notations* marking specific numerical values of heart action. We might also "read" the line as a
stock-market report in which the line must have a notational system of
ups and downs, indicating dollar gains and dollar losses. In these kinds
of *notational* or nonart readings, the reader looks "through" the sign
above to the information represented within the single frame of reference of electrocardiograms or stock-market graphs.

However, if the line in Figure 22 is read as an imaginative sketch of a
mountain, placed in the context of a drawing exhibit in an art museum,
we give the line an aesthetic reading in which the *density* and *color* of
the line and the *color* and *texture* of the page all communicate meaning
within the multiple frames of reference of density, color, texture, a person's direct experience of other "texts" about mountains, and our
imagination. In this poetic or art reading, the reader examines the sign
itself as a nontransparent pattern in which every variation from thick-
ness of the *line* to shade of *color* could have significance. The density of
color and density of the *line* can be ignored in stock-market or electrocardiogram trends, but in a poetic reading these issues of *density, texture,* and *color* cannot be ignored. They might suggest the imaginative
image of snow or rocks on the mountains or the hazy perspective of a
spectator standing far away from the mountain.

Yet another difference between art and nonart is that art always has
the personal signature of the "author" and nonart often does not. If the
line in Figure 22 is a sketch, we will probably know the artist's name. If
the line is the result of an electrocardiogram test, then we know there
will be no signature. The fact that the nonpoetic work has a conventionalized notational system (meaning "institutionalized" system) that
governs references means that the work is not based on strictly individual authorship. Thus, stock reports, weather reports, and life insurance
contracts are "authored" by the extensive collaborations of many people who constructed the notational systems of stocks, the weather, and
legal contracts. These are not personal documents and, therefore, do

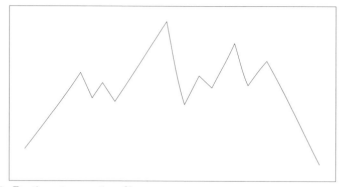

Fig. 22. Poetic or transactional?

not typically have bylines or personal credit lines. A platoon march from the boat to the barracks will not have an author's signature, but a dance on stage often will, even if the dance is a platoon march.

Sometimes the poetic work changes into a nonpoetic work and loses its signature. Contemporary maps do not now have author signatures, but old maps did. The old maps were, of course, not part of a notational system. In a reverse trend, at one time only a few news features had bylines, but now many newspaper features and reports have bylines, suggesting an increasing public awareness of the influence of authorship on so-called information. In other words, newspaper reports, like poetic works, have begun to raise issues of personal intentions and rhetorical slant.

Yet another difference between the poetic and the nonpoetic is the distinction between significance and information. Barthes gives us an example of this distinction in his response to a magazine photograph of a black French soldier drafted during the Algerian War (Barthes 1972, 128). In my reading of Barthes, the *photograph-as-message* or *information* tells us that the black French soldier is fighting in the Algerian War. But the *photograph-as-angle-of-vision*—the camera shot the soldier from below—tells us the soldier's heroic *significance* and *intertextuality*. In this last perspective, he is a heroic black soldier (Text 1) standing tall over all of us, being drafted and trained by the Western European French (Text 2) to defeat the Third World nation of Algeria (Text 3). In the first stance, the photograph is "read" as a transactional object with information, and in the last stance, the photograph is "read" as a poetic object with ironic intertextual connections to culture and history. In the first, we are anchored in the notational references about occupations and ethnic identity, and in the second, we are engaged in an imaginative construction of relationships and significance (a tricky difference, I admit). Both of these readings depend upon a historical framework which makes these readings possible. Students will not find this history on their own through expressive reading.

This shifting of our stance between the *nonpoetic* and *poetic*, between *information* and *significance*, between *notationality* and *density* of reference, between *no-signature* and *signature*, is a common way of being literate in our postmodern world. My wife and I, painting our first home, were looking at the mess we had to clean up when we noticed that one paint rag suddenly looked like a possible painting. So we framed it, giving it a new context and form, and for years afterward were asked, "Who is the painter?" We had shifted the rag from its *notational*, pragmatic use as a paint rag—it absorbed paint—to its aesthetic use as an abstract "painting" or "work." The frame gave the paint blotches intertextual "significance" and created the form and institutional context which invited, one might say required, a poetic reading. If left on the floor of a garage, these "rags" would obviously *not* have invited such a reading.

This critical difference between the pretend or imaginative reading (the poetic) and the "real" or informational reading begins to develop as a distinction in children when at age three, a biological clock seems to trigger periods of play in which children experiment with signs and objects in games, distinguishing roughly between the "actual" (nonplay) and "pretend" (play) (Vygotsky 1978, 96) and later evolving into the conventionalized distinction between the poetic/transactional and art/nonart. For example, in the preschool child's object-permanence games of peek-a-boo, hide-and-seek, and where-did-it-go, the child learns that if something is out of sight, it can still exist. In fact, not only may an object still exist, one can predict and guess with some accuracy where the object is likely to reappear if it does reappear. Thus, the learning of object permanence—in other words, that the invisible is nevertheless actual—is one of the child's important steps toward developing a distinction between the imaginative and the real and, in fact, developing a what-if or hypothesis-testing habit of mind.

Around the age of nine the explosion of symbolic play in drawing stops, and a period of literalness begins in which children become concerned about following the rules of "actual" life and copying "reality." Gardner reports the comment of Kay, age 9, that "I used to draw much better. My drawings were more interesting, but my perspective is three thousand times better now" (H. Gardner 1980, 143). The distinction between the imaginary and the "practical," between pretend and "actual," between play and "serious," begins initially as a way to create a shelter for learning in which the pretend/imaginary/play provides a no-risk setting for learning—in which mistakes cause no permanent harm. One can, for example, play house or circus and, thereby, learn new "adult" roles and their attendant ethical risks without getting seriously hurt.

Later, the contrast between "pretend" and "actual" evolves into conventionalized poetic and transactional forms of cultural activity distinguishing between museum paintings and police sketches, between literary dramas and television news footage, between dances and army marches—in other words, between the poetic and the transactional dimensions. In all of this, pretense is a key principle of learning for all, providing a stance for entering new imaginative worlds, even giving us a stance from which to examine the structure of our own responses as we pretend to watch ourselves as strangers.

Yes, play and pretend readings give us a role for discovering things about ourselves which we do not know. In *Boys and Girls: Superheroes in the Doll Corner* (1984), Vivian Paley, one of the nation's gifted teacher-researchers, describes what she discovered when she asked Franklin, a boy in her kindergarten class, to pretend to know how to share:

> Suddenly I recognize the difference between telling a child he must share and saying instead, "Pretend you are a boy who knows how to share." The first method announces that a child has done something wrong. "Pretend" disarms and enchants; it suggests heroic possibilities for making changes, just as in the fairy tales. (Paley 1984, 87)

Similarly, when my wife and I were unable to engage our oldest child in a conversation about his first days at kindergarten, I suggested to him that we play a pretend game in which I would call him up on the telephone, as if I were his friend Tony, and ask him what happened at school. Then he told all—and more!

Now let's examine how stance shifting might contribute to our readings of specific materials. To carry out this examination, I have collected and studied responses to the selection in Figure 23 from two classes at the University of Illinois at Urbana-Champaign and from eight groups of teachers in eight parts of the country. Both teachers and students start by saying that the calendar form suggests, at first, that the status of the document is nonliterary, but by the fourth line, most readers report that they recognize the possibility of a poetic reading because they are seeing an emerging structure in which "roses" contrasts with "violets." This kind of binary opposition does not seem accidental to most readers because these oppositions suggest we are possibly beginning to read the outlines of a pattern of a literary intention, the pattern of a cultural code or story. Of course, a few readers have suggested

Oct. 1	Ad for female stenographer	1.00
Oct. 4	Violets for new stenographer	1.50
Oct. 6	Week's salary for new stenographer	45.00
Oct. 9	Roses for stenographer	5.00
Oct. 10	Candy for wife	.90
Oct. 13	Lunch for stenographer	7.00
Oct. 15	Week's salary for stenographer	60.00
Oct. 16	Movie tickets for wife and self	1.20
Oct. 18	Theater tickets for steno and self	16.00
Oct. 19	Ice cream sundae for wife	.30
Oct. 22	Mary's salary	75.00
Oct. 23	Champagne & dinner for Mary & self	32.00
Oct. 25	Doctor for stupid stenographer	375.00
Oct. 26	Mink stole for wife	1,700.00
Oct. 28	Ad for male stenographer	1.50

TOTAL EXPENSES FOR MONTH	$2,321.40

Fig. 23. Calendar form of document. (Source: Rader 1974, 251. Used by permission of the University of Chicago Press.)

that a transactional, nonpoetic reading is, of course, still possible because we could use the calendar form as a source of information about changes in prices from one historical period to another, maybe from 1974 to 1992. Remember: I am presenting this problem in the institutional context of an English class on a university campus, and I found this selection originally in a journal of literary criticism. This institutional context tends to invite a poetic reading.

By the time we get to "theater tickets," almost all readers agree that the poetic reading seems clearly dominant. By then, the contrasts between "violets" and "roses," "candy" and "roses," "movie tickets" and "theater tickets," "lunch" and "ice cream sundae" have established the text as having a particular poetic structure and as conveying an imaginative experience. Students and teachers report that by the October 18 line, they recognize particular forms they have seen in other literary texts. They are, in some sense, recalling those other works and reconstructing them and their relationships to this text, moving from a narrative and descriptive reading to an expository reading. One reader, for example, asked why everyone assumed the boss was male, and pointed to his own experience with a female boss who lived with a female companion. These various reconstructions of the text begin to push out the boundary of a text's potential meaning as we collect other versions. A key teaching skill in a literature class is to keep all of these possible readings before the whole class (Langer 1994).

One of the issues in these readings is where does meaning come from. Readers find that the distinction between "violet" and "roses," for example, comes from their experiences and other texts (books, movies, TV) and that the distinction is culture-ridden. Knowing how to identify these two flowers as plants does not mean a student knows the cultural code represented by these two flowers. My students told me about how not knowing the code leads to problems. For instance, one young man sent his girl friend a potted plant on Valentine's Day, complete with dirt and bug spray, and she understood this act as being distinctly off the mark. Another young man reported sending roses to a friend, and she interpreted this act as going beyond the category of "mere friendship," something she did not want and something, she later discovered, he did not intend.

By the end of the reading, a few readers are proposing a "pregnancy theory," insisting that "this story is a fake" because from October 4 to October 25, the stenographer could not know whether or not she was pregnant. Some readers argue that she is suffering from some other physical problem. One student suggested that she might have gotten sick from "something else." Several suggest the secretary got attacked by the wife. One suggested the secretary attempted to attack the wife and lost. But most readers have a "pregnancy theory," and most agree that the period from October 22, when she is first called Mary, to October 25 is not enough time for the pregnancy to be detected. However, this factual inconsistency does not trouble most readers. Most readers read the selection for its story value and do not pay much attention to "factual" or notational accuracy. In fact, many readers claim that they do not care about the notational accuracy of the pregnancy when other readers bring up the issue.

A few readers insist, of course, that we could establish notational accuracy by adding nine months of calendar entries—say, 270. Objection, say most of the other readers! 120? Objection, say many readers!!! 14. Fewer objections! Almost everyone objects to correcting factual inconsistencies by adding many more calendar entries because most people say the "joke" of the story will be lost. In other words, satisfying the requirements of a nonliteracy reading—adding enough days to satisfy the factual requirements of a "pregnancy theory"—destroys the literary requirements. Brevity is needed to make the joke work. The "joke," they say, depends upon a quick, short structure, a structure which even 10 entries could destroy. Some have suggested lapses of time, skipping entries for a week. Many object to this. But a two-hour joke is not funny, no matter what! In summary, those who insist on a notational system in an informational reading are vigorously opposed by other readers who insist that we set aside issues of "believability" in order to enjoy the form—the joke, if you will. In literature classes, aesthetic considerations can overwhelm "facts." This is usually not the case in chemistry classes.

This tension between a poetic and nonpoetic stance is only one of the reasons I like to use this calendar to explore issues of a literary reading with my students. There is also the problem of ethics. That is, in every instance where I have tried this story, several students have raised questions about ethics. One asked, "Should we really laugh at this as a joke? After all, the boss hurt the secretary!" Another asked at another time, "Is it really funny? Whatever happened to the secretary? We leave her, after all, with a doctor and the narrator calling her stupid." "That's wrong!" said another. The form—the joke structure—seems to give us society's permission to laugh. But is the sexism of the situation really funny? Was it funny at one time? If so, what has changed? Should we as readers resist this "joke" because from one point of view the reading is so abhorrent? Many readings in English classes provide a similar test of our ethics. Remember Conrad and how uncomfortable we can feel about his racial and gender assumptions. Or remember Huck and how much he "sees" and does "not see" in racism. Should one historical period use its knowledge of racism and gender assumptions to judge another? The problem of ethics is pervasive in translation/critical English.

The NRA was right, of course, about the story of Peter Rabbit. I had never noticed any unfairness in our honoring such stories. The issue is, at bottom, ethical. Should we give Farmer Brown and the NRA its "day in court," a chance to put forward its views in our classroom? In our classroom, yes, I think we should. In our NCTE awards, we have no such obligation. In the classroom, the NRA is likely to point out our meat-eating habits, our leather shoes, and some of our other contradictions with respect to animals. These challenges can teach us to play out the ethics of various roles, and literature, especially, gives us a chance to look at ourselves and our ethics as we shift from the "pretend" to the "real," between the "real now" and the "unknowable future," between one historical period and another. Says Wayne Booth, "Many of the virtues that we most honor are originally gained by practices that our enemies might call faking, our friends perhaps something like aspiring or emulating. We pretend to be scholars long before we can produce a piece of scholarship that is not visibly faked. . . . We must fake—must practice—playing the cello (say) long before we can really play it, and each stage of improvement requires new levels of faking" (Booth 1988, 253). The practice of pretense—of being a mock reader, of pretending—

is the way one learns various worldviews—the ethics of the presentational/ironic/tough style, the ethics of the "modern" conversational style, the ethics of the intellectual/stuffy style, and the ethics of various points of view. And by pretending not to laugh at the "joke" above, we learn the ethics of those who have stopped laughing.

And by pretending to see the story from Farmer Brown's point of view, we learn about our animal-dependent ways. Increasingly, in this postmodern world, aware of our multiple frames of reference through practice in stance shifting, selections like the story in the calendar have, for many readers, ceased to be funny or, at the very least, have become ambiguous experiences. At the end, we face the question of the ethics of our personal response. Stance shifting in the reading of literature, then, is a way to learn to read, to learn the multiple points of reference of our fellow citizens, and finally to learn about our own ethical commitments.

In secondary English classes, a key difference between literary study in *decoding/analytic literacy* and in *translation/critical literacy* is that students in a secondary English class of *translation/critical literacy* are asked to write imaginative literature and asked to describe the negotiations of meaning in the literary readings in the class discussions. These descriptions are like classroom ethnographies and show how the meaning of a story or poem is influenced by the conversational interactions in class. Students, then, are expected both to participate in class and in small-group discussions and at the same time to observe and to describe the negotiations of meaning in class. Examples of how a literature class might be structured in this way have been elaborated upon by David Bleich (1988, 186).

In summary, then, one of the key differences between literature study in decoding/analytic literacy and in translation/critical literacy is that literature study in translation/critical literacy will at times involve the literary reading of what are typically regarded as nonliterary materials. For example, a secondary English class can "read" the tenth-grade science book in the same way that such a class might read a short story, beginning with the questions "Who is speaking and when?" "Is the speaker reliable?" and "Who has the authority to speak?" and moving to "Who am I?" "Who are we?" and "What are or are not the 'objects' of knowledge in this world?" I experimented with this approach in a reading of a tenth-grade science book, which began one chapter with the following sentences:

> Neglecting friction, all bodies, large and small, fall with the same acceleration. This, the law of falling bodies, is a physical paradox for it contradicts the conclusion the average person might reach from general observations.

The first question was "Who is speaking and when?" or "Who is able to say ... 'all bodies, large and small, fall with the same acceleration' and 'the law of falling bodies.'" One question I put to students was "Could you think of yourself writing these sentences in this voice? Could you announce a law to others? Why? Why not?" This same kind of interrogation can be applied to commercials, to editorials, to popular songs. This approach requires that English and English language arts take as their texts a wide variety of literature and public discourse.

The introduction of a variety of texts to be read as literature and public discourse has changed somewhat the literary texts typically found in English classes. *Recitation literacy*, remember, replaced ancient texts from Greece and Rome with Dryden, Bacon, Shakespeare, and other British works, and *decoding/analytic literacy* added American literature to K–12 English classes. *Translation/critical literacy* keeps much of the traditional literature (see Applebee's [1989] survey of books used in secondary classes), but it attempts to pair traditional texts with the contemporary voices of those who have been previously marginalized or excluded (Morrison, Wilson, and so forth). In addition, the translation/critical literacy classroom adds public discourse, film, paintings, TV, personal diaries, and tapes. This mixture of forms helps students stretch their own abilities to express themselves in their own imaginative writing and to comprehend, appreciate, and criticize literary texts within the context of other cultural artifacts. Finally, the teacher encourages (needs) diversity of response, unlike the classrooms of decoding/analytic literacy where the students aim for one reading, the one in the teacher's head (Applebee 1993).

14 Style and Worldviews in Literature and Public Discourse

Rationalists, wearing square hats,
Think, in square rooms,
Looking at the floor,
Looking at the ceiling.
They confine themselves
To right-angled triangles.
If they tried rhomboids,
Cones, waving lines, ellipses—
As, for example, the ellipse of the halfmoon—
Rationalists would wear sombreros

—Wallace Stevens*

In the classrooms of the new literacy of English and English language arts, students are engaged in literacy events: writing assignments embedded in the issues of the day; participating in a class discussion of two short stories; publishing a class newspaper; conducting an opinion survey in the community; participating in the radio and TV performances produced, written, and taped by students; carrying out research projects examining language use in texts and in school neighborhoods; reviewing and critiquing one's learning as reflected in one's portfolio. They are explicitly studying patterns of language use in those events.

All of these activities enable students to participate in society's larger cultural conversations of which these events are a part. Says Gerald Graff:

> In short, reading books with comprehension, making arguments, writing papers, and making comments in a class discussion are *social* activities. They involve entering into a cultural or disciplinary conversation, a process not unlike an initiation into a social club. (G. Graff 1992, 77)

Within discussions of paired readings—*Amazing Grace* and *Amelia Bedelia*, *Wuthering Heights* and *I Know Why the Caged Bird Sings*, *Wind in the Willows* and *Charlotte's Web*, or *Woman Warrior* and *Pride and Prejudice*,

---

*From: "Six Significant Landscapes." In *Collected Poems* by Wallace Stevens. Copyright © 1923 and renewed 1951 by Wallace Stevens. Reprinted by permission of Alfred A. Knopf, Inc.

to name four examples—students in English classes participate in the stories of literature and in conversations about those stories and, at the same time, are asked to step back and study the patterns of language use in those stories and conversations.

This unified focus on participation in events with defined purposes and on observation and explicit study represents a shift in school instruction away from decoding/analytic literacy. With its nearly exclusive focus on observation and explicit study of the steps in the reading/writing processes and on the parts of the reading/writing product, decoding/analytic literacy generally deemphasized participation in communicative events. Applebee was one of those who led the shift to a new literacy organized around participation in events with authentic purposes: "Because writing processes are a function of context and task, the current research emphasis on process may ultimately be as fruitless as the earlier emphasis on product. The most rewarding approaches to the study of writing may be those which include writing processes as strategies that are orchestrated in the course of a particular communicative event, with its own network of purposes and outcomes" (Applebee 1984, 187).

Langer and Applebee also emphasized the importance of observation and study—that we "view the classroom as a community of scholars (or of scholars and apprentices) with its own rules of evidence and procedures for carrying the discussion forward. Students must learn, then, not only the 'basic facts' around which the discussion is structured but the legal and illegal ways in which those facts can be mustered in the disciplinary community defined by the classroom" (Langer and Applebee 1987, 150).

Translation/critical literacy, therefore, is organized around apprenticeships which are situated first in communicative events requiring participation and second in peripheral contexts requiring the observation and study of language and "facts" in those events (see Lave and Wenger 1991). What is a communicative event? Communicative events are defined first by signs (Is the event verbal, visual, or action?), and second by stance (Is the event literary or nonliterary?), speech events (Is the event conversational, presentational, or academic?), modes (Is the event a narrative or a paradigmatic event?), and style (Is the worldview clear or hazy?). What is a peripheral context? Peripheral contexts are located on the margins of these communicative events, where students observe and study the patterns of language (syntax, figures of speech), self-fashioning (the universal in the particular and the perspectives of individual gender, ethnicity, race, and class), and tool use (distributed knowledge).

This chapter will focus on different styles and their worldviews toward various ideas (M. Myers 1981). In decoding/analytic literacy, worldviews or stylistic differences were usually discussed as "themes in literature." Ohmann has suggested, however, that in English, we need some simple yet broad way to talk about how "worldviews" shape ideas—where these themes came from—because we need to "sketch out to some purpose competing ways of conceptualizing action, mind, the past, cause, space, society, etc." (Ohmann 1971, 70). Stylistic differences are one way of talking about the different worldviews which shape ideas: "A style, like a culture or climate of opinion, sets up a horizon of expectation, a mental set, which registers deviations and modifications with exaggerated sensitivity. In noticing relationships, the mind registers tendencies. The history of art is full of reactions that can only be understood in this way" (Gombrich 1960, 60).

Lanham, calling style one of our motives for eloquence, one of the reasons behind our way of talking, has, like Ohmann, argued that we should begin "admitting stylistic self-consciousness into the community of human thinking and feeling" (Lanham 1976, 26). In order to admit style into the knowledge structures consciously studied in K–12 schools, we need a coherent framework for different styles and their worldviews. How are we to describe such a framework? Most scholars of style have used contrasting dimensions to define a framework for style. For example, Martin Joos (1962) used the contrasts between formal and informal, frozen and consultative, and John Carroll (1960) used pairs of contrasting adjectives: personal-impersonal, ornamented-plain, abstract-concrete, serious-humorous, and characterizing-narrating. Using these contrasting pairs, Carroll created a style scale which judges were asked to use to rank differences of style among selected authors. For example, judges were asked to use a scale much like the following one (my paraphrase of Carroll's scale) to describe whether a writer had a plain or an ornamented style:

| Ornamented | 1 | 2 | 3 | 4 | 5 | 6 | 7 | Plain |

(Put a check on degree of trait)

This scale worked well enough, but it turns out that a style scale probably needs more than two categorical dimensions. Two categories usually leave something important out, and Carroll, for example, is, on his scale, leaving out "elaborated." "Ornamented" is attempting to see things which are hazy and unclear, tending toward the gothic, and "elaborated" is the flourish of impersonal points of view attempting to explain that which is being clearly lighted, tending toward the academic. The scale I am proposing has five categories—gothic expressionism; sweet impressionism; tough/neutral; realistic journalism; elaborated rationalism.

Different dimensions or points on a style scale often overlap. One example of overlap occurs in the scales of Miles and Auerbach. Josephine Miles (1967) has proposed that the dimensions of style be organized around parts of speech—verbs (predicative), modifiers (adjectival), and conjunctions (the connective subordinative), while Auerbach (1953) has suggested distinguishing styles through examples of the great works: the classical (the *Odyssey*), the Biblical (the Old Testament), and the subjective. For Miles, the predicative emphasizes action, as does Auerbach's Old Testament; the connective-subordinative emphasizes order and logic, as does Auerbach's classical; and finally, Miles's adjectival style is very similar to Auerbach's subjective style.

In another example of overlap, "clarity" often tends to be associated with the "impersonal" because the "highly personal" is often associated with language only a few people can understand. The stylistic shift from "babble" to "geometry" in Lanham's seven-point scale below, for example, is generally associated with the shift from the unclear and personal to the clear and impersonal[1]:

—babble
—religious chant
—Henry James

—neutral reportage

—Hemingway
—telegraphese
—geometry (Lanham 1976, 25)

Lanham's seven-point scale captures the personal-impersonal and clear-unclear dimensions of style, both emphasized by Joos and Carroll, but what is left out of Lanham's description, as Lanham himself notes, is the author's effort to hide eloquence, producing a transparent style, or to show eloquence, producing an opaque style. Therefore, in addition to the several vertical dimensions above, Lanham proposes to add to these dimensions an interacting horizontal dimension (see Figure 24) with the transparent, plain, and unadorned style at one end, and the opaque, ornamented, and elaborate at the other end. Lanham, fearing the power of decoding/analytic literacy's demands for clarity, wants us to give due respect to both ends of the scale where language may have different degrees of difficulty: "Self-conscious posturing [the opaque style] attempts to keep faith with dramatic reality. . . . From a rhetorical point of view, transparent language seems dishonest, false to the world" (Lanham 1976, 28). These new distinctions do not, of course, cure any problems of overlap. On any stylistic scale, including the one in Figure 24, there will be styles which fall between the categories or points on the scale.

Third, in addition to having overlap and more than two categories, an adequate framework of style will often have a midpoint, and this midpoint is usually Lanham's transparent or neutral language. Barthes (1979), for example, proposed a zero (0) or neutral point on his style scale, and this "zero-degree writing," as Barthes called it, attempts to be factual and plain—what Lanham calls "transparent" or "neutral reportage." "Zero-degree writing" is a style which pretends it is not there. Style, of course, presents a screen through which one views the world—as personal or impersonal, as clear or unclear, as plain or ornamented—and the stylistic pretense that the screen is not there—is, in fact, zero—is a convenient center point being pulled in the other two directions (see Figure 24).

Fourth, style dimensions, in addition to being labeled with nouns and adjectives, can be "personified" as different voices representing a set of values which act as screens for looking at the world and shaping the ideas of that world. Walker Gibson (1966) has proposed that style be understood as three voices—tough, sweet, and stuffy—and Chris Anderson (1987, 55) has suggested that style be understood as the difference between a voice of purposeful rhetorical silence and a voice of talkativeness. Both Gibson and Anderson suggest that these stylistic masks or personae represent a screen through which people represent their values about language—its limits and its successes—and their values about knowledge—what can be known, what cannot. In the classroom, teachers often use value-laden popular figures to characterize the voice of a particular style. For example, the different voices on the scale can be illustrated by Bela Lugosi (also Frankenstein), the prototypical voice in popular culture for the scary, the gothic, and the opaque; Ann Landers (later, Dr. Ruth), the prototypical voice in pop culture of sweet impressionism, always friendly, often comic; Clint Eastwood (also Humphrey Bogart), the "just-the-facts-ma'am" voice of tough, zero writing, always noncommittal, often tight-lipped; Margaret Mead (also Albert Einstein), the prototypical voice of the super-brain, the academic, always super rational, often talkative; and Connie Chung (also Ed Bradley), the protypical journalist voice of realism and newspaper reports, always descriptive, usually accurate (M. Myers 1981, 28–29).

Frye, for example, has suggested that different kinds of heroes represent different views toward the world and that "[f]ictions . . . may be

Magazines	Mystic Magazine	True Confessions	Hardware Catalogue	Newsweek	Scientific American
	Expressionism	Impressionism	Neutral	Realism	Rationalism
Lamp with Hazy Light	Gothic	Sweet	Tough	Journalistic	Stuffy — Lamp with Focused, Clear Light
	Ornamented Opaque	Personal Episodic	Transparent Plain	Impersonal Organized	Developed Structured
Examples	Poe	Salinger	Hemingway	Steinbeck	James
Babble	Gothic Mirror: Things as dreamed	Romanticism Mirror: Things as gossiped	Zero Mirror: Things as they are	Realism Mirror: Things as reported	Logical Mirror: Things as enhanced — Verbal Geometry
Personas:	Bela Lugosi	Ann Landers	Clint Eastwood	Jane Pauley	Albert Einstein
	Magical, Other-worldly Hero of Legend, with more power	Comic Everyday Hero like us	Ironic Anti-Heroic Hero	Above-Average/Reasonable Hero like us	Super Brain Hero of Tragedy, with more power

Fig. 24. The five styles of lamps-mirrors, personal-impersonal, ornamented-developed.

classified ... by the hero's power of action, which may be greater than ours, less or roughly the same" (Frye 1957, 33). Some historical periods view the world with "irrational combinations," where magic and the other-worldly "run" the world. This world has either the Egyptian Sphinx as hero, an impossible combination of man and animal, or a Romantic human hero who talks to animals and jumps rivers. Other historical periods view the world with "super-rational" assumptions, where heroic men run the world with their reason, logic, and theories. Other periods view the world with ironic detachment, adopting the perspective of the anti-hero, the detached man. Still others adopt a mimetic or comic perspective (Frye 1957, 33–67), using either the average, reasonable man as comic hero or using the average person who is like us as an everyday hero. Four of Frye's heroes represent, in many ways, the ideas behind the five styles on the scale in Figure 24. On that scale, Frye's comic or everyman hero hovers between the magical, mythic hero and the anti-heroic hero of "zero-degree writing," and his reasonable hero hovers between the anti-hero and the super hero of the logical and intellectual. In Figure 24, Frye's mythic and legend heroes, who have more power than we do, are combined into one, the gothic and otherworldly, and the worldly hero, who is like us, is divided into the comic and the above-average reasonable hero.

Instead of voices or heroes, Abrams proposes a scale shifting between instruments of perception—between mirrors, which claim to reflect what is there, and lamps, which claim to show the world in different shades of light (Abrams 1953, 30–69). Zero-degree writing, for example, holds up to the world a mirror which gives us clean, sharp, neutral images, very simply stated, and realism holds up to the world a mirror showing more of the world's historical details and personal complexities, very accurately stated. The cracked mirror gives us the image of the gothic world, and the enhanced mirror gives us the structured, elaborated world of the academic. In Figure 24, each of these mirrors has a comparable lamp, showing the world in different shades of light. Each kind of lamp or mirror represents a set of values through which humans can know about their world.

The scale in Figure 24 incorporates these four points of contrasting dimensions, a midpoint, voices, more than two categories. In the middle of all styles in Figure 24 is the "tough style" (W. Gibson 1966)—what Barthes (1979) calls "writing degree zero"—which excludes journalism's emphasis on complete details and the Ann Lander's emphasis on exclamations and emotional expressions. Truman Capote, Ernest Hemingway, Shirley Jackson, and Emily Dickinson, who are tough writers, hold up to the world an impersonal mirror which gives us the sharp, clear outline of things as they appear in a clean, clear light which never reflects glare or haze or dark. In *In Cold Blood,* Capote describes a murder scene as follows:

> The detective moved from room to room. He had toured the house many times; indeed, he went out there almost everyday....The telephones, their wires still severed, were silent. The great quiet of the prairies surrounded him. He could sit in Herb's parlor rocking chair, and rock and think. (Capote 1965, 152–53)

Here are bare details, only a few, not the full details of a newspaper report. Here are short, no-talk sentences, not the loquaciousness of other styles.

Hemingway is one of those neutral, zero-degree writers who, says Mark Schorer, believes dignity is the stiff upper lip in the face of nothingness and who conveys this toughness in a style which eliminates wonder and innocence: "When these sentences are long, they are long because of coordinating conjunctions, *ands* and *buts,* which suggest that the several elements in the sentence have equal importance or unimportance, exactly as the story tells us that everything has equal value, therefore no value" (Schorer 1950, 426). Walker Gibson, after an analysis of selected passages from "tough" speakers, estimates that monosyllables are used over seventy percent of the time (W. Gibson 1966, 136). In the no-talk, tough style, there is no *justice,* only events; there is no *love,* only relationships.

To the left of "writing degree zero" in Figure 24 is the sweet, conversational style (W. Gibson 1966), the style of Ann Landers. Ann Landers—who is anything but tough—is informal, genial, as if the reader and the narrator were equals. Ann Landers, who is definitely more talkative than Truman Capote and Emily Dickinson, can be heard in the sweet voice of the TV commercial, in Erma Bombeck's columns in *True Confessions,* or in the voice of speakers like Salinger's Holden Caulfield. These voices invite you into a close, personal exchange, into an intimate acquaintance, as an equal who accepts the narrator's values. Walker Gibson calls this modern voice a "sweet" style, which is fragmentary at times, using different dialects, somewhat irregular in rhythm, and which aims for everyday speech and a good-buddy relationship to the reader, always acknowledging in a conversational perspective the uncertainty, the looseness, the fragmentary quality of modern life:

> A few of the writer's obvious attempts to echo a conversational tone in that paragraph can be quickly summarized. Contractions (let's). Colloquialisms (well . . . the next fellow). Some very short sentences. Capitalization in an effort to place an ironical turn on a Big Fat Abstraction (Truth)—an effort that is of course much easier

> to accomplish with the actual voice. Italics (*except,* like *this!*), again
> in mimicry of the way one speaks in conversation. And so on. The
> purpose of such devices, to compensate for the loss of oral intona-
> tion, is strictly speaking impossible to achieve. If only you were
> here I could *say* all this to you! (W. Gibson 1962, 105)

Some readers, of course, may refuse to accept the value assumptions of this style, turning away from the intimacy, the looseness. In this style of sweet impressionism, justice is a hazy concept but a "warm" feeling, and *love* is a wonderful feeling, beyond explanation but something to talk about, a lot.

On the far left in Figure 24 is Bela Lugosi's style, the mystical, dark, uncertain, gothic style of Edgar Allan Poe's characters or Shelley's Frankenstein. These talkers, too, are more talkative than Capote or Dickinson, and not as intimate and sweet as Ann Landers. Shelley sees the world with lamps of dark, hazy light, and Ann Landers sees the world with lamps of bright light with a somewhat hazy focus. Somewhere between Bela Lugosi's "gothic" and Ann Landers' "sweet" is Joan Didion, who gives us the images of dark, mindless murder with a personal "you," a world somewhere between the everyday gas stations in the world of Ann Landers and the hazy, frightening holdups in the world of Bela Lugosi: "to imagine the audience for whom [such murderous images] are tailored, maybe you need to have sat in a lot of drive-ins yourself, to have gone to school with boys who majored in shop and worked in gas stations and later held them up" (Didion 1979, 101). Didion, like many writers, shows some variation in her style. In a few works, she writes like Capote, who has a tough, zero-degree style, but most frequently she moves over to a point between Bela Lugosi and Ann Landers. In the world of Bela Lugosi, *justice* is irrational and accidental when it happens, and *love* is accidental or improbable because the world is too dark, too threatening.

The fourth style is the logical, explanatory, intellectual style at the far right of the scale in Figure 24—what Walker Gibson (1966) calls the stuffy style. Unlike the gothic style, the academic uses lamps with clear, focused light. The gothic attempts, of course, to light up the dark and fails—all remains uncertain and mysterious—and the academic style attempts to cast light on the world and succeeds, revealing the developed logic and order of things or, in some cases, the difficulty of our own logic. This style is the structured, elaborated style (W. Gibson 1966) of rationalist writers like Winston Churchill or William James or Margaret Mead or Homer, Jane Austen and Henry James (see also Auerbach 1953; J. Miles 1967). This elaborated, logical style uses controls and conventions which move the materials away from the so-called "realistic" flow of events—the journalistic discovery of life's details—and away from the conversational intimacy of the sweet style and toward distance and the logical forms illuminating the connections and the causes and effects of the world. Some students often think this style is "too difficult," "too abstract," a violation of the requirements for simple clarity. But in this style *justice* can be explained, its logical connections clearly revealed. *Love*, too, can be analyzed as a cause-effect sequence, the result of psychological causes.

The academic does not aim for simple clarity. Lanham insists that "the dogma of clarity is based on a false theory of knowledge" (Lanham 1974, 19). Obscurity can result from the attempt to explain all. One of Lanham's interesting examples is a layoff letter from a college official who avoids simple clarity to "hide" or "soften the blow" of the layoff. The letter itself is a good example of the rationalist and the academic explaining all the connections, all of the causes and effects, the logic of it all.

As Lanham observes, the style of the rationalist and the academic is not always the worldview one needs to get work done. Joseph Williams, although insisting that clarity is one of the first principles of good writing, also gives us some excellent examples of how unclear writing is shaped by one's worldview, one's clear sense of rhetorical purpose (J. Williams 1989, 24–25). One very compelling example of the potential and limits of "clarity" in different contexts is Williams's contrast of Lincoln's Gettysburg address and Lincoln's second inaugural address (see J. Williams 1986). The first is clear and classically structured, claiming large principles for the Civil War, an example of the intellectual and the logical. The second is purposefully unclear, ornamented, almost opaque, attempting to soften the wounds of the war by not stating North-South differences explicitly and clearly, avoiding connections (see Wills 1992).

The fifth style is the informational worldview of *Newsweek* and Steinbeck. This is the style of the journalist-realist, the world of Jane Pauley or Ed Bradley, who believes the world can be described clearly but not without accidental and irrational elements. The purpose of the knowledgeable, academic writer, of course, is to remove the accidental and irrational, to describe the world as logical and fitting some theory or overall structure. The purpose of the journalist is to give a report of what happened, not all of its logical connections. For the journalist, *justice* is an event surrounded by claims of a larger ethical purpose. The same is true of *love*. It is an event surrounded by claims of logical connections.

Now, let's examine the uses of this framework for style.

The style of the journalist-innocent is the style of everyday mimesis or simple "realism," a style which imitates the world as "seen," which holds both a lighted "lamp" and a clear "mirror" up to the world. The "mirror" reports what is there, and the "lamp" adds background and history. John Steinbeck and Walter Cronkite (Jane Pauley and Ed Bradley) are realists, and the scale provides a simple way to explain to students how a John Steinbeck or Walter Cronkite talks and thinks. But some students do not like playing the role of the innocent Walter Cronkite who asks people dozens of questions, as if he did not know many things. For these students, question asking is a public admission of vulnerability, and they, for whatever reason, are not prepared for that admission. For them, the authoritative voice of the academic, or the tough voice of Hemingway, or the sweet talk of impressionism may be far more comfortable than the realism of the prototypical journalist.

Let me illustrate this problem with a story. We were sitting in a circle, ten high school students and I, listening intently to a student read aloud her narrative about her first airplane trip, in which she flew from San Francisco to Hong Kong to visit her grandmother, with a one-night stopover in Tokyo. She described the parts of the airplane's interior, her view out the airplane window, the light, the blackness, the stop in Hawaii, and then her exploration of her hotel room during her Tokyo stopover, looking in all the drawers, describing the postcards, the stationery, the menus, and the tourist brochures. When she finished her reading, the students began their editing comments, the first asking, "Why don't you drop that stuff about postcards, stationery, and other things?" and a second chiming in, "Those parts tell us zip." The writer immediately shrugged, "O.K., I'll take those parts out."

My spirits dropped. The problem here is that the young writer did not know why she had given us that information about the flight, the parts of the airplane's interior, the hotel postcards and stationery. She did not have enough understanding of her role in the story as a journalist-innocent-abroad to support her intuition about the postcards, the stationery, the menu, the brochures. A couple of students and I asked the writer to keep those parts. We suggested that she gave us those pieces not as information, which we might use if we planned a trip to Tokyo, but as descriptions of a narrator who was the wide-eyed innocent-abroad, who explored like a curious journalist the world's assumed order, and who looked for that order in all the parts of her new surroundings. One or two of us had even had similar experiences—for example, going around opening all the drawers in a new hotel room and then telling others about it. We urged her not to drop the postcards and the other hotel-room details because they were an expression of her wonder, her faith in the world's order, her kind of journalist faith that the world can be known. In fact, without that faith, she would have drawn back from her new surroundings. She would not have reached out.

Several students in the group kept insisting that the postcards did not add anything; they were not efficient details. From one point of view, these students were correct. The postcards did not, in fact, add any essential information about geography or the calendar of the trip. The postcards did, however, add to the worldview, the style of the story—that is, the details added to the portrait of the journalist-innocent-abroad. In Walker Gibson's (1950) terms, those students who objected to the details did not want to play the role of the mock reader who was required to be sympathetic to the wide-eyed journalist-innocent-abroad. In fact, they may have felt that the role of the mock reader sympathizing with the journalist-innocent challenged their personal sense of their own "sophistication" or allowed others to see them playing the vulnerable role of journalist-innocent. In other words, these readers might not look in the hotel drawers, even though they wanted to, because they were afraid someone might see their innocence and, thus, their vulnerability. In addition, they might not ask questions like a typical journalist because these questions may reveal or suggest their innocence. Whatever their reasons, they did not want to be caught dead endorsing the worldview of the wide-eyed journalist-innocent.

The five styles in Figure 24 ask readers to enter a particular worldview with a particular attitude toward the world's "order," its causes and effects, and one would expect readers to recognize their own acceptance or resistance to these various worldviews, just as students recognize their acceptance or rejection of the journalist's investigation in the hotel story. I have tested this hypothesis of student acceptance or rejection by putting at the front of the classroom different magazines with several different styles and assumptions (*Sports Illustrated, Mystic Magazine, True Confessions, Dragnet Magazine, Atlantic Monthly*, and *Scientific American*). The magazines are themselves simplifications of the worldviews of the gothic and other-worldly, the casual and the impressionistic, the mimetic and realistic, the anti-heroic and zero-degree writing, and the super-rational and intellectual. Simplifications, yes, but they are a start. They help us summarize competing ways of conceptualizing causes, effects, the scene before us, the impact of individual action.

Notice here that I am trying to complicate the problem of clarity in writing by contextualizing the uses of clarity. I am also trying to deal with the problem of the separation of composition instruction, in which decoding/analytic literacy emphasized generic efficiency and simple clarity, from literary and literature instruction, which emphasized contextualizing clarity and difficulty. In the world of decoding/analytic literacy, as Edward Corbett has noted, "literary texts will more often than not serve as a distraction from, rather than a promoter of, the objectives of a writing course" (Corbett 1983, 183). Lanham has made the same point, arguing that in the composition classes of decoding/analytic literacy, we have taught a transparent theory of language in which composition is efficient communication, and then, in the first literature courses, the "resolute insistence on transparent prose gives way to a symbiotic exchange in which a prose surface both creates the reality beneath and in turn is affected by it" (Lanham 1983, 19). Both literature and composition need to study language as shaping reality and being shaped by it.

The magazines of pop culture are an area where the principles of composition and literature can be brought together. My experiment with these magazines is an attempt to make the patterns of language the visible screens through which we view the world. By asking students to explain which magazines they would read and not read while waiting in a crowded checkout line at the local grocery store, I have found that the students reveal much understanding about the conventions governing the style of different voices. They know that the voice of *True Confessions*, for example, calls for readers who believe in establishing a conversational, casual, personal relationship with a "sweet" narrator who exposes private feelings through casual impressions and fragmented memories which are often comic. The students know that if one were seen reading *True Confessions* in the checkout line in a grocery store, one would probably be marked as someone who was emotion-driven and seeking intimate, casual, possibly comic details about the lives of others.

The readers of *Sports Illustrated*, on the other hand, are marked as information-driven, like the young lady going to Hong Kong, a journalist-innocent who wants to know more about things. The readers of *Sports Illustrated* are expected to be fairly impersonal and well-organized consumers of news and journalism and are expected to be broadly interested in the everyday culture of the world. They are also, of course, sports fans. (They also wonder whether the journalist's mask is slipping.) The readers of *Scientific American*, however, play the intellectual roles of those who want to know rational cause-and-effect, logical connections, the theoretical forms of things. These readers are interested in analysis and explanation, why things happen, not just information about what happened.

But *Mystic Magazine* readers are, like the fans of Edgar Allan Poe, recognized as seekers after the irrational, the emotionally charged but hazily uncertain. These readers like magic magazines and other types of science fiction with wildly improbable stories of monsters and elves, Frankenstein and E.T. being notable examples. These readers like watching a sweet speaker like Ann Landers or a rationalist like Albert Einstein stumble across a monster like Frankenstein and descend into an opaque, hazy language.

Finally, the readers of *Dragnet Magazine* are attracted to the plain, tough, "just-the-facts-ma'am" world of the hard-boiled detective who keeps everything at a distance and claims only to hold up a mirror to the world, who retreats to a clean, well-lighted place and maintains an anti-heroic stance toward the world.

We, as English teachers, have all had students who resisted one style or another. We have had students who wanted to know why Poe did not tell us the name (and address?) of the person wearing the masque of red death. These kinds of readers read Poe as if he wrote for *Newsweek* magazine, as if Poe were a journalist instead of a seeker after magic and the other-worldly. If such readers would allow themselves to be the mock readers Poe asks for, they would release themselves to the experience of the unexpected, the mysterious, the world of the "The Tell-Tale Heart," "The Fall of the House of Usher," and, of course, *Mystic Magazine.* Names and addresses are not that important in Poe's world of the hazy and the irrational, and asking for the details of realism is a resistance to Poe's style.

Of course, we have also had students who asked just the right questions, like the one who asked me, "Do I have to use a lot of details for every little thing, the way this book says Hemingway does it?" The student was sitting at his desk with his composition text open to a selection from Hemingway's "The Big Two-Hearted River." The text said that the passages on cooking the fish were good examples of how writers use details to show sight, sound, smell, and so forth. I noticed for the first time that the text had turned the Hemingway selection into an exercise to teach students to use detail about everything—as if all writers should always go around asking themselves how does every little thing smell, taste, look, feel, sound. But, of course, not *all* writers should do that.

Furthermore, not even Hemingway did it. The impulse toward the details of things is the impulse of the journalist-realist who seeks the accurate information that shapes the world. Hemingway does not use a journalistic style. Hemingway's few, elaborated details are well selected. For Hemingway, the details about cooking fish are talk to escape from talk, not a journalistic report. In fact, the details about cooking fish are surrounded by a plot and scene for which we have *no* information, no "opening of furniture drawers" as happened in the journalist's pursuit in the hotel scene. In "The Big Two-Hearted River," Hemingway's main character concentrates on the immediate, sensory details of the cooking fish in order to escape from the journalist's details about what happened in all the other possible details of the story and to ignore the academic's questions about whether human experience has any order or logic. Barthes, using Camus as his example, describes how this neutral style differs from that of the journalist:

> It would be accurate to say that it is a journalist's writing, if it were not precisely the case that journalism develops, in general, optative or imperative (that is, emotive) forms. The new neutral writing takes its place in the midst of all of those ejaculations and judgments, without becoming involved in any of them; it consists precisely in their absence. (Barthes 1979, 76)

In the historical setting of "The Big Two-Hearted River," Hemingway's character has just returned from the world's first World War, in which almost everyone's theory about morality, justice, and truth has been destroyed. The character in the Hemingway story uses the tough style to speak for those who have lost their faith in the world's order. The character also uses these few details to speak for those who resist their curiosity about the details of things and who turn to a few of the sensory, concrete details of the cooking fish as a way to escape all the other details of life, as a way to find a safe haven in a few details of something—in this case, fishing and open-fire cooking. Hemingway's ironic, tough style becomes a code of escape, of noncommitment.

Why doesn't the narrator tell us all of this? He does, in a way; he does it in the whole collection of stories in *In Our Time*. In these stories, the narrator describes his lost faith in the world's order and in a talkative intellectual world. In *A Farewell to Arms*, Hemingway says that words like "glory" and "honor" "were obscene beside the concrete names of villages, numbers of roads, the names of rivers, the numbers of regiments and dates" (qtd. in Fussell 1975, 21). Says Paul Fussell, "In the summer of 1914 no one would have understood what on earth he was talking about" (Fussell 1975, 21). According to Fussell, this was not just an American experience. Other parts of the world had also lived through the same historical experience and developed the same worldview and style:

> I am saying that there seems to be one dominating form of modern understanding; that it is essentially ironic; and ... [that] it originates largely in the application of mind and memory to the events of the Great War. (Fussell 1975, 35)

For both American and British soldiers, World War I was a jarring experience in which the tough style of "no talk" was a way out—out of the Great War and out of a worldwide economic depression. Readers of this literature are asked to play the role of those who give themselves over to a tough, no talk, anti-intellectual, anti-journalistic style—the style, in other words, of Hemingway, Emily Dickinson, Camus, Mike

Hammer. To understand this style, students need the historical setting, the text-on-text, which Fussell or others provide.

One learns style by looking out at the writing, painting, and sculpture of others in a historical setting, not by looking closely at one's own writing. In fact, comments about style should probably be withheld when talking about the writing of individual students. Let me illustrate with two examples. Several years ago, a piece of my own writing was returned with a note saying, in part, "The voice rings true because it is part of a man presented as rugged, in straight-forward, even stark prose." I was taken aback for a moment. I had become so deeply involved in the writing of that piece that I had thought of the speaker as myself. I had viewed the writing as an attempt to set aside some of my own reflex moods and feelings about a particular subject and to find what I thought was true about both myself and the subject. To be told that the voice in my writing was "a man presented as" was to suffer a momentary feeling of emptiness of role-playing: Who was I anyway?

This experience brought home to me how many times I have made the same mistake with students: "Your voice here is a person who.... Your persona is that of the wide-eyed innocent. . . . You remind me of Kurt Vonnegut. . . ." The last example triggers my memory of a student's face, quizzical and hurt. When teachers say such things to young people, they rob them of a sense of self. To approach pieces of student writing as if they were examples of students role-playing the voices of other writers is to empty the writing of the levels of meaning in the contextualized voice and to demean students' efforts to understand their experiences. In summary, then, style is a way of understanding the patterns or worldviews of different writers or artists, but comments about style should probably be withheld when talking about the work of individual students.

One way to examine style in the classroom is to try Phyllis Brooks's (1973) approach to imitation. In this approach, students are asked to imitate a passage from a particular author, say the following passage from William Faulkner, whose style I would place somewhere between the realism of Steinbeck and the rationalism of Winston Churchill:

> Behind the smokehouse that summer, Ringo and I had a living map. Although Vicksburg was just a handful of chips from the woodpile and the River a trench scraped into the packed earth with the point of a hoe, it (river, city, and terrain) lived, possessing even in miniature that ponderable though passive recalcitrance of topography which outweighs artillery, against which the most brilliant of victories and the most tragic of defeats are but the loud noises of a moment. (Faulkner 1938, 3)

Students are asked to underline the words they intend to change in their rewrites, leaving untouched the connective prepositions, conjunctions, and verbs. Then they rewrite the passage, often drawing on personal experience:

> On top of the garage every spring, Vince and Bud had a flagpole. Although "Old Glory" was just a torn sheet from the mending basket, and the pole assembled from leftover beanpoles nailed together with Daddy's hammer, it (flag and pole) stood, providing even in its shabbiness that symbolic though limited means of communication which proclaims patriotism, by which the largest of nations and the most timid of peoples are still identified in a moment. (M. Myers and Gray 1983, 17)

> In the schoolyard that fall, Cathy and he had a torrid affair. Although sex was but a dream on the horizon, and love a bargain struck between the enamoured pair with the delicacy of a detente, it (sex, love, and relationship) flowered, obeying even in quietude that forceful though nebulous passion of youth that withstands parents, against which the most stubborn of attacks and the most humble of pleas are but the inconsequential mutterings of a substitute teacher. (M. Myers and Gray 1983, 17)

The reading aloud and drafting of these passages helps develop the students' "ear" for style. And an "ear," as I have argued earlier, is part of understanding.

The different categories of style have some overlap with speech events, but style is not the same as speech events. The style of sweet impressionism is always conversational, and the style of tough talk is usually presentational. The style of the rationalist is either an academic or a presentational speech event, and the mimetic-journalistic is either presentational or conversational. The tough is sometimes close to, but not equivalent to, the notational speech event. The gothic is a combination of the academic and the conversational, a combination which never works in institutions but which does work for individuals lost in a hazy, uncertain world. The difference between style and speech events is that speech events are institutionalized forms of speaking, taking place in particular social settings for particular social purposes. Style is the role, voice, or worldview of individuals toward the themes of love, reality versus appearance, and tolerance of ambiguity. Because style is the worldview of individual speakers, style may be the voice of those who are unreliable, those who are confused, those who tell, those who show (see Booth 1961 for further elaboration). A journalist-realist, acting as a stenographer or as a collector of documents from all sources (letters, reports), could obviously include speech from many different speech events. The overlap between style and speech events occurs because one's institutional setting often influences one's worldview, but they remain distinctly different ways of speaking and writing, ways of understanding what we read and hear. Within style, the ideas of love, friendship, hate, revenge, envy, generosity, loyalty, dishonesty, brotherhood, sisterhood, otherness, ethnicity, alienation, and other ideas are viewed and historically shaped in different ways. Ideas can be viewed as illusive in the sweet style, as a threatening or puzzling irrationality in Poe, as recognizable and reasonable in journalism, as rational and analyzable in the academic style, and as events which happen like weather and from which narrators retreat in a no-talk, tough style. Style structures our relationship to reality, giving us a worldview in which narrators are irrational or rational, tight-lipped or casually conversational, realistic or comic. The study of style seems like an impossible task—unless we approach our definitions of styles as prototypes to help us solve a learning problem, not as a complete summary of humanity's intellectual life. The style scale described here is a way to summarize some worldviews. This scale, which obviously does not exhaust all possibilities, enables us to help students understand differences in worldviews, one of the responsibilities of English teachers. Says Ohmann:

> The student who understands that world views differ, and that he himself employs one, has prepared himself for the informed encounter with experience that precedes good writing. He becomes a voting citizen of his world, rather than a bound vassal to an inherited ontology. (Ohmann 1971, 70)

Note

1. Eisner arranges what he calls the modes and what is here called style into three types: the *expressive*, the *mimetic* or *imitative* (what is here called the realistic), and finally, the *conventional* (Eisner 1982, 56–63). Eisner suggests that the types are often combined (62) and that people may arrange these in some kind of sequence for problem solving. Einstein is quoted by Eisner as saying, "Conventional words or other signs have to be sought for laboriously only in a secondary stage" (Eisner 1982, 42).

15 Conclusion: "I Think It Happened Again"

Using the resources of the physical and biological world (World-1), the strategies, schemas, and internalized voices of the cognitive world (World-2), and the influences of the world of ideas (World-3) (see Popper and Eccles 1977), a society constructs a form of literacy which contributes to shaping the habits of mind, the interests, and the affiliations of the educated person at a given time and place. A new form of literacy is now challenging the traditional curriculum of English and English language arts, changing in K–12 schools the recommended books and processes for reading, the subjects and audiences for writing, the models of development and "appropriateness" for each grade level, and the tests and assessments for reporting results.

For the individual student who comes to school with different forms of literacy from family and neighborhood, the literacy challenge in school is an accommodation between local forms of literacy in neighborhood and family and the dominant form of literacy in the national culture. During periods of transition from one dominant form of literacy to another, the usual stable tension among different forms of literacy turns into an open struggle. Now is such a time.

Today, the struggle is between parents whose jobs are organized around the old industrial models of decoding/analytic literacy and parents whose jobs are organized around the problem-solving models of translation/critical literacy. The struggle is also between those who fear the loss of the concept of nationhood in the multicultural interpretive models of translation/critical literacy and those who fear social exclusion in the universal melting pot of decoding/analytic literacy. One example of this open struggle is the current debate about how to teach reading. Recently, for example, Barak Rosenshine and Carla Meister (1994) reported that reciprocal reading programs, one of the emerging pedagogical forms of translation/critical literacy, produced significantly better reading achievement results on experimenter-developed comprehension tests than they did on the machine-scored standardized reading tests. Experimenter-developed comprehension tests showed significant increases in reading achievement 8 out of 10 times, while standardized reading tests like the Gates-MacGinitie showed significant increases in reading achievement only 2 out of 13 times (Rosenshine and Meister 1994, 519). Rosenshine and Meister asked, "Why are [these two tests] ... producing different results?" (Rosenshine and Meister 1994, 519).

Fifteen years earlier, Rosenshine had reported that direct instruction, which emphasized a "teacher-centered focus," "factual questions and controlled practice" (Peterson 1979, 58), seemed to produce better reading results on particular machine-scored standardized reading tests than did other kinds of instruction, particularly approaches using more open-ended responses—for example, like those in reciprocal reading (Rosenshine 1979; Peterson 1979, 58). However, students who learned through direct instruction did "worse on tests of abstract thinking ... and problem solving" than did students who received more open-ended instruction (Peterson 1979, 63).

Because direct instruction and open-ended responses represent two different definitions of literacy, they produce different test results. Even after Rosenshine and Meister complete the future study they called for in 1994, they will not have an answer to "Which one is the right one for this time and place?" The answer to that question resides in a social and historical decision about what kind of K–12 literacy the public thinks it needs and thinks it can afford at a given time and place. The decision is, of course, always a contingent answer. There is no absolute answer here, as I hope this book has made clear.

Another example of the open struggle over different forms of literacy is the debate over whether U.S. students are smarter or dumber than students in other countries and whether they are smarter or dumber than U.S. students used to be. In a recent summary of test results, the historian Lawrence Stedman concludes:

> (1) American 9-year-olds ranked second in the world in reading ... 14-year-olds had reading scores in the top third.... Students have done well internationally in reading;

> (2) Scores on the College Board achievement tests—which do measure academic achievement—rose over the past decade even as more students took them;

> (3) While [NAEP] 17-year-old reading ... scores have been basically level, their science scores fell ... NAEP reading scores of 9- and 13-year-olds have generally held steady for the last two decades;

> (4) In reading and elementary school science, American students have been among the world leaders;

> (5) Most high school students are competent in punctuation and grammar....

Stedman also notes:

> (6) In the 1992 NAEP reading assessment, only 37 percent of
> our seniors demonstrated proficiency [a new NAEP reading level
> above "basic"];
>
> (7) Most high school students . . . have weak expository, narra-
> tive, and compositional skills. . . . (Stedman 1995, 80–83)

These test results above tell us that students *are* learning decoding/an-
alytic literacy (items 1 through 5), but they *are not* learning transla-
tion/critical literacy (items 6 and 7). The point is that comparisons like
"ahead" and "behind" make no sense at all if the literacy being measured is not adequately described.

Literacy, then, is not an unchanging absolute and neither are intelligence, mind, schooling, teaching, learning, and testing. The mind is
an adaptation of basic biological equipment to meet new social needs,
and schools, as institutions, translate a nation's dominate literacy
policies into constructions of students and teachers, into pedagogical
processes for the teaching of English, into various assessment instruments to monitor public policies on literacy development, into book
lists and cultural artifacts, and into subject area disciplines—for example, literature, rhetoric, cognitive and social psychology, linguistics, and grammar.

Cultural processes and artifacts are never an unproblematic representation of a form of literacy. Books, for example, can be read in many different ways, one age group reading Milton as a traditionalist and another
reading him as a revolutionary. Therefore, when we talk about an entity
called "a book" or about "reading" or "writing," we need to ask "what
kind of book or reading or writing?" Do you mean "writing-as-hand-
writing," a dominant form of literacy in the signature period, or do you
mean "writing-as-five-paragraph-essay," a dominant form of writing in
the K–12 classes of decoding/analytic literacy? Do you mean "reading-
as-memorized-oration" or oral catechism, a dominant form of literacy
during recitation literacy, or do you mean "reading-as-silent-decoding,"
a dominant form of reading during decoding/analytic literacy? Do you
mean a "book-as-object-to-be-analyzed" through "objective" methods,
as in decoding/analytic literacy, or do you mean a "book-as-experience-
to-be-stored-in-memory," as in recitation literacy? Or do you mean a
"book-as-sacred-object," as in oracy, or do you mean a "book-as-a-con-
struction-to-be-produced," as in translation/critical literacy?

Each form of literacy has its favorite genres. In the world of decod-
ing/analytic literacy, the *Encyclopaedia Britannica* (or any other cultural
list, for that matter) was a favored form because the world was stable

and unified and, therefore, lists like the ninth edition of the *Encyclopaedia Britannica* could claim to present a unified worldview which "was widely, if not quite universally, shared by [its editor's] contributors" (MacIntyre 1990, 56). But by the fifteenth edition in 1974, that unified worldview was about gone, and lists began to lose their old coherence: "Heterogeneous and divergent contributions, which recognize the diversity and fragmentation of standpoints in central areas, are deeply at odds with the overall scheme" (MacIntyre 1990, 56). A new literacy was emerging in which the same cultural objects could be "read" in different ways and in which different readings were not to be wished away.

Each form of literacy adopts its own rules for access. In some literacies, for example, the reading of books is restricted to an elite. During recitation literacy, special education students, "delinquent" children and youth, and black and other "minority" children were excluded from the private and common schools that were teaching the nation's dominant literacy, and, instead, were sent to black, charity, reform, industrial, or vocational schools, as well as to state schools for the "deaf, dumb, and blind" (Richardson 1994, 696), where local forms of literacy were taught or where literacy was ignored altogether. During decoding/analytic literacy, legislation in juvenile justice, in special education, and in civil rights brought most children into the "integrated" public common schools where children were separated by faculty into different tracks, thereby denying college preparation or higher-order thinking skills to many students, while at the same time providing basic skills or the nation's decoding/analytic literacy for everyone.[1] By limiting tracking within the school and offering students a complex array of choices, translation/critical literacy provides for everyone the opportunity to attend a core program of higher-order thinking skills.

Each form of literacy is attempting to help solve its own set of social problems. By offering to more students a range of opportunities for higher-order thinking skills, translation/critical literacy hopes to increase democratic participation in public forums, to enrich our cultural resources through writing, to increase the skill and pay level of jobs, and to enable individuals to reimagine themselves in different ways for the shifting roles of contemporary life—as political participants, as parents, as workers, as husbands or wives or single persons, as critical consumers. Literacy is not, of course, the only solution to the nation's problems in citizenship, personal growth, and work. Literacy policies alone, for example, will not solve problems of equal educational opportunity. Increasing numbers of the nation's children live in poverty at the same time that public schools have started to charge for services which were formerly tax-supported—special classes, yearbooks, textbooks, dances, and so forth. Neither will literacy policies alone solve problems of family support. About one-third of our students at every age level come to school without both parents living in the home, and when both parents do live in the home, it's often the case that they both must work to support the household.

Neither will these policies alone give everyone a job. One of the important areas of research in economics "currently is on the returns of education, both monetary and non-monetary" (McMahon 1995, 1). In 1970, the unemployment rate of high school dropouts was 7 percent above the unemployment rate of those with a high school diploma, but by 1992, that 7 percent gap had grown to 20 percent (Tucker 1994). In addition, for the first time in our nation's history, high school graduates, their tenuous positions threatened by low-wage workers in other parts of the world, are entering jobs which, after corrections for inflation, pay them less than the salaries earned by their parents for the same jobs. McMahon reports, "The social rates of return to completion of only middle school, and also 9 to 12 years of schooling, have both been falling steadily" from 1960 to 1995 (McMahon 1995, 49). The *New York Times* reports (Kilborn 1995) that since 1979, wages are up for those with four years of college, 5.2 percent up for men and 19.1 percent up for women, and down for those who are high school dropouts, 23.3 percent down for men and 7.4 percent down for women. McMahon reports, "Annual earnings of college graduates in relation to high school graduates, 170% in 1995, have been increasing since 1960 when they were 152% for both males and females" (McMahon 1995, 6). As a result, college graduates and others with education beyond high school (two-year or four-year) are entering jobs which pay them more than the salaries earned by their parents, who were usually not college educated (House 1994, 28–29; Phillips 1993).

One result of these trends is an increasing wage gap between the college or post-high school educated and the high school or the less-than-high school educated. As a result, the number of people earning middle-income wages declines as the numbers in top and bottom incomes grow. Today, the United States leads all major industrial nations in the size of the gap separating incomes in the upper fifth from incomes in the lower fifth (Phillips 1990, 8). The huge changes in distribution of wealth, with the rich getting richer, the poor getting poorer, and the large middle disappearing (Levy 1987), is a scandal that no literacy program alone can correct. Furthermore, as long as most citizens do not understand what is happening, economic disparities are also not likely to be corrected with tax policies and programs for redistributing wealth. One long-range solution to this problem is a well-educated citizenry active in democratic debate and able to work in an information age. In summary, a new form of literacy will not give children all the supports they need, but a new form of literacy is one of the things children do need. Those who claim little or no relationship between income and education, higher-order thinking skills and democratic processes, literacy and one's opportunities in life are, I think, fundamentally incorrect.

When we change our minds about a form of literacy, we are also changing our minds about the structure of the mind. In signature literacy, the mind was a moral muscle which improved its discipline with drill. In recitation literacy, the mind was a memory bank of moral touchstones which shaped character. In decoding/analytic literacy, the mind was an epistemological instrument with a hierarchy of logical operations which could be used for the "objective" decoding and analysis of delivered objects and texts. To develop this mind-as-epistemological-instrument, the child moved in Piagetian-like fashion from egocentrism to socialized behavior, from personal audiences to the larger audiences in the universe of discourse, and from concrete actions to the higher-logical operations of autonomous third persons ("remove subjectivity") and thesis-evidence rules ("state logical relations between propositions and facts").

In decoding/analytic literacy, the mind was, like the factories of the period, a fixed hierarchy of parts, with one measure of production or intelligence:

> To say that one person is more intelligent than another can only mean that he or she uses information more efficiently to serve his or her purposes. The efficiency of the factory is not to be located in this or that part of the operation. Rather the purchasing division, the mechanics, the operators, the inspectors, and shippers do their tasks with few errors and little lost time. (Cronbach 1990, 275)

This general ability or general productivity measure of mind, a useful adaptation for the period of 1916 to 1983, is still a useful measure of basic skills, but in translation/critical literacy, the "G," or general aptitude measure, needs to be accompanied by descriptions of component processes (Sternberg 1985) and various domains of talent and knowledge (H. Gardner 1983).

In translation/critical literacy, these component processes and domains of talent are[2] (see Figure 25):

1. *a situated-language intelligence:* the habit of situating language in use/participation and in study/observation, in the models of whole language use and in the analysis of such parts as metaphor and grammar (phonemes, syntax, morphology);

2. *a self-fashioning and embodied intelligence:* the habit of embodied self-fashioning, actively engaged in meaning making, bringing together

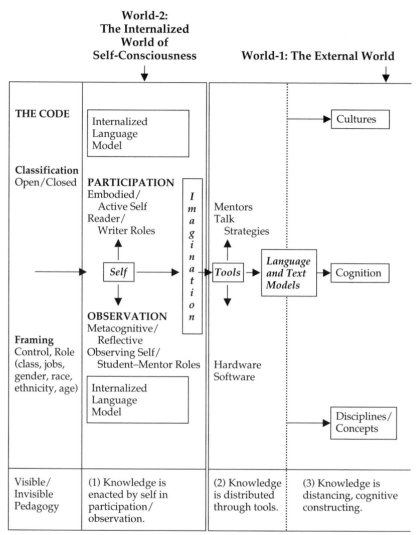

Fig. 25. A language model for translation/critical literacy.

in action a sense of one's individuality and one's common commitments, including those from democratic traditions; the development of roles for the self in believing and disbelieving, translating
and criticizing;

3. *a distributed intelligence:* knowing how to distribute problems to
   various resources, including tools, expert networks, and cognitive strategies;

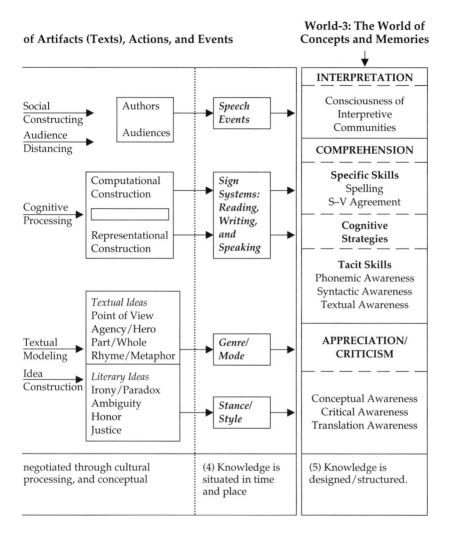

4. *a sign-system, representation, or cognitive-processing intelligence:* understanding how a range of representations can be used to express and explore an idea;

5. *a speech-event or social-construction intelligence:* knowing how to use a variety of speech events both to communicate to others and to think about an idea;

6. *a mode or textual-modeling intelligence:* being able to shift from one mode to another;

7. *a stance intelligence* (also part of textual modeling): understanding the structure of poetic and nonpoetic stances in reading and composing; and

8. *a style or idea-construction intelligence:* understanding differences among styles in literature and public discourse and contrasting ideas about how the world is put together (Table 8).

First, *a situated-language intelligence.* For our age, decoding/analytic literacy's exclusive emphasis on "observation and imitation" is in all probability wrong in every particular (see Lave and Wenger 1991, 103). In the new translation/critical literacy, the learner fluctuates between the "visible" observation of the patterns of language and the "invisible" participation in language as a mediated activity in literacy events (Lave and Wenger 1991, 103). Thus, in translation/ critical literacy, the learner is engaged in legitimate peripheral participation in which the learner is "both absorbing and being absorbed in the 'culture of practice'" surrounding literacy events (Lave and Wenger 1991, 95). Observation helps the learner make confusing language experiences comprehensible, and participation or use helps the learner acquire and assimilate comprehensible language practices (Krashen 1993). Observation is the process of standing back from language participation and use through editing, revising, practicing, and reviewing. Language participation and use is the process of involvement in the community or "literacy club" (F. Smith 1988) that sponsors literacy events or enterprises which produce purposeful speeches, talk, and writing.

This need for some fluctuation between participation and observation is important in many contemporary cultural practices—not just the literacy activities in schools. In decoding/analytic literacy, observation seemed to work in schools for teaching only basic skills in an age of slow-moving, slow-changing information. One learned basic skills through observation in school, and one used these prescribed skills in carefully defined jobs. In today's world—where information changes at a fast rate in all areas of contemporary life and in which interpretation is essential at every point of one's work, requiring one to modify one's work while doing it—more and more groups are fluctuating between learning by participation in their work and learning in retreats and conventions for observation of their work.

Lave and Wenger (1991) report that apprentice butchers in the workplace complain that they spend all of their time in participation at the counter, taking and filling orders, and, thus, do not get adequate time in the back room to study charts, to learn the names and shapes of the different cuts, to read the latest information that changes their craft. The same complaint comes from some apprentices of Alcoholics Anonymous who report that they spend all of their time participating in group interaction and not enough time in the explicit study of the latest information about alcoholism as a disease. And, of course, the same complaint comes from contemporary medical students and student teachers who say they need a balance of participation and observation, not the present all-or-nothing situation. The same complaint used to come from autoworkers who felt they needed the observation time or a staff development meeting to meet the demands of modern assembly lines. Staff training and observation have been added to participation in workplaces like auto plants, and now participation and use have been added to K–12 schools. The point is that in the postmodern workplace, there is a new way of working which balances participation and study. In decoding/analytic literacy, learning through participation was good enough in the workplace. No longer.

Parents and some professionals are not necessarily comfortable with this fluctuation between participation and observation in the teaching of the new literacy, even though they recognize that this fluctuation has become an essential practice in schools and in many areas of contemporary life. In California in 1989, Professor Siegfried Engelmann charged that the California State Board of Education had violated the California State Constitution by adopting a literature-based reading text which provided participation in stories but which did not provide explicit observation of the parts of the reading process. Engelmann argued that the state constitution required the state to adopt a reading text and that a reading text had to have an explicit observation of parts (see *Engelmann vs. State Board of Education et al.* 1989).

In Engelmann's view, his Distar program satisfied the constitutional requirement for a reading textbook, but a literature-based textbook could not. But the California Curriculum Commission rejected Distar as an adequate model for a reading text, arguing that Distar "sequences rote memorization, recitation, and workbook drills in a lock-step manner…few attempts are made to teach the language arts as an interactive process" (*Engelmann vs. State Board of Education et al.* 1989, 11). Notice that, in this dispute, a basic definition of literacy is at stake, Engelmann apparently emphasizing decoding/analytic literacy's observation of parts and the California Curriculum Commission apparently emphasizing participation, leaning away from decoding/analytic literacy toward translation/critical literacy.

What is proposed in translation/critical literacy is a unification of participation and observation. There are those who claim that the California

Table 8. Contrast of two forms of literacy.

DECODING/ANALYTIC LITERACY: BEHAVIORISM AND INFORMATION PROCESSING		CRITICAL/TRANSLATION LITERACY: COGNITIVE APPRENTICESHIP	
(1)	Learning a language requires one to learn the autonomous structures, semantics (word meanings), and syntax of text and figures of speech.	(1)	Learning a language requires one to begin with purposes, intention, and meaning—*various models of people doing things* in the world. From these acts comes syntax, text, figures of speech, and other units of language.
TEACHING PRACTICE:	Vocabulary lessons are separate from drills in syntactic patterns, and syntax is separate from purposes within literacy events.	TEACHING PRACTICE:	Initiate students into various literacy events both in and out of school, recognizing how vocabulary shapes syntax. (Language)
(2)	Learning in school focuses on cognition, not affective issues.	(2)	Learning in school recognizes that self-fashioning is part of all cognitive activities.
TEACHING PRACTICE:	Avoid the personal "I" in one's writing. Ignore personal responses and attend only to the "objective" text.	TEACHING PRACTICE:	Practice playing the believing and disbelieving game in reading and discussion, shifting point of view. (Self-fashioning)
(3)	Learning in school is an individual activity. Intelligence is in the individual's mind.	(3)	Learning in school is a process of developing distributed intelligence, involving collaborative work with people and machines
TEACHING PRACTICE:	Always work alone. Do not use technology (like spell checkers).	TEACHING PRACTICE:	Work with other people and tools (calculators, pencils, pens, computers, and so forth). (Tool Shifting)
(4)	To learn, one focuses on words and numbers and uses computational model of thinking processes.	(4)	To learn, one transfers problems from one sign system (body and action) to another (visuals, words, numbers) and back again. Every sign system is silent in some areas, exuberant in others.
TEACHING PRACTICE:	Focus in school on letters, numbers, and segmented processes.	TEACHING PRACTICE:	Engage in frequent sign shifting (or translation) around a problem. (Sign Shifting)

Table 8. *Continued.*

DECODING/ANALYTIC LITERACY: BEHAVIORISM AND INFORMATION PROCESSING		CRITICAL/TRANSLATION LITERACY: COGNITIVE APPRENTICESHIP	
(5)	Learning in school focuses on academic language as the primary language of thought.	(5)	Learning in school transfers problems from one speech event (conversations) to another (academic events or presentations) and back again. Language use is always an interpersonal event.
TEACHING PRACTICE:	Use academic language through individual practice.		
		TEACHING PRACTICE:	Engage in frequent speech event shifting. (Speech-Event Shifting)
(6)	The Paradigmatic Argument and Definition are the primary ways of writing in English. Narrative is only a way to begin to grow toward the paradigmatic.	(6)	The Narrative must become at least as important as the Paradigmatic in English classes. The Narrative is its own way of knowing. One essential skill is some facility with mode shifting.
TEACHING PRACTICE:	Learn to write the paradigmatic essay.	TEACHING PRACTICE:	Practice shifting modes. Give special attention to Narrative writing. (Mode Shifting)
(7)	Learning focuses on either the real (information) or the imaginary (the literary). Learn the independent, objective structure of these two types of texts.	(7)	Learning focuses on stance shifting in which the "real" and the "literary" are ways of reading, not necessarily different texts.
TEACHING PRACTICE:	Read literature and then read nonliterature. Write only nonliterary pieces in English. Literary pieces are reserved for "creative writing," a special, low-status course for a few students.	TEACHING PRACTICE:	Practice literary and non-literary readings of same text, and write literary and nonliterary pieces on the same topic. Give status to literary writing in English. (Stance Shifting)

Curriculum Commission did not establish a unification (Honig 1995). Unification, of course, is not easy to maintain, especially in public forums where extremes make news. One recent example of pop culture's imbalance-for-profit is Art Levine's *Atlantic Monthly* characterization of whole language instruction as opposing the explicit study and observation of phonics (or, I assume, any other pattern of language) (Levine 1994). He begins his article by describing a reading crisis which pits phonics instruction against whole language, thereby blessing an old either/or debate which probably made some sense during decoding/analytic literacy, but which makes little sense during translation/critical literacy. At the end of his article, after establishing phonics as the essential of reading instruction, Levine attempts to establish a balance he ignores at the beginning: "whatever its limitations, whole language does have something to offer. Its stress on reading enjoyable children's literature is surely worthwhile. . . . The emphasis on early writing wins broad support. . . . For its part, traditional phonics instruction also has limitations" (Levine 1994, 44). Levine's gesture toward balance was largely ignored in the public discussion that followed his article. In summary, then, language learning in translation/critical literacy emphasizes a unification of participation and observation, use and practice, and fluctuation between models of purposeful literacy events and classification of parts of those events, between problem solving and information retrieval.

Second, *a self-fashioning and embodied intelligence.* Decoding/analytic literacy focused on the efforts of individuals to become the ideal universal person who, shaped by melting-pot values, expressed commonalities, not differences. The "I" or individual self was to be refined out of existence, beginning with an emphasis on third-person essays and on "objective" readings or analyses. The learner was fashioned as passive. In translation/critical literacy, the learner is active, attempting to embody ideas in action. The new translation/critical literacy describes self-fashioning as the effort of individuals to define their individualism both as the "I" of their individual experiences and responses and as the "we" of interpretive groups and democratic communities with diverse populations. The attention to pluralism and diversity (geography, class, race, ethnicity, gender) is intended to add to our understanding of both our individualism and our commonalities, including our commitments to democratic traditions, to integration, and to traditional values of compassion, courage, honesty.

The need in English classes for attention to self-fashioning, organized around a sense of one's individuality and intercultural existence, is not an invention of English teachers which they put to the test in the selection of particular books. The need for a self-fashioning intelligence is the direct result of radical changes in the world. Daughters who watch their mothers enter careers formerly reserved for men will inevitably come to K–12 English classes and read traditional books differently, even Dickens, and add to their own reading new voices that describe their experiences. These readings in K–12 schools primarily grow out of family values, then, not the political agendas of English teachers. Teenagers who hear news interviews and musical lyrics from every part of the world cannot be expected to ignore the diversity of worldwide perspectives when they write essays or read books. The readings of these teenagers are a direct result of the growth of worldwide communication landing in the family living room.

These same teenagers live within the middle of the country's second largest wave of immigration in this century. In the first wave, from 1901 to 1910, 85 percent of the immigrants were from Europe (Germany, Italy, Ireland, and so forth), and in this the second wave, 10 percent of the immigrants are from Europe while the rest are from Mexico, the Philippines, Korea, China, Taiwan, Cuba, Vietnam, and so forth (Hodgkinson 1995, 32). Says Harold Hodgkinson, "By 2025, youths in the United States will be about half white and half 'minority'" (Hodgkinson 1995, 32). Children who interact with these immigrants at school and in the community cannot be expected to ignore this experience when they read and write.

Some parents fear that English teachers are politicizing everything by turning self-fashioning into continuous role-playing of different forms of group-think from perspectives of gender and race and thereby promoting separation of groups by race and gender while ignoring individuality and our common democratic values. The English Coalition Conference, in 1987, struggled with the question of whether there is a set of common values which all students should share. The Coalition gave an unequivocal answer: all English classes in the U.S. should be based on a commitment to democratic values as outlined in the founding documents of the country (Lloyd-Jones and Lunsford 1989).

Many parents fear that English classes are rushing to group-separation theories, attempting to classify all individual perspectives as group memberships with competing interests. In California, a group of parents got the State Board of Education to remove two stories from the state testing program on the grounds that one story promoted vegetarianism by telling a story from a vegetarian's point of view while the other promoted religious and gender tensions by telling a story from the point of view of a Moslem female who was marrying a Christian male.

In the heated atmosphere of public debate, the public did not take the time to read carefully the stories under attack. In these two stories, the central character is attempting to fashion a sense of self out of individual experience, which involved but was not restricted to religious, gender, or vegetarian theory. These theories were not irrelevant to the struggle each character endured, but the theories themselves are, as good literature always asserts, incomplete portraits of individuals. For example, *Maniac Magee,* as Irene Rosenthal argues, can be read as social studies or as literature. In the first, the nonpoetic reading, students set the cultural maps of their own lives "against the world of the text." In the second, the poetic or literary reading, students use literature's "imagined world that is real enough to engage us...to help us consider ourselves and others in ways that might be completely new" (Rosenthal 1995, 115). I would add that in high school, students in English must do both, adding historical setting to their ways of examining tensions in a given society.

The problem of the common culture in individual self-fashioning is also illustrated by the Smithsonian Institution's decision in 1995 not to carry out its plans for an exhibit of the *Enola Gay.* The Smithsonian attempted to bring together two stories embedded in the history of the *Enola Gay,* the story of American heroes who fought in World War II and the story of dead Japanese at the beginning of the Atomic Age. The objections of the Veterans of Foreign Wars, peace groups, and others ultimately killed the project in January of 1995—but not before an extensive debate about whether or not an individual can sustain a sense of the courage and heroism of the World War II soldiers from the U.S. and, at the same time, sustain a sense of the horror and sorrow at the Japanese dead at the beginning of the Atomic Age. This kind of mixture, of ambiguity, is the kind of self-fashioning which translation/critical literacy requires and which literature invites. Simply racing to a theory of gender or race, as Barbara Christian (1992) has noted, or simply insisting on commonality, as others have insisted, are both inadequate reflections of the complexity of the individual self in contemporary democracies. It is the job of English teachers, through literature and public discourse, to challenge students to deal with these issues of self-fashioning.

Third, *a distributed intelligence.* Decoding/analytic literacy emphasized individualized authorship, individualized technology (pencils, typewriters), and individualized memory, but translation/critical literacy emphasizes the distributed intelligence of collaborative work, internalized voices, expert networks, and information-processing machines. Translation/critical literacy's notion that the educated person must be able to distribute problems to machines, experts, and internalized strategies has changed radically the nation's concept of individual authorship and intellectual property. For one thing, collaborative author-ship, which appears to be increasing in many disciplines, raises the question of who gets credit for what in university merit reviews, who owns and collects royalties, if any, on computer group-generated drafts of work. And how does the notion of distributed intelligence under-mine individual responsibility for one's actions. Does it turn everything into a collaborative act without individual agency? Again, distributed intelligence worries parents. They wonder whether collaborative work allows cheating and weakens individual responsibility. Again, these practices and problems have become pervasive in contemporary life. They are not the inventions of English teachers.

Fourth, *a sign-system, representation, or cognitive-processing intelli-gence.* Decoding/analytic literacy in English and English language arts classes focused primarily on a silent, alphabetic discourse, but transla-tion/critical literacy focuses on the discourse of many different sign systems, shifting among the visual, the alphabetic, and the action-se-quence, thereby introducing into English classes improvisational drama, film studies, computerized simulations, TV dramas, radio and TV talk shows, and the use of charts and diagrams for thinking through problems. Not too many years ago, high school, college, and university English departments rejected film study as a serious part of the English curriculum. That rejection is now long gone.

Parents, however, worry that sign shifting may be carried too far in K–12 English classes, to the point that we show too many movies and, in the process, abandon the reflective habit of silent, print reading. Par-ents (and professionals) point to the fact that TV's habit of mind is usu-ally fast and often unreflective and that in print reading, the reader usually controls the pace, engaging in rereading and in other habits es-sential to reflection. Print reading, in other words, may be one way to teach a habit of mind useful in many situations needing reflection, even in the playback of TV scenes. But the emphasis in English on viewing and on other sign systems may undermine adequate attention to the re-flective reading of print. The challenge, once again, is to find a balance.

Fifth, *a speech-event or social-construction intelligence.* Decoding/analytic literacy focused primarily on the audiences and logic of lectures and aca-demic speech events, stressing in writing the third person and the formal structure of a clear thesis sentence followed by enumerated evidence. Be-cause of the stress on writing as silent decoding and analysis, by the 1930s and 1940s, speech, drama, and debate began to disappear from many K–12 English classes and from many university English departments. In universities, these areas sometimes formed their own departments, be-coming the Department of Speech, later the Department of Rhetoric, and finally the Department of Communication Studies on many campuses.

The renewed interest in speech events in translation/critical literacy means that the interests of some of these departments will return to the sphere of English studies.

The emphasis on speech events in translation/critical literacy is essentially an effort to help students understand how ways of talking are also ways of knowing. In some speech-event situations, especially *conversational* ones, teachers often start with such questions as, "How does this scene make you feel?"—a question connecting the text to students' feelings. In a suit filed in Los Angeles Superior Court, one group of parents charged that these "feelings" questions were illegal in California assessments because such questions, the parents said, were an illegal invasion of privacy. But the American Civil Liberties Union argued that feelings questions are a source of ideas and that "we must be ever vigilant not to 'strangle the free mind at its source'" (Ehrlich 1994), a position with which the judge generally concurred (O'Brien 1994, 4). The ACLU argument, incidently, bears an interesting consistency with James Britton's notion that expressive language, like conversation, does, in fact, enable students to learn to shape ideas at the initial point of utterance and that the initial point of utterance is uniquely close to the intuitive and impressionistic source of the student's individualism (Britton 1970).

From the point of view of many parents, who assume that the primary purpose of writing is decoding/analytic literacy's finished "communication," the conversational events reflected in diaries and learning logs are deeply troubling. Parents who see this conversational writing in student folders ask why the writing has not been "corrected." When teachers try to explain the importance of learning to use writing for thinking, not just for communication, parents wonder why all writing is *not* communication and all errors are *not* public embarrassments. Some of these parents seem to carry with them the assumptions of *oral* and *signature literacy* that printed marks on paper were always a public icon. For the parents, the misspelling of a title of a book is a sign of disrespect toward the book. Many parents also worry that conversational talk may become an end in itself in English classes and that the principles of logic and of content in traditional academic speech events may get downplayed or lost altogether.

Sixth, *a mode or textual-modeling intelligence.* In both decoding/analytic literacy and translation/critical literacy, the paradigmatic modes of exposition, comparison-contrast, and argument use classification with a hierarchy of features and logical sequences to organize knowledge, and the narrative modes use the chronology of stories and the spatial relations of descriptions to describe knowledge. In the contemporary world, both kinds of truth testing are essential in all areas of knowledge, but decoding/analytic literacy conceived of these modes as steps on a ladder of abstraction. Narratives, for example, were near the bottom of the ladder, and persuasion or arguments were near the top. Thus, the writing of the "research" report was considered more intellectually demanding for students, a better test of truth, than the writing of a narrative, and even the social sciences (and sometimes even the humanities) were thought to be evolving toward the paradigmatic modes used in physics and chemistry, leaving behind their narrative impulses (Geertz 1983, 21).

During translation/critical literacy, there has been a growing recognition that the narrative (narration and description) and paradigmatic (comparison-contrast and argument or persuasion) modes are distinctly different but equally useful ways of organizing experience. Says Geertz, "[M]any social scientists have turned away from a laws and instances [paradigmatic] ideal of explanation toward a cases and interpretation [narrative] one, looking less for the sort of thing that connects planets and pendulums and more for the sort of thing that connects chrysanthemums and swords" (Geertz 1983, 19).

In the English classes of translation/critical literacy, there is an equal status afforded the different modes at all grade levels. In other words, narratives are not restricted to fourth grade and persuasion to tenth, the ladder or hierarchy at work in the curriculum sequences of decoding/analytic literacy. Instead, there is increasing differentiation of each mode from one grade to another. For instance, fourth grade could begin with narrative, and eighth grade could differentiate narrative into autobiography and biography. This is essentially the sequence proposed by California in its curriculum framework. Some states, however, still use the sequence proposed by decoding/analytic literacy.

Seventh, *a stance intelligence* (also part of textual modeling). Decoding/analytic literacy classified literature and public discourse as distinct codes producing distinctly different texts or works and, at the same time, classified the reading of these texts or works as the same. As a result, "across the U.S., literature is taught and tested in an unliterary manner" (Langer 1992, 42). Translation/critical literacy, on the other hand, classifies texts as typically inviting a poetic or transactional reading, as asking the reader to play a spectator (poetic) or participant (transactional) role, as invoking aesthetic (poetic) or commodity (transactional) purposes. The practice of stance shifting in translation/critical literacy opens up texts to new readings and refines the distinctions between literary and nonliterary readings—for example, the classified ad can be read as a poem or as an ad, while the novel can be read as a novel or as history, leading to fictionalizations of real life and historicizing of fiction.

Parents are worried, however, that the stance shifting of translation/critical literacy may have undermined some important behaviors associated with decoding/analytic literacy's assigned codes for literature and nonliterature. Literary codes, for example, prescribe a legitimate voyeurism, while nonliterary codes do not (Potok 1994). Parents worry that the literary reading of nonliterary "actual lives," as if real people were fictionalized entities, has encouraged an illegitimate voyeurism into everyday lives. Parents complain that the legitimate peeping-Tomism allowed by literature has now been extended into nonliterary areas where peeping-Tomism was formerly, and still should be, illegitimate. Grocery-counter magazines are one example. Newspaper coverage of private lives is another. The imaginative writing of students has produced other examples. To meet this public challenge, English teachers need to begin to assess what kind of reading is socially appropriate in which contexts. The blurring of literary and nonliterary codes or stance may not be a good idea in all contexts. At the least, the issue needs investigation.

Eighth, *a style or idea-construction intelligence.* Decoding/analytic literacy tended to treat composition as the study of a single style, the clear, efficient, rationalism of the traditional expository essay. Translation/critical literacy opens up the study of composition to a broader range of styles. Also, decoding/analytic literacy tended to organize literary study in K–12 schools around themes, genres, or chronologies. Translation/critical literacy adds to these methods of organization issues of gender, class, race, and ethnicity, which represent the perspectives of particular groups, and individual style, which represents a worldview that cuts across many groups. Style is the overarching worldview or set of ideas which shapes and contextualizes details. The gothic and the formalist, writing-degree-zero and impressionism, the formalist and the realist—these are the stylistic ideas and worldviews which can help us think about the values of events, character, and setting which shape the "facts" of our stories, showing us that facts are always embedded in values. Each of these worldviews, for example, has a different assumption about cause-and-effect relationships. In English classes, students experience these different worldviews in their own reading. These worldviews are, then, special tools for analysis from the disciplines of English and English language arts, and they illustrate quite clearly why disciplinary knowledge cannot be abandoned as a method of analysis, even in interdisciplinary projects.

There appear to be social-class differences in the way the new literacy is accepted by the public, which has created tensions between the profession and that public. Licensed professionals, managers, information processors and interpreters, workers in restructured factories, some salespersons, public-service occupations—these workers at all economic levels appear to demand translation/critical literacy to help them solve the unstructured problems of their work and family lives. But workers and managers from traditional factories, unskilled workers, some salespersons, and many others appear to demand decoding/analytic literacy, which requires habits of mind closer to their work and to their family traditions. Translation/critical literacy has within it a negotiating, flexible attitude toward work roles and the boundaries of gender, age, race, and ethnicity—a flexibility reflected in attitudes toward historical judgments, literary and nonliterary distinctions, and mode distinctions, to name three features of English. In decoding/analytic literacy, boundaries between one gender and another, literature and nonliterature, narrative and the paradigmatic, and young and old are usually predetermined and not negotiated. It is important to remember that these social-class differences cut across economic, gender, racial, and ethnic categories. It is also important to remember that in this time of transition, most people share a few attitudes from both classes. Finally, we need to return to insights from Bernstein (1990) and Lisa Delpit (1995), who have shown us that translation/critical literacy's flexible, negotiating attitude in teaching style may make the new literacy incomprehensible and possibly invisible to students from a social class more accustomed to decoding/analytic distinctions. To make the distinctions of translation/critical literacy visible, teachers may need to begin with decoding/analytic literacy's visible parts and then describe the transition to translation/critical literacy. In other words, we may need to teach some of the history of our differences over literacy.

A new form of literacy will not alone improve schools (or factory production, for that matter). The U.S. schoolteacher, who achieved the 1916 challenge of decoding/analytic literacy for nearly all, faces students today who are "100% more likely to be murdered" than they were in 1965 (Berliner 1992, 46), who are more likely to come from one-parent households and to live in poverty (45), and who may not have any health care. These problems cannot be solved with a good literacy lesson.

School structure must also change. To teach this new literacy of translation/critical literacy (see Figure 10 in Chapter 7; Table 8; and Figure 26), schools, among other things, will have to change radically the way students are scheduled, the way students are taught, the way achievement is assessed and reported, the way teacher professionalism is defined and practiced, and, yes, as in all new forms of literacy, to change the way students and teachers are constructed. These changes in the dominant form of literacy in schools require a new multiliteracy awareness which recognizes social-class differences in the way schools

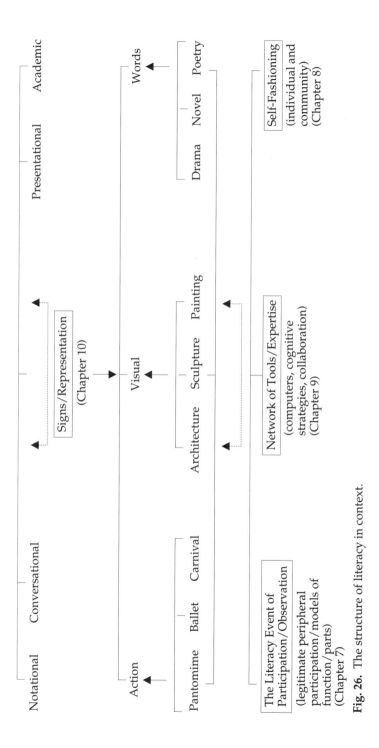

Fig. 26. The structure of literacy in context.

are understood. We may need to use older forms of literacy to help some students make the transition to understanding the new literacy. When we change from one form of literacy to another, we change our minds, in both senses of these terms. I think Virginia Woolf was about right when she said, "On or about December 1910, human nature changed" (Newman 1985, 17). I think that on or about December 1983, it happened again.

Notes

1. The Juvenile Justice and Delinquency Prevention Act of 1974, Public Law No. 93-415, Sec. 1, No. 5 stated: "Juvenile delinquency can be prevented through programs designed to keep students in elementary and secondary schools..." (Richardson 1994, 718).

2. Stanley Fish says, "It would be more accurate to say that an analytic perspective on a practice does not insulate one from experiencing the practice in all its fullness" (Fish 1994, 315).

Works Cited

Abbott, Jan. 1989. "NUMMI—Perspectives on the Role of Organizational Culture." *Labor Center Report* no. 267 (June). Institute of Industrial Relations, University of California–Berkeley.

Ablaza, Armano. 1989. Seminar comments at the Institute of Industrial Relations. University of California–Berkeley. June.

Abrams, M. H. 1953. *The Mirror and the Lamp: Romantic Theory and the Critical Tradition.* New York: Oxford University Press.

Adams, Hazard. 1972. "Literary Study at Irvine." *New Literary History* 4.1 (Fall): 193–203.

———. 1988. "The Fate of Knowledge." In *Cultural Literacy and the Idea of General Education,* edited by Ian Westbury and Alan C. Purves, 52–68. Chicago: University of Chicago Press.

Adamson, Walter L. 1980. *Hegemony and Revolution: Gramsci's Political and Cultural Theory.* Berkeley: University of California Press.

Adler, Mortimer. 1940. *How to Read a Book: The Art of Getting a Liberal Education.* New York: Simon and Schuster.

Alabama Coalition for Equity, Inc., et al. and Alabama Disabilities Advocacy Program, et al. v. Jim Folsom, Governor and as President of the State Board of Education. 1993. Decision: June 9, by Eugene W. Reese, Circuit Judge.

Allport, D. Alan. 1980. "Patterns and Actions: Cognitive Mechanisms Are Content-Specific." In *Cognitive Psychology: New Directions,* edited by Guy Claxton, 26–64. London: Routledge and Kegan Paul.

Altick, Richard D. 1983. *The English Common Reader: A Social History of the Mass Reading Public, 1800–1900.* Chicago: University of Chicago Press.

Anderson, Chris. 1987. *Style as Argument: Contemporary Nonfiction.* Carbondale: Southern Illinois University Press.

Anderson, Richard C., and William Nagy. 1990. "Word Meanings." In *Handbook of Reading Research,* Vol. II, edited by Rebecca Barr, Michael L. Kamil, Peter Mosenthal, and P. David Pearson, 690–724. New York: Longman.

Anderson, Richard C., and P. David Pearson. 1984. "A Schema-Theoretic View of Basic Processes in Reading Comprehension." In *Handbook of Reading Research,* Vol. I, edited by P. David Pearson, 255–91. New York: Longman.

Anderson, Wilda C. 1984. *Between the Library and the Laboratory: The Language of Chemistry in Eighteenth-Century France.* Baltimore: Johns Hopkins University Press.

Angoff, W. H., and H. S. Dyer. 1971. "The Admissions Testing Program." In *The College Board Admissions Testing Program: A Technical Report on the Research and Development Activities Relating to the Scholastic Aptitude and Achievement Tests,* edited by W. H. Angoff, 1–14, Princeton, NJ: Educational Testing Service.

APL Final Report: The Adult Performance Level Study. 1977. Washington, D.C.: U.S. Office of Education.

Applebee, Arthur N. 1974. *Tradition and Reform in the Teaching of English: A History.* Urbana, IL: National Council of Teachers of English.

———. 1978. *The Child's Concept of Story: Ages Two to Seventeen.* Chicago: University of Chicago Press.

———. 1981. *Writing in the Secondary School: English and the Content Areas.* Urbana, IL: National Council of Teachers of English.

———. 1984. *Contexts for Learning to Write: Studies of Secondary School Instruction.* Norwood, NJ: Ablex.

———. 1989. *A Study of Book-Length Works Taught in High School English Courses.* Report no. 12. Albany, NY: National Research Center on Literature Teaching and Learning, State University of New York.

———. 1993. *Literature in the Secondary School: Studies of Curriculum and Instruction in the United States.* Urbana, IL: National Council of Teachers of English.

———. 1994. *Toward Thoughtful Curriculum: Fostering Discipline-Based Conversation in the English Language Arts Classroom.* Albany, NY: National Research Center on Literature Teaching and Learning, State University of New York.

Applebee, Arthur N., Judith A. Langer, and Ina V.S. Mullis. 1987. *Learning to Be Literate in America: Reading, Writing, and Reasoning.* Washington, D.C.: National Assessment of Educational Progress.

Applebee, Arthur N., et al. 1994. *NAEP 1992 Writing Report Card.* Washington, D.C.: U.S. Department of Education.

"Are Boys Better at Math?" 1980. *New York Times* (December 7): 107, col. 1.

Atwell, Nancie. 1987. *In the Middle: Writing, Reading, and Learning with Adolescents.* Portsmouth, NH: Boynton/Cook Publishers.

Auerbach, Eric. 1953. *Mimesis: The Representation of Reality in Western Literature.* Princeton, NJ: Princeton University Press.

Bagg, Lyman H. 1871. *Four Years at Yale, by a Graduate of '68.* New Haven: Charles C. Chatfield.

Bailey, T. 1988. "Education and the Transformation of Markets and Technology in the Textile Industry." Technical Paper no. 2. Conservation of Human Resources Project. New York: Columbia University Press.

———. 1990. "Jobs for the Future and the Skills They Will Require." *American Educator* 14.1 (Spring): 10–15, 40–44.

Bain, Alexander. 1866. *English Composition and Rhetoric: A Manual.* New York: N.p. [1st U.S. edition.]

Bakhtin, Mikhail M. 1986. *Speech Genres and Other Late Essays.* Translated by Michael Holquist and edited by Caryl Emerson and Michael Holquist. Austin: University of Texas Press.

Barthes, Roland. 1972. *Mythologies.* New York: Hill and Wang.

———. 1979. *Writing Degree Zero: Elements of Semiology.* Translated by Annette Lavers and Colin Smith. New York: Hill and Wang.

Bartholomae, David. 1985. "Inventing the University When a Writer Can't Write: Studies in Writer's Block and Other Composing-Process Problems." In *When a Writer Can't Write: Studies in Writer's Block and Other Composing-Process Problems,* edited by Mike Rose, 134–65. New York: Guilford.

————. 1990. "Producing Adult Readers: 1930–50." In *The Right to Literacy*, edited by Andrea A. Lunsford, Helene Moglen, and James Slevin, 13–28. New York: Modern Language Association of America.

Bartholomae, David, and Anthony R. Petrosky, eds. 1986. *Facts, Artifacts, and Counterfacts: Theory and Method for a Reading and Writing Course*. Portsmouth, NH: Heinemann.

Bartine, David. 1989. *Early English Reading Theory: Origins of Current Debates*. Studies in Rhetoric/Communication. Carroll C. Arnold, series editor. Columbia: University of South Carolina Press.

————. 1992. *Reading, Criticism, and Culture: Theory and Teaching in the United States and England, 1820–1950*. Columbia: University of South Carolina Press.

Bartlett, Frederic Charles. 1932. *Remembering: A Study in Experimental and Social Psychology*. Cambridgeshire, England: Cambridge University Press.

Bartlett, John. 1855. *Familiar Quotations*. Boston: Little, Brown.

Barton, David. 1994. *Literacy: An Introduction to the Ecology of Written Language*. Cambridgeshire, England: Blackwell.

Beach, Richard W., and James D. Marshall. 1991. *Teaching Literature in the Secondary School*. San Diego: Harcourt, Brace, Jovanovich.

Becker, Alton L. 1992. "Humanistic Approaches to Linguistic Analysis." Speech delivered at the annual convention of the American Educational Research Association (AERA). San Francisco. April 23.

Beiber, Owen. 1982. "UAW Views Circles Not Bad At All." *The Quality Circles Journal* Vol. 3 (August). Cited in *The New United Motors Manufacturing, Inc.: A Joint Venture between General Motors and the Toyota Motor Corporation*. 1988 (June): 22. Fremont, CA: New United Motors Manufacturing, Inc.

Benbow, C. P., and J. C. Stanley. 1980. "Mathematical Ability: Is It a Sex Factor?" *Science* 210: 1264.

Benedict, Ruth. 1946. *Patterns of Culture*. New York: Mentor/New American Library.

Beniger, James R. 1986. *The Control Revolution: Technological and Economic Origins of the Information Society*. Cambridge, MA: Harvard University Press.

Bereiter, Carl. 1985. "Toward a Solution of the Learning Paradox." *Review of Educational Research* 55(2): 201–26.

————. 1994. "Constructivism, Socioculturalism, and Popper's World-3." *Educational Researcher* 23(7): 21–23.

————. 1995. Comments as a member of the Panel on Basics in Education at the annual convention of the American Educational Research Association (AERA). San Francisco. April.

Bereiter, Carl, and Marlene Scardamalia. 1987. *The Psychology of Written Composition*. Hillsdale, NJ: Lawrence Erlbaum.

Bereiter, Carl, et al. 1966. "An Academically Oriented Pre-School for Culturally Deprived Children." In *Pre-School Education Today*, edited by Fred M. Hechinger, 105–37. New York: Doubleday.

Berg, Ivar E. 1971. *The Literacy Process: A Practice in Domestication or Liberation?* New York: Writers and Readers Publishers Cooperative.

Berlin, James. 1990. "Writing Instruction in School and College English, 1890–1985." In *A Short History of Writing Instruction: From Ancient Greece to*

Twentieth-Century America, edited by James J. Murphy, 183–220. Davis, CA: Hermagoras.

Berliner, David C. 1992. "Educational Reform in an Era of Disinformation." Paper presented at the meeting of the American Association of Colleges for Teacher Education. San Antonio. February.

———. 1994. Personal communication.

Bernstein, Basil. 1971. "On the Classification and Framing of Educational Knowledge." In *Knowledge and Control,* edited by F. D. Young, 47–69. London: Collier-Macmillan.

———. 1972. "Social Class, Language, and Socialization." In *Language and Social Context: Selected Readings,* edited by Pier Paolo Giglioli, 167–78. Harmondsworth, England: Penguin.

———. 1975. *Toward a Theory of Educational Transmission.* Vol. 3 of *Class, Codes, and Control.* London: Routledge and Kegan Paul.

———. 1990. *The Structuring of Pedagogic Discourse.* Vol. 4 of *Class, Codes, and Control.* London: Routledge and Kegan Paul.

Bizzell, Patricia. 1990. "Beyond Foundationalism to Rhetorical Authority: Problems in Defining Cultural Literacy." *College English* 52.6 (October): 661–75.

———. 1992. *Academic Discourse and Critical Consciousness.* Pittsburgh: University of Pittsburgh Press.

Blackmur, R. P. 1955. *The Lion and the Honeycomb: Essays in Solicitude and Critique.* New York: Harcourt, Brace.

Blair, Hugh. 1783. *Lectures on Rhetoric and Belles Lettres.* Vol. 1. rpt. Carbondale: Southern Illinois University Press, 1965; Vol. 3. rpt. New York: Garland, 1970.

Blau, Sheridan. 1981. "Literacy as a Form of Courage." *Journal of Reading* 25(2): 101–5.

———. 1994. "The California Learning Assessment System Language Arts Test: A Guide for the Perplexed." Sacramento, CA: California State Department of Education.

Bleich, David. 1988. *The Double Perspective: Language Literacy and Social Relations.* New York: Oxford University Press.

Bloch, Maurice, ed. 1975. *Political Language and Oratory in Traditional Society.* London: Academic Press.

Bogdan, Deanne. 1990. "Censorship, Identification, and the Poetics of Need." In *The Right to Literacy,* edited by Andrea A. Lunsford, Helene Moglen, and James Slevin, 128–47. New York: Modern Language Association of America.

Bolter, J. David. 1984. *Turing's Man: Western Culture in the Computer Age.* Chapel Hill: University of North Carolina Press.

Booth, Wayne C. 1961. *The Rhetoric of Fiction.* Chicago: University of Chicago Press.

———. 1988. *The Company We Keep: An Ethics of Fiction.* Berkeley: University of California Press.

Borstelmann, L. J. 1983. "Children Before Psychology: Ideas About Children from Antiquity to the Late 1800s." In *Handbook of Child Psychology,* Vol. 1, edited by Paul Henry Mussen, 1–40. New York: Wiley.

Boulding, Kenneth E. 1956. *The Image: Knowledge in Life and Society.* Ann Arbor: University of Michigan Press.

Boyarin, Jonathan, ed. 1993. *The Ethnography of Reading.* Berkeley: University of California Press.

Boyer, Ernest. 1987. *College: The Undergraduate Experience in America.* New York: Harper & Row.

Bracey, Gerald W. 1991. "Why Can't They Be Like We Were?" *Phi Delta Kappan* 73.2 (October): 105–17.

Bransford, John D., and M. K. Johnson. 1973. "Consideration of Some Problems of Comprehension." In *Visual Information Processing: Proceedings of the 8th Symposium on Cognition, Carnegie-Mellon University,* edited by William G. Chase, 383–438. New York: Academic Press.

Braverman, Harry. 1974. *Labor and Monopoly Capital: The Degradation of Work in the Twentieth Century.* New York: Monthly Review Press.

Bremner, Robert H., ed. 1970. *Children and Youth in America: A Documentary History. Vol. 1: 1600–1865.* Cambridge, MA: Harvard University Press.

Breton, Nicholas. 1618. "The Court and The Country." Qtd. in Dunham, William Huse, and Stanley McCrory Pargellis, eds. 1938. *Complaint and Reform in England, 1436–1714,* 468. New York: Oxford University Press.

Britton, James N. 1970. *Language and Learning.* London: Allen Lane.

Britton, James N., Tony Burgess, Nancy Martin, Alex McLeod, and Harold Rosen. 1975. *The Development of Writing Abilities (11–18).* London: Macmillan Education.

Broadbent, Donald Eric. 1958. *Perception and Communication.* London: Pergamon.

Brontë, Emily. [1846] 1961. *Wuthering Heights.* New York: Dell.

Brooke, Robert E. 1991. *Writing and Sense of Self: Identity Negotiation in Writing Workshops.* Urbana, IL: National Council of Teachers of English.

Brooks, Phyllis. 1973. "Mimesis: Grammar and the Echoing Voice," *College English* 35.3 (November): 161–68.

Brown, Ann. 1990. "Distributed Expertise in the Classroom." Paper presented at the annual convention of the American Educational Research Association (AERA). Boston. April 18.

Brown, Ann L. and Jeanne D. Day. 1983. "Macrorules for Summarizing Texts: The Development of Expertise." *Journal of Verbal Learning and Verbal Behavior* 22(1): 1–14.

Brown, Claire, and George Nano. 1989. "UAW/NUMMI: The Fremont, California Experiment." *Labor Center Reporter* no. 254 (January): 1–2. Berkeley: University of California.

Brown, John Seely. 1991a. "Research That Reinvents the Corporation." *Harvard Business Review* 69.1 (January/February): 102–11.

———. 1991b. Panel comments at the annual convention of the American Educational Research Association (AERA). April.

Brown, Rollo. 1915. *How the French Boy Learns to Write.* Cambridge, MA: Cambridge University Press.

Bruner, Jerome S. 1973. "Culture and Cognitive Growth." In *Beyond the Informa-tion Given: Studies in the Psychology of Knowing*, by Jerome S. Bruner, selected and edited by Jeremy M. Anglin, 368–93. New York: Norton.

———. 1976. "Nature and Uses of Immaturity." In *Play—Its Role in Development and Evolution*, edited by Jerome S. Bruner, Kathy Sylva, and Alison Jolly, 28–64. New York: Basic Books.

———. 1978. "Learning the Mother Tongue." *Human Nature* 1 (September): 42–49.

———. 1985. "Narrative and Paradigmatic Modes of Thought." In *Learning and Teaching the Ways of Knowing*, edited by Elliot Eisner, 97–115. Eighty-fourth Yearbook of the National Society for the Study of Education. Chicago: University of Chicago Press.

———. 1990. *Acts of Meaning*. Cambridge, MA: Harvard University Press.

Bruner, Jerome S., Jacqueline J. Goodnow, and George A. Austin. 1956. *A Study of Thinking*. New York: Wiley.

Bruner, Jerome S., Rose R. Olvér, Patricia M. Greenfield, et al. 1966. *Studies in Cognitive Growth: A Collaboration at the Center for Cognitive Studies*. New York: Wiley.

Buckley, Marilyn and Owen Boyle. 1981. "Mapping the Writing Journey." In *Teaching Writing: Essays from the Bay Area Writing Project*, edited by Gerald Camp, 184–220. Portsmouth, NH: Boynton/Cook.

Burgess, John W. 1921. Qtd. in Hofstadter, Richard. 1959. *Social Darwinism in American Thought*. Rev. ed. New York: G. Braziller.

Burke, Peter. 1986. "Strengths and Weaknesses of the History of Mentalities." *History of European Ideas* 7(5): 439–51.

Burns v. Spiker. 1921. Qtd. in Stevens, Edward. 1983. "Illiterate American and Nineteenth-Century Courts: The Meaning of Literacy." In *Literacy in Histori-cal Perspective*, edited by Daniel P. Resnick, 59–83. Washington, D.C.: Library of Congress.

Burrows, Alvina Trent. 1977. "Composition: Prospect and Retrospect." In *Read-ing and Writing Instruction in the United States: Historical Trends*, edited by H. Alan Robinson, 17–43. Urbana: Education Resources Information Clearing-house and International Reading Association.

California State Department of Education. 1985. *California Mathematics Frame-work*. Sacramento: California State Department of Education.

Callahan, Raymond E. 1962. *Education and the Cult of Efficiency: A Study of the So-cial Forces That Have Shaped the Administration of the Public Schools*. Chicago: University of Chicago Press.

Campbell, George. [1776] 1823. *The Philosophy of Rhetoric*. Boston: Charles Ivers.

Campbell, Oscar James, and Edward G. Quinn. 1966. *The Reader's Encyclopedia of Shakespeare*. New York: Crowell.

Cannell, John. 1987. *Nationally Normed Elementary Achievement Testing in Amer-ica's Public Schools: How All Fifty States Are Above Average*. Daniels, WV: Friends for Education.

Capote, Truman. 1965. *In Cold Blood*. New York: Random House.

Carpenter, Charles H. 1963. *History of American Schoolbooks*. Philadelphia: University of Pennsylvania Press.

Carroll, John. 1960. "Vectors of Prose Style." In *Style in Language*, edited by Thomas A. Sebeok, 283–92. Cambridge, MA: MIT Press.

Carroll, John Bissell, and Jeanne Sternlicht Chall, eds. 1975. *Toward a Literate Society: The Report of the Committee on Reading of the National Academy of Education.* New York: McGraw-Hill.

Case, Robbie. 1975. "Gearing the Demands of Instruction to the Developmental Capacities of the Learner." *Review of Educational Research* 45: 59–87.

———. 1985. *Intellectual Development: Birth to Adulthood.* Orlando, FL: Academic Press.

———. 1991. *The Mind's Staircase: Stages in the Development of Human Intelligence.* Hillsdale, NJ: Lawrence Erlbaum.

Cazden, Courtney B. 1995. "Visible and Invisible Pedagogies in Literacy Education." In *Discourse and Reproduction: Essays in Honor of Basil Bernstein*, edited by Paul Atkinson, Brian Davies, and Sara Delamont, 159–72. Cresskill, NJ: Hampton Press.

Chafe, Wallace L. 1982. "Integration and Involvement in Speaking, Writing, and Oral Literature." In *Spoken and Written Language: Exploring Orality and Literacy*, edited by Deborah Tannen, 35–53. Norwood, NJ: Ablex.

Channing, Edward Tyrrell. 1856. *Lectures Read to the Seniors in Harvard College.* Boston: Ticknor and Fields.

Chapman, P. 1979. *Schools as Sorters: Lewis Terman and the Intelligence Testing Movement, 1890–1930.* Unpubl. Doct. Diss. Stanford University.

Chi, Michelene T.H., Miriam Bassock, Matthew W. Lewis, and Peter Reimann, et al. 1989. "Self-Explanations: How Students Study and Use Examples in Learning to Solve Problems." *Cognitive Science* 13(2): 145–82.

Chomsky, Noam. 1957. *Syntactic Structures.* The Hague: Mouton.

———. 1965. *Aspects of the Theory of Syntax.* Cambridge, MA: MIT Press.

Christensen, Francis. 1967. *Notes Toward a New Rhetoric: Six Essays for Teachers.* New York: Harper & Row.

Christian, Barbara T. 1992. Presentation at the NCTE Summer Institute for Teachers of Literature. Myrtle Beach, South Carolina. June 8.

Cipolla, Carlo M. 1980. *Literacy and Development in the West.* Baltimore: Penguin.

Clanchy, Michael. 1979. *From Memory to Written Record: England, 1066–1307.* Cambridge, MA: Harvard University Press.

———. 1988. "Hearing and Seeing and Trusting Writing." In *Perspectives on Literacy*, edited by Eugene R. Kintgen, Barry M. Kroll, and Mike Rose, 135–58. Carbondale: Southern Illinois University Press.

Clark, Beverly Lyon, and Sonja Wiedenhaupt. 1992. "On Blocking and Unblocking Sonja: A Case Study in Two Voices." *College Composition and Communication* 43.1 (February): 55–74.

Clark, S. H. 1899. *How to Teach Reading in the Public Schools.* Chicago: Scott, Foresman.

Cleveland, Charles D. [1849] 1851. *A Compendium of English Literature, Chronologically Arranged, from Sir John Mandeville to William Cowper.* Philadelphia: E. C. and J. Biddle.

Clifford, Geraldine Joncich. 1984. "*Buch und Lesen:* Historical Perspectives on Literacy and Schooling." *Review of Educational Research* 54(4): 472–500.

Cobb, Lyman. 1844. *Cobb's Spelling Book: Being a Just Standard for Pronouncing the English Language.* Ithaca, NY: Andrus, Woodruff & Gauntlett.

Coe, Michael D. 1992. *Breaking the Maya Code.* New York: Thames and Hudson.

Cohen, Patricia Kline. 1982. *A Calculating People: The Spread of Numeracy in Early America.* Chicago: University of Chicago Press.

Cohen, Ralph. 1984. "The Autobiography of a Critical Problem." Lecture presented at annual meeting of the Midwest Modern Language Association. Bloomington, Indiana. November 4.

Cole, Nancy. 1990. "Conceptions of Educational Achievement." *Educational Researcher* 19.3 (April): 2–19.

Coley, Richard J. 1995. *Dreams Deferred: High School Dropouts in the United States.* Princeton, NJ: Educational Testing Service.

Collins, Allan M., John Seely Brown, and Susan E. Newman. 1989. "Cognitive Apprenticeship: Teaching the Craft of Reading, Writing, and Mathematics." In *Cognition and Instruction: Issues and Agendas,* edited by Lauren B. Resnick. Hillsdale, NJ: Lawrence Erlbaum.

Collins, Allan M., and M. Ross Quillian. 1969. "Retrieval Time from Semantic Memory." *Journal of Verbal Learning and Verbal Behavior* 18.2 (April): 240–47.

Commission on English. 1965. *Freedom and Discipline in the Teaching of English.* New York: College Entrance Examination Board.

Committee of Ten of the National Education Association (NEA). 1894. *Report of the Committee of Ten on Secondary School Studies, with the Reports of the Conferences Arranged by the Committee.* New York: American Book Company.

Committee on the National Interest and Teaching of English. 1961. *A Report on the Status of the Profession.* Urbana, IL: National Council of Teachers of English.

Conant, James B. 1961. *Slums and Suburbs: A Commentary on Schools in Metropolitan Areas.* New York: New American Library.

The Confessions of Saint Augustine. 1956. Translated by Edward B. Pusey. New York: Pocket Books.

Connors, Robert J. 1987. "Personal Writing Assignments." *College Composition and Communication* 38.2 (May): 166–83.

Copperman, Paul. 1978. *The Literacy Hoax: The Decline of Reading, Writing, and Learning in the Public Schools and What We Can Do about It.* New York: Morrow.

Corbett, Edward P.J. 1983. "Literature and Composition: Allies or Rivals in the Classroom?" In *Composition and Literature: Bridging the Gap,* edited by Winifred Bryan Horner, 168–84. Chicago: University of Chicago Press.

Corson, Hiram. [1896] 1908. *The Voice and Spiritual Education.* New York: Macmillan. [Rpt. of the 1896 edition.]

Cory, William. 1897. *Extracts from the Letters and Journals of William Cory.* Edited by F. W. Cornish. Oxford: Oxford University Press.

Cox, Brian. 1988. *Cox on Cox: An English Curriculum for the 1990s.* London: Hoder and Stoughton.

Crawford, James. 1989. *Bilingual Education: History, Politics, Theory, and Practice.* Trenton: Crane.

Cremin, Lawrence A. 1961. *The Transformation of the School: Progressivism in American Education*. New York: Vintage.

Cressy, David. 1980. *Literacy and the Social Order: Reading and Writing in Tudor and Stuart England*. London: Cambridge University Press.

Cronbach, Lee J. 1990. *Essentials of Psychological Testing*. 5th ed. New York: Harper & Row.

Crowley, Sharon. 1990. *The Methodical Memory: Invention in Current-Traditional Rhetoric*. Carbondale: Southern Illinois University Press.

Cuban, Larry. 1983. "Effective Schools: A Friendly but Cautionary Note." *Phi Delta Kappan* 64(10): 695–96.

———. 1984. *How Teachers Taught: Constancy and Change in American Classrooms, 1800–1980*. New York: Longman.

Cubberly, Ellwood Patterson. 1916. *Public School Administration: A Statement of the Fundamental Principles Underlying the Organization and Administration of Public Education*. Boston: Houghton-Mifflin.

———. 1924. "Public School Administration." In *Twenty-Five Years of American Education: Collected Essays*, edited by Isaac Leon Kandel. New York: Macmillan.

Culler, Jonathan. 1975. *Structuralist Poetics: Structuralism, Linguistics, and the Study of Literature*. Ithaca, NY: Cornell University Press.

Damon, William. 1990. "Reconciling the Literacies of Generations." *Daedalus* 119.2 (Spring): 33–53.

Dandridge, Sarah, John Harter, Rob Kessler, and Miles Myers. 1979. *Independent Study and Writing*. Berkeley: Bay Area Writing Project, University of California.

D'Angelo, Frank J. 1975. *A Conceptual Theory of Rhetoric*. Cambridge, MA: Winthrop.

Darrah, C. N. 1990. "An Ethnographic Approach to Workplace Skills." Unpubl. mss. Qtd. in Hull, Glynda. 1993. "Hearing Other Voices: A Critical Assessment of Popular Views on Literacy and Work." *Harvard Educational Review* 63.1 (Spring): 20–49.

Davis, Natalie Zemon. 1975. "Printing and the People." In *Society and Culture in Early Modern France: Eight Essays*. Stanford, CA: Stanford University Press.

De Bono, Edward. 1968. *New Think: The Use of Lateral Thinking in the Generation of New Ideas*. New York: Basic Books.

DeJesus, Tony. 1989. Seminar comments at the Institute of Industrial Relations. University of California–Berkeley. June.

de Jongh, Elena M. 1992. *An Introduction to Court Interpreting: Theory and Practice*. Lanham, MD: University Press of America.

Delain, Marsha, P. David Pearson, and Richard C. Anderson. 1985. "Reading Comprehension and Creativity in Black Language Use: You Stand to Gain by Playing the Language Game." *American Educational Research Journal* 22(2): 155–73.

Delpit, Lisa. 1986. "Skills and Other Dilemmas of a Progressive Black Educator." *Harvard Educational Review* 56: 280–88.

———. 1995. *Other People's Children*. New York: The New Press.

Dennis, John. 1939. *The Critical Works*. Vol. 1. Edited by Edward Niles Hooker. Baltimore: Johns Hopkins University Press.

Dennison, George. 1969. *The Lives of Children: The Story of the First Street School.* New York: Vintage.

Dewey, John. 1904. Qtd. in Tyack, David B. 1974. *The One Best System: A History of American Urban Education.* Cambridge, MA: Harvard University Press.

———. 1931. *The Way Out of Educational Confusion.* Cambridge, MA: Harvard University Press.

Didion, Joan. 1979. *The White Album.* New York: Simon and Schuster.

Dixon, John. 1975. *Growth Through English: Set in the Perspective of the '70s.* 3rd ed. London: Oxford University Press.

———. 1994. "Categories to Frame an English Curriculum." *English Education* 28.1 (Spring): 3–8.

Doddridge, Philip. 1748. *Rise and Progress of Religion in the Soul.* London: N.p.

Donaldson, Margaret C. 1979. *Children's Minds.* New York: Norton.

Donaldson, Margaret C., and J. McGarrigle. 1974. "Some Clues to the Nature of Semantic Development." *Journal of Child Language* 1: 185–94.

Douglas, Wallace. 1976. "Rhetoric for the Meritocracy: The Creation of Composition at Harvard." In *English in America: A Radical View of the Profession,* edited by Richard Ohmann, 97–132. New York: Oxford University Press.

Dreyfus, Stuart, Herbert Dreyfus, Eleanor Rosch, and William Cole. 1983. "A Model of Cognitive Skill Acquisition." Paper presented at the Cognitive Science Seminar. University of California–Berkeley.

Dunlap, G. D., and H. H. Shufeldt. 1969. *Dutton's Navigation and Piloting.* 12th ed. Annapolis, MD: United States Naval Institute.

Dyson, Anne Haas. 1993. *Social Worlds of Children Learning to Write in an Urban Primary School.* New York: Teachers College Press.

Eagleton, Terry. 1983. *Literary Theory: An Introduction.* Minneapolis: University of Minnesota Press.

Ede, Lisa, and Andrea Lunsford. 1990. *Singular Texts/Plural Authors: Perspectives on Collaborative Writing.* Carbondale: Southern Illinois University Press.

Edelman, Gerald M. 1992. *Bright Air, Brilliant Fire: On the Matter of the Mind.* New York: Basic Books.

Ehrlich, Dorothy M., Executive Director, ACLU Foundation of Northern California. 1994. Letter to William Dawson, Acting Superintendent, California State Department of Education. February 23.

Eisenstein, Elizabeth L. 1979. *The Printing Press as an Agent of Change: Communications and Cultural Transformations in Early Modern Europe.* 2 Vols. New York: Cambridge University Press.

———. 1985. "On the Printing Press as an Agent of Change." In *Literacy, Language, and Learning: The Nature and Consequences of Reading and Writing,* edited by David R. Olson, Angela Hildyard, and Nancy Torrance, 19–33. New York: Cambridge University Press.

Eisner, Elliot W. 1982. *Cognition and Curriculum: A Basis for Deciding What to Teach.* New York: Longman.

Elbow, Peter. 1986. *Embracing Contraries: Explorations in Learning and Teaching.* New York: Oxford University Press.

———. 1990. *What Is English?* New York: Modern Language Association of America; Urbana, IL: National Council of Teachers of English.

Ellul, Jacques. 1964. *The Technological Society.* New York: Vintage.

Emig, Janet. 1971. *The Composing Processes of Twelfth Graders.* Urbana, IL: National Council of Teachers of English.

Empson, William. 1930. *Seven Types of Ambiguity.* New York: New Directions.

Engelmann, Siegfried vs. State Board of Education, et al. 1989. Petition for Writ of Mandate (July 21, 1989); Memorandum of Points and Authorities in Opposition to Petition for Writ (October 6, 1989).

Engestrom, Yrjö. 1987. *Learning by Expanding.* Helsinki: Orienta-Konsulti Oy.

———. 1993. "Developmental Studies of Work as a Test Bench of Activity Theory: The Case of Primary Care Medical Practice." In *Understanding Practice: Perspectives on Activity and Context,* edited by Seth Chaiklin and Jean Lave, 64–103. New York: Cambridge University Press.

Epstein, Arnold Leonard. 1953. *The Administration of Justice and the Urban African: A Study of Urban Native Courts in Northern Rhodesia.* Colonial Research Studies: 7. London: H. M. Stationery Office.

———. 1954. *Juridical Techniques and the Judicial Process: A Study in African Customary Law.* The Rhodes-Livingstone Papers 23. Manchester: Manchester University Press and Rhodes-Livingstone Institute.

Erickson, Frederick. 1986. "Qualitative Methods in Research on Teaching." In *Handbook of Research on Teaching,* 3rd ed., edited by Merlin C. Wittrock, 119–61. New York: Macmillan.

Erikson, Erik H. 1968. *Identity, Youth, and Crisis.* New York: Norton.

Fahnestock, Jeanne. 1986. "Accommodating Science: The Rhetorical Life of Scientific Facts." *Written Communication* 3(3): 275–96.

Faigley, Lester. 1992. *Fragments of Rationality: Postmodernity and the Subject of Composition.* Pittsburgh: University of Pittsburgh Press.

Fallers, Lloyd A. 1969. *Law Without Precedent: Legal Ideas in Action in the Courts of Colonial Busoga.* Chicago: University of Chicago Press.

Farr, Roger, Leo Fay, and Harold H. Negley. 1978. *Then and Now: Reading Achievement in Indiana, 1944–1945 and 1976.* Bloomington: Indiana University School of Education.

Farrell, Thomas J. 1979. "Male and Female Modes of Discourse." *College English* 40.8 (April): 909–21.

Faulkner, William. 1938. *The Unvanquished.* New York: Random House.

Felton, Rebecca L. 1919. *Country Life in Georgia in the Days of My Youth.* 2nd ed. Atlanta: Index Printing.

Ferrerio, Emilia. 1984. "The Underlying Logic of Literacy Development." In *Awakening to Literacy: The University of Victoria Symposium on Children's Response to a Literate Environment: Literacy before Schooling,* edited by Hillel Goelman, Antoinette A. Oberg, and Frank Smith, 154–73. Portsmouth, NH: Heinemann.

Fillmore, Charles. 1977. "Topics in Lexical Semantics." In *Current Issues in Linguistic Theory,* edited by Roger W. Cole, 76–138. Bloomington: Indiana University Press.

———. 1982. "Frame Semantics." In *Linguistics in the Morning Calm: Selected Papers from SICOL-1981,* edited by the Linguistic Society of Korea, 111–38. Seoul: Hanshin.

Finkelstein, Barbara Joan. 1970. "Governing the Young: Teacher Behavior in American Primary Schools, 1820–1880." Unpublished Educ. Doct. Diss. Teachers College, Columbia University.

Fish, Stanley. 1994. *There's No Such Thing as Free Speech, and It's a Good Thing, Too.* New York: Oxford University Press.

Fisher, Donald L. 1978. *Functional Literacy and the Schools.* Washington, D.C.: National Institute of Education.

Fishlow, Albert. 1966. "Levels of Nineteenth-Century American Investment in Education." *Journal of Economic History* 26(4): 418–36.

Flower, Linda S., and John R. Hayes. 1980. "The Dynamics of the Composing Process: Making Plans and Juggling Constraints." In *Cognitive Processes in Writing,* edited by Lee W. Gregg and Erwin R. Steinberg, 31–50. Hillsdale, NJ: Lawrence Erlbaum.

———. 1981. "A Cognitive Process Theory of Writing." *College Composition and Communication* 32.4 (February): 365–87.

Fodor, Jerry A. 1983. *The Modularity of Mind: An Essay on Faculty Psychology.* Cambridge, MA: MIT Press.

Folger, John K., and Charles B. Nam. 1967. *The Education of the American Population.* Washington, D.C.: U.S. Government Printing Office.

Ford Foundation. 1959. *The Basic Issues in the Teaching of English.* New York: Ford Foundation. Rpt. in Shugrue, Michael F. 1968. *English in a Decade of Change.* New York: Pegasus.

Foucault, Michel. 1970. *The Order of Things: An Archaeology of the Human Sciences.* New York: Vintage.

———. 1972. *The Archaeology of Knowledge.* Translated by A. M. Sheridan Smith. New York: Pantheon.

Fox, Helen. 1994. *Listening to the World: Cultural Issues in Academic Writing.* Urbana, IL: National Council of Teachers of English.

Franklin, Bruce. 1970. "The Teaching of Literature in the Highest Academies of the Empire." *College English* 31.6 (March): 548–57.

Freedman, Diane P. 1992. *An Alchemy of Genres: Cross-Genre Writing by American Feminist Poet-Critics.* Charlottesville, VA: University Press of Virginia.

Freedman, Sarah Warshauer. 1994. *Exchanging Writing, Exchanging Cultures: Lessons in School Reform from the United States and Great Britain.* Urbana, IL: National Council of Teachers of English; New York: Harvard University Press.

French, James. 1840–1842. *School Writing Book.* Boston, MA: James French.

Fries, Charles Carpenter. 1940. *American English Grammar.* New York: Appleton-Century.

Frye, Northrop. 1957. *Anatomy of Criticism: Four Essays.* Princeton, NJ: Princeton University Press.

———. 1982. *The Great Code: The Bible and Literature.* New York: Harvest/Harcourt Brace Jovanovich.

Furet, François, and Jacques Ozouf. 1982. *Reading and Writing: Literacy in France from Calvin to Jules Ferry.* Cambridge, MA: Cambridge University Press.

Fussell, Paul. 1975. *The Great War and Modern Memory.* New York: Oxford University Press.

Gadway, Charles J., and Harlalee Allen Wilson. 1976. *Functional Literacy: Basic Reading Performance.* Denver, CO: National Assessment of Educational Progress.

Gardner, Howard. 1980. *Artful Scribbles: The Significance of Children's Drawings.* New York: Basic Books.

———. 1982. *Art, Mind, and Brain: A Cognitive Approach to Creativity.* New York: Basic Books.

———. 1983. *Frames of Mind: The Theory of Multiple Intelligences.* New York: Basic Books.

Gardner, Martin. 1982. *Logic Machines and Diagrams.* 2nd ed. Chicago: University of Chicago Press.

Gates, Henry Louis, Jr. 1984. *Black Literature and Literary Theory.* New York: Methuen.

Gazzaniga, Michael S. 1967. "The Split Brain in Man." *Scientific American* 217 (August): 24–29.

Gaur, A. 1987. *A History of Writing.* London: British Library.

Gebhardt, Richard. 1993. "Forms of Scholarly Publications: Some Trends and Some Risks." *FOCUS* 8.2 (Winter): 93–96.

Geertz, Clifford. 1983. *Local Knowledge: Further Essays in Interpretive Anthropology.* New York: Basic Books.

Gelb, Ignace Jay. 1952. *A Study of Writing: The Foundations of Grammatology.* Chicago: University of Chicago Press.

Gelman, Rochel, and C. R. Gallistel. 1978. *The Child's Understanding of Number.* Cambridge, MA: Harvard University Press.

"The Gender Factor in Math." 1980. *Time* 116.24 (December 15): 57.

Gibbs, John C. 1977. "Kohlberg's Stages of Moral Judgment: A Constructive Critique." *Harvard Educational Review* 47.1 (February): 43–61.

Gibson, Walker W. 1950. "Authors, Speakers, Readers, and Mock Readers." *College English* 11.5 (February): 265–69.

———. 1966. *Tough, Sweet, and Stuffy: An Essay on Modern American Prose Styles.* Bloomington: Indiana University Press.

———, ed. 1962. *The Limits of Language.* Clinton, MA: Colonial Press.

Gilbert, G. Nigel, and Michael Mulkay. 1984. *Opening Pandora's Box: A Sociological Analysis of Scientists' Discourse.* New York: Cambridge University Press.

Gilyard, Keith. 1991. *Voices of the Self: A Study of Language Competence.* Detroit: Wayne State University Press.

Giroux, Henry A. 1983. *Theory and Resistance in Education: A Pedagogy for the Opposition.* South Hadley, MA: Bergin & Garvey.

Gladwin, Thomas. 1970. *East Is a Big Bird: Navigation and Logic on the Puluwat Atoll.* Cambridge, MA: Harvard University Press.

Gombrich, Ernst Hans. 1960. *Art and Illusion: A Study in the Psychology of Pictorial Representation.* New York: Pantheon.

Gonzalez, Roseann Dueñas. 1993. "Demographics of Change." Speech given at the "Reclaiming the Dream" Conference of the National Council of Teachers of English. Washington, D.C. August.

Goodlad, John I. 1984. *A Place Called School: Prospects for the Future.* New York: McGraw-Hill.

Goodman, Kenneth S. 1993. Comments at the end of a speech given by Lauren Resnick. National Conference on Research in English meeting. Pittsburgh.

Goodman, Kenneth S., Lois Bridges Bird, and Yetta M. Goodman, eds. 1991. *The Whole Language Catalog*. Santa Rosa, CA: American School Publishers.

Goodman, Kenneth S., et al. 1988. *Report Card on Basal Readers*. Katonah, NY: Richard C. Owen.

Goodman, Nelson. 1968. *Languages of Art: An Approach to a Theory of Symbols*. Indianapolis: Bobbs-Merrill.

———. 1978. *Ways of Worldmaking*. Indianapolis: Hackett.

Goody, Jack. 1986. *The Logic of Writing and the Organization of Society*. New York: Cambridge University Press.

———, ed. 1968. *Literacy in Traditional Societies*. New York: Cambridge University Press.

Goody, Jack, and Ian P. Watt. 1968. "The Consequences of Literacy." In *Literacy in Traditional Societies*, edited by Jack Goody, 27–68. New York: Cambridge University Press.

Gould, James L., and Peter Marler. 1987. "Learning by Instinct." *Scientific American* 256(1): 74–85.

Gould, Stephen Jay. 1983. *Hen's Teeth and Horse's Toes*. New York: Norton.

Gowan, S. 1990. "'Yes on a Different Prose': A Critical Ethnography of Workplace Literacy Programs." Unpubl. Doct. Diss. Georgia State University.

Grace, Gerald. 1995. "Theorizing Social Relations within Urban Schooling: A Sociohistorical Analysis." In *Discourse and Reproduction: Essays in Honor of Basil Bernstein*, edited by Paul Atkinson, Brian Davies, and Sara Delamont, 209–28. Cresskill, NJ: Hampton Press.

Graff, Gerald. 1987. *Professing Literature: An Institutional History*. Chicago: University of Chicago Press.

———. 1992. *Beyond the Culture Wars: How Teaching the Conflicts Can Revitalize American Education*. New York: Norton.

Graff, Harvey J. 1979. *The Literacy Myth: Literacy and Social Structure in a Nineteenth-Century City*. New York: Academic Press.

———. 1987. *The Legacies of Literacy: Continuities and Contradictions in Western Culture and Society*. Bloomington: Indiana University Press.

Grant, W. V., and L. J. Eiden. 1982. *Digest of Education Statistics*. Washington, D.C.: U.S. Government Printing Office.

Graves, Donald H. 1975. "An Examination of the Writing Processes of Seven-Year-Old Children." *Research in the Teaching of English* 9.3 (Winter): 227–241.

Graves, Donald H., and Bonnie S. Sunstein, eds. 1992. *Portfolio Portraits*. Portmouth, NH: Heinemann.

Greenblatt, Stephen J. 1980. *Renaissance Self-Fashioning: From More to Shakespeare*. Chicago: University of Chicago Press.

Greene, Maxine. 1986. "Toward Possibility: Expanding the Range of Literacy." *English Education* 18.4 (December): 231–43.

Greenfield, Norman, Gary Thomason, and DOES 2,000–3,000 (Petitioner) v. Los Angeles Unified School District and DOES 2,000–3,000 (Respondents and Real Party in Interest). 1994. Case no. BS-028-375. Superior Court of the State of California for the County of Los Angeles. Judge Robert H. O'Brien. May 10.

Greenfield, Patricia M. 1972. "Oral or Written Language: The Consequences for Cognitive Development in Africa, the U.S., and England." *Language and Speech* 15: 169–78.

Greenfield, Patricia M., and Jerome S. Bruner. 1973. "Culture and Cognitive Growth." In *Beyond the Information Given: Studies in the Psychology of Knowing*, selected and edited by Jeremy M. Anglin, 368–93. New York: Norton.

Griffin, P., and Michael Cole. 1984. "Current Activity for the Future: The Zo-Ped." In *Children's Learning in the "Zone of Proximal Development."* New Directions for Child Development, no. 23, edited by Barbara M. Rogoff and James V. Wertsch. San Francisco: Jossey-Bass.

Gudschinsky, Sarah. 1979. "Some Misperceptions about Prereading." *Notes on Literacy. Selected Articles. Issues 1–19.* Dallas: Summer Institute of Linguistics.

Haley, Margaret. 1904. Qtd. in Tyack, David B. 1974. *The One Best System: A History of American Urban Education.* Cambridge, MA: Harvard University Press.

Hall, D. B. 1983. "The Uses of Literacy in New England, 1600–1850." In *Printing and Society in Early America*, edited by William Leonard Joyce, et al. Worcester, MA: American Antiquarian Society.

Hall, Edward T. 1977. *Beyond Culture.* New York: Anchor.

Halliday, M.A.K. 1978. *Language as Social Semiotic: The Social Interpretation of Language and Meaning.* Baltimore: University Park Press.

Halliday, M.A.K., and J. R. Martin. 1993. *Writing Science: Literacy and Discursive Power.* Pittsburgh: University of Pittsburgh Press.

Halloran, S. Michael. 1990. "From Rhetoric to Composition: The Teaching of Writing in America to 1900." In *A Short History of Writing Instruction: From Ancient Greece to Twentieth-Century America*, edited by James J. Murphy, 151–82. Davis, CA: Hermagoras.

Hammersley, Martyn, and Paul Atkinson. 1983. *Ethnography: Principles in Practice.* London: Tavistock.

Harding, D. W. 1937. "The Role of the Onlooker." *Scrutiny* 6: 247–58.

Harre, Rom. 1984. *Personal Being: A Theory for Individual Psychology.* Cambridge, MA: Harvard University Press.

Harris, Joseph. 1989. "The Idea of Community in the Study of Writing." *College Composition and Communication* 40.1 (February): 11–22.

Harris, Louis, and Associates, Inc. 1970. *Survival Literacy: Conducted for the National Reading Council.* New York: Louis Harris and Associates.

———. 1971. *The 1971 National Reading Difficulty Index: A Study of Functional Reading Ability in the United States for the National Reading Center.* Washington, D.C.: National Reading Center.

Harris, William T., and Duane Dorty. 1874. *A Statement of the Theory of Education in The United States as Approved by Many Leading Educators.* Washington, D.C.: U.S. Government Printing Office.

Harrison, Anna J. 1984. "Common Elements and Interconnections." *Science* 224 (June): 939–42.

Harste, Jerome C., Virginia A. Woodward, and Carolyn L. Burke. 1984. *Language Stories and Literacy Lessons.* Portsmouth, NH: Heinemann Educational Books.

Hatfield, W. Wilbur. 1935. *An Experience Curriculum in English: A Report of the Curriculum Committee of the National Council of Teachers of English*. New York: Appleton-Century.

Havelock, Eric Alfred. 1963. *Preface to Plato*. Cambridge, MA: Harvard University Press.

———. 1978. *The Greek Concept of Justice: From Its Shadow in Homer to Its Substance in Plato*. Cambridge, MA: Harvard University Press.

Hawkes, Terence. 1977. *Structuralism and Semiotics*. Berkeley: University of California Press.

Healy, Jane M. 1990. *Endangered Minds: Why Our Children Don't Think—and What We Can Do About It*. New York: Simon and Schuster.

Heath, Shirley Brice. 1983. *Ways with Words: Language, Life, and Work in Communities and Classrooms*. New York: Cambridge University Press.

———. 1986a. "Critical Factors in Literacy Development." In *Literacy, Society, and Schooling: A Reader*, edited by S. de Castell, A. Luke, and K. Egan, 209–29. Cambridgeshire, England: Cambridge University Press.

———. 1986b. "Separating 'Things of the Imagination' from Life: Learning to Read and Write." In *Emergent Literacy: Writing and Reading*, edited by William H. Teale and Elizabeth Sulzby, 156–72. Norwood, NJ: Ablex.

———. 1986c. "Sociocultural Contexts of Language Development." In *Beyond Language: Social and Cultural Factors in Schooling Language Minority Students*, edited by California Office of Bilingual Bicultural Education, 143–86. Los Angeles: California State University Evaluation Dissemination and Assessment Center.

———. 1989. "Oral and Literate Traditions among Black Americans Living in Poverty." *American Psychologist* 44.2 (February): 367–73.

———. 1990. "The Fourth Vision: Literate Language at Work." In *The Right to Literacy*, edited by Andrea A. Lunsford, Helene Moglen, and James Slevin, 288–306. New York: Modern Language Association of America.

Hemingway, Ernest. 1925. "The Big Two-Hearted River." In *In Our Time: Stories*. New York: Scribner.

———. 1929. *A Farewell to Arms*. New York: Grosset & Dunlap.

Herndon, James. 1969. *The Way It Spozed To Be*. New York: Bantam.

Hildyard, Angela, and David R. Olson. 1982. "On the Comprehension and Memory of Oral versus Written Discourse." In *Spoken and Written Language: Exploring Orality and Literacy*, edited by Deborah Tannen, 19–33. Norwood, NJ: Ablex.

Hillocks, George, Jr. 1986. *Research on Written Composition: New Directions for Teaching*. New York: National Conference on Research in English; Urbana, IL: ERIC Clearinghouse on Reading and Communication Skills.

Hirsch, E. D., Jr. 1977. *The Philosophy of Composition*. Chicago: University of Chicago Press.

———. 1987. *Cultural Literacy: What Every American Needs to Know*. Boston: Houghton-Mifflin.

Hodges, R. E. 1977. "In Adam's Fall: A Brief History of Spelling Instruction in the United States." In *Reading and Writing Instruction in the United States: Historical Trends*, edited by H. Alan Robinson, 1–16. Urbana, IL: Educational Resources Information Center; Newark, DE: International Reading Association.

Hodgkinson, Harold L. 1992. *A Demographic Look at Tomorrow.* Washington, D.C.: Center for Demographic Policy.

———. 1995. "A True Nation of the World." *Education Week* 14.17 (January 18): 32.

Hofstadter, Richard. 1959. *Social Darwinism in American Thought.* Rev. ed. New York: G. Braziller.

Honig, Bill. 1995. *How Should We Teach Our Children to Read?* San Francisco: Bill Honig. [Monograph distributed by the author.]

Horowitz, J. 1976. "The Historical Foundations of Modern Contract Law." *Harvard Law Review* 87. Rpt. in Wythe, Holt, ed. 1976. *Essays in Nineteenth-Century American Legal History.* Westport, CT: Greenwood.

Hosic, James Fleming, comp. 1917. *Report on the Reorganization of English in Secondary Schools* [Report of the Joint Committee on English]. Bureau of Education Bulletin no. 2. Washington, D.C.: U.S. Government Printing Office.

House, Ernest. 1994. "Policy and Productivity in Higher Education." *Educational Researcher* 23.5 (June/July): 27–32.

Huber, Carole H. 1987. Review of *Teaching Writing: Pedagogy, Gender, and Equity,* edited by Cynthia Caywood and Gillian R. Overing. *College, Composition and Communication* 28.3 (October): 355–57.

Huey, Edmund Burke. [1908] 1968. *The Psychology and Pedagogy of Reading with a Review of the History of Reading and Writing and of Methods, Texts, and Hygiene in Reading.* New York: Macmillan.

Hull, Glynda. 1993. "Hearing Other Voices: A Critical Assessment of Popular Views on Literacy and Work." *Harvard Educational Review* 63.1 (Spring): 20-49.

Hundert, E. J. 1987. "Enlightenment and the Decay of Common Sense." In *Common Sense: The Foundations of Social Science,* edited by Fritz van Holthoon and David R. Olson. Lanham: University Press of America.

Hunt, Kellogg W. 1965. *Grammatical Structures Written at Three Grade Levels.* Champaign, IL: National Council of Teachers of English.

Hutchins, Edwin. 1980. *Culture and Inference: A Trobriand Case Study.* Cambridge, MA: Harvard University Press.

———. 1983. "Understanding Micronesian Navigation." In *Mental Models,* edited by Dedre Gentner and Albert L. Stevens. Hillsdale, NJ: Lawrence Erlbaum.

Hymes, Dell. 1974. *Foundations in Sociolinguistics: An Ethnographic Approach.* Philadelphia: University of Pennsylvania Press.

Innis, Harold A. 1972. *Empire and Communications.* Toronto: University of Toronto Press.

Iran-Nejad, Asghar. 1990. "Active and Dynamic Self-Regulation of Learning Processes." *Review of Educational Research* 60(4): 573–602.

Iran-Nejad, Asghar, Wilbert J. McKeachie, and David C. Berliner. 1990. "The Multisource Nature of Learning: An Introduction." *Review of Educational Research* 60(4) (Winter): 509–15.

Ishikawa, Kaory. 1972. *Guide to Quality Control.* Tokyo: Asian Productivity Association.

Jackendoff, Ray. 1994. *Patterns in the Mind: Language and Human Nature.* New York: Basic Books.

Jackson, Jim. 1989. Seminar comments at the Institute of Industrial Relations. University of California–Berkeley. June.

Jacoby, Russell. 1994. *Dogmatic Wisdom: How the Culture Wars Direct Education and Distract America.* New York: Doubleday.

Jakobson, Roman, and Morris Halle. 1956. *Fundamentals of Language.* The Hague: Mouton.

Jenkins, John. [1813] 1823. *The Art of Writing, Reduced to a Plain and Easy System.* In 7 books. Elizabethtown, NJ: J. & E. Sanderson. [Rpt. of the 1813 edition.]

Johns, C.H.W. 1904. *Babylonian and Assyrian Laws, Contracts, and Letters.* Edinburgh: T. & T. Clark.

Johnson, Mark. 1987. *The Body in the Mind: The Bodily Basis of Meaning, Imagination, and Reason.* Chicago: University of Chicago Press.

Johnson, Scott, and Ruth Thomas. In progress. "Technology Education and the Cognitive Revolution." Paper prepared for the National Center for Research in Vocational Education and Technical Education. University of California–Berkeley.

Johnson v. The State [Texas], 21 Texas Court of Appeals. 1886. Qtd. in Stevens, Edward. 1983. "Illiterate Americans and Nineteenth-Century Courts: The Meaning of Literacy." In *Literacy in Historical Perspective,* edited by Daniel P. Resnick, 59–83. Washington, D.C.: Library of Congress.

Joos, Martin. 1962. "The Five Clocks." *International Journal of American Linguistics* 28.2 (April): 1–62.

Joyce, James. 1939. *Finnegans Wake.* London: Faber and Faber; New York: Viking.

Joyce, William Leonard, et al., eds. 1983. *Printing and Society in Early America.* Worcester, MA: American Antiquarian Society.

Kaestle, Carl F. 1985. "The History of Literacy and the History of Readers." *Review of Research in Education* 12: 11–53.

Kaestle, Carl F., Helen Damon-Moore, Lawrence Stedman, Katherine Tinsley, and William Vance Trollinger, Jr. 1991. *Literacy in the United States: Readers and Reading Since 1880.* New Haven: Yale University Press.

Kaestle, Carl F., and Eric Foner. 1983. *Pillars of the Republic: Common Schools and American Society, 1780–1860.* New York: Hill and Wang.

Kahneman, Daniel, and Amos Tversky. 1973. "On the Psychology of Prediction." *Psychological Review* 80(4): 237–51.

Kantor, Kenneth. 1975. "Creative Expression in the English Curriculum: An Historical Perspective." *Research in the Teaching of English* 9.1 (Spring): 5–29.

Katz, Michael B. 1968. *The Irony of Early School Reform: Educational Innovation in Mid-Nineteenth Century Massachusetts.* Cambridge, MA: Harvard University Press.

Keller, Helen. 1954. *The Story of My Life.* New York: Doubleday.

Kelly, Louis G. 1969. *25 Centuries of Language Teaching: An Inquiry into the Science, Art, and Development of Language Teaching Methodology, 500 B.C.—1969.* Rowley, MA: Newbury House.

Kempe, William. 1588. *The Education of Children in Learning: Declared by the Dignitie, Utilitie, and Method Thereof.* London: T. Orwin.

Kermode, Frank. 1979. *The Genesis of Secrecy: On the Interpretation of Narrative.* Cambridge, MA: Harvard University Press.

Kilborn, Peter. 1995. "Up from Welfare: It's Harder and Harder." *New York Times* (April 16): Sec. 4, 1, 4.

Kingsley, C. D., ed. 1918. *The Cardinal Principles of Secondary Education: A Report of the Commission on the Reorganization of Secondary Education* appointed by National Education Association. Bulletin no. 35. Washington, D.C.: Department of Interior, Bureau of Education, Government Printing Office.

Kinneavy, James L. 1971. *A Theory of Discourse: The Aims of Discourse.* Englewood Cliffs, NJ: Prentice-Hall.

Kirsch, Irwin S., and Ann Jungeblut. 1986. *Literacy: Profiles of America's Young Adults.* Princeton, NJ: Educational Testing Service.

Kirsch, Irwin S., et al. 1993. *Adult Literacy in America: A First Look at the Results of the National Adult Literacy Survey.* Washington, D.C.: Office of Educational Research and Improvement, U.S. Department of Education.

Knoblauch, C. H. 1990. "Literacy and the Politics of Education." In *The Right to Literacy,* edited by Andrea A. Lunsford, Helene Moglen, and James Slevin, 74–80. New York: Modern Language Association of America.

Krashen, Stephen. 1993. *The Power of Reading: Insights from the Research.* Englewood, CO: Libraries Unlimited.

Krug, Edward A. 1961. *Charles W. Eliot and Popular Education.* New York: Teachers' College Press, Columbia University.

Kuhn, Thomas S. 1970. *The Structure of Scientific Revolutions.* 2nd ed. Chicago: University of Chicago Press.

Labov, William. 1972a. *Language in the Inner City: Studies in the Black English Vernacular.* Philadelphia: University of Pennsylvania Press.

———. 1972b. "The Logic of Non-Standard English." In *Language and Social Context: Selected Readings,* edited by Pier Paolo Giglioli, 179–215. Harmondsworth, England: Penguin.

———. 1972c. "Negative Attraction and Negative Control in English Grammar." *Language* 48: 773–818.

Lafleur, Laurence J., trans. 1951. *Meditations on First Philosophy,* by René Descartes [1641]. New York: Library on Liberal Arts, Liberal Arts Press.

Lakoff, George. 1987. *Women, Fire, and Dangerous Things: What Categories Reveal about the Mind.* Chicago: University of Chicago Press.

Lakoff, George, and Mark Johnson. 1980. *Metaphors We Live By.* Chicago: University of Chicago Press.

Lakoff, Robin T. 1982. "Some of My Favorite Writers Are Literate: The Mingling of Oral and Literate Strategies in Written Communication." In *Spoken and Written Language: Exploring Orality and Literacy,* edited by Deborah Tannen, 239–60. Norwood, NJ: Ablex.

———. 1990. *Talking Power: The Politics of Language in Our Lives.* New York: Basic Books.

Langer, Judith A. 1989. *The Process of Understanding Literature.* Albany: National Research Center on Literature Teaching and Learning, State University of New York.

———. 1992. "Rethinking Literature Instruction." In *Literature Instruction: A Focus on Student Response*, edited by Judith A. Langer, 35–53. Urbana, IL: National Council of Teachers of English.

———. 1994. *A Response-Based Approach to Reading Literature*. Albany: National Research Center on Literature Teaching and Learning, State University of New York.

Langer, Judith A., and Arthur N. Applebee. 1987. *How Writing Shapes Thinking: A Study of Teaching and Learning*. Urbana, IL: National Council of Teachers of English.

Lanham, Richard A. 1974. *Style: An Anti-Textbook*. New Haven: Yale University Press.

———. 1976. *The Motives for Eloquence: Literary Rhetoric in the Renaissance*. New Haven: Yale University Press.

———. 1983. "One, Two, Three." In *Composition and Literature: Bridging the Gap*, edited by Winifred Bryan Horner, 14–29. Chicago: University of Chicago Press.

Laqueur, Thomas. 1976. "The Cultural Origins of Popular Literacy in England, 1500–1850." *Oxford Review of Education* 2: 255–75.

Lasch, Christopher. 1984. *The Minimal Self: Psychic Survival in Troubled Times*. New York: Norton.

Lashley, K. S. 1951. "The Problem of Serial Order in Behavior." In *Cerebral Mechanisms in Behavior: The Hixon Symposium*, edited by Lloyd A. Jeffress, 112–46. New York: Wiley.

Latour, Bruno. 1987. *Science in Action: How to Follow Scientists and Engineers through Society*. Cambridge, MA: Harvard University Press.

Laughren, M. 1992. "A Preliminary Description of Propositional Particles in Warlpiri." In *Papers in Warlpiri Grammar*. Working Papers of the Summer Institute of Linguistics, Australian Aborigines Branch, Series A, Vol. 6, edited by S. Swartz. Darwin: SIL-AAB.

Lave, Jean, M. Murtaugh, and O. de la Rocha. 1984. "The Dialectic of Arithmetic in Grocery Shopping." In *Everyday Cognition: Its Development in Social Context*, edited by Jean Lave and Barbara M. Rogoff. Cambridge, MA: Harvard University Press.

Lave, Jean, and Etienne Wenger. 1991. *Situated Learning: Legitimate Peripheral Participation*. Cambridgeshire, England: Cambridge University Press.

Ledoux, J. E., G. Risse, S. P. Springer, D. H. Wilson, and M. S. Gazzaniga. 1977. "Cognition and Commissurotomy." *Brain* 100: 87–104. [See also Gazzaniga, Michael S., and Joseph E. Ledoux. 1978. *The Integrated Mind*. New York: Plenum.]

Lee, Carol D. 1993. *Signifying as a Scaffold for Literature Interpretation: The Pedagogical Implications of an African American Discourse Genre*. Urbana, IL: National Council of Teachers of English.

Lemann, Nicholas. 1991. *The Promised Land: The Great Black Migration and How It Changed America*. New York: Knopf.

Lemke, Jay L. 1995. *Textual Politics: Discourse and Social Dynamics*. Bristol, PA: Taylor and Francis.

Lerner, Daniel. 1958. *The Passing of Traditional Societies: Modernizing the Middle East*. Glencoe, IL: Free Press.

Lessinger, Leon, and Dwight W. Allen. 1969. "Performance Proposals for Educational Funding: A New Approach to Federal Resource Allocation." *Phi Delta Kappan* 51 (November): 136–37.

Levin, Henry. 1987. "Improving Productivity through Education and Technology." In *The Future Impact of Technology on Work and Education*, edited by Gerald Burke and Russell W. Rumberger, 194–214. New York: Falmer Press.

Levin, Henry, and Russell W. Rumberger. 1983. "The Low-Skill Future of High Tech." *Technology Review* 86(6): 18–21.

Levine, Art. 1994. "The Great Debate Revisited." *The Atlantic Monthly* 274.6 (December): 38–44.

Levy, Frank. 1987. *Dollars and Dreams: The Changing American Income Distribution.* New York: Russell Sage Foundation.

Linn, R. L., M. E. Graue, and N. M. Sanders. 1990. "Comparing State and District Test Results to National Norms: The Validity of Claims that 'Everyone Is Above Average'." *Educational Measurement: Issues and Practice* 9.3 (Fall): 5–14.

Lloyd-Jones, Richard, and Andrea Lunsford, eds. 1989. *The English Coalition Conference: Democracy through Language.* Urbana, IL: National Council of Teachers of English.

Locke, John. [1690] 1962. *An Essay Concerning Human Understanding,* edited by Mary Whiton Calkins. LaSalle, IL: Open Court.

Lockridge, Kenneth. 1974. *Literacy in Colonial New England: An Enquiry into the Social Context of Literacy in the Early Modern West.* New York: Norton.

Lord, Albert Bates. 1960. *Singer of Tales.* Cambridge, MA: Harvard University Press.

Luria, Aleksandr R. 1976. *Cognitive Development: Its Cultural and Social Foundations.* Translated by Martin Lopez-Morillas and Lynn Solotoroff. Edited by Michael Cole. Cambridge, MA: Harvard University Press.

Lynd, Robert Staughton, and Helen Merrell Lynd. 1929. *Middletown: A Study in Contemporary American Culture.* New York: Harcourt, Brace.

MacIntyre, Alasdair C. 1990. *Three Rival Versions of Moral Enquiry: Encyclopaedia, Genealogy, and Tradition.* Notre Dame, IN: University of Notre Dame Press.

Macrorie, Ken. 1980. *Searching Writing: A Contextbook.* Rochelle Park, NJ: Hayden.

Madaus, George. 1993. "A National Testing System: Manna from Above." *Educational Assessment* 1.1 (Winter): 9–26.

Magaziner, Ira. 1992. Comments on radio interview from Washington, D.C. December.

Maheu, R. 1965. Address. World Conference of Ministers of Education on the Eradication of Illiteracy. UNESCO. Teheran.

Mann, Horace. 1842. *Fifth Annual Report of the Secretary of the Board of Education.* Boston, MA.

Manno, Bruno V. 1993. "Deliver Us from Clinton's Schools Bill." *Wall Street Journal* 221.120 (June 22): A-14.

Marckwardt, Albert H., and Fred G. Walcott. 1938. *Facts about Current English Usage.* New York: Appleton-Century.

Marshall, Ray, and Marc Tucker. 1992. *Thinking for a Living*. New York: Basic Books.

Martin, Laura M.W., and King Beach. 1992. "Technical and Symbolic Knowledge in CNC Machining: A Study of the Technical Workers of Different Backgrounds." National Center for Research in Vocational Education, University of California–Berkeley. November.

Mathews, Mitford McLeod. 1966. *Teaching to Read, Historically Considered*. Chicago: University of Chicago Press.

Mauss, Marcel. 1985. "A Category of the Human Mind: The Notion of the Person, The Notion of the Self." In *The Category of the Person: Anthropology, Philosophy, History*, edited by Michael Carrithers, Steven Collins, and Steven Lukes, 1–25. Cambridgeshire, England: Cambridge University Press.

Mayher, John S., and Rita S. Brouse. 1986. "Learning through Teaching: Is Your Classroom Like Your Grandmother's?" *Language Arts* 63.6 (October): 617–20.

McCloskey, Michael, and Robert Kargon. 1988. "The Meaning and Use of Historical Models." In *Ontogeny, Phylogeny, and Historical Development*, edited by Sidney Strauss, 49–67. Norwood, NJ: Ablex.

McGill-Franzen, Anne. 1992. "The Role of Literature in the School Experiences of 4-to-7-Year-Old Children." Report to the National Research Center on Literature Teaching and Learning, State University of New York. Albany. June 1.

———. 1993. *Shaping the Preschool Agenda: Early Literacy, Public Policy, and Professional Beliefs*. Albany: State University of New York Press.

McGill-Franzen, Anne, and Cynthia Lanford. 1993. *Exposing the Edge of the Preschool Curriculum: Teachers Talk about Text and Children's Literary Understandings*. Albany: National Research Center on Literature Teaching and Learning, State University of New York.

McGuffey, William Holmes. 1836. *McGuffey's Eclectic First Reader*. Cincinnati, OH: Truman and Smith.

———. 1869. *McGuffey's New Eclectic Primer in Pronouncing Orthography*. Cincinnati, OH: Wilson, Hinckle.

———. 1879. *McGuffey's Fifth Eclectic Reader*. Rev. ed. Cincinnati, OH: Van Antwerp, Bragg.

McLaughlin, Milbrey W., Merita A. Irby, and Juliet Langman. 1994. *Urban Sanctuaries: Neighborhood Organizations in the Lives and Futures of Inner-City Youth*. San Francisco: Jossey-Bass.

McMahon, Walter W. 1995. "Conceptual Framework for the Analysis of the Social Returns to Education." Paper. Department of Economics, University of Illinois at Urbana-Champaign.

McNeill, Daniel, and Paul Freiberger. 1993. *Fuzzy Logic*. New York: Simon and Schuster.

McQuade, Donald. 1992. "Living In—and On—the Margins." *College Composition and Communication* 43.1 (February): 11–22.

Mead, Margaret. 1970. *Culture and Commitment: A Study of the Generation Gap*. New York: Anchor/Doubleday.

Medawar, Peter. 1964. "Is the Scientific Paper Fraudulent? Yes, It Misrepresents Scientific Thought." *Saturday Review* (August 1): 42–43.

Mellon, John C. 1969. *Transformational Sentence Combining: A Method of Enhancing the Development of Syntactic Fluency in English Composition.* Champaign, IL: National Council of Teachers of English.

Michaels, Sarah. 1986. "Narrative Presentations: An Oral Preparation for Literacy with First Graders." In *The Social Construction of Literacy,* edited by Jenny Cook-Gumperz, 94–116. New York: Cambridge University Press.

Miles, Josephine. 1967. *Style and Proportion: The Language of Prose and Poetry.* Boston: Little, Brown.

Miller, Arthur I. 1987. *Imagery in Scientific Thought: Creating 20th-Century Physics.* Cambridge, MA: MIT Press.

Miller, George. 1967. "The Magical Number Seven, Plus or Minus Two." In *The Psychology of Communication: Seven Essays,* 14–44. New York: Basic Books.

Miller, Susan, et al. 1990. "Cross-Curricular Underlife: A Collaborative Report on Ways with Academic Words." *College Composition and Communication* 41.3 (February): 11–36.

Minard, John Stearns. 1905. *Recollections of the Log School House Period and Sketches of Life and Customs in Pioneers Days.* Cuba, NY: Free Press Printers.

Moffett, James. 1968. *Teaching the Universe of Discourse.* Boston: Houghton-Mifflin.

———. 1988. *Storm in the Mountains: A Case Study of Censorship, Conflict, and Consciousness.* Carbondale: Southern Illinois University Press.

Moffett, James, et al., comps. 1987. *Active Voice.* 3 vols. Upper Montclair, NJ: Boynton/Cook.

Moon, Cliff, and Gordon Wells. 1979. "The Influence of Home on Learning to Read." *Journal of Research in Reading* 2: 53–62.

Morison, Elting. 1966. *Men, Machines, and Modern Times.* Cambridge, MA: MIT Press.

Moskowitz, Breyne Arlene. 1978. "The Acquisition of Language." *Scientific American* 239(5): 92–108.

Moynihan, Daniel Patrick. 1993. *Pandemonium: Ethnicity in International Politics.* New York: Oxford University Press.

———. 1994. "Defining Deviancy Down." *American Educator* 17.4 (Winter) 10–18.

Mullis, Ina V.S., Jay R. Campbell, Alan E. Farstrup. 1993. *Executive Summary of the NAEP 1992 Reading Report Card for the Nation and the States: Data from the National and Trial State Assessments.* Washington, DC: National Center for Education Statistics.

Mumford, Lewis. 1934. *Technics and Civilization.* London: Routledge.

Murnane, Richard J., and Frank Levy. 1993. "Why Today's High School Educated Males Earn Less Than Their Fathers Did: The Problem and an Assessment of Responses." *Harvard Educational Review* 63.1 (Spring): 1–19.

Murphy, Sandra, and Mary Ann Smith. 1990. "Talking about Portfolios." *The Quarterly* 12(2): 1–3, 24–27. Berkeley: Bay Area Writing Project and Center for the Study of Writing.

Murray, Donald M. 1987. *Write to Learn.* 2nd ed. New York: Holt, Rinehart & Winston.

Myers, Greg. 1985. "The Social Construction of Two Biologists' Proposals." *Written Communication* 2.3 (July): 219–45.

———. 1990. *Writing Biology: Texts in the Social Construction of Scientific Knowledge.* Madison: University of Wisconsin Press.

Myers, Miles A. 1971. "English as Woodshop." *English Journal* 60.3 (March): 317–25.

———. 1980. *A Procedure for Writing Assessment and Holistic Scoring.* Urbana, IL: National Council of Teachers of English.

———. 1981. "What Kind of People Talk That Way." *English Journal* 70.7 (November): 24–29.

———. 1982a. "Learning Logs in Secondary Classrooms." Unpubl. paper as part of a federally funded study of secondary schools in Oakland, California (1980–1982). Berkeley: Bay Area Writing Project.

———. 1982b. *The Speech Events Underlying Written Composition.* Unpubl. Doct. Diss. University of California–Berkeley.

———. 1984. "Shifting Standards of Literacy: The Teacher's Catch-22." *English Journal* 73.4 (April): 26–32.

Myers, Miles, and James Gray. 1983. *Theory and Practice in the Teaching of Composition: Processing, Distancing, and Modeling.* Urbana, IL: National Council of Teachers of English.

Nano, George. 1989. Comments as a panelist at a conference seminar of the Institute of Industrial Relations. University of California–Berkeley. June.

Nash, Ray. 1969. *American Penmanship 1800–1850: A History of Writing and a Bibliography of Copybooks from Jenkins to Spencer.* Worchester, MA: American Antiquarian Society.

National Assessment of Educational Progress. 1981. *Three National Assessments of Reading.* A project of the Education Commission of the States. Washington, D.C.: U.S. Department of Health, Education, and Welfare.

———. 1984. *The Reading Report Card: Progress Toward Excellence in Our Schools: Trends in Reading Over Four National Assessments, 1971–1984.* Washington, D.C.: U.S. Department of Health, Education, and Welfare.

National Center for Education Statistics. 1976, 1979, 1980, 1993. *The Condition of Education: A Statistical Report.* Washington, D.C.: U.S. Dept. of Health, Education, and Welfare. [Issued annually.]

National Commission on Excellence in Education. 1983. *A Nation at Risk: The Imperative for Educational Reform.* Report of the National Commission on Excellence in Education. David Gardner, chair. Washington, D.C.: U.S. Department of Education.

National Education Association. 1912. *51st Annual Meeting: Addresses and Proceedings.*

Neisser, Ulric. 1976. *Cognition and Reality: Principles and Implications of Cognitive Psychology.* San Francisco: W. H. Freeman.

"A New Battle of the Books or Throwing Out the Middle Ages." 1914. *The Nation* 99: 315–16.

New England Association Standing Committee on Courses of Study. 1907. "The Course of Study in English—The Call for It, the Character of It, and the Construction of It." *School Review* 15: 559–75.

Newman, Charles. 1985. *The Post-Modern Aura: The Act of Fiction in an Age of Inflation.* Evanston, IL: Northwestern University Press.

Noble, David F. 1984. *Forces of Production: A Social History of Industrial Automation.* New York: Knopf.

Nunes, Terezinha. 1992. "Sylvia Scribner: A Mind in Action." *The Quarterly Newsletter of the Laboratory of Comparative Human Cognition* 14.4 (October): 136–38.

O'Brien, Robert, Judge of the Los Angeles Superior Court. 1994. Tentative decision in *Thomason vs. Los Angeles Unified School District and the State Board of Education.* May 10. Case Number: B5-028-375.

O'Donnell, Roy C., William J. Griffith, and Raymond C. Norris. 1967. *Syntax of Kindergarten and Elementary School Children: A Transformational Analysis.* NCTE Research Report no. 8. Champaign, IL: National Council of Teachers of English.

O'Hare, Frank. 1975. *Sentencecraft: An Elective Course in Writing.* Lexington, MA: Ginn.

Ohmann, Richard. 1971. "In Lieu of a New Rhetoric." In *Contemporary Theories of Rhetoric: Selected Readings,* edited by Richard L. Johannesen, 63–71. New York: Harper & Row.

———. 1982. "Reflections on Class and Language." *College English* 44.1 (January): 1–17.

Olson, David R. 1977. "From Utterance to Text: The Bias of Language in Speech and Writing." *Harvard Educational Review* 47(3): 257–81.

———. 1984. Personal correspondence with Janet Astington.

———. 1986. "Learning to Mean What You Say: Toward a Psychology of Literacy." In *Literacy, Society, and Schooling: A Reader,* edited by Suzanne de Castell, Allan Luke, and Kieran Egan, 145–58. Cambridgeshire, England: Cambridge University Press.

———. 1994. *The World on Paper: The Conceptual and Cognitive Implications of Writing and Reading.* New York: Cambridge University Press.

Ong, Walter J. 1981. *Fighting for Life: Contest, Sexuality, and Consciousness.* Ithaca: Cornell University Press.

———. 1982. *Orality and Literacy: The Technologizing of the Word.* New York: Methuen.

———. 1983. *Ramus, Method, and the Decay of Dialogue.* Cambridge, MA: Harvard University Press.

Ortega y Gasset, José. 1963. *Man and People.* Translated by Willard R. Trask. New York: Norton.

Paley, Vivian Gussin. 1984. *Boys and Girls: Superheroes in the Doll Corner.* Chicago: University of Chicago Press.

Palincsar, Annemarie Sullivan. 1994. Discussant comments at the symposium "Examining the Contexts of Community, Classrooms, and Activities: The Effects of Instructional Variations on Special Education Students' Literacy Performance." Annual convention of the American Educational Research Association (AERA). New Orleans. April 6.

Parry, Milman. 1971. *The Making of Homeric Verse: The Collected Papers of Milman Parry,* edited by Adam Parry. Oxford: Clarendon Press.

Pepper, Stephen. 1942. *World Hypotheses: A Study in Evidence.* Berkeley: University of California Press.

Perkins, David N. 1990. "Person Plus: A Distributed View of Thinking and Learning." Paper presented at symposium at the annual convention of the American Educational Research Association (AERA). Boston. April 18.

Peterson, Penelope L. 1979. "Direct Instruction Reconsidered." In *Research on Teaching: Concepts, Findings, and Implications,* edited by Penelope L. Peterson and Herbert J. Walberg, 57–69. Berkeley: McCutchan.

———. 1988. "Teachers and Students' Cognitional Knowledge for Classroom Teaching and Learning." *Educational Researcher* 17(5): 5–14.

Petroski, Henry. 1990. "Of Styluses and Diamonds: Annals of the Pencil." *Education Week* 9 (April 18): 36, 56.

Petrosky, Anthony. 1990. "Rural Poverty and Literacy in the Mississippi Delta: Dilemmas, Paradoxes and Conundrums." In *The Right to Literacy,* edited by Andrea A. Lunsford, Helene Moglen, and James Slevin, 61–73. New York: Modern Language Association of America.

———. 1994. "Schizophrenia, National Board for Professional Teaching Standards' Policies, and Me." *Council Chronicle* 5.3 (June): 10–11, 13.

Phillips, Kevin. 1990. *The Politics of Rich and Poor.* New York: Random House.

———. 1993. *Boiling Point: Democrats, Republicans, and the Decline of Middle-Class Prosperity.* New York: Random House.

Pinker, Steven. 1994. *The Language Instinct: How the Mind Creates Language.* New York: Morrow.

Plimpton, George. 1990. Speech given at the spring conference of the National Council of Teachers of English. Colorado Springs, Colorado. March 8.

Pooley, Robert C. 1946. *Teaching English Usage.* New York: Appleton-Century-Crofts.

Popper, Karl, and John Eccles. 1977. *The Self and the Brain.* 2 vols. New York: Springer International.

Porter, Ebenezer. 1838. *The Rhetorical Reader.* 43rd ed. Andover, MA: Gould and Newman.

Postman, Neil. 1993. *Technopoly: The Surrender of Culture to Technology.* New York: Vintage.

Potok, Chaim. 1994. "Rebellion and Authority: The Writer and the Community." Speech delivered at the annual convention of the National Council of Teachers of English. Orlando, Florida. November 20.

Pound, Ezra. [1931] 1971. *How to Read.* New York: Haskell House. [Rpt. of original edition.]

Powell, Arthur G., Eleanor Farrar, and David K. Cohen. 1985. *The Shopping Mall High School: Winners and Losers in the Educational Marketplace.* Boston: Houghton-Mifflin.

Pratt, Mary Louise. 1991. "Arts of the Contact Zone." *Profession 91,* 33–40. New York: Modern Language Association of America.

Prawat, Richard S. 1991. "The Value of Ideas: The Immersion Approach to the Development of Thinking." *Educational Researcher* 20(2): 3–10, 30.

———. 1993. "The Value of Ideas: Problems versus Possibilities in Learning." *Educational Researcher* 22(6): 5–16.

Price-Williams, D. R. 1961. "A Study Concerning Concepts of Conservation of Quantities among Primitive Children." *Acta Psychologica* 18: 297–305.

Probst, Robert. 1984. *Adolescent Literature: Response and Analysis.* Columbia, OH: Charles Merrill.

Purves, Alan C. 1973. *Literature Education in Ten Countries: An Empirical Study. International Studies in Evaluation, Vol. II.* New York: Wiley.

———. 1984. "The Potential and Real Achievement of U.S. Students in School Reading." *American Journal of Education* 93: 82–106.

———. 1987. "Literature, Culture, and Community." In *The Future of Literacy in a Changing World,* edited by Daniel A. Wagner, 216–32. New York: Pergamon.

———. 1990. *The Scribal Society: An Essay on Literacy and Schooling in the Information Age.* White Plains, NY: Longman.

Purves, Alan C., and Sauli Takala, eds. 1982. *An International Perspective on the Evaluation of Written Composition. Evaluation in Education: An International Review Series,* Vol. 5, no. 3. Oxford: Pergamon.

Rader, Ralph. 1974. "Fact, Theory, and Literary Explanation." *Critical Inquiry* 1.2 (December): 245–72.

Reddy, Michael. 1979. "The Conduit Metaphor." In *Metaphor and Thought,* edited by Andrew Ortony, 284–324. New York: Cambridge University Press.

Reed, Alonzo, and Brainerd Kellogg. [1885] 1894a. *Higher Lessons in English Grammar and Composition: In Which the Science of Language Is Made Tributary to the Art of Expression: A Course of Practical Lessons Carefully Graded and Adapted to Everyday Use in the School-room.* New York: Maynard, Merrill.

———. 1894b. *Graded Lessons in English. An Elementary English Grammar, Consisting of One Hundred Practical Lessons, Carefully Graded and Adapted to the Class-room.* Rev. ed. New York: Maynard, Merrill.

Reich, Robert B. 1983. *The Next American Frontier.* New York: Times Books.

———. 1992. *The Work of Nations: Preparing Ourselves for 21st Century Capitalism.* New York: Vintage Books.

Reid, William A. 1987. "Institutions and Practices: Professional Education Reports and the Language of Reform." *Educational Researcher* 16.8 (November): 10–18.

Resnick, Daniel P. 1991a. "Historical Perspectives on Literacy and Schooling." *Daedalus* 119.2 (Spring): 15–32.

———. 1991b. Personal communication.

Resnick, Daniel P., and Lauren B. Resnick. 1977. "The Nature of Literacy: An Historical Exploration." *Harvard Educational Review* 47 (August): 371–84.

———. 1985. "Standards, Curriculum, and Performance: An Historical and Comparative Perspective." *Educational Researcher* 14.4 (April): 5–20.

Resnick, Lauren B. 1983. "Mathematics and Science Learning: A New Conception." *Science* 220 (4596): 477–78.

———. 1987. "Learning in School and Out." *Educational Researcher* 16.9 (December): 13–20.

———. 1993. Speech given at the National Conference on Research in English meeting. Pittsburgh.

Rice, Joseph Mayer. 1893. *The Public-School System of the United States.* New York: Century.

Richards, I. A. 1948. "Science and Poetry." In *Criticism: The Foundations of Modern Literary Judgment,* edited by Mark Schorer, Josephine Miles, and Gordon McKenzie, 505–23. New York: Harcourt, Brace.

Richardson, John G. 1994. "Common, Deliquent, and Special: On the Formalization of Common Schooling in the American States." *American Educational Research Journal* 31.4 (Winter): 695–723.

Robinson, H. Alan, ed. 1977. *Reading and Writing Instruction in the United States: Historical Trends.* Newark, DE: International Reading Association; Urbana, IL: ERIC Clearinghouse on Reading and Communication Skills.

Robinson, H. Alan, Vincent Farone, Daniel R. Hittleman, and Elizabeth Unruh. 1990. *Reading Comprehension Instruction 1783–1987: A Review of Trends and Research,* edited by Jill Fitzgerald. Newark, DE: International Reading Association.

Rodriguez, Richard. 1983. *Hunger of Memory: The Education of Richard Rodriguez.* New York: Bantam.

Roemer, Marjorie, Lucille Schultz, and Russel Durst. 1991. "Portfolios and the Process of Change." *College Composition and Communication* 42.4 (December): 455–69.

Rorty, Richard. 1989. *Contingency, Irony, and Solidarity.* New York: Cambridge University Press.

Rosch, Eleanor. 1973. "On the Internal Structure of Perceptual and Semantic Categories." In *Cognitive Development and the Acquisition of Language,* edited by Timothy E. Moore, 111–14. New York: Academic Press.

———. 1977. "Human Categorization." In *Studies in Cross-Cultural Psychology,* Vol. 1, edited by Neil Warren. London: Academic Press.

———. 1978. "Principles of Categorization." In *Cognition and Categorization,* edited by Eleanor Rosch and Barbara Lloyd, 27–48. Hillsdale, NJ: Lawrence Erlbaum.

———. 1983. "Prototype Classification and Logical Classification: The Two Systems." In *New Trends in Conceptual Representation: Challenges to Piaget's Theory?* edited by Ellin Kofsky Scholnick, 73–86. Hillsdale, NJ: Lawrence Erlbaum.

Rosch, Eleanor, and Carolyn Mervis. 1975. "Family Resemblances: Studies in the Internal Structure of Categories." *Cognitive Psychology* 7(4): 573–605.

Rose, Mike. 1989. *Lives on the Boundary: The Struggles and Achievements of America's Underprepared.* New York: Free Press.

Rose, Stephen J. 1992. *Social Stratification in the United States: The American Profile Poster Revised and Expanded.* New York: New Press.

Rosenblatt, Louise M. 1968. *Literature as Exploration.* Rev. ed. New York: Noble & Noble.

———. 1978. *The Reader, the Text, the Poem: The Transactional Theory of the Literary Work.* Carbondale, IL: Southern Illinois University Press.

Rosenfield, Israel. 1988. *The Invention of Memory: A New View of the Brain.* New York: Basic Books.

Rosenshine, Barak. 1979. "Content, Time, and Direct Instruction." In *Research on Teaching: Concepts, Findings, and Implications,* edited by Penelope L. Peterson and Herbert J. Walbert, 28–56. Berkeley: McCutchan.

Rosenshine, Barak, and Carla Meister. 1994. "Reciprocal Teaching: A Review of Research." *Review of Education Research* 64.4 (Winter): 479–530.

Rosenthal, Irene. 1995. "Education through Literature: Flying Lessons from *Maniac Magee*." *Language Arts* 72.2 (February): 113–19.

Russell, David R. 1991. *Writing in the Academic Disciplines, 1870–1990: A Curricular History.* Carbondale, IL: Southern Illinois University Press.

Ryle, Gilbert. 1949. *The Concept of Mind.* New York: Barnes and Noble.

Salomon, Gavriel, Tamar Globerson, and Eva Guterman. 1990. "The Computer as a Zone of Proximal Development: Internalizing Reading-Related Metacognitions From a Reading Partner." *Journal of Educational Psychology* 81: 620–27.

Salomon, Gavriel, David Perkins, and Tamar Globerson. 1991. "Partners in Cognition: Extending Human Intelligence with Intelligent Technologies." *Educational Research* 20.3 (April): 2–9.

Sampson, Geoffrey. 1985. *Writing Systems: A Linguistic Introduction.* Stanford, CA: Stanford University Press.

Samuelson, F. 1987. "Was Early Mental Testing (a) Racist Inspired, (b) Objective Science, (c) a Technology for Democracy, (d) the Origin of Multiple-Choice Exams, (e) None of the Above?" In *Psychological Testing and American Society, 1890–1930,* edited by M. M. Sokal, 113–27. New Brunswick, NJ: Rutgers University Press.

Saxe, Geoffrey. 1988a. "Candy Selling and Math Learning." *Educational Researcher* 17(6): 14–21.

———. 1988b. "The Mathematics of Child Street Vendors." *Child Development* 59: 1415–25.

SCANS (Secretary [of Labor]'s Commission on Achieving Necessary Skills). 1991. *Learning A Living: A SCANS Report for America 2000.* Washington, D.C.: U.S. Government Printing Office.

Schaafsma, David. 1993. *Eating on the Street: Teaching Literacy in a Multicultural Society.* Pittsburgh: University of Pittsburgh Press.

Schieffelin, Bambi B. 1979. "Getting it Together: An Ethnographic Approach to the Study of the Development of Communicative Competence." In *Developmental Pragmatics,* edited by Bambi B. Schieffelin and Elinor Ochs, 73–108. New York: Academic Press.

Schlovsky, Viktor. 1917. "Art as Device." Cited in Eagleton 1983, i.

Schmandt-Besserat, Denise. 1978. "The Earliest Precursor of Writing." *Scientific American* 238(6): 50–59.

Schofield, R. S. 1968. "The Measurement of Literacy in Pre-Industrial England." In *Literacy in Traditional Societies,* edited by Jack Goody, 311–25. Cambridge, MA: Cambridge University Press.

Scholes, Robert E. 1985. *Textual Power: Literary Theory and the Teaching of English.* New Haven, CT: Yale University Press.

———. 1992. "Canonicity and Textuality." In *Introduction to Scholarship in Modern Languages and Literature,* edited by Joseph Gibaldi, 138–58. New York: Modern Language Association of America.

Schon, Donald A. 1971. *Beyond the Stable State.* New York: Norton.

Schonberger, Richard. 1986. *World-Class Manufacturing: The Lessons of Simplicity Applied.* New York: Free Press.

Schorer, Mark, ed. 1950. *The Story: A Critical Anthology*. New York: Prentice-Hall.

———. 1964. "Technique as Discovery." In *Forms of Modern Fiction*, edited by William Van O'Connor, 9–30. Bloomington: Indiana University Press.

Schrag, Peter. 1986. "What the Test Scores Really Mean." *The Nation* 243.10 (October 4): 297+ .

Schramm, Wilbur, and W. Lee Ruggels. 1967. "How Mass Media Systems Grow." In *Communication and Change in the Developing Countries*, edited by Daniel Lerner and Wilbur Schramm, 57–75. Honolulu: East-West Center Press.

Schudson, Michael. 1978. *Discovering the News: A Social History of American Newspapers*. New York: Basic Books.

Scribner, Sylvia. 1984. "Studying Working Intelligence." In *Everyday Cognition: Its Development in Social Context*, edited by Jean Lave and Barbara M. Rogoff, 9–41. Cambridge, MA: Harvard University Press.

———. 1987. Report from Center for Research in Vocational Education, University of California, Berkeley; similar findings described in: Scribner, Sylvia, L. Martin, and King Beach (in preparation at the time of Sylvia Scribner's death in the summer of 1991) *Technical and Symbolic Knowledge in CNC Machining: A Study of Technical Workers*. Also discussed in Scribner, Sylvia. 1989. "Project II.9: Learning to Integrate Technical and Symbolic Knowledge in Computer-Controlled Machining." Project Abstracts Center for Research in Vocational Education.

———. 1992. "Mind in Action: A Functional Approach to Thinking," *The Quarterly Newsletter of the Laboratory of Comparative Human Cognition* 14.5 (October): 103–10.

Scribner, Sylvia, and Michael M. Cole. 1981. *The Psychology of Literacy*. Cambridge, MA: Harvard University Press.

———. 1988. "Unpacking Literacy." In *Perspectives in Literacy*, edited by Eugene R. Kintgen, Barry M. Kroll, and Mike Rose, 57–70. Carbondale: Southern Illinois University Press.

Searle, John. 1972. "Chomsky's Revolution in Linguistics." *The New York Review of Books* 18.12 (29 June): 16–24.

Shaiken, H. 1984. *Work Transformed: Automation and Labor in the Computer Age*. New York: Holt, Rinehart & Winston.

Shanker, Albert. 1987. "Where We Stand." *New York Times* (November 15): 6, 8.

Shavelson, Richard J., N. B. Carey, and N. M. Webb. 1990. "Indicators of Science Achievement: Options for a Powerful Policy Instrument." *Phi Delta Kappan* 71(9): 692–97.

Shores-Mueller Co. v. Lonning. 1913. Qtd. in Stevens, Edward. 1983. "Illiterate Americans and Nineteenth-Century Courts: The Meaning of Literacy." In *Literacy in Historical Perspective*, edited by Daniel P. Resnick, 59–83. Washington, D.C.: Library of Congress.

Sims, Rudine. 1982. *Shadow and Substance: Afro-American Experience in Contemporary Children's Fiction*. Urbana, IL: National Council of Teachers of English.

Sizer, Theodore R. 1984. *Horace's Compromise: The Dilemma of the American High School*. New York: Houghton-Mifflin.

Skinner, B. F. 1957. *Verbal Behavior.* New York: Appleton-Century-Crofts.

Slama, E. A. 1923. "A Silent Reading Poster Lesson." *Chicago Schools Journal* 6: 142–44.

Smith, Barbara Herrnstein. 1978. *On the Margins of Discourse: The Relation of Literature to Language.* Chicago: University of Chicago Press.

Smith, Frank. 1988. *Joining the Literacy Club: Further Essays into Education.* Portsmouth, NH: Heinemann.

Smith, Joel. 1988. "Literacy in the Workplace." Paper presented at the Conference in Broadening the Definition of Literacy. California Federation of Teachers and the Central California Council of Teachers of English. May 5.

Smith, Louise Z. 1993. "Commentary on *College English.*" *FOCUS* 6.2 (Winter): 78–80.

Smith, Nila Banton. 1965. *American Reading Instruction: Its Development and Its Significance in Gaining a Perspective on Current Practices in Reading.* Newark, DE: International Reading Association.

Smitherman, Geneva. 1977. *Talkin' and Testifyin': The Language of Black America.* Boston: Houghton-Mifflin.

———. 1993. "Cultural Demographics." Speech delivered at the "Reclaiming the Dream" Conference of the National Council of Teachers of English. Washington, D.C. August.

Smuts, Robert W. 1971. *Women and Work in America.* New York: Schocken.

Snyder, Thomas D., ed. 1993. *120 Years of American Education: A Statistical Portrait.* Washington, D.C.: National Center for Education Statistics.

Soltow, Lee, and Edward Stevens. 1981. *The Rise of Literacy and the Common School in the United States: A Socioeconomic Analysis to 1870.* Chicago: University of Chicago Press.

Sommers, Nancy. 1992. "Between the Drafts." *College Composition and Communication* 43.1 (February): 3–31.

Spedding, J., ed. 1868. *The Letters and Life of Francis Bacon. Vol. 4.* London: Longman, Green.

Spencer, Platt Rogers. [1866] 1872. *Spencerian Key to Practical Penmanship.* New York: Ivison.

Spolsky, Bernard, and Patricia Irvine. 1980. "Sociolinguistic Aspects of Literacy in the Vernacular." In *Speaking, Singing, and Teaching.* Proceedings of Swallow VIII Anthropological Research Papers. Tempe: Arizona State University.

Sprat, Thomas. [1667] 1972. *History of the Royal Society of London.* New York: Reader's Microprint Corp. [Rpt. of the original work.]

Squire, James R., and Roger K. Applebee. 1968. *High School English Instruction Today: The National Study of High School English Programs.* New York: Appleton-Century-Crofts.

St. Augustine's Confessions. 1979. With an English translation by William Watts (1631). 2 vols. Cambridge, MA: Harvard University Press.

Starch, D., and E. C. Elliot. 1912. "Reliability of Grading High School Work in English." *School Review* 21: 442–57.

Stedman, Lawrence C. 1995. "The New Mythology about the Status of U.S. Schools." *Educational Leadership* 52.5 (February): 80–85.

Stedman, Lawrence C., and Carl F. Kaestle. 1987. "Literacy and Reading Performance in the United States, from 1800 to the Present." *Reading Research Quarterly* 22: 8–46.

Steiner, George. 1975. *After Babel: Aspects of Language and Translation.* New York: Oxford University Press.

Stern, David. 1983. Seminar comments at the Forum of the School of Education, University of California–Berkeley. April.

Sternberg, Robert J. 1985. *Beyond IQ: A Triarchic Theory of Human Intelligence.* Cambridgeshire, England: Cambridge University Press.

Sterne, Laurence. [1759–1767] 1991. *Tristram Shandy.* New York: Knopf.

Stevens, Edward. 1983. "Illiterate Americans and Nineteenth-Century Courts: The Meaning of Literacy." In *Literacy in Historical Perspective,* edited by Daniel P. Resnick, 59–83. Washington, D.C.: Library of Congress.

Stevens, Wallace. [1923] 1957. "Six Significant Landscapes." In *The Collected Poems of Wallace Stevens,* 73–75. New York: Knopf.

Stevenson, Harold W., and James W. Stigler. 1992. *The Learning Gap: Why Our Schools Are Failing and What We Can Learn from Japanese and Chinese Education.* New York: Summit Books.

Sticht, Thomas, G. 1992. Discussion at roundtable entitled "Cultural Influences in Workplaces and Schoolplaces: The Intergeneration Transfer of Cognition." Conference of American Educational Research Association (AERA), San Francisco. April 21. [See also Cole, J. Y., and T. G. Sticht, eds. 1981. *The Textbook in American Society: A Volume Based on a Conference at the Library of Congress* on May 2–3, 1979. Also see Sticht, Thomas G., William B. Armstrong, Daniel Hickey, and John S. Caylor. 1987. *Cast-Off Youth: Policy Training Methods from the Military Experience.* New York: Praeger. (Part III, "Developing an Experimental Function-Context Curriculum," describes an experimental course for electronics technicians.)]

Stock, Brian. 1983. *The Implications of Literacy: Written Language and Models of Interpretation in the Eleventh and Twelfth Centuries.* Princeton, NJ: Princeton University Press.

Stone, George Winchester, Jr., ed. 1964. *Issues, Problems, and Approaches in the Teaching of English.* New York: Holt, Rinehart & Winston.

Stone, Lawrence. 1969. "Literacy and Education in England 1640–1900," *Past and Present* 42: 69–139.

Strang, Ruth. 1942. *Exploration in Reading Patterns.* Chicago: University of Chicago Press.

Straussman, P. 1983. "Information Systems and Literacy." In *Literacy for Life: The Demand for Reading and Writing,* edited by Richard W. Bailey and Robin Melanie Fosheim, 115–21. New York: Modern Language Association of America.

Street, Brian V. 1984. *Literacy in Theory and Practice.* New York: Cambridge University Press.

Strong, William. 1973. *Sentence Combining: A Composing Book.* New York: Random House.

Stuckey, J. Elspeth. 1991. *Violence of Literacy.* Portsmouth, NH: Boynton/Cook.

Stuckey, J. Elspeth, and Kenneth Alston. 1990. "Cross-Age Tutoring: The Right to Literacy." In *The Right to Literacy,* edited by Andrea A. Lunsford, Helene Mogden, and James Slevin, 245–54. New York: Modern Language Association of America.

Stuller, Jay. 1986. "War Is Peace." *PSA Magazine* (February). San Diego: Pacific Southwest Airlines.

Sullivan, Zohreh. 1991. "Theory for the Untheoretical: Rereading and Reteaching Austen, Brontë, and Conrad." *College English* 53.5 (September): 571–78.

Super, R. H., ed. 1973. *The Complete Prose Works of Matthew Arnold.* Ann Arbor: University of Michigan Press. [An eleven-volume series started in 1960.]

Swift, Jonathan. 1704. *A Tale of a Tub. Written for the Universal Improvement of Mankind . . . to Which Is Added, an Account of a Battel between the Antient and Modern Books in St. James's Library. . . .* London: J. Nutt.

Tambiah, S. J. 1968. "Literacy in a Buddhist Village In North-East Thailand." In *Literacy In Traditional Societies,* edited by Jack Goody, 85–131. New York: Cambridge University Press.

Tannen, Deborah. 1984. "Spoken and Written Narrative in English and Greek." In *Coherence in Spoken and Written Discourse,* edited by Deborah Tannen, 21–41. Norwood, NJ: Ablex.

———. 1985. "Relative Focus on Involvement in Oral and Written Discourse." In *Literacy, Language, and Learning: The Nature and Consequences of Reading and Writing,* edited by David R. Olson, Nancy Torrance, and Angela Hildyard, 124–47. Cambridgeshire, England: Cambridge University Press.

———. 1990. *You Just Don't Understand: Women and Men in Conversation.* New York: Morrow.

Taylor, Charles. 1989. *Sources of the Self: The Making of the Modern Identity.* Cambridge, MA: Harvard University Press.

Taylor, Denny, and Catherine Dorsey-Gaines. 1988. *Growing Up Literate: Learning from Inner-City Families.* Portsmouth, NH: Heinemann.

Taylor, Frederick W. [1911] 1967. *Principles of Scientific Management.* New York: Norton.

Taylor, Susan Champlin. 1987. "The Numbers Game." *Modern Maturity* 30.6 (December/January): 29.

Terkel, Studs. 1970. *Hard Times: An Oral History of the Great Depression.* New York: Avon.

Thelen, Esther. 1990. "Dynamic Systems and the Generation of Individual Differences." In *Individual Differences in Infancy: Reliability, Stability, Prediction,* edited by Jeffrey Fagen, John Colombo, and the Society for Research in Child Development, 19–43. Hillsdale, NJ: Lawrence Erlbaum.

Theobald, Paul. 1991. "Country School Curriculum and Governance: The One-Room School Experience in the Midwest to 1918." Unpublished paper.

Thompson, E. P. 1975. "The Crime of Anonymity." In *Albion's Fatal Tree: Crime and Society in Eighteenth-Century England,* edited by Douglas Hay, et al., 279–80. New York: Pantheon.

Thorndike, Edward L. 1904. *An Introduction to the Theory of Mental and Social Measurement.* Part I. New York: Science Press.

————. 1906. *The Principles of Teaching: Based on Psychology*. New York: A. G. Seiler.

————. 1918. *An Introduction to the Theory of Mental and Social Measurement*. Part II. New York: Science Press.

Tompkins, Jane. 1988. "Fighting Words: UnLearning to Write the Critical Essay," *Georgia Review* 42 (Fall): 585–90.

Traugott, Elizabeth Cross. 1987. "The Special Case of Speech-Act Verbs." In *Language, Literacy, and Culture: Issues of Society and Schooling*, edited by Judith A. Langer, 111–27. Norwood, NJ: Ablex.

Tucker, Marc. 1994. Personal communication.

Tuddenham, Read D. 1948. "Soldier Intelligence in World Wars I and II." *American Psychologist* 3(2): 54–56.

Tufte, Edward R. 1983. *The Visual Display of Quantitative Information*. Cheshire, CT: Graphics Press.

Tuman, Myron C. 1986. "From Astor Place to Kenyon Road: The NCTE and the Origin of English Studies." *College English* 48.4 (April): 339–49.

————. 1987. *A Preface to Literacy: An Enquiry into Pedagogy, Practice, and Progress*. University, AL: University of Alabama Press.

————. 1992. "First Thoughts." In *Literacy Online: The Promise (and Peril) of Reading and Writing with Computers*, edited by Myron C. Tuman, 3–15. Pittsburgh: University of Pittsburgh Press.

Tyack, David B. 1974. *The One Best System: A History of American Urban Education*. Cambridge, MA: Harvard University Press.

Tyler, Ralph. 1990. Personal communication.

U.S. Bureau of the Census. 1953. *School Enrollment, Educational Attainment, and Illiteracy October, 1952*. Current Population Reports, Ser. P-20, no. 45. Washington, D.C.: U.S. Government Printing Office.

————. 1971. *Illiteracy In The United States: November 1969*. Current Population Reports, Ser. P-20, no. 217. Washington, D.C.: U.S. Government Printing Office.

————. 1976. *Historical Statistics of the United States: Colonial Items to 1970 (pt. 1)*. Washington, D.C.: U.S. Bureau of the Census.

U.S. Department of Education. 1986. *Update on Adult Literacy*. Washington, D.C.: U.S. Government Printing Office.

U.S. Department of Labor. 1993. *Workplace Literacy and the Nation's Unemployed Workers*. Washington, D.C.: U.S. Government Printing Office.

Valentine, Kristin B. 1992. Presentation at the annual convention of the Speech Communication Association. Chicago.

Van Lehn, Kurt, Randolph M. Jones, Michelene T.H. Chi. 1992. "The Model of the Self-Explanation Effect." *The Journal of the Learning Sciences* 2(1): 1–59.

Vinovskis, Maris A. 1981. *Fertility in Massachusetts from the Revolution to the Civil War*. New York: Academic Press.

Vygotsky, L. S. [Vygotskii, Lev Semenovich]. 1962. *Thought and Language*. Cambridge, MA: M.I.T. Press.

————. 1978. *Mind in Society: The Development of Higher Psychological Processes*, edited by Michael Cole, Vera John-Steiner, Sylvia Scribner, and Ellen Souberman. Cambridge, MA: Harvard University Press.

Wagner, Daniel. 1991. "Literacy as Culture." In *Literate Systems and Individual Lives: Perspectives on Literacy and Schooling,* edited by Edward M. Jennings and Alan C. Purves, 11–19. Albany: State University of New York Press.

Walker, Alice. 1982. *The Color Purple: A Novel.* New York: Harcourt, Brace, Jovanovich.

Watson, Bruce, and Richard Konicek. 1990. "Teaching for Conceptual Change: Confronting Children's Experience." *Phi Delta Kappan* 71(9): 680–85.

Watson, John B. 1925. *Behaviorism.* New York: Norton.

Weaver, Warren. 1947. "Science and Complexity." In *The Scientists Speak,* edited by Warren Weaver. New York: Boni & Gaer.

Webb, Noreen M. 1989. "Peer Interaction and Learning in Small Groups." *International Journal of Educational Research* 13(1): 21–39.

Webster, Daniel. 1875. *The Private Correspondence of Daniel Webster,* edited by Fletcher Webster. 2 vols. Boston: Little, Brown.

Webster, Noah. 1783. *American Spelling Book.* Boston: Isaiah Thomas and Ebenezer T. Andrews. [Originally entitled *Blue-Backed Speller,* this speller assumed this name in a later edition. This book went through tens of editions, and in its early years, editions varied from state to state.]

———. [1789] 1967. *Dissertations on the English Language.* Menston, England: Scholar Press.

Wellborn, Stanley N. 1982. "Ahead: A Nation of Illiterates?" *U.S. News and World Report* 92.19 (May 17): 53–56.

Wellek, René, and Austin Warren. 1949. *Theory of Literature.* New York: Harcourt, Brace.

Wells, C. Gordon. 1981. *Learning through Interaction: The Study of Language Development.* Cambridgeshire, England: Cambridge University Press.

Wertsch, James V. 1986. "Mind in Context: A Vygotskian Approach." Speech delivered at the annual convention of the American Educational Research Association.

Whalley, Joyce Irene. 1980. *The Pen's Excellencie: Calligraphy of Western Europe and America.* New York: Taplinger.

Wheelock, Anne. 1992. *Crossing the Tracks: How Untracking Can Save America's Schools.* New York: New Press.

White, Hayden V. 1981. "The Value of Narrativity in the Representation of Reality." In *On Narrative,* edited by W.J.T. Mitchell, 1–24. Chicago: University of Chicago Press. [The articles in this volume originally appeared in *Critical Inquiry* 7.1 (Autumn 1980).]

Wilkinson, Andrew. c1970s. Personal communication.

Williams, D. A., and P. King. 1980. "Do Males Have a Math Gene?" *Newsweek* 96 (December 15): 73.

Williams, Joseph M. 1986. "Non-Linguistic Linguistics and the Teaching of Style." In *The Territory of Language: Linguistics, Stylistics, and the Teaching of Composition,* edited by Donald A. McQuade, 174–91. Carbondale: Southern Illinois University Press.

———. 1989. *Style: Ten Lessons in Clarity and Grace.* 3rd ed. Chicago: University of Chicago Press.

Williams, Raymond. 1976. *Keywords: A Vocabulary of Culture and Society*. New York: Oxford University Press.

Wills, Garry. 1992. *Lincoln at Gettysburg: The Words That Remade America*. New York: Simon & Schuster.

Wilson, Edward O. 1975. *Sociobiology: A New Synthesis*. Cambridge, MA: Belknap/Harvard University Press.

Wimsatt, William K., Jr. 1954. *The Verbal Icon: Studies in the Meaning of Poetry*, by William K. Wimsatt, Jr., with two preliminary essays written in collaboration with Monroe C. Beardsley. Lexington: University of Kentucky Press.

Wimsatt, William K., Jr., and Cleanth Brooks. 1957. *Literary Criticism: A Short History*. New York: Knopf.

Wirth, Arthur G. 1987. "Contemporary Work and the Quality of Life." In *Society as Educator in an Age of Transition*, edited by Kenneth D. Benne and Steven Tozer, 54–87. Eighty-sixth Yearbook of the National Society for the Study of Education. Chicago: University of Chicago Press.

Wood, Gordon S. 1992. *The Radicalism of the American Revolution*. New York: Knopf.

Wundt, Wilhelm Max, James Edwin Creighton, and Edward Bradford Titchener. 1896. *Lectures on Human and Animal Psychology*. New York: Macmillan.

Yancey, Kathleen Blake, ed. 1992. *Portfolios in the Writing Classroom: An Introduction*. Urbana, IL: National Council of Teachers of English.

Yates, Frances Amelia. 1966. *The Art of Memory*. London: Routledge & Kegan Paul.

Young, Richard E. 1978. "Paradigms and Problems: Needed Research in Rhetorical Invention." In *Research on Composing: Points of Departure*, edited by Charles R. Cooper and Lee Odell, 29–47. Urbana, IL: National Council of Teachers of English.

Zadeh, Lofti Asker. 1973. "Outline of a New Approach to the Analysis of Complex Systems and Decision Processes." *IEEE Transactions on Systems, Man, and Cybernetics* 3: 28–44.

———. 1978. "Fuzzy Sets as a Basis for a Theory of Possibility." *Fuzzy Sets and Systems* 1: 3–28.

Ziff, Paul. 1972. *Understanding Understanding*. Ithaca, NY: Cornell University Press.

Subject Index

Author Index

Author

Miles Myers received his B.A. in rhetoric, his M.A. in English and M.A.T. in English and education, and Ph.D., from the Language and Learning Division, at the University of California–Berkeley. He has served as the Executive Director of the National Council of Teachers of English since 1990, and has been president of the Central California Council of Teachers of English (in the 1960s), a vice president of the California Association of Teachers of English (in the 1970s), president of the Oakland Federation of Teachers, AFT (in the 1960s), and president of the California Federation of Teachers-AFT (in the 1980s). He was the administrative director of the Bay Area (California) and National Writing Projects during the first ten years of their development, and for almost thirty years, he has been secretary-treasurer and later president of Alpha Plus Corporation, a nonprofit corporation of preschools in Oakland, California. He taught high school English for many years, primarily at Oakland High School, where he was department chair until 1975, when he left for the University of California–Berkeley. He taught English methods courses at the University of California–Berkeley for five years, at the University of Illinois Urbana-Champaign for three years, and at various other institutions for shorter periods of time. He is co-director of the literacy unit of the New Standards Project, and he serves on the advisory boards of the Center for the Study of Writing at the University of California–Berkeley and the National Research Center on Literature Teaching and Learning at the State University of New York at Albany, as well as the Board on Testing and Assessment of the National Academy of Science. He has received the Distinguished Service Award from the California Association of Teachers of English (CATE), the Ben Rust Award for Service from the California Federation of Teachers-AFT, and an Exemplary Service Award from the California Council of Classified Employees. He has authored five books and monographs as well as many articles on the teaching of English.